Accounting for Non-accounting Students

J R Dyson

Department of Accounting, Napier College, Edinburgh

Pitman

PITMAN PUBLISHING
128 Long Acre, London WC2E 9AN

A Division of Longman Group UK Limited

First edition 1987
Reprinted 1988, 1989, 1990

British Library Cataloguing in Publication Data

Dyson J. R.
Accounting for non-accounting students
1. Accounting
I. Title
657 HF5635

ISBN 0-273-02563-5

Printed and bound in Great Britain by
Richard Clay Ltd, Bungay, Suffolk

To Auntie Clarice

Contents

Preface xi
Acknowledgements xv

Part 1: Introduction to accounting xvii

1 **The accounting world** 1
Nature and purpose of accounting · Accounting and the non-accountant · Branches of accounting · The accountancy profession · Types of organizations · Conclusion · Questions

2 **Accounting rules** 13
Boundary rules · Measurement rules · Ethical rules · Summary · Conclusion · Questions

Part 2: Financial accounting 27

3 **Recording accounting information** 29
The dual aspect rule · Recording information · A ledger account example · Balancing the accounts · The trial balance · Conclusion · Questions

4 **Basic financial statements** 54
The measurement of profit · Preparation of the basic financial statements · An illustration of the basic financial statements · Format of accounts · Post trial balance adjustments · A comprehensive example · Estimating accounting profit · Conclusion · Questions

5 **Manufacturing accounts** 87
Contents · Construction · A comprehensive example · Conclusion · Questions

6 **Partnership and company accounts** 103
Partnerships · Limited liability companies · Structure and operation · The profit and loss account · The balance sheet · A comprehensive example · Conclusion · Questions

7 **Source and application of funds** 125
Accounting profit and liquidity · Format and contents · Construction · The recommended format · A comprehensive example · Conclusion · Questions

8 **Interpretation of accounts** 144
The need for ratios · Profitability ratios · Liquidity ratios · Efficiency ratios · Investment ratios · Summary of the main ratios · An illustrative example · Analysing the accounts · Interpreting the accounts · Conclusion · Questions

Part 3: Cost and management accounting 171

9 **Basic costing principles** 173
Historical review · Planning and control · Implementation procedure · Costing procedure · Conclusion · Questions

10 **Direct costs** 185
Direct materials · Direct labour · Direct expenses · Conclusion · Questions

11 **Indirect costs** 200
Factory overhead · A comprehensive example · Non-factory overhead · Pre-determined rates · Conclusion · Questions

12 **Recording cost data** 220
Cost book-keeping · Basic costing methods · Costing techniques · Conclusion · Questions

13 **Marginal costing** 227
The problem of fixed costs · The marginal cost technique · The application of marginal costing · Criticisms of marginal costing · Marginal costing formulae · An illustrative example · Limiting factors · Conclusion · Questions

14 **Budgeting control** 243
The nature of budgeting · Budget procedure · Functional budgets: an illustrative example · Fixed and flexible budgets · Conclusion · Questions

15 **Standard costing** 262
Administration · Control ratios · Variance analysis · Variance analysis formulae · An illustrative example · Sales variances · Operating statements · Conclusion · Questions

16 **Capital investment** 284
Project profitability · Source of funds · Conclusion · Questions

Part 4: Annual reports 297

17 **Disclosure of information** 299
Minimum disclosure requirements · Contents of an annual report
Conclusion

18 **The principal reports** 303
The chairman's report · The directors' report · The auditors' report · Conclusion

19 **The main financial statements** 307
The background to published accounts · Additional features · The group profit and loss account · The group balance sheet · Group statements of source and application of funds · Conclusion

20 **Supplementary statements and reports** 317
Inflation adjusted reports · Value added statements · Statistical summaries · Employee reports · Conclusion · Assignment

Appendix 1: Discount table 328
Appendix 2: Answers to questions 330
Index 429

Preface

This is a book for non-accountants. It is intended primarily for students who are required to study accounting as part of a non-accounting degree or professional studies course. It should also be of value to those working in commerce, government or industry who find that their work involves them in dealing with accounting information. It is hoped that the book will help to explain why there is a need for such information.

Non-accounting students (such as engineers, personnel managers, purchasing officers, and sales managers) are sometimes unable to understand why they are required to study accounting. This is often found to be the case when they have to take an examination in the subject, and they are then presented with a paper of some considerable technical rigour.

Accounting books written specifically for the non-accountant are also often extremely demanding. The subject needs to be covered in such a way that non-accounting students do not become confused by too much technical information. They do not require the same detailed analysis that is only of relevance to the professional accountant. Some accounting books specially written for the non-accountant go to the opposite extreme. They outline the subject so superficially that they are of no real practical help either to examination candidates or to those non-specialists requiring some guidance on practical accounting problems.

The aim of this book is to serve as a good introduction to the study of accounting. The subject is not covered superficially. In parts, the book goes into considerable detail, but only where it is necessary for a real understanding of the subject. It is appreciated that non-accountants are unlikely to be involved in the *detailed* preparation of accounting information such as, for example, in the compilation of a company's annual accounts. However, if such accounts are to provide the maximum possible benefit to their users, it is desirable that users should have a good knowledge of how they are prepared and how to extract the maximum possible information from them.

This concept is analogous to that of driving a car. It is perfectly possible to drive a car without knowing anything about how it works. However, to get the best possible performance from the car, it is useful to know something about the engine. It is not necessary to know as much about the car as a motor mechanic. All that is required is just sufficient knowledge to be able to drive the car so that it operates at its maximum efficiency. Similarly, it is not absolutely necessary to know how to prepare accounts to be able to use them, but they will mean a great deal more if the user knows something about their construction.

The background to the book

Many colleges and polytechnics now run a number of degree and diploma courses which include accounting as a compulsory subject. Whilst the syllabi for such courses have usually to be approved by external bodies (such as by the CNAA or by a number of various professional associations and institutes), the detailed contents of such syllabi are often left to the individual college lecturer to decide. This book has been written with that type of course especially in mind.

The material contained in the book has been designed so that it can be covered in about 90 class contact hours. If more time is available, there will be an opportunity for students to tackle additional exercises in the classroom under the general supervision of their lecturer, but if less class contact time is available, it will probably be necessary for students to work largely unsupervised.

The book is divided into four parts. Part 1 puts the subject of accounting into context. Part 2 deals with financial accounting, and Part 3 with cost and management accounting. It is possible that most students will more readily identify with Part 3 of the book, since cost and management accounting probably relates more directly to their current day-to-day responsibilities. It might seem more logical, therefore, to begin by studying that branch of accounting, but experience suggests that students find it very difficult to understand cost and management accounting if they have not first studied financial accounting. Part 4 of the book outlines the contents of a limited liability company's annual report. Some lecturers may prefer to cover this part of the book before moving on to cost and management accounting. It would then be possible to link directly and immediately the material covered in Chapter 8 on the interpretation of accounts with the information contained in a company's annual report.

However, the section on annual reports has been placed at the end of the book for two main reasons:

1 The contents may not be of immediate interest to most non-accounting students until they become senior officers in their respective companies;
2 This subject requires an almost unlimited amount of class contact hours, so that it is perhaps best left to the end of the course when lecturers will know how much spare time they have available.

How to use the book

Lecturers will have their own way of introducing the various subjects. We would hope, however, that they will still use the various exhibits in the book to demonstrate particular accounting procedures. It is our view that lecturers spend far too much time photocopying questions for use in lectures. The students then spend their time in lectures trying to take down what the lecturer is writing on the blackboard without really listening to what he is saying.

If this book is used as it is intended, there is no need for lecturers to photocopy additional exhibits and answers. The book contains sufficient exhibits for most one year courses, and every exhibit is followed by a detailed solution. Thus there is no need for students to copy answers that have been written on the blackboard: they should be able to listen to the lecturer as he demonstrates each point step by step.

Most chapters are also followed by a number of tutorial exercises. Since detailed solutions for these questions are contained in Appendix 2, lecturers will also be spared having to provide solutions of their own.

A word to students

If you are using this book as part of a formal course, your lecturer will provide you with a work scheme which will outline just how much of the book you are expected to cover each week. In addition to the work done in your lecture, you will probably have to read each chapter two or three times. As you read a chapter work through each exhibit, and then have a go at doing it without reference to the solution.

You are also recommended to attempt as many of the questions which follow each chapter as you can, but do not look at the solutions until you are absolutely certain that you do not know how to do the question. The more questions that you attempt, the more confident you will be that you really do understand the subject matter. However, you must not spend all your time studying accounting, so make sure that you put enough time into your other subjects.

Many students study accounting without having the benefit of attending lectures. If you fall into this category, we suggest that you adopt the following study plan:

1 Organize your private study so that you have covered every topic in your syllabus by the time of your examination. You will probably need to allow for extra time to be spent on Chapters 3, 4, 8, 13 and 15.
2 Read each chapter slowly, being careful to work through each exhibit. Do not worry if you do not immediately understand each point: read on to the end of the chapter.

3 Read the chapter again, this time making sure that you do understand each point. Try doing each exhibit without looking at the solution.
4 Attempt as many questions at the end of the chapter as you can, but do not look at the solutions until you have finished or you are certain that you cannot do the question.
5 If you have time, re-read the chapter.

One word of caution. Accounting is not simply a matter of elementary arithmetic. The solution to many accounting problems often calls for a considerable amount of personal judgement, and hence there is bound to be some degree of subjectivity attached to the solution.

The problems demonstrated in this book are not readily solved in the real world, and the suggested answers ought to be subject to a great deal of argument and discussion. It follows that non-accountants ought to be severely critical of any accounting information that is supplied to them, although it is difficult to be constructive in your criticism unless you have some knowledge of the subject matter.

By the end of this book, we think that you will have a sufficient knowledge of accounting to be able to examine critically and constructively much of the accounting information that you are likely to meet. In addition, if you have to take an examination in accounting, it is to be hoped that you will be able to do so and pass with flying colours!

Acknowledgements

Like most authors, I could not have written this book without the help of a considerable number of other people. Many of them have contributed directly to the ideas that have gone into the writing of the book, whilst in other cases I know that I have absorbed their views without being conscious of doing so.

I am indebted to far too many people for me to name them individually, but it would be remiss of me if I did not at least place on record my thanks to Douglas Sievewright of Napier College, Edinburgh. I am grateful to Douglas for reading an earlier draft of the manuscript, and for making very many valuable suggestions for improving it. Most of his recommendations have been incorporated into the final draft. There will, no doubt, still be very many imperfections in it for which I am, of course, entirely responsible.

I have always found that my students are usually extremely tolerant of any mistakes that I make (often unintentional, sometimes deliberate) in my attempts to teach them something about accounting. I can only hope that my readers will be just as tolerant!

Part 1
Introduction to accounting

1 The accounting world

This chapter is an introduction to the world of accounting. It begins with an explanation of the nature and purpose of the subject, and then outlines the relevance of accounting to non-accountants. Modern accounting has now developed into a considerable number of specialisms, and these are briefly described in a subsequent section. A brief outline of the structure of the accountancy profession then follows. The final section describes the major types of organizations covered in the book.

Nature and purpose of accounting

The word *account* in everyday language is often used as a substitute for an *explanation* or a *report* of certain actions or events. Employees may, for example, have to account for how they have been spending their time, or managers of a business may be asked to report upon its progress. In order to do so it is necessary, of course, for them to remember what they have done or to know what has happened. This may come entirely from personal observation or because someone has supplied them with the necessary information. As it is difficult, even in the smallest of businesses, to remember everything of importance for very long, it is usually necessary to write down those events that may need to be reported. Such records can be said to form the basis of a rudimentary accounting system.

In a primitive sense, man has always been involved in some form of accounting. It may have gone no further than measuring wealth by (say) counting the number of cows a farmer owned, but the advent of the monetary system enabled a more sophisticated system to be developed. It then became possible not only to calculate much more meaningfully the increase or decrease in individual wealth over a period of time, but also to assess whether a farmer with (say) ten cows was wealthier than one with fifty sheep.

It took a very long time for formal recording systems to develop on any scale, although it is possible to trace the origins of modern book-keeping as far back as the twelfth century. It was from about then that traders began to adopt a system of recording information that we now refer to as *double-entry book-keeping*. By the end of the fifteenth century, double-entry was widely used in business, especially by the Venetian merchants of that time. The first known book on the subject was published in 1494 by an Italian mathematician called Pacioli. Modern book-keeping systems are still based on the principles of double-entry book-keeping first established in mediaeval times and as outlined by Pacioli.

Put at its simplest, such systems supply managers and proprietors with the answers to three basic questions which can be summarized as follows:

1 What profit has the business made?
2 How much does the business owe?
3 How much is owed to it?

In a small business, a basic double-entry book-keeping system still provides sufficient information to be able to answer these three questions. In larger and more complex business enterprises this is not the case.

Following the industrial revolution, many enterprises grew at an enormous rate, as well as becoming much more complex. It also became quite common for ownership to become divorced from managership. In such situations, it became almost impossible for managers (still less owners) to exercise day-to-day control based largely on personal observation and intervention. It became apparent that if businesses were to be controlled effectively, managers needed to be supplied with more detailed information. As a traditional double-entry book-keeping system was not designed for this purpose, it became necessary to convert the traditional form of recording information into a form that met the requirements of management.

In summary, therefore, it can be argued that modern accounting is now primarily concerned with meeting the demand for information from two main sources:

1 from business owners who want to monitor the progress of their investment – this is known as *financial* accounting; and
2 from the internal management of the company who want information so that they can plan and control the activities of the business – this is known as *management* accounting.

Whilst it is useful to categorize accounting into financial and management accounting, the subject covers an enormously wide range of information supply that ranges far beyond that required by just business managers and proprietors. Other interested parties include creditors, employees, central and local government, investors, journalists, financial analysts and the general public.

This book is mainly concerned with the supply of information to proprietors and business managers. We examine the importance of the subject in that context in the next section.

Accounting and the non-accountant

Some types of business organizations (such as limited liability companies) have a statutory obligation to publish a certain amount of information about their affairs. In order to ensure that the required information is available for publication, a considerable amount of data have to be collected, collated and summarized. We referred to this process in the last section as *financial* accounting.

It is unlikely that non-accountants will be directly involved in the preparation of financial accounts unless they are at a very senior level. They may, however, be required to provide some information for eventual incorporation into them. It is more likely that non-accountants will be involved in supplying information for management purposes, that is, as part of the *management* accounting function. The main purpose of management accounting is to provide management with information for planning and control purposes. Besides supplying information, the non-accountant may also *receive* a great deal of management accounting data. As a result of having more information on which to base plans and monitor their progress, the non-accountant should be able to do his or her job far more effectively.

Employees at all levels are increasingly asked to supply a great deal of information to senior employees. These requests are often directed through the accounting function, but it is not always apparent why such information is required. It may be because it forms part of the annual reporting system, or it may be because it is part of the information-for-management system. Such requests can be highly irksome to those employees who are asked for the information, especially if they do not understand why it is wanted.

Companies must publish their annual financial accounts, but there is no legislation requiring them to publish management accounts. Consequently, it is sometimes very difficult to see why it is necessary to collect a vast amount of data simply for internal consumption. Thus if the job is to be done properly, it is very important that employees are made aware of the purpose and the need for such information. Unfortunately, many management accounting information systems are largely ineffective because they are not properly explained to those employees who are involved in them.

More information does not necessarily mean, of course, that managers take better decisions, since there is no comparative test that can be applied to decisions that might have been taken in the absence of additional information. The test has to be a fairly subjective one. If managers *feel* that they have made a better decision as a result of having more information, then it has probably been worthwhile supplying it to them. This point helps to explain why accounting is such an important subject for non-accountants to study. Until they know something about accounting, it is difficult for them to judge whether accounting information can help them, and if it can, what form it should take.

In brief, therefore, it is suggested that non-accountants need to know something about accounting for two main reasons:

1 in order to ensure that their organizations comply with statutory disclosure requirements; and
2 to ensure that information supplied to them can help them do a far better job.

The purpose of this book is to explain how accounting can be of assistance to the non-accountant. By the end of it, the conscientious student should have a sound grasp of basic accounting techniques. The knowledge acquired should be sufficient for him or her to judge the importance and relevance of much accounting information that he or she comes across.

As modern accounting systems embrace a considerable number of specialisms, it may be helpful to outline some of the major branches of accounting that the non-accountant may meet during his or her career. We review them briefly in the next section.

Branches of accounting

The work which accountants now undertake ranges far beyond that of simply collating data in order to assess business profitability and states of indebtedness. Although this work is still very important, accountants have gradually extended the scope of their responsibilities. Other disciplines (such as operational research and work study) have similarly evolved in order to satisfy an ever-increasing demand for more and more information.

At one time, some observers expected accounting to be superseded by the newer and more scientifically based disciplines. As yet this has not happened, although many accountants now work in those areas, whilst others have absorbed the methods into the solution of accounting problems.

Accountants have always been well placed in this respect, since specialist techniques have to be translated into a language that the layman can understand if he is to benefit from them. The accountant uses money as his language, and since everyone understands the language of money, the accountant has always been at an advantage.

A brief explanation of the main branches of accounting is given in the following sub-sections.

Accountancy and accounting

The accountancy profession is engaged in the collection, collation and distribution of information as an aid towards the control of resources and as a contribution towards decision-making. Many writers use accountancy and accounting as synonymous terms, but in this book *accountancy* will be used to refer to the profession and *accounting* to the subject.

Auditing

Auditing forms a most important branch of the accountancy profession. Once accounts have been prepared they may be checked in order to ensure that they do not present a distorted picture. Such a process is known as *auditing*. Not all businesses have their accounts audited, but it is compulsory for some organizations such as limited liability companies.

Auditors are usually accountants acting under another title. If they are appointed from outside the organization they are sometimes referred to as the *external* auditors. In the case of a limited liability company, they are appointed by the shareholders and not by the company's management. Their job is to protect the interests of the shareholders, and as such, they are answerable to the shareholders. This contrasts with *internal* auditors who are employees of the company, and therefore answerable to the management of the company.

Internal auditors perform routine and detailed checking of the company's accounting and management procedures. In practice, external and internal auditors usually work very closely together, but the distinction made between their respective employers is an important one.

Whilst internal auditors expect to be given a great deal of freedom in performing their duties and to be free from direct interference, they are still employees of the company. Ultimately, therefore, they have to report to the company's senior management. By contrast, external auditors *should* be completely independent, but as the directors of the company normally make a recommendation to the shareholders about the appointment of the auditors, even external auditors may be subject to some indirect pressure. It may be suggested to them, for example, that the directors are considering another firm of auditors. It is not always easy for external auditors to appeal directly to the shareholders, although this is sometimes done when the auditors feel that their freedom is being jeopardized.

Bankruptcy, liquidation and receivership

The work involved in dealing with bankruptcy, liquidation and receivership is all very similar. Individuals and businesses are said to be insolvent if they cannot pay their debts when they are asked to do so. If an individual cannot pay his debts, a legal procedure known as *bankruptcy* may be instituted. His assets may be sold to pay off as many of his debts as possible, and he is then given the chance to begin a new life not burdened by his former debts. He may be subject, however, to some very severe legal restrictions before he is allowed to take on new debts.

In a similar way, a company unable to pay its debts may have to be liquidated; in other words, it will be wound-up and it will go out of existence. In both cases, those parties who are owed money by the bankrupt individual or the liquidated company may lose all or most of what is owed to them.

The treatment of the affairs of a bankrupt individual or that of a company going into liquidation is very complex. The aim is to ensure that the assets are realized in such a way that everyone who is involved is treated in the fairest possible manner.

Companies who are in financial difficulties sometimes anticipate that they may have to go into liquidation by calling in a *receiver*. Sometimes he may be appointed by the creditors or by some other group who is owed money by the company. The receiver's task is to ascertain whether it is possible to reorganize the company in such a way that it can continue to operate. If it can continue to operate, then the receiver will try to ensure that at least some (if not all) of his or her client's debts are settled. It follows that a company is not always put into liquidation when a receiver is called in.

Bankruptcy, liquidation and receivership work is a highly specialist accounting and legal function. It also involves a great deal of business and managerial expertise. Few accountants have much experience of this type of work, and it is usually left to a small number of specialist firms of practising accountants.

Book-keeping

Book-keeping is a mechanical task involving the collection of basic information and the entry of it in special records known as *books of account*. At the end of an agreed period of time, the data are extracted and summarized. This is usually in the form of a periodic statement, known as a *profit and loss account*, and a statement of assets and liabilities, known as a *balance sheet*.

The book-keeping function ends when the periodic statements have been prepared. At that stage, the specific *accounting* function takes over. Although accounting is a generic term, covering almost anything to do with the collection and supply of information, it should be more properly applied to the use and conversion of that information once it has been extracted from the books of account. Book-keeping is a routine operation, whilst accounting requires the ability to assess a problem from certain facts obtained from, *inter alia*, the books of account.

Cost book-keeping, costing and cost accounting

These branches of accounting deal with the collection, collation and supply of *detailed* information, mainly for management purposes. The object is to have sufficient information available in order to help management control the resources of the entity and to provide information for decision-making.

The difference between costing (or cost accounting) and accounting is only one of degree: a costing system requires a great deal more information to be collected. The difference between cost book-keeping and cost accounting is very similar to that between book-keeping and accounting. The collection and storage of information is known as cost book-keeping, whilst the use of it for planning and decision-making is known as cost accounting. A cost book-keeping system contains much more information than a financial book-keeping system and hence the accounts have to be re-adapted to deal with the additional information.

Executorship and trusts

Executorship work involves dealing with the affairs of deceased persons. The deceased may, for example, have left a will which requires the estate to be disposed of in a certain way. A solicitor would normally deal with the legal disposition of the assets and settling of any debts, but an accountant may be responsible for looking after any investments and the calculation and distribution of any income on them in accordance with the will. It is possible that the estate will not be wound-up for many years, and an accountant may act in this capacity for some time.

An accountant may also be involved in administering the affairs of a minor. The minor may be a beneficiary of an estate, but may not be able to control what has been bequeathed until of a certain age. Until that time, a trustee will look after the minor's affairs in strict accordance with both trustee law and the conditions laid down by the person setting up the trust.

Executorship and trustee work is another highly specialist accounting function, and few accountants will have had any experience of it.

Financial accounting

Financial accounting is the more specific term applied to the publication of periodic financial data. Such information is usually prepared for the owner of the business, but it may also be used by management for control and decision-making purposes. Other interested parties will include creditors, employees, central and local government, financial analysts, investors, journalists, and the general public.

Management accounting

Management accounting is another all-embracing term. It was suggested earlier that cost book-keeping deals with the routine collection and summary of information for internal management purposes, whilst cost accounting is more orientated towards supplying information for control and decision-making. Management accounting covers any type of information provided for management. It often necessitates using cost accounting data and adapting it for highly specific decisions which management may be called upon to make. A management accounting system can, therefore, incorporate *all* types of information. Such information may be obtained from a wide range of sources which stretch far beyond those used in a conventional accounting system.

Taxation

Taxation is a highly complex and technical branch of accounting. Accountants involved in tax work are responsible for computing the amount of tax payable both by business entities and by individuals. Neither companies nor individuals need pay more tax than is lawfully demanded, and so tax experts spend much of their time trying to reduce their clients' tax bills. If this is done strictly in accordance with the law, it is known as tax *avoidance* and is a perfectly legitimate exercise. Tax lawfully due but not paid is known as tax *evasion*, and is a very serious offence. The borderline between tax avoidance and tax evasion is a fairly narrow one.

The major accounting specialisms outlined above illustrate the many diverse jobs in which an accountant may be involved. Some are highly specialist functions and most accountants will have had little experience of them. Accountants in practice, for example, are usually specialists in auditing, financial accounting and taxation. Although many accountants in industry also work in these areas, their major specialism tends to be in management accounting. This book is mainly concerned with financial and management accounting.

As it is likely that the non-accountant will be in contact with members of the different accountancy bodies, it may be helpful to describe briefly the organizational structure of the accountancy profession itself. We do so in the next section.

The accountancy profession

Anyone can practise in the United Kingdom as an accountant. Irrespective of training and experience, there is almost complete freedom to perform accounting work. Some work is, however, legally restricted to those who are considered to be *qualified* accountants or who have been specially approved by the Department of Trade and Industry. This restriction applies particularly to the audit of limited liability companies.

A qualified accountant is generally regarded as someone who has been admitted to membership of one of the major accountancy bodies. Many non-qualified accountants would, however, strongly dispute that they also were not 'qualified', and hence not be able to act in a professional capacity.

It follows that the accountancy profession is very diverse. There are, in fact, *six* major professional accountancy bodies. They are as follows:

1 the Institute of Chartered Accountants in England and Wales;
2 the Institute of Chartered Accountants in Ireland;
3 the Institute of Chartered Accountants of Scotland;
4 the Chartered Association of Certified Accountants;
5 the Chartered Institute of Management Accountants; and
6 the Chartered Institute of Public Finance and Accountancy.

Chartered accountants have to undergo their training in practice (like a solicitor), much of their time being spent on auditing and taxation work. After qualifying, many chartered accountants move out of a practitioner's office and go to work in industry, commerce or government. Certified accountants may also obtain their training in practice, but relevant experience elsewhere counts towards their training. Management accountants usually train and work mainly in industry, whilst public sector accountants specialize almost exclusively in central and local government work, the nationalized industries and other quasi-government entities (such as the health authorities and the water boards).

Apart from the six major bodies, there are a number of important, although less well known, smaller accountancy associations and institutes. There is also another association known as the *Association of Accounting Technicians*. The Association was formed in 1980 especially for those who *assist* qualified accountants in the preparation of accounting information. In order to become an accounting technician, it is necessary to take the Association's examinations. The examinations are, however, less demanding than those of the major accountancy bodies.

It is clear from this brief outline of the accountancy profession that there are a bewildering number of individuals who may call themselves an accountant. Many such accountants are employed in commerce, industry and government, and the non-accountant is likely to meet a considerable number of them. The accountants that he does meet may perhaps all be members of different accountancy bodies, but they will all have one thing in common: their job is to help the *non*-accountant perform more effectively. Accountants are employed to provide a service. They have much to offer to the non-accountant, and it is up to the latter to make the best use of their services.

This book will help to explain what the accountant has to offer. Before moving on, however, it would be helpful to examine the main *types* of organizations which will be encountered in the book. These are reviewed in the next section.

Types of organizations

In a book of this nature it is not possible to consider *all* the types of organizations in which non-accountants might be working, but the main ones which will be used as examples are examined in the following sub-sections.

Sole traders

Like much else in accounting, this term is misleading. The term refers to an organization owned and controlled by one individual, although the owner may employ many other people to help operate it.

Similarly, the term is not restricted to *trading* organizations. It can be used to refer to any type of organization regardless of whether it is a manufacturing, a trading, a service or a not-for-profit-making entity, such as a charity. The main requirement is that it should be owned by one individual.

Sole trader organizations usually operate on an informal basis, and the private affairs of the proprietor may be difficult to distinguish from those of the entity.

Chapters 3, 4 and 5 of this book are primarily concerned with sole trader organizations. This is the simplest type of organization, so you will be able to understand much more clearly the procedures involved in recording and extracting accounting information than if a much more involved form of organization was used.

Partnerships

A partnership exists where two or more individuals share the ownership and control of an entity. It is often the case, for example, that an individual starts out in business on his or her own. After some time, the individual may find that he or she is short of funds or of managerial expertise. The individual may then be willing to let someone else come into the business as a partner. Each partner becomes a joint owner of business (although they may not necessarily be *equal* partners). It is also not unusual to find that new businesses are formed immediately as partnerships, partly to help finance the business and partly to share the burden of running it.

The precise arrangements between the partners (such as over the sharing of profits) should be agreed between them. In the absence of any formal agreement, the provisions of the Partnership Act 1890 are deemed to apply. Otherwise, partnerships are not covered by any specific legislation.

The accounting procedures involved in dealing with partnerships are similar to those which apply to sole trader organizations, and will not be covered in too much detail.

Companies

A limited liability company is a much more formal type of organization than that of either a sole trader or of a partnership. By law, a company is regarded as a *being* quite separate from its owners. As such, therefore, the operation of a company is bound by some extremely severe legal restrictions on how it may be operated. These restrictions are now largely contained within the Companies Act 1985.

Company accounts will be examined in Chapter 6, and thereafter the remaining chapters will be mainly concerned with this type of organization.

Other organizations

Besides sole traders, partnerships and companies, there are, of course, many other types of organizations, such as charities, local authorities and voluntary organizations. There are also specialist types of organizations which the layman might regard as being a form of company, for example, banks, building societies, and unit trusts. This book will not be dealing with these types of organizations, since it is mainly concerned with *basic* accounting practices. These basic practices apply to almost any type of organization, although some specific changes may be necessary depending upon the precise nature and size of the organization's operations.

Conclusion

The aim of this chapter has been to introduce the non-accountant to the world of accounting. The chapter has emphasized that the main objective of accounting is to supply information to a number of interested parties.

Information must be of benefit to those for whom it is intended. Non-accountants are often reluctant to question the value of some accounting information because they are not quite sure either what it means or what purpose it serves. By the end of this book, the non-accountant should have sufficient knowledge to be able to judge the value of almost any accounting information that is encountered.

Now that the world of accounting has been outlined, it is time to turn to the detailed subject matter, and the first task is to learn the basic rules of accounting. These rules are explained in the next chapter.

Questions

1 State briefly the main reasons for which a company employs a team of accountants.
2 Why does a limited liability company have to engage a firm of external auditors, and for what purpose?
3 Why should a non-accountant study accounting?
4 Are there any statutory obligations requiring the preparation of management accounts?
5 Are there any statutory obligations supporting the publication of financial accounts?
6 Describe briefly the nature and purpose of accounts.

2 Accounting Rules

It was suggested in Chapter 1 that accountancy is a profession engaged in the supply of information to a wide range of interested parties. In fact, the amount of information that is available is so enormous that it is necessary to place some limit on what is to be supplied.

Modern accounting systems have evolved over a long period of time. They have not been developed out of any sort of theoretical model, but out of practical necessity. As a result, a number of basic procedures have been developed. These procedures may perhaps best be described as the *basic rules of accounting*. Some authors refer to them under a variety of other names, the most common being: assumptions, axioms, concepts, conventions, postulates, principles and procedures.

In preparing and presenting information, accountants have considerable freedom over which rules to adopt and how to interpret them. Since 1971, the accountancy profession has tried to restrict the room for manoeuvre by issuing a series of accounting guides. These guides are known as Statements of Standard Accounting Practice (SSAPs), and qualified accountants are supposed to adopt them in the preparation of accounting statements. It is impossible, however, to lay down totally rigid rules, because information is only useful if it has been prepared to suit individual circumstances, and individual circumstances may vary enormously. Consequently, accountants are still able to use a great deal of discretion in the preparation and presentation of accounting information.

It is possible, of course, to ignore all of the generally recognized accounting rules and to prepare accounts in an entirely novel way. This would be like trying to play football under different rules than the ones laid down by the Football Association. If the accepted rules are abandoned, however, any match played under entirely new rules would result in a game that would be incomprehensible to most of the spectators. The same situation would apply in accounting if the conventional rules were abandoned. These rules govern the amount and type of information to be collected and the length of the accounting period. They are practical rules, like those in football covering the size of the pitch and the length of the match. Other accounting rules are more of an ethical nature, for example that the rules should be applied consistently and information should not be presented in a deliberately distorted fashion. These rules may again be compared with those in football that cover misconduct, for example that the ball must not be handled and an opponent should not be intentionally kicked.

The basic accounting rules will be outlined in subsequent sections. For convenience, they have been classified as follows:

1 boundary rules;
2 measurement rules; and
3 ethical rules.

This classification is largely arbitrary, although it should prove helpful to explain more clearly the basic accounting rules than if they were listed in random order. There are something like 150 recognized accounting rules. The 14 rules that are considered the most relevant for our purposes have been chosen.

Boundary rules

In small businesses the proprietor can probably obtain all the information that he needs from personal observation. In larger organizations, however, this is much more difficult. It is then essential to give an account of the entity's results at frequent intervals. To cope with this situation, a number of accounting rules have gradually evolved. These rules deal with the amount and the type of information that interested parties may generally require. For convenience, we shall classify such rules as *boundary* rules.

There are four main boundary rules, and we shall examine them in the following sub-sections.

Entity

There is so much information available that accountants start by drawing a boundary around what is known as an *entity*. An entity could be a profit-making business, such as a shop buying and selling goods, or a firm of solicitors offering a service. Such businesses are usually referred to as *profit-making* entities. A profit-making entity may be organized in the form of a sole trader, a partnership or of a limited liability company. However, an entity might well be a *not-for-profit* entity, such as a charity or a local authority. The primary purpose of such organizations is to provide a service to the public, the profit motive being either irrelevant or of secondary consideration.

The accountant tries to restrict the amount of information to that of the entity itself. This is sometimes very difficult, especially in small businesses. In small businesses there is often no clear distinction between the affairs of the business and the private affairs of the proprietor. It is quite common for the proprietor to finance his household expenditure through the business, and he might also pay for some business transactions out of his private bank account. In such a situation, the accountant has to decide what are the business transactions and what are the private transactions of the proprietor. He has then to establish exactly what the business owes the proprietor and what the proprietor owes the business. He will, however, only be interested in recording the effect on the *business* and not on the proprietor's private affairs.

It would be an entirely different exercise if the accountant did deal with the private affairs of the proprietor. In effect, he would be accounting for a different entity. That entity would be considered to be quite distinct from that of the business, although there would obviously be a very close link between them.

Periodicity

Most entities have an unlimited life. They are usually started in the expectation that they will operate for an indefinite life. Consequently, it is clearly impractical for interested parties to wait until the entity eventually ceases before a report is received on its progress. Such parties almost certainly wish to receive regular reports at frequent intervals.

If an entity has an unlimited life, any report must be prepared at the end of what is inevitably an arbitrary period of time. In practice, it is customary to prepare accounting statements for a period of twelve months. Such a time period has arisen largely as a matter of custom, although in the westernized agrarian world it does reflect the four seasons. There is also a natural tendency to compare recent events with those of a year ago. Where entities have an unlimited life, the preparation of annual accounts presents considerable problems in relating specific transactions to appropriate accounting periods.

Apart from custom, there is no reason why an accounting period could not be shorter or longer than twelve months. Indeed, management accounts are often prepared more frequently than once every twelve months, whilst in the construction industry a very long accounting period may be adopted because of the time that it takes to complete a building contract. Nonetheless, current legislation requires limited liability companies to prepare annual accounts, and as tax computations are also calculated on a twelve months basis, it would not be possible for an entity to ignore altogether the conventional twelve months period. In any case, it must be appreciated that given the unlimited life of most entities, *any* period must be somewhat arbitrary no matter how carefully a particular entity tried to relate its accounting period to the nature of its business.

Going concern

The periodicity rule requires a regular period of account to be established irrespective of the life of the entity and of the arbitrary nature of the accounting period. The going concern rule arises out of the periodicity rule. If an arbitrary accounting period is adopted, it is assumed that the entity will continue in existence for the foreseeable future unless there is information to the contrary. It is important to make absolutely certain that the entity's existence is assured for the immediate future, because if this is not the case, then different measurement rules are used in preparing accounts for entities that have a limited life.

Quantitative

Accounting information is usually restricted to information that is easily quantifiable. If a company uses a fleet of vans in the operation of its business, for example, it is normally very easy to count them and to check their ownership. Similarly, it is usually very easy to count the number of employees employed by a company. They may also be very *skilled* employees, but skill is a concept which is hard to quantify. We would, therefore, normally ignore such a concept in preparing the traditional form of accounts.

Measurement rules

The boundary rules state *what* should be included in an accounting system, whereas the measurement rules explain *how* that information should be recorded. There are six main measurement rules, and they are outlined in the following sub-sections.

Money measurement

It would be very cumbersome to record information simply in terms of quantifiable amounts. It would also be impossible to make any fair or meaningful comparisons between different types of assets or different types of transactions. In order to do so, we need to convert the information that we have quantified into a common and recognizable measure. It was argued in the first chapter that the monetary unit has been used for this purpose for many centuries. The monetary unit enables meaningful comparisons to be made between different events and different types of transaction.

Money is an ideal means of converting accounting data into a common unit, and since most quantifiable information is capable of being translated into monetary terms, there is usually no difficulty in adopting the monetary measurement rule.

Historic cost

The historic cost rule is an extension of the money measurement rule. It requires transactions to be recorded at their *original* cost. Consequently, subsequent changes in prices or values are usually ignored. Increased costs may arise because of a combination of an improved product and changes in the purchasing power of the monetary unit, that is, through inflation.

There have been several attempts in the United Kingdom since 1975 to change the historic cost rule in order to allow for the effect of inflation in preparing the traditional financial accounts. As yet, there has been no general agreement on what should replace historic cost accounting (HCA). This subject is examined further in Chapter 20, but for the time being the historic cost rule should be adopted.

Realization

One of the problems of putting the periodicity rule into practice is that it is often difficult to relate a particular transaction to a specific period. A business may order, for example, some goods in period 1, receive them in period 2 and pay for them in period 3. It is not easy to decide in which period the goods were actually *purchased*. In conventional accounting, it would be most unusual to include them in the accounts for period 1, because the business at that stage has not got a legal title to them. They could be included in period 3's accounts when the goods have been paid for. This method is not uncommon, and is known as *cash flow accounting*, transactions only being entered in the books of account when a cash exchange has taken place.

Normally, however, it is customary to enter most transactions in the books of account when the legal title of the goods has been transferred from one party to another and when there is an obligation to pay for them. This means that in most circumstances the goods would have been considered to have been purchased in period 2.

This concept is generally applied. All goods and services are considered to have been purchased when the legal title has been transferred, irrespective of the period in which they are paid for. As long as there is an obligation to pay for such goods and services at some future time, they are said to be *realized*. They should, therefore, be entered in the books of account when they are realized, that is, when the legal title to them has been transferred to the purchaser.

The realization rule also applies to sales of goods to customers and the receipt of other incomes. Goods are treated as having been sold when the legal title to them has been transferred to the customer.

The realization rule can produce some rather misleading results. A company can, for example, treat some goods as being realized in one period, only to find in a subsequent period that the customer cannot pay for them. This means that if the sales have been included in the earlier period, the profit for that period has been overstated (by the amount of profit on the sales). When the bad debt becomes certain, the profit for that period will be reduced, because the bad debt will have to be charged against that year's profit. As it happens, there is an accounting procedure which enables the effect of these distortions to be smoothed out. How the procedure works is explained in Chapter 4.

Matching

The realization rule applies largely to the purchase and sale of goods and services, but a similar procedure can be adopted for other incomes and expenses. This procedure is covered by what is known as the *matching* rule.

An unfair comparison could be made if cash received during a period was simply matched against the cash paid out during the same period. The exact period in which the cash was either received or paid may bear no relationship to the period in which the transactions took place. Consequently, accountants normally adjust cash received and cash paid on to what is known as an *accruals'* and a *prepayments'* basis. An accrual is an amount owed at the end of a period for services supplied during that period. A prepayment is an amount paid or received in advance for services expected to be supplied during a future period.

The conversion of cash received and cash paid on to an accruals' and a prepayments' basis at a period end often involves a considerable amount of arithmetical adjustment. An allowance has to be made for accruals and prepayments calculated at the end of the previous period (that is, for *opening* accruals and prepayments), as well as for accruals and prepayments at the end of the current period (that is, for *closing* accruals and prepayments. We shall be returning to the subject of accruals and prepayments in Chapter 4.

An accruals' and prepayments' system of accounting enables a much fairer comparison to be made between one accounting period and another. It enables the incomes of one period to be matched against the costs of the same period. The comparison is not distorted by the accidental timing of cash receipts and payments. However, the matching rule does require the accountant to estimate the accruals and prepayments at the end of a period, and a degree of subjectivity is, therefore, built into the system.

Dual aspect

The dual aspect rule is a useful practical rule, although it really only states a truism. Every type of transaction that the entity is engaged in has a two-fold effect. If, for example, the amount of cash that the business has is increased, then someone must have provided the money for it to be increased. Similarly, if the business pays out some money, then it must be giving it to someone. In other words, every time something is given, someone else must be receiving it.

In Chapter 1, it was explained that this two-fold effect was recognized many centuries ago. It gave rise to the system of recording information known as double-entry book-keeping. This system of book-keeping is still widely used, and even computerized recording systems are based on it. Double-entry book-keeping is a most convenient system to adopt, because it provides accessible information about an entity's profitability and indebtedness. It also provides a double-check on the accuracy of the transactions that have been entered into the system, thereby enabling errors to be traced more speedily.

There is no real necessity to adopt the dual aspect rule in recording information, but experience has shown that it is a convenient way of storing much basic data. The incorporation of the dual aspect rule into an accounting system is considered in detail in the next chapter.

Materiality

Strict application of the various accounting rules may not always be practical. It could involve a considerable amount of work that may be out of all proportion to the information that is eventually obtained. The materiality rule permits other rules to be ignored if the effects are not considered to be material, that is, if they are not significant. Hence the materiality rule avoids the necessity to follow other accounting rules to the point of absurdity. Normally, for example, it would be considered unnecessary to value the closing stock of small amounts of stationery, or to maintain detailed records of inexpensive items of office equipment. Immaterial items may, therefore, be treated in the accounting system quite differently from material items, even if they are of a similar nature.

Ethical rules

There is an old story in accounting about the company chairman who asks his chief accountant how much profit the company has made. The chief accountant replies by asking how much profit the chairman would like to make. Accountants recognize that there is some truth in this story. It is quite possible for different accountants to use the same basic data in calculating profit, and yet still obtain different results.

It might be thought that by obeying all the same accounting rules, it would be impossible to arrive at different levels of profit. Unfortunately, this is not the case, since all of the main accounting rules are capable of wide intepretation. As we have seen in an earlier section, for example, the matching rule involves making an estimate of accruals and prepayments, whilst the materiality rule allows the accountant to decide what is material. Both rules involve an element of subjective judgement, and no two accountants are likely to agree precisely on how these rules should be applied in specific instances.

In order to limit the room for individual manoeuvre, a number of other rules have been evolved. These rules are somewhat ethical in nature, and indeed some authors refer to them as accounting *principles*. (Other authors, however, sometimes refer to *all* of the basic accounting rules as principles.) The ethical rules require accountants to follow not just the letter but the spirit of the basic rules.

There are four main accounting rules of an ethical nature, and they are reviewed individually in the following sub-sections.

Prudence

The prudence rule (which is sometimes known as *conservatism*) arises out of the need to make a number of estimates in preparing periodic accounts. Business managers and proprietors are often naturally over-optimistic about future events. As a result, there is a tendency to be too confident about the future, and not to be altogether realistic about the entity's prospects. There may be, for example, some undue optimism over the creditworthiness of a particular customer.

Such optimism may result in a gross over-estimation of profit, because insufficient allowance is made for the level of doubtful debts. The prudence rule is sometimes expressed in the form of a simple maxim:

If in doubt, overstate losses and understate profits.

Consistency

As we have seen, the traditional accounting statements necessitate a considerable amount of discretion in the application of the basic accounting rules. The consistency rule requires that once the various accounting rules have been adopted, they must be followed in all subsequent accounting periods.

It would be considered quite unethical to change those rules just because they were unfashionable, or because alternative ones gave better results. Once adopted, the rules must be applied *consistently*, unless circumstances change which make it necessary to adopt new ones. If the rules are consistently followed, the users of the accounts can be confident that fair and undistorted comparisons can be made between different accounting statements.

It is permissible to adopt new rules (or to interpret them differently) if circumstances change, but the effect of such changes must be clearly highlighted and any comparative figures adjusted accordingly.

Objectivity

Accounts should be prepared with the minimum amount of bias. This is not an easy task, since individual judgement is required in interpreting the rules and adapting them to suit particular circumstances. Proprietors may want, for example, to adopt a policy which would result in higher profit figures or to disguise poor results. Accounts prepared on such a basis would be considered to lack objectivity if the facts did not support that kind of interpretation.

If optional policy decisions are possible within the existing rules, it is advisable to fall back on the prudence rule. Indeed, the prudence rule tends to be an overriding one. If in doubt about which rule to adopt (or how it should be interpreted), the prudence rule should always take precedence.

It should be recognized, however, that if the prudence rule is always adopted as the easy way out of a difficult problem, the accountant could be accused of a lack of objectivity. In other words, he must not use this rule to avoid making a difficult decision. Indeed, it is just as unfair to be excessively cautious as it is to be widely optimistic. Extremism of any kind suggests a lack of objectivity, and both over-caution and over-optimism should be avoided.

Relevance

The amount of information that could be supplied to any interested party is practically unlimited. If too much information is disclosed, it becomes very difficult to absorb. It should, therefore, be presented only if it is relevant.

The selection of relevant information requires much experience and judgement, as well as calling for a great understanding of the user's requirements. It needs to be designed in such a way that it meets the *objectives* of specific user groups. If too much information is given it may be thought to be an attempt to mislead the users. As a result, the information may be rejected altogether.

In this context, accountants try to present accounts in such a way that they represent 'a true and fair view'. In fact, the Companies Act 1985 requires company accounts to reflect this precise criterion. The Act does not define what is meant by 'true and fair', but it is assumed that accounts will represent a true and fair view if a company has followed the rules laid down in the respective statements of standard accounting practice.

Accounting standards are formulated by a committee comprising senior members of the accountancy profession, industry and commerce. The implementation of their recommendations becomes the responsibility of the six major professional accountancy bodies, and once approved, they have to be followed by all professionally qualified accountants. By the end of 1985, 23 statements of standard accounting practice had been issued (although two had been withdrawn). Such statements are considered to represent the most authoritative view of how certain matters should be dealt with in the accounts of those entities which are intended to give a true and fair view. This is perhaps rather a strange way of requiring compliance with the standards, because it suggests that some accounts are not meant to give a true and fair view!

The standards cover such diverse subjects as the accounting policies adopted by an entity, and the treatment of depreciation, taxation and stock valuations in the accounts of entities intended 'to give a true and fair view'. Although professionally qualified accountants are supposed to follow the recommendations contained within the standards, they still leave room for considerable individual intepretation. Indeed, some accountants have chosen to ignore the standards, but as yet, no disciplinary action seems to have been taken against anyone for ignoring them.

Summary

It may be convenient at this stage to summarize the basic accounting rules outlined in the previous section, since a summary will be useful to refer back to when studying later chapters. In brief, therefore, the basic accounting rules may be summarized as follows:

Boundary rules

1 *Entity*. Accounting information must be restricted to the entity itself. It should not be extended to the private affairs of those individuals connected with it.
2 *Periodicity*. Accounts should be prepared at the end of a defined period of time. This period should be adopted as the regular period of account.
3 *Going concern*. The accounts should be prepared on the assumption that the entity will continue in existence for the foreseeable future.
4 *Quantitative*. Only information that is capable of being easily quantified should be included in an accounting system.

Measurement rules

1 *Money measurement*. Quantifiable information must be translated into monetary terms before being included in an accounting system.

2 *Historic cost*. Transactions should be recorded in the books of account at their historic cost, that is, at their original purchase cost.
3 *Realization*. Transactions should be entered in the books of account when the legal title to them has been transferred from one party to another party, irrespective of when the cash settlement takes place.
4 *Matching*. Cash received and cash paid during a particular accounting period should be adjusted in order to match the cost of sales against the sales revenue for the same period.
5 *Dual aspect*. All transactions should be recorded in a double-entry format so that the giving and the receiving effect of each transaction is reflected within the accounting system.
6 *Materiality*. The basic accounting rules must not be rigidly applied if the treatment of some transactions would be out of all proportion to the results obtained by adopting an inflexible interpretation of the rules.

Ethical rules

1 *Prudence*. If there is some doubt over the treatment of a particular transaction, income should be underestimated and expenditure overestimated, so that profit is more likely to be understated and losses overstated.
2 *Consistency*. Accounting rules should not be amended unless there is a fundamental change in circumstances that necessitates a reconsideration of the original rules.
3 *Objectivity*. Personal prejudice must be avoided in the interpretation of the basic accounting rules.
4 *Relevance*. Accounting statements should not include information that prevents the user from obtaining a true and fair view of the information being communicated to him.

Conclusion

In this chapter 14 basic accounting rules have been identified that are commonly adopted in the preparation of accounting statements. Four of these rules have been described as boundary rules, six as measurement rules and four as ethical rules. It has been argued that the boundary rules limit the amount and type of information that is traditionally collected and stored in an accounting system. The measurement rules provide some guidance on how that information should be recorded, and the ethical rules lay down a code of conduct on how all the other rules should be interpreted.

The exact number, classification and description of these various accounting rules is subject to much debate amongst accountants. Most entities can, in fact, adopt what rules they like. However, it should be noted that as far as limited liability companies are concerned, four of the basic accounting rules must be followed. These are the going concern, matching, prudence, and consistency rules. In addition, most companies and other entities will also adopt the other ten accounting rules outlined in this chapter.

The next chapter deals with the practical application of the dual aspect rule. This rule is at the heart of double-entry book-keeping and most modern accounting systems are based upon it.

Questions

In each of the following questions you are required to state which accounting rule the accountant would most probably adopt in dealing with the problem.

1
1 Electricity consumed in period 1 and paid for in period 2.
2 Equipment originally purchased for £20,000 which would now cost £30,000.
3 The company which has a good industrial relations' record.
4 A five year construction contract.
5 A customer who might go bankrupt owing the company £5,000.
6 The company's vehicles which would only have a small scrap value if it goes into liquidation.

2
1 A demand by the company's chairman to include every detailed transaction in the presentation of the annual accounts.
2 A sole-trader business which has paid the proprietor's income tax based partly on the business profits for the year.
3 A proposed change in the method of valuing stock.
4 The valuation of a gallon of petrol in one vehicle at the end of accounting period 1.
5 A vehicle which could be sold for more than it was purchased.
6 Goods which were sold to a customer in period 1, but for which the cash was only received in period 2.

3
1 The proprietor who has supplied the business capital out of his own private bank account.
2 The sales manager who is always very optimistic about the credit-worthiness of prospective customers.
3 The managing director who does not want annual accounts prepared as the company operates a continuous 24 hours a day/365 days a year process.
4 At the end of period 1, it is difficult to be certain whether the company will have to pay legal fees of £1,000 or £3,000.
5 The proprietor who argues that the accountant has got a motor vehicle entered twice in the books of account.
6 Some goods were purchased and entered into stock at the end of period 1, but they were not paid for until period 2.

4 The following is a list of problems which an accountant may well meet in practice:

1 The transfer fee of a footballer.
2 Goods sold in one period, but the cash for them is received in a later period.
3 The proprietor's personal dwelling house has been used as security for a loan which the bank has granted to the company.
4 What profit to take in the third year of a five year construction contract.
5 Small stocks of stationery held at the accounting year end.
6 Expenditure incurred in working on the improvement of a new drug.

Required:
State:
(a) which accounting rule the accountant would most probably adopt in dealing with each of the above problems; and
(b) the reasons for your choice.

Part 2

Financial accounting

3 Recording accounting information

In the last chapter a number of basic accounting rules were outlined. In this chapter one of those rules, the dual aspect rule, will be examined in more depth.

Most modern book-keeping systems adopt the dual aspect rule, irrespective of whether they are handwritten, mechanized or computer based. Whilst it is unlikely that the non-accountant will be involved in the detailed recording of accounting information he may well be presented with summaries of it. Such summaries are often prepared in a format that presupposes some knowledge of double-entry book-keeping.

This chapter has been specially designed to introduce the *non-accountant* to the subject of double-entry book-keeping. The chapter contains a number of book-keeping examples, and whilst it might seem unnecessary for a non-accountant to work through them, you are recommended to do so for two main reasons:

1 it will help you to become familiar with accounting terminology; and
2 a knowledge of the methods used in collating accounting information will help you to assess its *usefulness* in whatever context you are going to use it, for example, in decision-making.

You are advised that this will not be an easy chapter to work through. Indeed, it is essential that it is *worked*, as opposed to merely read. Most sections in the chapter contain an exhibit which illustrates the book-keeping procedure being examined in that particular section. These exhibits must be studied most carefully. To help you work through this chapter, you are recommended to adopt the following approach:

1 Read the descriptive material in each section very carefully.
2 Make sure that you understand the requirements of each exhibit.
3 Examine the answer to each exhibit, paying particular attention to the following points:
(a) the way in which it has been presented, i.e. its format; and
(b) how the data in the exhibit have been converted in response to the requirements of the question.
4 Once you have worked through the answer, try and do the question

on your own without reference to the printed answer.
5 If you get the wrong answer, or you find that you do not know how to do the question, re-read the earlier parts of the chapter and then have another attempt at the question.

The study of the dual aspect rule begins with an examination of its fundamental concept in the next section.

The dual aspect rule

The dual aspect rule arises from a recognition that every time a transaction takes place, there must always be a double-sided effect *within* the entity itself. A few examples may help to establish the point.

1 If the proprietor pays £10,000 into a business bank account out of his private resources, the business bank account will go *up* by £10,000, but the amount owed by the business to the proprietor will also go *up* by £10,000.
2 If the business owes Jones £3,000 and it sends him a cheque for £2,000, the amount that it owes Jones will go *down* by £2,000, but its bank account will also go *down* by £2,000.
3 If a business receives £1,000 in cash from someone who owes it some money, its cash will go *up* by £1,000, but the amount that it is owed will go *down* by £1,000.
4 If the business pays £5,000 in cash for a motor car, then the total value of its motor cars will go *up* by £5,000, but the amount of cash that it has available will go *down* by £5,000.

Transaction 1 results in an *up/up* effect. Transaction 2 results in a *down/down* effect. Transactions 3 and 4 result in an *up/down* effect. Thus although some transactions result in a consequent movement in the same direction, other transactions cause a movement to take place in the opposite direction. Nonetheless, there is *always* a two-fold effect: there are *no* exceptions to this phenomenon. We can state quite categorically, therefore, that *within* an entity, any transaction results in a corresponding and equal effect taking place elsewhere within the entity: the effect is always two-fold.

It is this recognition of the two-fold effect of all transactions that has given rise to the system of recording information that we know as double-entry book-keeping. The main objective of double-entry book-keeping is very simple: it is to record the dual nature of all transactions. The method that has evolved to record information in this way is deceptively simple: all that it requires is for each transaction to be recorded *twice* within the system.

The recording is achieved by classifying all transactions into appropriate groupings. These are then stored separately in what are known as *accounts*. An account is simply a history or a record of a particular type of transaction, and accounts used to be kept in bound books known as ledgers. Nowadays, many entities store information in mechanized or in computer-based systems, although old fashioned recording methods are still to be found.

The effect of a particular transaction on an account is to cause the balance on the account either to go up or to go down. In other words, the monetary value of the transaction could either *increase* the total value of all transactions contained within the account, or it could have the opposite effect and *decrease* them. The account can, therefore, *receive* an extra amount, or it can *give* (or release) something that it already contains. It is this receiving and giving effect that has given rise to two terms used in accounting, and with which you must become familiar. The two terms are as follows:

- *Debit:* from the Latin meaning to receive or value received; and
- *Credit:* also from the Latin meaning to give or value given.

Accountants judge the two-fold effect of all transactions on particular accounts from a receiving and giving point of view, and each transaction is recorded on that basis. Thus when a transaction takes place, it is necessary to ask the following questions:

1 Which account should *receive* this transaction, i.e. which account should be debited?
2 Which account has *given* this amount, i.e. which account should be credited?

Accounts have been designed to keep the debit entries separate from the credit entries, thereby emphasizing the opposite (although equal) effect of each transaction. The separation is achieved by recording the *debit* entries on the *left*-hand side of the account, and the *credit* entries on the *right*-hand side. In a handwritten system, each account is normally kept on a separate page (known as a *folio*) in a *book of account* (although if there are a lot of entries, it may be necessary to keep several books of account). A book of account is also sometimes known as a *ledger*, and hence accounts are often referred to as ledger accounts. The format of a typical handwritten ledger account is illustrated in Exhibit 3.1.

There is no logical reason why debits should be entered on the left-hand side of an account, and credits on the right-hand side. It is purely a matter of custom, just as in some countries motorists drive on the left-hand side of the road, while in others they drive on the right-hand side.

The way in which particular transactions are recorded in ledger accounts are examined in the next section.

DATE	DESCRIPTION	FOLIO	AMOUNT £	DATE	DESCRIPTION	FOLIO	AMOUNT £
	DEBIT SIDE				CREDIT SIDE		

Exhibit 3.1: Example of a ledger account

Tutorial notes

1 The columnar headings would normally be omitted.
2 The description of each entry is usually limited to the *title* of the corresponding account in which the equal and opposite entry may be found.
3 The folio column is used to refer to the folio (or page) number of the corresponding account.
4 This example of a ledger account may nowadays only be found in a fairly basic handwritten book-keeping system. Computerized and mechanized systems of recording information usually necessitate an alternative format.

Recording information

It would not be helpful to record information haphazardly, and so what has evolved is a systematic method of capturing the two-fold nature of all transactions in separate accounts. The book-keeper has first to decide in which two accounts the respective transactions should be recorded. In the following sub-sections how a book-keeper comes to that decision is looked at in detail.

Choice of accounts

As it happens, most transactions can be relatively easily grouped into appropriate categories without too much difficulty. The exact number and type of account will depend upon the amount of detail that the proprietor wishes to extract from the system. He or she might be interested, for example, in having a separate analysis for both salaries and wages, or it might be thought that just one account would be sufficient. In practice, there are a number of accounts that are common to most entities, but if there is any doubt about which account to use, the following rule should be adopted:

If in doubt, open another account.

If an account becomes superfluous, it can always be combined with other accounts at a later stage in the analysis.

Whilst some accounts are common to most entities, it will not always be clear from their description what type of transaction they are supposed to record. Listed below, therefore, is a brief summary of the main types of accounts:

Capital	The capital account records what the proprietor has contributed (or given) to the entity out of his private resources in order to start the business and to keep it going.
Cash at bank	The bank account records what money the entity keeps at the bank. It shows what has been paid in (usually in the form of cash and cheques) and what has been taken out (usually by cheque payments).
Cash in hand	The cash account works on similar lines to that of the bank account, except that it records the physical cash received, such as notes, coins and cheques, before it is paid into the bank. The cash may be used to purchase goods and services, or it may be paid straight into the bank. From a control point of view, it is best not to pay for purchases directly from such cash receipts, but to draw an amount out of the bank specifically for sundry purchases.
Creditors	Creditors' accounts record what the entity owes its suppliers for goods or services purchased by or supplied on credit.
Debtors	Debtors' accounts record what is owed to the entity for goods or services sold to its customers on credit.
Discounts allowed	Discounts allowed are cash discounts granted to the entity's customers for the prompt settlement of any debts due to the entity. As a result, the amount of cash received from debtors who claim a cash discount will be less than the total amount for which they have been invoiced.
Discounts received	Discounts received relate to cash discounts given by the entity's suppliers for the prompt payment of any amounts due to them. As a result of

claiming a cash discount, the amount paid to the entity's creditors will be less than the amounts stated on their respective invoices.

Drawings — The description *drawings* is a special term used in accounting. The drawings account is used to record what cash (or goods) the proprietor has withdrawn from the business for his own personal use during a particular accounting period.

Petty cash — The petty cash account works like the bank and the cash accounts. It is usually limited to the recording of minor cash transactions, such as bus fares and small items of office expenses. The cash used to finance this account will either be transferred out of the main cash account or withdrawn from the bank account.

Purchases — The term *purchases* has a restricted meaning in accounting. It relates to those goods that are bought primarily with the intention of selling them (normally at a profit). The purchase of a motor car, for example, would not usually be recorded in the purchases account if it had not been bought with the intention of selling it to a customer. Goods not bought for resale are usually recorded in separate accounts of their own. It should be noted that purchases may require further work to be done on them, or they may be sold exactly in the same form that they were bought.

Sales — The sales account records the value of goods sold to customers during a particular accounting period. The account includes both cash and credit sales. It does not include receipts from the sale of a motor car, for example, originally purchased for use within the business.

Stock — Stock includes the value of goods which had not been sold at the end of the accounting period. In accounting terminology, this would be referred to as *closing* stock. The closing stock at the end of one period becomes the *opening* stock at the beginning of the next period.

Trade creditors — Trade creditor accounts are similar to creditors' accounts except that they relate specifically to amounts owing to suppliers for goods purchased on credit terms.

Trade debtors — Trade debtor accounts are similar to debtors' accounts except that they relate specifically to amounts owing by customers for goods sold to them on credit terms.

Trade discounts — Trade discounts are a form of special discount given, for example, for large orders or to special customers. They result in a reduction of the purchase price or the selling price of goods bought or sold. Trade discounts are not recorded in books of account.

Once the book-keeper has chosen the accounts in which to record all the transactions that have taken place during a particular accounting period, he has then to decide which account should be debited and which account should be credited. We examine this problem in the next sub-section.

Entering transactions in accounts

There is one simple rule to follow in entering transactions in their relevant accounts. It can be summarized as follows:

Debit the account which receives
and
credit the account which gives.

The application of this rule is illustrated below with some common ledger account entries:

1 The proprietor contributes some cash to the business.

Debit: Cash account *Credit:* Capital account
Reason: The cash account receives some cash given to the business by the proprietor. His capital account is the giving account and the cash account is the receiving account.

2 Some cash-in-hand is paid into a business bank account.

Debit: Bank account *Credit:* Cash account
Reason: The cash account is the giving account because it is releasing some cash to the bank account.

3 A van is purchased for use in the business; it is paid for by cheque.

Debit: Van account *Credit:* Bank account
Reason: The bank account is giving some money in order to pay for a van, so the bank account must be credited since it is the giving account.

4 Some goods are purchased for cash.

Debit: Purchases account *Credit:* Cash account
Reason: The cash account is giving up an amount of cash in order to pay for some purchases. The cash account is the giving account and it must be credited.

5 Some goods are purchased on credit terms from Fred.

Debit: Purchases account *Credit:* Fred's account.
Reason: Fred is supplying the goods on credit terms to the business. He is, therefore, the giver and his account must be credited.

6 Some goods are sold for cash.
Debit: Cash account *Credit:* Sales account
Reason: The cash account receives the cash from the sale of goods, the sales account being the giving account.

7 Some goods are sold on credit terms to Sarah.
Debit: Sarah's account *Credit:* Sales account
Reason: Sarah's account is debited because she is receiving the goods, and the sales account is credited because it is supplying (or giving) them.

It is not easy for beginners to think of the receiving and of the giving effect of each transaction. Furthermore, it is especially easy to get them mixed up and reverse the entries. If we look at transactions 6 and 7, for example, it is difficult to understand why the sales account should be credited. Why is the sales account the giving account? Surely it is *receiving* an amount and not giving anything? In one sense it is, of course, because all accounts have an extra amount entered in them if a transaction takes place which affects that account. However, the sales account is a supplying account because it has given (or released) something to another account.

If you find this concept difficult to understand, think of the effect on the *opposite* account. A cash sale, for example, results in the amount of cash-in-hand being increased (not decreased). The cash account must, therefore, be the receiving account, and it must be debited. Somebody must have given the cash, but instead of calling the other account by the name of a person, we call it the sales account.

Most students find it easier, in fact, to work out the double-entry effect of respective transactions by relating them to the movement of cash, and you might find it useful to remember the following procedure:

Either *Debit:* the cash (or bank) account
Credit: the corresponding account
if the entity *receives* some cash;

Or *Debit:* the corresponding account

Credit: the cash (or bank) account
if the entity *gives* some cash.

If a movement of cash is not involved in a particular transaction, work out the effect on the corresponding account on the assumption that one account *is* affected by a cash transaction. In the case of credit sales, for example, the account that benefits from the *receipt* of the goods must be that of an individual, so that individual's account must be debited (instead of the cash account). The corresponding entry must, therefore, be *credited* to some other account. In this case it will be the sales account.

Always remember the general rule used in double-entry book-keeping:

For every debit there must be a credit
and
for every credit there must be a debit.

There are no exceptions to this rule. As this chapter develops, more practice will be obtained in deciding which account to debit and which account to credit. After some time, it becomes largely a routine exercise, and you will find yourself making the correct entries automatically.

It would now be helpful to illustrate the entry of a number of transactions in specific accounts. We do so in the next section.

A ledger account example

This section illustrates the procedure adopted in entering various transactions in ledger accounts. The section brings together the basic material covered so far in this chapter and demonstrates the types of account to be adopted, and the effect of each transaction in terms of debit and credit.

The example given in Exhibit 3.2 and its answer below relates to a sole trader commencing business on his own account. Most non-accountants will not be involved in sole trader entities, but this type of entity has been chosen in order to illustrate the principles of double-entry book-keeping. If we used a more involved form of entity, those principles would become somewhat obscured.

The example is also confined to a business that purchases and sells goods on cash terms. Businesses that buy and sell goods on credit terms will be a feature of later examples.

Exhibit 3.2: Joe Simple: A sole trader

The following information relates to Joe Simple who started a new business on 1 January 19X1:

1 1.1.X1 Joe started the business with £5,000 in cash.
2 3.1.X1 He paid £3,000 of the cash into a business bank account.

3 5.1.X1 Joe bought a van for £2,000 paying by cheque.
4 7.1.X1 He bought some goods for cash costing £1,000.
5 9.1.X1 Joe sells some of the goods for £1,500 for cash.

Required:
Enter the above transactions in Joe's ledger accounts.

The answer to this exhibit is shown below. Work through the solution making sure that you understand the treatment of each transaction. If you are not sure why a transaction has been treated in a particular way, refer back to the earlier sections of this chapter.

Answer to Exhibit 3.2
Joe Simple's books of account:

Cash Account

		£			£
1.1.X1	Capital (1)	5,000	3.1.X1	Bank (2)	3,000
9.1.X1	Sales (5)	1,500	7.1.X1	Purchases (4)	1,000

Capital Account

		£			£
			1.1.X1	Cash (1)	5,000

Bank Account

		£			£
3.1.X1	Cash (2)	3,000	5.1.X1	Van (3)	2,000

Van Account

		£			£
5.1.X1	Bank (3)	2,000			

Purchases Account

		£			£
7.1.X1	Cash (4)	1,000			

Sales Account

		£			£
			9.1.X1	Cash (5)	1,500

Tutorial notes

1 The numbers in brackets after each entry refer to the question notes and have been inserted for tutorial guidance only.
2 The description in each account relates to that account in which the equal and opposite entry may be found.

It is unnecessary for the non-accountant to spend too much time on detailed ledger account work, but before moving onto the next section you are recommended to work through Exhibit 3.2 without reference to the answer. This exercise will help you to familiarize yourself with the dual aspect concept and so help you to understand the rest of the book much more clearly.

After entering all the transactions for a particular period in the ledger accounts, the next stage in the exercise is to calculate the balance on each account at the end of the accounting period. This procedure is outlined in the next section.

Balancing the accounts

During a particular accounting period, some accounts (such as the bank and cash accounts) will contain a great many entries on both sides of the account. Other accounts may contain largely debit entries (for example, the purchases account), whilst other accounts may contain largely credit entries (for example, the sales account). It would be extremely cumbersome to allow the entries (whether they are all debit entries, all credit entries or a mixture of both) to build up without occasionally obtaining a total balance. Indeed, the proprietor will almost certainly want to know not just the detailed composition of each account, but also its overall or *net* balance. Consequently, it will be necessary to balance the accounts at regular intervals. Balancing the accounts requires the book-keeper to add up all the respective debit and credit entries in each account, take one total away from the other, and arrive at a net balance for each account.

Accounts may be balanced extremely frequently (for example, once a week or once a month), although some entities only balance their books once a year prior to the preparation of the annual accounts. For control purposes, however, it is useful to balance the books fairly regularly. The frequency will depend upon the size of the organization, but once a month is probably sufficient for most entities.

The balancing of the accounts is part of the double-entry procedure, and the method is quite formal. The balancing of an account with a *debit* balance on it (that is, when its total debit entries exceed its total credit entries) is illustrated in Exhibit 3.3.

Exhibit 3.3: Balancing an account with a debit balance

Cash Account

		£			£
1.1.X1	Sales (1)	2,000	10.1.X1	Jones (1)	3,000
15.1.X1	Rent received (1)	1,000	25.1.X1	Davies (1)	5,000
20.1.X1	Smith (1)	4,000			
31.1.X1	Sales (1)	8,000	31.1.X1	Balance c/d (2)	7,000
	(3)	£15,000		(3)	£15,000
1.2.X1	Balance b/d (4)	7,000			

Note: The number shown after each narration relates to the tutorial notes below.

Tutorial notes

1. The total debit entries equal £15,000 (£2,000 + £1,000 + £4,000 + £8,000). The total credit entries equal £8,000 (£3,000 + £5,000). The net balance on this account, therefore, at 31 January 19X1 is a *debit* balance of £7,000 (£15,000 − £8,000). Until both the debit entries and the credit entries have been totalled, of course, it will not usually be apparent whether the balance is a debit one or a credit one. However, it should be noted that there can never be a credit balance in a cash account, because it is impossible to pay out more cash than has been received.
2. The debit balance of £7,000 is inserted on the *credit* side of the account at the time that the account is balanced (in the case of Exhibit 3.3 at 31 January 19X1). This then enables the total of the credit column to be balanced so that it agrees with the total of the debit column. The abbreviation 'c/d' means carried down, i.e. the debit balance is carried down in the account in order to start the new period on 1 February 19X1.
3. The £15,000 shown as a total in both the debit and the credit columns demonstrates that the columns balance (they do so, of course, because we have inserted £7,000 in the credit column to make them balance). The totals are double-underlined with the currency sign placed in front of them in order to signify that they are a final total.
4. The balancing figure of £7,000 is brought down ('b/d') in the account to start the new period on 1 February 19X1. The double-entry has been completed because we have debited £7,000 *below* the line (i.e. below the £15,000 debit total). and credited the £7,000 balancing figure *above* the line (i.e. above the £15,000 total).

Exhibit 3.3 demonstrates how an account with a *debit* entry is balanced. Exhibit 3.4 illustrates how an account with a *credit* entry is balanced.

Exhibit 3.4: Balancing an account with a credit entry

Scott's Account

		£			£
31.1.X1	Bank (1)	20,000	15.1.X1	Purchases (1)	10,000
31.1.X1	Balance c/d (2)	5,000	20.1.X1	Purchases (1)	15,000
	(3)	£25,000		(3)	£25,000
			1.2.X1	Balance b/d (4)	5,000

Note: The number shown after each narration relates to the tutorial notes below.

Tutorial notes

1. Apart from the balance, there is only one debit entry in this account: the bank entry of £20,000. The total credit entries amount to £25,000 (£10,000 + £15,000). There is a *credit* balance, therefore, in this account at 31 January 19X1 of £5,000 (£10,000 + £15,000 − £20,000). With many more entries in the account we could not always immediately tell whether the balance was a debit one or a credit one.
2. The credit balance of £5,000 at 31 January 19X1 is inserted on the *debit* side

of the account in order to enable us to balance the account. The balance is then carried down (c/d) to the next period.

3 The £25,000 shown as the total for both the debit and the credit columns identifies the balancing of the account. This has been made possible because of the insertion of the £5,000 balancing figure on the debit side of the account.

4 The balancing figure of £5,000 is brought down (b/d) in the account in order to start the account in the new period beginning on 1 February 19X1. The double-entry has been completed because the debit entry of £5,000 *above* the £25,000 line on the debit side equals the credit entry *below* the £25,000 line on the credit side.

Exhibits 3.3 and 3.4 demonstrate the importance of always obeying the cardinal rule of double-entry book-keeping:

For every debit there must be a credit
and
for every credit there must be a debit.

This rule must still be followed even if the two entries are made in the same account (as is the case when an account is balanced). If this rule is not obeyed the accounts will not balance. This could mean that a lot of time is spent looking for the error, or it could even mean that some incorrect information is supplied to the proprietor, since there is bound to be a mistake in at least one account.

In fact, after balancing each account, the next stage in the procedure is to check that the double-entry has been completed throughout the system. This is done by compiling what is known as a *trial balance*. This procedure is examined in the next section.

The trial balance

A trial balance is a statement compiled at the end of a specific accounting period listing all of the ledger account debit balances and all of the ledger account credit balances. The preparation of a trial balance is a convenient method of checking that the double-entry has been completed throughout the system.

Once all the debit balances and credit balances have been listed, we then compare the total of all the debit balances with the total of all the credit balances. If the two totals agree, we can be reasonably confident that the double-entry has been completed.

It should be noted that a trial balance is a working paper: it does not form part of the double-entry process.

The preparation of a trial balance is illustrated in Exhibit 3.5 which also gives more examples of how transactions are entered in ledger accounts.

Exhibit 3.5: Edward—Compilation of a trial balance

Edward started a new business on 1 January 19X1. The following transactions took place during his first month in business:

19X1	
1.1	Edward commenced business with £10,000 in cash.
3.1	He paid £8,000 of the cash into a business bank account.
6.1	He bought a van on credit from Perkin's garage for £3,000.
9.1	Edward rented shop premises for £1,000 per quarter; he paid for the first quarter immediately by cheque.
12.1	He bought goods on credit from Roy Limited for £4,000.
15.1	He paid shop expenses amounting to £1,500 by cheque.
18.1	Edward sold goods on credit to Scott and Company for £3,000.
21.1	He settled Perkin's account by cheque.
24.1	Edward received a cheque from Scott and Company for £2,000; this cheque was paid immediately into the bank.
27.1	Edward sent a cheque to Roy Limited for £500.
31.1	Goods costing £3,000 were purchased from Roy Limited on credit.
31.1	Cash sales for the month amounted to £2,000.

Required:

(a) Enter the above transactions in appropriate ledger accounts, balance off each account as at 31 January 19X1, and bring down the balances as at that date; and

(b) extract a trial balance as at 31 January 19X1.

The answer to Exhibit 3.5 is shown below. Before moving on to part (b) of the exhibit, make sure that you can do part (a). Follow through the transactions, checking that you understand the respective debit and credit entries. Note carefully how each account has been balanced off. When you are confident that you can do part (a), move on to part (b).

Answer to Exhibit 3.5(a)
Edward's accounts:

Cash Account

		£			£
1.1.X1	Capital (1)	10,000	1.1.X1	Bank (2)	8,000
31.1.X1	Sales (12)	2,000	31.1.X1	Balance c/d	4,000
		£12,000			£12,000
1.2.X1	Balance b/d	4,000			

Capital Account

		£			£
			1.1.X1	Cash (1)	10,000

Bank Account

		£			£
3.1.X1	Cash (2)	8,000	9.1.X1	Rent payable (4)	1,000
24.1.X1	Scott and Company (9)	2,000	15.1.X1	Shop expenses (6)	1,500
			21.1.X1	Perkin's garage (8)	3,000
			27.1.X1	Roy Limited (10)	500
			31.1.X1	Balance c/d	4,000
		£10,000			£10,000
1.2.X1	Balance b/d	4,000			

Van Account

		£			£
6.1.X1	Perkin's Garage (3)	3,000			

Perkin's Garage Account

		£			£
21.1.X1	Bank (8)	3,000	6.1.X1	Van (3)	3,000

Rent Payable Account

		£			£
9.1.X1	Bank (4)	1,000			

Purchases Account

		£			£
12.1.X1	Roy Limited (5)	4,000			
31.1.X1	Roy Limited (11)	3,000	31.1.X1	Balance c/d	7,000
		£7,000			£7,000
1.2.X1	Balance b/d	7,000			

Roy Limited Account

		£			£
27.1.X1	Bank (10)	500	12.1.X1	Purchases (5)	4,000
31.1.X1	Balance c/d	6,500	31.1.X1	Purchases (11)	3,000
		£7,000			£7,000
			1.2.X1	Balance b/d	6,500

Shop Expenses Account

		£			£
15.1.X1	Bank (6)	1,500			

Sales Account

		£			£
			18.1.X1	Scott & Company (7)	3,000
31.1.X1	*Balance* c/d	5,000	31.1.X1	Cash (12)	2,000
		£5,000			£5,000
			1.2.X1	*Balance* b/d	5,000

Scott and Company Account

		£			£
18.1.X1	Sales (7)	3,000	24.1.X1	Bank (9)	2,000
			31.1.X1	Balance c/d	1,000
		£3,000			£3,000
1.2.X1	Balance b/d	1,000			

Tutorial notes

1 The number shown after each narration has been inserted for tutorial guidance only in order to illustrate the insertion of each entry in the appropriate account.
2 There is no need to balance off and carry down the balance where there is a single entry in one account (for example, Edward's Capital Account).
3 Note that some accounts have no balance in them at all at 31 January 19X1 (for example, Perkin's Garage Account).

When you are confident that you can do part (a) of the question, move on to part (b). Note the format of the trial balance, and the listing of all those accounts that have balances on them as at 31 January 19X1.

Answer to Exhibit 3.5(b)

Trial Balance at 31 January 19X1

	Dr	Cr
	£	£
Cash	4,000	
Capital		10,000
Bank	4,000	
Van	3,000	
Rent Payable	1,000	
Purchases	7,000	
Roy Limited		6,500
Shop Expenses	1,500	
Sales		5,000
Scott and Company	1,000	
	£21,500	£21,500

Tutorial notes

1 The total debit balance agrees with the total credit balance, and therefore the trial balance balances. This confirms that the transactions appear to have been entered in the books of account correctly.
2 The total amount of £21,500 shown in both the debit and credit columns of the trial balance does not have any significance, except to prove that the trial balance balances.

Once we have got the trial balance to balance, we can be reasonably confident that we have carried out most of the double-entry procedures correctly throughout the system. However, there are some errors that do not affect the balancing of the trial balance. These errors are as follows:

1 *Omission*. A transaction could have been completely omitted from the books of account.
2 *Complete reversal of entry*. A transaction could have been entered in (say) Account A as a debit and in Account B as a credit, when it should have been entered as a credit in Account A and as a debit in Account B.
3 *Principle*. A transaction may have been entered in the wrong *type* of account; for example the purchase of a new delivery van may have been debited to the purchases account, instead of the delivery vans account.
4 *Commission*. A transaction may have been entered in the correct type of account, but in the wrong *personal* account, for example in Bill's Account instead of in Ben's Account.
5 *Compensating*. An error may have been made in (say) adding the debit side of one account, and an identical error in adding the credit side of another account, the two errors thereby cancelling each other out.
6 *Original entry*. A transaction may be entered incorrectly in both accounts, for example, as £291 instead of as £921.

Even allowing for the types of errors listed above, the trial balance still serves a useful purpose. In fact, it has three main functions:

1 to check the general accuracy of the accounts;
2 to provide a summary of the balance on each account; and
3 to serve as a basis for the preparation of the annual accounts.

As far as function 3 is concerned, how the annual accounts are prepared from a trial balance is explained in the next chapter.

Conclusion

It is most unlikely that non-accountants will become involved in entering transactions in ledger accounts. We have, therefore, avoided going into too much detail about double-entry book-keeping. However, as part of the managerial role, the non-accountant will almost certainly be supplied with information which has been extracted from such a system. In order to assess its real value, it is most important that the non-accountant should know something about where it has come from, what it means, and what reliability can be placed on it. Before leaving this chapter it is recommended that you make absolutely sure that you are familiar with the following features of a double-entry book-keeping system:

- the types of account generally used in practice;
- the meaning of the terms *debit* and *credit*;
- the meaning of the terms *debtor* and *creditor*;

- the way in which transactions are entered in ledger accounts;
- how accounts are balanced; and
- the significance of the trial balance.

This chapter has attempted to provide the basic information necessary to become familiar with the six features listed above. If you are reasonably confident that you now have a basic grasp of double-entry book-keeping, you can move on to an examination of how financial accounts are prepared, but before doing so, you are recommended to test your knowledge of the contents of this chapter by attempting some of the questions that now follow.

Questions

3.1 Adam has just gone into business. The following is a list of his transactions for the month of January 19X1:

1 Cash paid into the business by Adam.
2 Goods for resale purchased on cash terms.
3 Van bought for cash.
4 One quarter's rent for premises paid in cash.
5 Some goods sold on cash terms.
6 Adam buys some office machinery for cash.

Required:
State which account in Adam's books of account should be debited and which account should be credited.

3.2 The following is a list of Brown's transactions for February 19X2:

1 Transfer of cash to a bank account.
2 Cash received from sale of goods.
3 Purchase of goods paid for by cheque.
4 Office expenses paid in cash.
5 Cheques received from customers from sale of goods on cash terms.
6 A motor car for use in the business paid for by cheque.

Required:
State which account in Brown's books of account should be debited and which account should be credited.

3.3 Corby is in business as a retail distributor. The following is a list of his transactions for March 19X3:

1 Goods purchased from Smith on credit.
2 Corby introduces further capital in cash into the business.
3 Goods sold for cash.
4 Goods purchased for cash.
5 Cash transferred to the bank.
6 Machinery purchased, paid for in cash.

Required:
State which account in Corby's books of account should be debited and which account should be credited.

3.4 Davies buys and sells goods on cash and credit terms. The following is a list of his transactions for April 19X4:

1 Capital introduced by Davies paid into the bank.
2 Goods purchased on credit terms from Swallow.
3 Goods sold to Hill for cash.
4 Cash paid for purchase of goods.
5 Dale buys goods from Davies on credit.
6 Motoring expenses paid by cheque.

Required:
State which account in Davies' books of account should be debited and which account credited.

3.5 The following is a list of Edgar's transactions for May 19X5:

1 Goods purchased on credit from Gill.
2 Goods sold on credit to Ash.
3 Goods sold for cash to Crosby.
4 Goods purchased in cash from Lowe.
5 Cheque sent to Gill.
6 Cash received from Ash.

Required:
State which account in Edgar's books should be debited and which account should be credited.

3.6 Ford buys and sells goods on cash and credit terms. The following is a list of his transactions for June 19X6.

1 Goods sold on cash terms to Orange.
2 Goods purchased from Carter on credit.
3 Goods sold to Holly on credit.
4 Goods bought on cash terms from Apple.
5 Holly returns some of the goods.
6 Goods returned to Carter.

Required:
State which account in Ford's books should be debited and which account should be credited.

3.7 The following transactions relate to Gordon's business for the month of July 19X7:

1 Bought goods on credit from Watson.
2 Sold some goods for cash.
3 Sold some goods on credit to Moon.
4 Sent a cheque for half the amount owing to Watson.
5 Watson grants Gordon a cash discount.
6 Moon settles most of his account in cash.
7 Gordon allows Moon a cash discount that covers the small amount owed by Moon.

8 Gordon purchases some goods for cash.

Required:

State which accounts in Gordon's books of account should be debited and which account should be credited.

3.8 Harry started a new business on 1 January 19X8. The following transactions cover his first three months in business:

1 Harry contributed an amount in cash to start the business.
2 He transferred some of the cash to a business bank account.
3 He paid an amount in advance by cheque for rental of business premises.
4 Bought goods on credit from Paul.
5 Purchased a van paying by cheque.
6 Sold some goods for cash to James.
7 Bought goods on credit from Nancy.
8 Paid motoring expenses in cash.
9 Returned some goods to Nancy.
10 Sold goods on credit to Mavis.
11 Harry withdrew some cash for personal use.
12 Bought goods from David paying in cash.
13 Mavis returns some goods.
14 Sent a cheque to Nancy.
15 Cash received from Mavis.
16 Harry receives a cash discount from Nancy.
17 Harry allows Mavis a cash discount.
18 Cheque withdrawn at the bank in order to open a petty cash account.

Required:

State which account in Harry's books of account should be debited and which account should be credited.

3.9 The following is a list of transactions relating to Ivan for the first month that he is in business:

1.9.X9	Started the business with £10,000 in cash.
2.9.X9	Paid £8,000 into a business bank account.
3.9.X9	Purchased £1,000 of goods in cash.
10.9.X9	Bought goods costing £6,000 on credit from Roy.
12.9.X9	Cash sales of £3,000.
15.9.X9	Goods sold on credit terms to Norman for £4,000.
20.9.X9	Ivan settles Roy's account by cheque.
30.9.X9	Cheque for £2,000 received from Norman.

Required:

Enter the above transactions in Ivan's ledger accounts.

3.10 Jones has been in business since 1 October 19X1. The following is a list of his transactions for October 19X1:

1.10.X1	Capital of £20,000 paid into a business bank account.
2.10.X1	Van purchased on credit from Lang for £5,000.

6.10.X1	Goods purchased on credit from Green for £15,000.
10.10.X1	Cheque drawn on the bank for £1,000 in order to open a petty cash account.
14.10.X1	Goods sold on credit for £6,000 to Haddock.
18.10.X1	Cash sales of £5,000.
20.10.X1	Cash purchases of £3,000.
22.10.X1	Miscellaneous expenses of £500 paid out of petty cash.
25.10.X1	Lang's account settled by cheque.
28.10.X1	Green allows Jones a cash discount of £500.
29.10.X1	Green is sent a cheque for £10,000.
30.10.X1	Haddock is allowed a cash discount of £600.
31.10.X1	Haddock settles his account in cash.

Required:
Enter the above transactions in Jones' ledger accounts.

3.11 The transactions listed below relate to Ken's business for the month of November 19X2:

1.11.X2	Started the business with £15,000 in cash.	
2.11.X2	Transferred £14,000 of the cash to a business bank account.	
3.11.X2	Paid rent of £1,000 by cheque.	
4.11.X2	Bought goods on credit from the following suppliers:	
	Ace	£5,000
	Mace	£6,000
	Pace	£7,000
10.11.X2	Sold goods on credit to the following customers:	
	Main	£2,000
	Pain	£3,000
	Vain	£4,000
15.11.X2	Returned goods costing £1,000 to Pace.	
22.11.X2	Pain returned goods sold to him for £2,000.	
25.11.X2	Additional goods purchased from the following suppliers:	
	Ace	£3,000
	Mace	£4,000
	Pace	£5,000
26.11.X2	Office expenses of £2,000 paid by cheque.	
27.11.X2	Cash sales for the month amounted to £5,000.	
28.11.X2	Purchases paid for in cash during the month amounted to £4,000.	
29.11.X2	Cheques sent to the following suppliers:	
	Ace	£4,000
	Mace	£5,000
	Pace	£6,000
30.11.X2	Cheques received from the following customers:	
	Main	£1,000
	Pain	£2,000
	Vain	£3,000

30.11.X2 The following cash discounts were claimed by Ken:

Ace	£200
Mace	£250
Pace	£300

30.11.X2 The following cash discounts were allowed by Ken:

Main	£100
Pain	£200
Vain	£400

30.11.X2 Cash transfer to the bank of £1,000.

Required:
Enter the above transactions in Ken's ledger accounts.

3.12 The following transactions relate to Pat's business for the month of December 19X3:

1.12.X3 Started the business with £10,000 in cash.

2.12.X3 Bought goods on credit from the following suppliers:

Grass	£6,000
Seed	£7,000

10.12.X3 Sold goods on credit to the following customers:

Fog	£3,000
Mist	£4,000

12.12.X3 Returned goods to the following suppliers:

Grass	£1,000
Seed	£2,000

15.12.X3 Bought additional goods on credit from Grass for £3,000 and from Seed for £4,000.

20.12.X3 Sold more goods on credit to Fog for £2,000 and to Mist for £3,000.

24.12.X3 Paid office expenses of £5,000 in cash.

29.12.X3 Received £4,000 in cash from Fog and £6,000 in cash from Mist.

31.12.X3 Pat paid Grass and Seed £6,000 and £8,000 respectively in cash.

Required:
(a) Enter the above transactions in Pat's ledger accounts.
(b) Balance off the accounts as at 31 December 19X3.
(c) Bring down the balances as at 1 January 19X4.
(d) Compile a trial balance as at 31 December 19X3.

3.13 Vale has been in business for some years. The following balances were brought forward in his books of account as at 31 December 19X2:

	£ Dr	£ Cr
Bank	5,000	
Capital		20,000
Cash	1,000	
c/fwd	6,000	20,000

	b/fwd	6,000	20,000
Dodd			2,000
Fish		6,000	
Furniture		10,000	
		£22,000	£22,000

During the year to 31 December 19X3 the following transactions took place.

1 Cash purchases of £15,000.
2 Cash sales of £20,000.
3 Goods bought from Dodd on credit of £30,000.
4 Goods sold to Fish on credit for £50,000.
5 Cheques sent to Dodd totalling £29,000.
6 Cheques received from Fish totalling £45,000.
7 Cash received from Fish amounting to £7,000.
8 Office expenses paid in cash totalling £9,000.
9 Purchase of delivery van costing £12,000 paid by cheque.
10 Cash transfers to bank totalling £3,000.

Required:

(a) Compile Vale's ledger accounts for the year 31 December 19X3, balance off the accounts and bring down the balances as at 1 January 19X4.

(b) Extract a trial balance as at 31 December 19X3.

3.14 Brian started in business on 1 January 19X4. The following is a list of his transactions for his first month of trading:

1.1.X4	Opened a business bank account with £25,000 obtained from private resources.
2.1.X4	Paid one month's rent of £2,000 by cheque.
3.1.X4	Bought goods costing £5,000 on credit from Linda.
4.1.X4	Purchased motor car from Savoy Motors for £4,000 on credit.
5.1.X4	Purchased goods costing £3,000 on credit from Sydney.
10.1.X4	Cash sales of £6,000.
15.1.X4	More goods costing £10,000 purchased from Linda on credit.
20.1.X4	Sold goods on credit to Ann for £8,000.
22.1.X4	Returned £2,000 of goods to Linda.
23.1.X4	Paid £6,000 in cash into the bank.
24.1.X4	Ann returned £1,000 of goods.
25.1.X4	Withdrew £500 in cash from the bank to open a petty cash account.
26.1.X4	Cheque received from Ann for £5,500; Ann also claimed a cash discount of £500.
28.1.X4	Office expenses of £250 paid out of petty cash.
29.1.X4	Sent a cheque to Savoy Motors for £4,000.
30.1.X4	Cheques sent to Linda and Sydney for £8,000 and £2,000 respectively. Cash discounts were also claimed from Linda and Sydney of £700 and £100 respectively.
31.1.X4	Paid by cheque another month's rent of £2,000.
31.1.X4	Brian introduced £5,000 additional capital into the business by cheque.

Required:

(a) Enter the above transactions in Brian's ledger accounts for January 19X4, balance off the accounts and bring down the balances as at 1 February 19X4.

(b) Compile a trial balance as at 31 January 19X4.

3.15 The following balances have been extracted from Field's ledger accounts as at 28 February 19X5:

	£
Bank	13,000
Cash	2,000
Capital	15,000
Creditors	4,000
Debtors	10,000
Drawings	5,000
Electricity	4,000
Furniture	7,000
Office expenses	3,000
Purchases	50,000
Sales	100,000
Wages	25,000

Required:
Compile Field's trial balance as at 28 February 19X5.

3.16 An accounts clerk has compiled Trent's trial balance as at 31 March 19X6 as follows:

	Dr £	Cr £
Bank (overdrawn)	2,000	
Capital	50,000	
Discount allowed		5,000
Discount received	3,000	
Dividends received	2,000	
Drawings		23,000
Investments		14,000
Land and buildings	60,000	
Office expenses	18,000	
Purchases	75,000	
Sales		250,000
Suspense (unexplained balance)		6,000
Rates		7,000
Vans	20,000	
Van expenses		5,000
Wages and salaries	80,000	
	£310,000	£310,000

Required:
Compile Trent's corrected trial balance as at 31 March 19X6.

3.17 The following balances have been extracted from Severn's books of account as at 30 April 19X7:

	£000
Purchases	300
Cash	8
Discount received	2
Rents received	5
Wages	44
Discount allowed	5
Creditors	12
Telephone	3
Sales	500
Capital	100
Sales returns	20
Bank interest received	1
Furniture and fittings	18
Bank (deposit)	50
Advertising	14
Motor cars	22
Bank (current)	5
Purchases returns	15
Land and buildings	40
Debtors	30
Plant and equipment	37
Drawings	45
Fees received	10
Motor car expenses	4

Required:
Compile Severn's trial balance at 30 April 19X7.

4 Basic financial statements

It was suggested in Chapter 1 that business proprietors want to know the answers to three fundamental questions:

1 What profit has the business made?
2 How much does the business owe?
3 How much is owed to it?

The last chapter concluded by illustrating how a trial balance is constructed. The trial balance not only provides a check on the accuracy of the double-entry book-keeping, but it also enables us to prepare the *basic financial statements*. It is from such statements that the three questions posed by business proprietors can be answered. The preparation of the basic financial statements forms the subject of this chapter.

In this chapter, as in the last, sole trader accounts will be used as examples, as a more complicated type of entity would obscure the accounting principles that are being illustrated.

The measurement of profit

Before the preparation of the basic financial statements is examined in detail, it would be useful to examine what accountants mean by *profit*. In this section, therefore, the nature of accounting profit is considered, and later sections will deal with the preparation of financial statements.

Proprietors often try to measure business profit (that is, how well the business has done) by comparing how much cash the business had at the beginning of a period with how much cash it had at the end. This is not usually what accountants mean by profit.

As we argued in Chapter 2, accounts are normally prepared by adopting a certain number of accounting rules. Two of the rules that were examined, the realization rule and the matching rule, require the matching of the cost of sales against the sales revenue for a particular period irrespective of whether the respective transactions have been settled in cash during that period. It follows that the difference between cash received during a period and the cash paid out during the same period is not the same as accounting profit. Cash transactions may relate to earlier or later periods, whereas incomes and expenses (as defined in accounting) try to measure the *precise* activity which has occurred during a strictly defined period of time.

There are great problems, of course, in trying to measure income and expenditure rather than cash receipts and cash payments. Some expenditure, for example, may benefit more than one time period. Thus if the entity purchases a machine, and it is estimated to have a life of 20 years, how should the cost of the machine be matched against the sales revenue earned during each year of the life of that machine?

To cope with this problem, accountants classify expenditure into *capital* and *revenue*. Capital expenditure is expenditure that benefits more than one accounting period. Revenue expenditure is expenditure that relates only to one accounting period. Since the basic financial statements are normally prepared on an annual basis, we can regard revenue expenditure as being virtually synonymous with annual expenditure. If during the next year, we want to receive the benefit of the service that revenue expenditure provides, we will have to re-order or renew the service from the supplier during that year.

Examples of revenue expenditure include goods purchased with the intention of resale, electricity charges, expenditure on rates, and wages and salaries. Examples of capital expenditure include land and buildings, plant and machinery, motor vehicles, and furniture and fittings. Such items are described as *fixed assets*, because they are intended for long-term use within the business. It is also possible to classify income into capital and revenue, although the terms *capital income* and *capital revenue* are not commonly adopted. Income of a revenue nature would include the revenue from the sale of goods to customers, rents received, and dividends received. Income of a capital nature would include the proprietor's capital, and loans made to the business, such as a long-term bank loan.

In practice, it is not always easy to distinguish between capital and revenue items, and the distinction is often an arbitrary one. Some items of expenditure are particularly difficult to distinguish, although most transactions fall into recognizable categories.

The distinction between capital and revenue items is very important, because, essentially, accounting profit is the difference between revenue income and revenue expenditure. If capital and revenue items are not classified as accurately as possible, therefore, a misleading level of accounting profit would be reported.

We examine how accounting profit is calculated in the next section.

Preparation of the basic financial statements

It is now possible to examine how financial statements are prepared.

It may be assumed that a trial balance has been prepared and that the books balance. There are two main stages in preparing the financial statements, and each stage will be dealt with separately.

The trading and profit and loss account stage

The first stage in compiling the basic financial statements is to prepare a profit and loss account. In a trading organization, this stage will first require the preparation of a trading account, followed by the profit and loss account. In order to compile the accounts, it is necessary to extract from the trial balance all the revenue income and expenditure items. These are then matched against each other in the form of a statement called a *trading and profit and loss account*. By deducting the total of the revenue balances from the total of the revenue expenditure balances, we can determine the level of the accounting profit (or loss) for the period. There are two important points to note. These are as follows:

1 It is customary for the trading account to come before the profit and loss account (as will be seen when manufacturing organizations are dealt with in the next chapter). The trading account matches the sales revenue against the cost of goods sold (mainly the cost of purchasing goods). The difference between the sales revenue and the cost of goods sold is known as *gross profit*. The gross profit is then transferred to the profit and loss account where it is added to the other revenue incomes of the business, the total then being matched against all the other expenses of the business (such as heat and light, and wages and salaries). The difference between the gross profit plus other non-trading incomes, less the other expenses is known as *net profit* (or net loss). In other words:

(Gross profit + Other revenue incomes)
− Revenue expenditure = Net profit (or net loss)

2 Both the trading account and the profit and loss account are accounts in their own right. This means that any transfer to them forms part of the double-entry system, and so a corresponding and equal entry has to be made in some other account.

The balance sheet stage

The second stage in the preparation of the basic financial statements is to summarize all the balances that remain in the trial balance once all the trading account and profit and loss account balances have been extracted. The remaining balances are summarized in the form of a statement called a *balance sheet*. A balance sheet is simply a listing of all the remaining balances. Unlike the trading and profit and loss accounts, it does not form part of the double-entry: it is merely a listing of balances.

It would be helpful at this stage to illustrate with a simple example the preparation of the basic financial statements; this is done in the next section.

An illustration of the basic financial statements

In this section, Exhibit 4.1 shows how to prepare a trading account, a profit and loss account, and a balance sheet.

Exhibit 4.1

The following trial balance has been extracted from Bush's books of account as at 30 June 19X7:

Name of account		Dr £	Cr £
Bank (1)		5,000	
Capital (at 1 July 19X6) (2)			11,000
Cash (3)		1,000	
Drawings (4)		8,000	
Motor vehicle at cost (5)		6,000	
Motor vehicle expenses (6)	(R)	2,000	
Office expenses (7)	(R)	3,000	
Purchases (8)	(R)	30,000	
Trade creditors (9)			4,000
Trade debtors (10)		10,000	
Sales (11)	(R)		50,000
		£65,000	£65,000

Note: There were no opening or closing stocks.

Required:

(a) Prepare Bush's trading and profit and loss account for the year to 30 June 19X7; and

(b) a balance sheet as at that date.

The answer to the exhibit is shown below. Note that account numbers have been inserted in the trial balance to help you trace the entries through the respective financial statements. The symbol 'R' (meaning revenue) has also been inserted to help show you which balances relate to the trading account and the profit and loss account.

Work through the solution, noting in particular two main features:

(1) which balance goes in which statement; and
(2) the format of the respective statements.

Answer to Exhibit 4.1(a)

BUSH

Trading, profit and loss account for the year to 30 June 19X7

	£		£
Purchases (8)	30,000	Sales (11)	50,000
Gross profit c/d	20,000		
	£50,000		£50,000
Motor vehicle expenses (6)	2,000	Gross profit b/d	20,000
Office expenses (7)	3,000		
Net profit c/d	15,000		
	£20,000		£20,000
		Net profit b/d	15,000

Tutorial notes

1 The number shown in brackets after each narration refers to the account number of each balance extracted from the trial balance.

2 Both the trading account and the profit and loss account cover a period of time. In this year it is for the year *to* (or alternatively, *ending*) 30 June 19X7.

3 It is not customary to keep the trading account totally separate from the profit and loss account. The usual format is the one shown above whereby the trading account balance (that is, the gross profit) is carried down into the profit and loss account with no natural break occurring between them.

4 Note that the proprietor's drawings (account (4)), are not an expense of the business. Proprietors' drawings are treated as an *appropriation*, i.e. amounts withdrawn by the proprietors in advance of any profit that the business might have made.

Now that we have completed part (a) of the question, we can move on to part (b).

Answer to Exhibit 4.1(b)

BUSH

Balance sheet at 30 June 19X7

	£	£		£	£
Capital			*Fixed assets*		
Balance at 1 July			Motor vehicle at		
19X6 (2)		11,000	cost (5)		6,000
Add: Net profit					
for the year*	15,000		*Current assets*		
Less: Drawings (4)	8,000		Trade debtors (10)	10,000	
		7,000	Bank (1)	5,000	
			Cash (3)	1,000	16,000
	c/fwd	18,000		c/fwd	22,000

BUSH
Balance sheet at 30 June 19X7

		£		£
	b/fwd	18,000	b/fwd	22,000
Current liabilities				
Trade creditors (9)		4,000		
		£22,000		£22,000

*This balance has been obtained from the profit and loss account.

Note: The number in brackets shown after each narration refers to the account number of each balance listed in the trial balance on p. 57.

Tutorial notes

1 The balance sheet is prepared *at* a particular moment in time. It depicts the balances as they were at a specific date. In this example, the balances are shown as at 30 June 19X7.

2 This type of balance sheet shows the capital and liability balances on the left-hand side of the page, and the assets balances on the right-hand side.

3 The left-hand side of the balance sheet is divided into two main sections:
   (a) the capital section shows how the business has been financed (usually from combination of the original capital contributed by the proprietor and profit he has left in the business); and
   (b) the current liabilities section shows what amounts are owed to various parties outside the entity, and which are due for payment within 12 months.

4 As far as the capital section is concerned, the net profit obtained from the profit and loss account must be added to it, because it is a remaining balance within the ledger system. In effect, it is a summary balance: it is merely a *net* balance obtained after matching the revenue income and expenditure balances. It is preferable to deduct any drawings that the proprietor may have made from the net profit for the year in order to show how much he has left in the business out of that year's profits.

5 The current liabilities should be listed in the order of those which are going to be paid last being placed before those that are going to be paid first, e.g. creditors should come before a bank overdraft.

6 The right-hand side of the balance sheet is also divided into two main sections:
   (a) the fixed assets section includes those assets which are intended for long-term use within the business; and
   (b) the current assets section includes assets which are constantly being turned over, for example stocks, debtors and cash.

7 Fixed assets are usually shown at their original, i.e. at their *historical* cost. The fact that they are stated at cost should be noted on the balance sheet.

8 Both fixed assets and current assets should be listed with the least liquid (or realizable) asset being placed first, e.g. property should come before machinery, and stocks before debtors.

9 The total of fixed assets and current assets is known as *total assets*.

You are now recommended to work through Exhibit 4.1 again, but this time without reference to the answer.

Format of accounts

In Exhibit 4.1, we adopted what is known as the *horizontal* format for both the trading and profit and loss accounts, and for the balance sheet. In the United Kingdom, it is now more fashionable to prepare such statements in a *vertical* format, that is so that the information can be read down the page on a line-by-line basis.

There are three good reasons for adopting this format:

1 It is believed that it is more helpful than the horizontal format for those users who are untrained in double-entry book-keeping since it is not presented in a ledger accounts format.
2 It highlights the various sections more clearly.
3 It is easier to read down a page than across it.

As you are probably more likely to meet financial statements prepared in the vertical format (although you will still come across examples of the horizontal format); we shall be adopting the vertical format throughout the rest of this book.

Exhibit 4.2 gives the answer to Exhibit 4.1 by way of illustration of the vertical format of presenting accounts.

Exhibit 4.2

BUSH

Trading and profit and loss account for the year to 30 June 19X7

	£	£
Sales		50,000
Less: Cost of goods sold:		
Purchases		30,000
Gross profit		20,000
Less: Expenses:		
Motor vehicle expenses	2,000	
Office expenses	3,000	
		5,000
Net profit for the year		£15,000

BUSH

Balance sheet at 30 June 19X7

	£	£
Fixed assets		
Motor vehicle at cost		6,000
Current assets		
Trade debtors	10,000	
Bank	5,000	
Cash	1,000	
c/fwd	16,000	6,000

BUSH
Balance sheet at 30 June 19X7

	£	£
b/fwd	16,000	6,000
Less: Current liabilities:		
Trade creditors	4,000	12,000
		£18,000
Financed by:		
Capital		
Balance at 1 July 19X6		11,000
Add: Net profit for the year	15,000	
Less: Drawings	8,000	7,000
		£18,000

Study Exhibit 4.2 carefully, noting how the information shown in Exhibit 4.1 has been rearranged. There are very few changes, except that the information now reads downwards, rather than across the page.

The preparation and format of the basic financial statements have now been outlined. The exhibits that have been used, of course, have been deliberately simple. Major complications may arise in the preparation of these statements, and these are considered in the next section. There is quite a lot of difficult material contained in the section, so take your time over it.

Post trial balance adjustments

After a trial balance has been prepared, it is usually necessary to make a number of last minute adjustments to the accounts. The normal procedure is to calculate a *provisional* balance for each account and then to prepare the trial balance. Any errors will be located at the provisional trial balance stage. Once the books have been balanced, any necessary further adjustments will be made. It is at that stage that the final accounts will be prepared. Only when the accounts have been finalized will the further adjustments be formally written into the ledger accounts. The ledger accounts will then be balanced, and the balances carried down to the next period.

There are four main types of year-end adjustments that are normally required after a provisional trial balance has been extracted. These adjustments are as follows:

1 closing stock adjustments;
2 depreciation adjustments;
3 accruals and prepayments adjustments; and
4 adjustments for bad debts and provisions for doubtful debts.

Each of these adjustments will be considered in some detail in the following subsections.

Stock adjustments

It is most unlikely that all of the purchases that have been made during a particular period will have been sold by the end of it. It is almost certain that some purchases will still be in store at the period end. In accounting terminology, purchases still on hand at the period end are referred to as *stock*.

In calculating the gross profit for the period, therefore, it is necessary to make some allowance for closing stock, since we want to match the cost of goods actually sold (and not the cost of all those goods purchased) with the sales revenue earned for the period. Consequently, we have to check the quantity of stock we have on hand at the end of the accounting period, and then put some value on it. In practice, this is an extremely difficult exercise, and we shall be examining it in more detail in Chapter 10. Most examples used in this part of the book assume that the value of the closing stock is readily available.

We also have another problem in dealing with stock. Closing stock at the end of one period becomes the *opening* stock at the beginning of the next period. In calculating the cost of goods sold, therefore, we also have to allow for opening stock. In fact, the cost of goods sold can be quite easily calculated by adopting the following formula:

Cost of goods sold = (Opening stock + Purchases) − Closing stock

The book-keeping entries are not quite so easy to understand, but they may be summarized as follows:

1 Transfer the opening stock to the trading account:

Required: *Debit:* Trading account *Credit:* Stock account with the value of the opening stock as estimated at the end of the previous period (this should have been brought down as a debit balance in the stock account at the beginning of the current period).

2 Estimate the value of the closing stock:

Required: *Debit:* Stock account *Credit:* Trading account with the value of the closing stock as estimated at the end of the current period.

By making these adjustments the trading account should now appear as in Exhibit 4.3.

Exhibit 4.3: Example of a trading account with stock adjustments

	£		£
Opening stock	1,000	Sales	4,000
Purchases	2,000	Closing stock	1,500
Gross profit c/d	2,500		
	£5,500		£5,500

Note: This format does not show clearly the cost of goods sold, so it is customary to deduct the closing stock from the total of the opening stock and the purchases, as shown below:

	£		£
Opening stock	1,000	Sales	4,000
Purchases	2,000		
	3,000		
Less: Closing stock	1,500		
	1,500		
Gross profit c/d	2,500		
	£4,000		£4,000

Study this amended format very carefully, because it will be encountered frequently in subsequent examples.

Depreciation adjustments

As has already been explained, expenditure which covers more than one accounting period is known as *capital* expenditure. Capital expenditure is not included in either the trading account or the profit and loss account. It would be misleading, however, to exclude it altogether from the calculation of profit.

Expenditure on fixed assets (such as plant and machinery, motor vehicles and furniture) is presumably necessary in order to help provide a general service to the business. The benefit received from the purchase of fixed assets must (by definition) extend beyond at least one accounting period. Nonetheless, it is just as much a charge against profit as that expenditure which provides a benefit for just one accounting period. The only difference is that it is difficult to know how much of the cost of fixed assets should be charged to each accounting period. In accounting terminology, such a charge is known as *depreciation*.

There is also another reason why fixed assets should be depreciated. By *not* charging each accounting period with a proportion of the cost of fixed assets, the level of profit in each period will be correspondingly higher. Thus the proprietor will be able to withdraw a higher level of the profit from the business. If this is the case, insufficient funds may be left in the business, and it may not be able to finance the replacement of its stocks and fixed assets in order to continue operating at the same level that it has done previously.

In practice, it is not easy to measure the benefit provided in each accounting period by the respective fixed assets. Most depreciation methods are very simple. The one most commonly adopted is known as *straight-line* depreciation. This method charges an equal amount of depreciation to each accounting period that benefits from the service that the fixed asset provides. The annual depreciation charge is calculated as follows:

$$\text{Annual depreciation charge} = \frac{\text{Original cost of the asset} - \text{estimated residual value}}{\text{Estimated life of the asset}}$$

In order to calculate the annual depreciation charge, it is necessary, therefore, to work out how long the asset is likely to last, and what it can be sold for when its useful life is ended.

Although it is customary to include fixed assets at their historical cost in the balance sheet, some fixed assets (such as property) may be frequently revalued. If this is the case then the depreciation charge will be based on the revalued amount, and not on the historic cost. It should also be noted that even if the asset is depreciated on the basis of its revalued amount, there is still no guarantee that it can be replaced at that amount. This is especially the case if depreciation is based on historic cost. A combination of inflation and obsolescence may mean that the eventual replacement cost is far in excess of the historic cost. It follows that when the fixed assets eventually come to be replaced, there may well be a short-fall of funds.

Besides straight-line depreciation, there are other methods that may be adopted. One other depreciation method that is sometimes used (although it is far less common than straight-line) is known as the *reducing balance* method. This method is similar to straight-line in that it is based on the historic cost of the asset. It also requires an estimate to be made of the life of the asset, and of its estimated residual value. The depreciation rate is usually expressed as a percentage, and the rate is then applied to the *reducing* balance of the asset, i.e. after the depreciation charge in previous years has been deducted.

Suppose, for example, that an asset costs £1,000, and that the depreciation rate is 50% of the reduced balance. The depreciation charge per year would then be as follows:

Year		£
1. 1.X1	Historic cost	1,000
31.12.X1	Depreciation charge for the year (50%)	500
	Reduced balance	500
31.12.X2	Depreciation charge for the year (50%)	250
	Reduced balance	250
31.12.X3	Depreciation charge for the year (50%)	125
	Reduced balance	125
		.
		.
		.

...and so on, until the asset has been written down to its estimated residual value.

The reducing balance depreciation rate may be found by formula, viz.:

$$r = 1 - \sqrt[n]{\frac{R}{C}}$$

where: r = the depreciation rate to be applied;
n = the estimated life of the asset;
R = its estimated residual value;
C = its historic cost.

The reducing balance method results in a much higher level of depreciation in the first few years of the life of an asset, and a much lower charge in later years. It is a more suitable method to adopt in depreciating vehicles, for example, because vehicles tend to have a high depreciation rate in their early years, and a low rate towards the end of their life. In addition, maintenance costs tend to be low initially, and become greater as the vehicles become older. Consequently, the combined depreciation charge plus the maintenance costs produce a more even pattern of *total* vehicle costs than is the case if the straight-line method of depreciation is used.

There are other methods of depreciating fixed assets, but since they are rarely used they are considered beyond the scope of this text.

The ledger account entries for depreciation are quite straightforward. The annual charge for depreciation will be entered into the books of account as follows:

Debit: Profit and loss account *Credit:* Accumulated depreciation account with the depreciation charge for the year.

Note: Each group of fixed assets will normally have its own accumulated depreciation account.

As far as the balance sheet is concerned, it is customary to disclose the following details for each group of fixed assets:

1 original cost;
2 accumulated depreciation; and
3 net book value (i.e. 1 less 2).

Exhibit 4.4 illustrates the balance sheet presentation.

Exhibit 4.4: Balance sheet disclosure of fixed assets

Fixed assets	*Cost*	*Accumulated depreciation*	*Net book value*
	£	£	£
Buildings	100,000	30,000	70,000
Equipment	40,000	25,000	15,000
Furniture	10,000	7,000	3,000
	£150,000	£62,000	88,000
Current assets			
Stocks		10,000	
Debtors		8,000	
Cash		2,000	
			20,000
			£108,000

Exhibit 4.4 shows how the accumulated depreciation is deducted from the original cost for each group of assets, thereby arriving at the respective net book value for each group. The total net book value (£88,000 in Exhibit 4.4) forms part of the balancing of the balance sheet. The total cost of the fixed assets and the total accumulated depreciation are shown purely for information. Such totals do not form part of the balancing process.

Accruals and prepayment adjustments

In Chapter 2 we described why it was sometimes necessary to make an adjustment for accruals and prepayments at the end of a particular accounting period. This procedure will now be examined in a little more detail.

Accruals

An *accrual* is an amount outstanding at the end of an accounting period for a service rendered during that period. The amount outstanding will be settled in cash in a subsequent period. The entity may, for example, have settled the last quarter's electricity bill one week before the year end. In its accounts for that year, therefore, it needs to allow (or *accrue*) for the amount it will owe for the electricity which it has consumed during the last week of its accounting year (since it is unlikely that it will be invoiced for it until the next period).

The accrual will be based on an estimate of the likely cost of a week's supply of electricity, or if it is preparing its accounts after the next quarter's invoice has been received, on an apportionment of that quarter's invoice.

The ledger account entries are reasonably straightforward. It is not normal practice to open a separate account for accruals, the double-entry being completed within the same account. Exhibit 4.5 illustrates the procedure.

Exhibit 4.5: Accounting for accruals

Electricity Account

		£			£
1.4.X1	Bank	400	1.4.X1	Balance b/d*	400
1.7.X1	Bank	300			
1.9.X1	Bank	100			
1.1.X2	Bank	500			
31.1.X2	Balance c/d**	600	31.3.X2	Profit and loss account	1,500
		£1,900			£1,900
			1.4.X2	Balance b/d	600

*This balance is assumed to be an accrual made in the year to 31 March 19X1.
**This amount is an accrual for the year to 31 March 19X2.

It will be noted from Exhibit 4.5 that the balance on the electricity account at 31 March 19X2 is transferred to the profit and loss account. The ledger account entry is as follows:

Debit: Profit and loss account *Credit:* Electricity account
with the electricity charge for the year.

The double-entry has been completed for the accrual by debiting it in the accounts for the year to 31 March 19X2 (i.e. above the line), and crediting it in the following year's account (i.e. below the line). The accrual of £600 will be shown on the balance sheet at 31 March 19X2 in the current liabilities section under the subheading 'accruals'.

Prepayments

A prepayment is an amount settled in cash during an accounting period for a service or a benefit which is to be received in a subsequent period. If a company, for example, buys a van half way through Year 1 and pays for 12 months tax on it, half of the tax will relate to Year 1 and half to Year 2. It is necessary, therefore, to adjust Year 1's accounts so that only half of the tax is charged to that year's accounts. The other half will eventually be charged to Year 2's accounts. The procedure is illustrated in Exhibit 4.6.

Exhibit 4.6: Accounting for prepayments

Van Tax Account

		£			£
1.1.X1	Balance b/d*	40			
1.7.X1	Bank	100			
			31.12.X1	Profit and loss account	90
			31.12.X1	Balance c/d**	50
		£140			£140
1.1.X2	Balance b/d	50			

*This balance is assumed to be a prepayment arising in the previous period.
**This amount is a prepayment made during the year to 31 December 19X1.

It will be noted from Exhibit 4.6 that the balance on the van tax account is transferred to the profit and loss account. The double-entry procedure is as follows.

Debit: Profit and loss account *Credit:* Van tax account
with the annual cost of the tax on the van.

The double-entry has been completed by debiting the prepayment in next year's accounts (i.e. below the line) and crediting it to this year's accounts (i.e. above the line).

The prepayment of £50 made at 31 December 19X1 will be shown in the balance sheet at that date in the current assets section under the subheading 'prepayments'.

Adjustments for bad debts and provisions for doubtful debts

The fourth main series of adjustments that need to be made in preparing the basic financial statements are those relating to bad debts and provisions for bad debts.

In Chapter 2 it was explained that the realization rule allows the claiming of profit for goods sold even if the cash for them is not received until a future accounting period. This means that a risk is taken in claiming the profit in the period when the goods are legally sold to the customer. If that customer defaults on settling the amount due, the proprietor might already have taken the profit out of the business, but by the time it is found that the debt is bad, it is usually too late to do anything about the miscalculation of profit in the earlier period. However, it is possible to build in an allowance in case any of the trade debtors do default.

We need, therefore, to explain: (1) how to account for bad debts; and (2) how to allow for the possibility that some of the trade debtors may default. Each of these matters is dealt with separately below.

Bad Debts

Once it is absolutely certain that a debt is bad, then it must be written off to the current period's profit and loss account. This means that it will be charged against the profit for a period to which it does not relate. If credit for it has already been taken in an earlier period, it is, of course, too late to correct that period's accounts (other than in a purely arithmetical sense because profit, for example, might already have been paid out on the basis of those accounts).

The double-entry procedure for writing off bad debts is quite straightforward. The entries are as follows:

Debit: Profit and loss account *Credit:* Trade debtor's account
with the amount of the bad debt to be written off.

As far as the balance sheet is concerned, trade debtors will be shown net of any bad debts that have been written off to the profit and loss account.

The provision for doubtful debts account

The profit in future accounting periods will be severely distorted if a number of bad debts occur. It appears prudent, therefore, to allow for the possibility that the profit could be overstated if we do not allow for the possibility that some debtors will default. This is achieved by setting up what is called a 'provision for doubtful debts account'.

An estimate is made of the likely level of bad debts. The estimate will be based on past experience, and it is usual to express it as a percentage of the outstanding trade debtors as at the period end. The double-entry procedure is as follows:

Debit: Profit and loss account *Credit:* Provision for doubtful debts account
with the amount of the provision needed to meet the expected level of bad debts.

The procedure is illustrated in Exhibit 4.7.

Exhibit 4.7: Accounting for doubtful debts

You are presented with the following information for the year to 31 March 19X3:

	£
Trade debtors at 1 April 19X2	20,000
Trade debtors at 31 March 19X3 (including £3,000 of specific bad debts)	33,000
Provision for doubtful debts at 1 April 19X2	1,000

Note: A provision for doubtful debts is maintained equivalent to 5% of the trade debtors as at the end of the year.

Required:

(a) Calculate the increase required in the doubtful debts provision account for the year to 31 March 19X3; and

(b) show how both the trade debtors and the provision for doubtful debts account would be featured in the balance sheet at 31 March 19X3.

Answer to Exhibit 4.7

(a)		£
Trade debtors as at 31 March 19X3		33,000
Less:	Specific bad debts to be written off to the profit and loss account for the year to 31 March 19X3	3,000
		30,000
Provision required: 5% thereof		1,500
Less: Provision at 1 April 19X2		1,000
Increase in the doubtful debts provision account to be charged to the profit and loss account for the year to 31 March 19X3		500

Tutorial note

The balance on the provision for doubtful debts account will be higher at 31 March 19X3 than it was at 1 April 19X2. This arises because the level of trade debtors is higher at the end of 19X3 than it was at the end of 19X2. The required increase in the provision of £500 will be *debited* to the profit and loss account. If it had been possible to reduce the provision (because of a lower level of trade debtors at the end of 19X3 compared with 19X2), the decrease would have been *credited* to the profit and loss account.

(b) Balance sheet extract at 31 March 19X3

	£	£
Current assets		
Trade debtors	30,000	
Less: Provision for doubtful debts	1,500	
		28,500

The treatment of bad debts and doubtful debts in ledger accounts is a fairly technical and complicated matter. However, as a non-accountant it is important for you to grasp just two essential points:

1 A debt should never be written off until it is absolutely certain that it is bad (because once written off, probably no further attempt will be made to recover it).

2 It is prudent to allow for the possibility of some doubtful debts, although it is rather a questionable decision to reduce profit in such an arbitrary manner.

A great deal of technical matter has been covered in this chapter. It would now be helpful to bring all the material together in the form of a comprehensive example; this is done in the next section.

A comprehensive example

In this section we bring together the procedures that are required in preparing the basic financial statements in Exhibit 4.8. This example is a fairly detailed one, so take your time in working through it.

Exhibit 4.8

Wayne has been in business for many years. His accountant has extracted the following trial balance from his books of account as at 31 March 19X5:

	£	£
Bank	1,200	
Capital		33,000
Cash	300	
Drawings	6,000	
Insurance	2,000	
Office expenses	15,000	
Office furniture at cost	5,000	
Office furniture: accumulated depreciation at 1 April 19X4		2,000
Provision for doubtful debts at 1 April 19X4		500
Purchases	55,000	
Salaries	25,000	
Sales		100,000
Stock at 1 April 19X4	10,000	
Trade creditors		4,000
Trade debtors	20,000	
	£139,500	£139,500

Notes: The following additional information is to be taken into account:

1 Stock at 31 March 19X5 was valued at £15,000.
2 The insurance included £500 worth of cover which related to the year to 31 March 19X6.
3 Depreciation is charged on office furniture at 10% per annum of its original cost (it is assumed not to have any residual value).
4 A bad debt of £1,000 included in the trade debtors balance of £20,000 is to be written off.
5 The provision for doubtful debts is to be maintained at a level of 5% of outstanding trade debtors as at 31 March 19X5, i.e. after excluding the bad debt referred to in note 4 above.
6 At 31 March 19X5, there was an amount owing for salaries of £1,000.

Required:
(a) Prepare Wayne's trading, and profit and loss account for the year to 31 March 19X5; and
(b) a balance sheet as at that date.

Answer to Exhibit 4.8

(a) WAYNE

Trading and profit and loss account for the year to 31 March 19X5

	£	£	*(Source of entry)*
Sales		100,000	(TB)
Less: Cost of goods sold:			
Opening stock	10,000		(TB)
Purchases	55,000		(TB)
	65,000		
Less: Closing stock	15,000		(QN 1)
		50,000	
Gross profit		50,000	
Less: Expenses:			
Insurance (£2,000 − £500)	1,500		(Wkg.1)
Office expenses	15,000		(TB)
Depreciation: office furniture	500		(Wkg.2)
Bad debt	1,000		(QN 4)
Increase in provision for doubtful debt	450		(Wkg.3)
Salaries (£25,000 + £1,000)	26,000		(Wkg.4)
		44,450	
Net profit for the year		£5,550	

(b) WAYNE

Balance sheet at 31 March 19X5

	£	£	£	*(Source of entry)*
Fixed assets	*Cost*	*Accumulated depreciation*	*Net book value*	
Office furniture	5,000	2,500	2,500	(TB & Wkg.5)
Current assets				
Stock		15,000		(QN 1)
Trade debtors (£20,000 − £1,000)	19,000			(Wkg.3)
Less: Provision for doubtful debts	950			(Wkg.3)
		18,050		
c/fwd		33,050	2,500	

b/fwd		33,050	2,500	
Prepayment		500		(QN 2)
Cash at bank		1,200		(TB)
Cash in hand		300		(TB)
		35,050		
Less: Current liabilities				
Trade creditors	4,000			(TB)
Accrual	1,000			(QN 6)
		5,000	30,050	
			£32,550	
Financed by:				
Capital				
Balance at 31 March 19X4			33,000	(TB)
Add: Net profit for the year		5,550		(P&L A/c)
Less: Drawings		6,000		
			(450)	
			£32,550	

Key:
TB = from trial balance.
QN = extracted straight from the question and related notes.
Wkg. = workings (see below).
P&L A/c = balance obtained from the profit and loss account.

Workings

		£
1	Insurance:	
	As per the trial balance	2,000
	Less: Prepayment (QN 2)	500
	Charge to the profit and loss account	£1,500
2	Depreciation:	
	Office furniture at cost	£5,000
	Depreciation: 10% of the original cost	£500
3	Increase in provision for doubtful debts:	
	Trade debtors at 31 March 19X5	20,000
	Less: Bad debt (QN 4)	1,000
		£19,000

continued

Workings	£
Provision required: 5% thereof	950
Less: Provision at 1 April 19X4	500
Increase in provision: charge to profit and loss	£450
4 Salaries:	
As per the question	25,000
Add: Accrual (QN 6)	1,000
Charge to profit and loss	£26,000
5 Accumulated depreciation:	
Balance at 1 April 19X4 (as per TB)	2,000
Add: Depreciation for the year (Wkg. 2)	500
Accumulated depreciation at 31 March 19X5	£2,500

After you have worked through Exhibit 4.8 as carefully as you can, try and do the question without referring to the answer.

Estimating accounting profit

Before leaving this chapter, it is considered helpful if the major defects in the traditional method of calculating accounting profit are summarized.

As a non-accountant, it is most important that you appreciate one vital fact: such a method results in an *estimate* of what the accountant thinks that the profit should be. You must not, therefore, place too much reliance on the ***absolute*** level of accounting profit. Accounting profit can only be as reliable and as accurate as the assumptions upon which it is based. If you regard it as a reasonable estimate (and you accept the assumptions adopted in measuring it), you will not go too far wrong in using the information for decision-making purposes.

Listed below is a summary of the main reasons why you should not place too much reliance on accounting profit.

1 Goods are treated as being sold when the legal title to them changes hands, and not when the customer has paid for them in cash. In practice, the cash for some sales may never be received.

2 Purchases are also regarded as having been purchased when the legal title to them is exchanged, although they may not be paid for until a future accounting period.

3 Goods that have not been sold at the period end have to be quantified and valued. This procedure involves a considerable amount of subjective judgement.

4 There is no clear distinction between capital and revenue items.

5 Estimates have to be made to allow for accruals and prepayments.

6 The cost of fixed assets is shared out amongst respective accounting

periods using methods that are fairly simplistic and highly questionable.
7 Arbitrary reductions in profit are made to allow for doubtful debts.
8 Historic cost accounting makes no allowance for inflation. In a period of inflation, for example, the *value* of £100 at the beginning of a period is not the same as £100 at the end of the period.

The above disadvantages of historical cost accounting are extremely serious, but as yet, accountants have not been able to suggest anything better to put in its place. If at this stage, therefore, you do not feel to have much confidence in accounting information, then take comfort in the old adage that 'it is better to be vaguely right than precisely wrong'!

Conclusion

The construction of the basic financial statements have been examined in some detail in this chapter. You should now be in a far better position to assess the relevance and reliability of any accounting information that you come across.

The material that has been covered so far in this book provides a broad foundation for all the remaining chapters. It is essential, therefore, that before moving on to the other chapters, you satisfy yourself that you really do understand the mechanics behind the preparation of the basic financial statements. To test your understanding of this subject, you are recommended to work through all of the exhibits once again, and then to attempt some of the chapter exercises which follow.

Questions

4.1 The following trial balance has been extracted from Ethel's books of account as at 31 January 19X1:

	Dr £	Cr £
Capital		10,000
Cash	3,000	
Creditors		3,000
Debtors	6,000	
Office expenses	11,000	
Premises	8,000	
Purchases	20,000	
Sales		35,000
	£48,000	£48,000

Required:
Prepare Ethel's trading, and profit and loss account for the year to 31 January 19X1, and a balance sheet as at that date.

4.2 **Marion has been in business for some years. The following trial balance has been extracted from her books of account as at 28 February 19X2.**

	Dr	Cr
	£000	£000
Bank	4	
Buildings	50	
Capital		50
Cash	2	
Creditors		24
Debtors	30	
Drawings	55	
Heat and light	10	
Miscellaneous expenses	25	
Purchases	200	
Sales		400
Wages and salaries	98	
	474	474

Required:
Prepare Marion's trading and profit and loss account for the year to 28 February 19X2 and a balance sheet as at that date.

4.3 **The following trial balance has been extracted from the books of Garswood as at 31 March 19X3.**

	Dr	Cr
	£	£
Advertising	2,300	
Bank	300	
Capital		55,700
Cash	100	
Discount allowed	100	
Discount received		600
Drawings	17,000	
Electricity	1,300	
Investments	4,000	
Investment income received		400
Office equipment	10,000	
Other creditors		800
Other debtors	1,500	
Machinery	20,000	
Purchases	21,400	
Purchases returns		1,400
c/fwd	78,000	58,900

	Dr	Cr
	£	£
b/fwd	£78,000	58,900
Sales		63,000
Sales returns	3,000	
Stationery	900	
Trade creditors		5,200
Trade debtors	6,500	
Wages	38,700	
	£127,100	£127,100

Required:
Prepare Garswood's trading, and profit and loss account for the year to 31 March 19X3, and a balance sheet as at that date.

4.4 The following information has been extracted from Lathom's books of account for the year to 30 April 19X4:

	£
Purchases	45,000
Sales	60,000
Stock (at 1 May 19X3)	3,000
Stock (at 30 April 19X4)	4,000

Required:
(a) Prepare Lathom's trading account for the year to 30 April 19X4; and
(b) state where the stock at 30 April 19X4 would be shown on the balance sheet as at that date.

4.5 Rufford presents you with the following information for the year to 31 March 19X5:

	£
Purchases	48,000
Purchases returns	3,000
Sales	82,000
Sales returns	4,000
Stock at 1 April 19X4	4,000

He is not sure how to value the stock as at 31 March 19X5. Three methods have been suggested. They all result in different closing stock values, viz.:

Method 1	£8,000
Method 2	£16,000
Method 3	£4,000

Required:
(a) Calculate the effect on gross profit for the year to 31 March 19X5 by using each of the three methods of stock valuation; and

(b) other things being equal, what would be the effect on gross profit for the year to 31 March 19X6 by using method 1 instead of method 2?

4.6 Standish has been trading for some years. The following trial balance has been extracted from his books of account as at 31 May 19X6:

	Dr £	Cr £
Capital		22,400
Cash	1,200	
Creditors		4,300
Debtors	6,000	
Drawings	5,500	
Furniture and fittings	8,000	
Heating and lighting	1,500	
Miscellaneous expenses	6,700	
Purchases	52,000	
Sales		79,000
Stock (at 1 June 19X5)	7,000	
Wages and salaries	17,800	
	£105,700	£105,700

Note: Stock at 31 May 19X6: £12,000.

Required:
Prepare Standish's trading, and profit and loss account for the year to 31 May 19X6, and a balance sheet as at that date.

4.7 Witton commenced business on 1 July 19X6. The following trial balance was extracted from his books of account as at 30 June 19X7:

	Dr £	Cr £
Capital		3,000
Cash	500	
Drawings	4,000	
Creditors		1,500
Debtors	3,000	
Motor car at cost	5,000	
Office expenses	8,000	
Purchases	14,000	
Sales		30,000
	£34,500	£34,500

Additional information:

1 Stocks at 30 June 19X7: £2,000.
2 The motor car is to be depreciated at a rate of 20% per annum on cost; it was purchased on 1 July 19X6.

Required:
Prepare Witton's trading, and profit and loss account for the year to 30 June 19X7, and a balance sheet as at that date.

4.8 Croxteth has been in the retail trade for many years. The following is his trial balance as at 31 July 19X8:

	Dr	Cr
	£	£
Bank	2,000	
Capital		35,000
Creditors		4,800
Delivery vans at cost	40,000	
Depreciation:		
Delivery vans (at 1 August 19X7)		12,000
Shop equipment (at 1 August 19X7)		2,400
Drawings	8,000	
Purchases	70,000	
Sales		85,000
Shop equipment at cost	8,000	
Shop expenses	7,200	
Stock (at 1 August 19X7)	4,000	
	£139,200	£139,200

Additional information:

1 Stock at 31 July 19X8: £14,000.
2 Depreciation on delivery vans at a rate of 30% per annum on cost, and on shop equipment at a rate of 10% per annum on cost.

Required:
Prepare Croxteth's trading, and profit and loss account for the year to 31 July 19X8, and a balance sheet as at that date.

4.9 The following is an extract from Barrow's balance sheet at 31 August 19X8:

Fixed Assets	*Cost*	*Accumulated depreciation*	*Net book value*
	£	£	£
Land	200,000	—	200,000
Buildings	150,000	60,000	90,000
Plant	55,000	37,500	17,500
Vehicles	45,000	28,800	16,200
Furniture	20,000	12,600	7,400
	£470,000	£138,900	£331,100

Barrow's depreciation policy is as follows:

1 a full year's depreciation is charged in the year of acquisition, but none in the year of disposal;
2 no depreciation is charged on land;

3 buildings are depreciated at an annual rate of 2% on cost;
4 plant is depreciated at an annual rate of 5% on cost after allowing for an estimated scrap value of £5,000;
5 vehicles are depreciated on a reduced balance basis at an annual rate of 40% on the reduced balance;
6 furniture is depreciated on a straight-line basis at an annual rate of 10% on cost after allowing for an estimated scrap value of £2,000.

Additional information:

1 During the year to 31 August 19X9, new furniture was purchased for the office. It cost £3,000 and it is to be depreciated on the same basis as the old furniture. Its estimated scrap value is £300.
2 There were no additions to or disposals of any other fixed assets during the year to 31 August 19X9.

Required:

(a) Calculate the depreciation charge for each of the fixed asset groupings for the year to 31 August 19X9; and
(b) show how the fixed assets would appear on Barrow's balance sheet as at 31 August 19X9.

4.10 Pine started business on 1 October 19X1. The following is his trial balance at 30 September 19X2:

	£	£
Capital		6,000
Cash	400	
Creditors		5,900
Debtors	5,000	
Furniture at cost	8,000	
General expenses	14,000	
Insurance	2,000	
Purchases	21,000	
Sales		40,000
Telephone	1,500	
	£51,900	£51,900

The following information was obtained after the trial balance had been prepared:

1 Stock at 30 September 19X2: £3,000.
2 Furniture is to be depreciated at a rate of 15% on cost.
3 At 30 September 19X2, Pine owed £500 for telephone expenses, and insurance had been prepaid by £200.

Required:

Prepare Pine's trading, and profit and loss account for the year to 30 September 19X2, and a balance sheet as at that date.

4.11 Dale has been in business for some years. The following is his trial balance at 31 October 19X3:

	Dr £	Cr £
Bank	700	
Capital		85,000
Depreciation (at 1 November 19X2):		
Office equipment		14,000
Vehicles		4,000
Drawings	12,300	
Heating and lighting	3,000	
Office expenses	27,000	
Office equipment, at cost	35,000	
Rates	12,000	
Purchases	240,000	
Sales		350,000
Stock (at 1 November 19X2)	20,000	
Trade creditors		21,000
Trade debtors	61,000	
Vehicles at cost	16,000	
Wages and salaries	47,000	
	£474,000	£474,000

Additional information (not taken into account when compiling the above trial balance) is as follows:

1 Stock at 31 October 19X3: £26,000.
2 Amount owing for electricity at 31 October 19X3: £1,500.
3 At 31 October 19X3, £2,000 had been paid in advance for rates.
4 Depreciation is to be charged on the office equipment for the year to 31 October 19X3 at a rate of 20% on cost and on the vehicles at a rate of 25% on cost.

Required:
Prepare Dale's trading, and profit and loss account for the year to 31 October 19X3, and a balance sheet as at that date.

4.12 The following information relates to Astley for the year to 30 November 19X4:

Item	*Cash paid during the year to 30 November 19X4*	*As at 1 December 19X3 Accruals/Prepayments*		*As at 30 November 19X4 Accruals/Prepayments*	
	£	£	£	£	£
Electricity	26,400	5,200	—	8,300	—
Gas	40,100	—	—	—	4,900
Insurance	25,000	—	12,000	—	14,000
Rates	16,000	—	4,000	6,000	—
Telephone	3,000	1,500	—	—	200
Wages	66,800	1,800	—	—	—

Required:

(a) Calculate the charge to the profit and loss account for the year to 30 November 19X4 for each of the above items.

(b) Demonstrate what amounts for accruals and prepayments would be shown in the balance sheet as at 30 November 19X4.

4.13 Duxbury started in business on 1 January 19X3. The following is his trial balance as at 31 December 19X3:

	Dr £	Cr £
Capital		40,000
Cash	300	
Delivery van, at cost	20,000	
Drawings	10,600	
Office expenses	12,100	
Purchases	65,000	
Sales		95,000
Trade creditors		5,000
Trade debtors	32,000	
	£140,000	£140,000

Additional information:

1 Stock at 31 December 19X3 was valued at £10,000.

2 At 31 December 19X3, an amount of £400 was outstanding for telephone expenses, and the rates had been prepaid by £500.

3 The delivery van is to be depreciated at a rate of 20% per annum on cost.

4 Duxbury decides to set aside a provision for doubtful debts equal to 5% of trade debtors as at the end of the year.

Required:

Prepare Duxbury's trading, and profit and loss account for the year to 31 December 19X3, and a balance sheet as at that date.

4.14 Beech is a retailer. Most of his sales are made on credit terms. The following information relates to the first four years that he has been in business:

Year:	19X4	19X5	19X6	19X7
Trade debtors as at 31 January:	£60,000	£55,000	£65,000	£70,000

The trade is one which experiences a high level of bad debts. Accordingly, Beech decides to set aside a provision for doubtful debts equivalent to 10% of trade debtors as at the end of the year.

Required:

(a) Show how the provision for doubtful debts would be disclosed on the respective balance sheets as at 31 January 19X4, 19X5, 19X6 and 19X7; and

(b) calculate the increase/decrease in provision for doubtful debts transferred to the respective profit and loss accounts for each of the four years.

4.15 The following is Ash's trial balance as at 31 March 19X5:

	Dr £	Cr £
Bank		4,000
Capital		20,500
Depreciation (at 1 April 19X4): furniture		3,600
Drawings	10,000	
Electricity	2,000	
Furniture, at cost	9,000	
Insurance	1,500	
Miscellaneous expenses	65,800	
Provision for doubtful debts (at 1 April 19X4)		1,200
Purchases	80,000	
Sales		150,000
Stock (at 1 April 19X4)	10,000	
Trade creditors		20,000
Trade debtors	21,000	
	£199,300	£199,300

Additional information:

1 Stock at 31 March 19X5: £15,000.

2 At 31 March 19X5 there was a specific bad debt of £6,000. This was to be written off.

3 Furniture is to be depreciated at a rate of 10% per annum on cost.

4 At 31 March 19X5, Ash owes the electricity board £600, and £100 had been paid in advance for insurance.

5 The provision for doubtful debts is to be made equal to 10% of trade debtors as at the end of the year.

Required:
Prepare Ash's trading, and profit and loss account for the year to 31 March 19X5, and a balance sheet as at that date.

4.16 Elm is a wholesaler. The following is his trial balance at 30 June 19X6:

	Dr	Cr
	£	£
Advertising	3,000	
Bank	400	
Capital		73,500
Cash	100	
Depreciation (at 1 July 19X5):		
furniture		1,800
vehicles		7,000
Discounts allowed	400	
Discounts received		500
Drawings	10,000	
Electricity	3,200	
Furniture, at cost	12,000	
General expenses	28,900	
Interest on investments		800
Investments, at cost	5,000	
Provision for doubtful debts (at 1 July 19X5)		2,300
Purchases	645,000	
Purchases returns		2,000
Rates	6,000	
Sales		820,000
Sales returns	4,000	
Stock (at 1 July 19X5)	47,000	
Telephone	1,300	
Trade creditors		13,000
Trade debtors	42,000	
Vehicles, at cost	35,000	
Wages and salaries	77,600	
	£920,900	£920,900

Additional information:

1. **Stock at 30 June 19X6: £50,000.**
2. **The provision for doubtful debts is to be made equal to 5% of trade debtors as at 30 June 19X6.**
3. **Furniture is to be depreciated at a rate of 15% on cost, and the vehicles at a rate of 20% on a reducing balance basis.**
4. **At 30 June 19X6 amount owing for electricity, £300, rates paid in advance £1,000.**

Required:
Prepare Elm's trading, and profit and loss account for the year to 30 June 19X6, and a balance sheet as at that date.

4.17 Lime's business has had liquidity problems for some months. The trial balance was extracted from his books of account as at 30 September 19X7:

	Dr	Cr
	£	£
Bank		15,200
Capital		19,300
Cash from sale of office equipment		500
Depreciation (at 1 October 19X6): office equipment		22,000
Drawings	16,000	
Insurance	1,800	
Loan (long-term from Cedar)		50,000
Loan interest	7,500	
Miscellaneous expenses	57,700	
Office equipment, at cost	44,000	
Provision for doubtful debts (at 1 October 19X6)		2,000
Purchases	320,000	
Rates	10,000	
Sales		372,000
Stock (at 1 October 19X6)	36,000	
Trade creditors		105,000
Trade debtors	93,000	
	£586,000	£586,000

Additional information:

1 Stock at 30 September 19X7: £68,000.

2 At 30 September 19X7, accrual for rates of £2,000 and insurance prepaid of £200.

3 Depreciation on office equipment is charged at a rate of 25% on cost. During the year, office equipment costing £4,000 had been sold for £500. Accumulated depreciation on this equipment amounted to £3,000. Lime's depreciation policy is to charge a full year's depreciation in the year of acquisition, and none in the year of disposal.

4 Specific bad debts of £13,000 are to be written off.

5 The provision for doubtful debts is to be made equal to 10% of outstanding trade debtors as at 30 September 19X7.

Required:
Prepare Lime's trading, and profit and loss account for the year to 30 September 19X7, and a balance sheet as at that date.

4.18 Teak has extracted the following trial balance from his books of account as at 31 December 19X8:

	Dr	Cr
	£	£
Building society deposit	20,000	
Capital		66,500
Cash at bank and in hand	400	
Depreciation:		
plant and equipment		
(at 1 January 19X8)		30,000
office (at 1 January 19X8)		16,000
Dividends received (interim)		100
Interest received from building society		700
Interest received from Gray		500
Investments at cost	5,000	
Loan to Gray (repayable 1.10.X9)	10,000	
Office expenses	39,000	
Plant and equipment at cost	50,000	
Purchases	83,000	
Sales		164,000
Stock (at 1 January 19X8)	2,800	
Trade debtors/trade creditors	13,200	22,200
Vehicles at cost	64,000	
Vehicle expenses	12,600	
	£300,000	£300,000

Additional information:

1 Stock at 31 December 19X8: £15,800.

2 During the year to 31 December 19X8, Teak had used some goods (purchased through the business) for his own personal consumption. At cost price these were estimated to be worth £6,000. No entries had been made in the books of account to record this transaction.

3 At 31 December 19X8 there was an amount owing for vehicles expenses of £1,200. At the same date Teak was due to receive interest from the building society of £800, and a final dividend of £600 from a company in which he had some investments.

4 Depreciation is to be charged on plant and equipment at a rate of 30% per annum on cost, and on vehicles at a rate of 25% on the reduced balance.

5 Office expenses include Teak's drawings for the year of £9,000.

Required:
Prepare Teak's trading, and profit and loss account for the year to 31 December 19X8, and a balance sheet as at that date.

5 Manufacturing accounts

In the two previous chapters, we have been dealing almost entirely with trading entities. It has been assumed that when goods have been purchased, no further work has been necessary to put them into a saleable condition before they were eventually sold at a profit.

There are, of course, many businesses whose main purpose is simply to buy *finished* goods and then to sell them to someone else at a profit. These types of businesses are known as *trading* entities. There are, however, other types of businesses who *manufacture* their own products. They may buy materials that require further work to be done on them before they can be sold. Such materials are known as *raw* materials.

In compiling a trading account for manufacturing entities, it is not possible to add purchases to the opening stock and then to deduct the closing stock. The entity will purchase raw materials and further work will need to be done on them before they can be put in their *finished* goods state. It may well be that in manufacturing entities, a considerable amount of work needs to be done to the raw materials before they can be sold to customers. The cost of such work is usually shown in a *manufacturing* account. Manufacturing accounts form the subject of this chapter.

Manufacturing accounts are similar to trading and profit and loss accounts in three respects:

1 they form part of the double-entry system;
2 they are used as summary statements at the end of the financial period; and
3 they can be presented in either the horizontal or the vertical format.

The chapter falls into two main parts: the contents of a manufacturing account, and then how it is constructed.

Contents

A manufacturing account mainly records manufacturing costs, and it is unlikely that many incomes will be found in such an account. The costs which are debited to the account can be divided into two important categories. These are as follows:

1 direct costs (i.e. direct to the product such as materials and labour), and
2 indirect costs (i.e. indirect to the product, such as canteen expenses and factory management).

Direct and indirect costs may be defined as follows:

- A direct cost is a cost which is easily identifiable with a particular department or product.
- An indirect cost is a cost which is *not* easily identifiable with a particular department or product.

The manufacturing account is usually broken down into the following three main sections:

1 direct materials;
2 direct labour; and
3 indirect costs.

These categories are sometimes known as the elements of cost, and Exhibit 5.1 gives a basic example. The account is shown in the vertical format which, as explained in the last Chapter, is considered easier to follow for non-specialists unused to double-entry book-keeping. A detailed explanation of the items in the account follows the exhibit.

Exhibit 5.1: Format of a basic manufacturing account

	£	£
Direct costs (1)		
Direct material (2)	X	
Direct labour (3)	X	
Other direct expenses (4)	X	
Prime cost (5)		X
Manufacturing overhead (6)		
Indirect material cost (7)	X	
Indirect labour cost (7)	X	
Other indirect expenses (7)	X	
Total manufacturing overhead incurred (8)		X
Total manufacturing costs incurred (9)		X
Work-in-progress (10)		
Opening work-in-progress	X	
Closing work-in-progress	(X)	X
Manufacturing cost of goods produced (11)		X
Manufacturing profit (12)		X
Market value of goods produced transferred to the trading account (13)		£X

Notes:

1 The number shown after each item refers to the tutorial notes (see below).

2 The term 'factory' or 'work' is sometimes substituted for the term *manufacturing*.

Tutorial notes

1 *Direct costs*. The exhibit relates to a *company's* manufacturing account. It is assumed that the direct costs listed for materials, labour and other expenses relate to those expenses which have been easy to identify with the specific products that the company manufactures.

2 *Direct materials*. The charge for direct materials will be calculated as follows:

Direct material cost = (Opening stock of raw materials + purchases of raw materials) − Closing stock of raw materials

The total of direct material cost is sometimes referred to as *materials consumed*. Direct materials will include all the raw material costs and component parts which have been easy to identify with particular products.

3 *Direct labour*. Direct labour will include all those employment costs that have been easy to identify with particular products.

4 *Other direct expenses*. Besides direct material and direct labour costs, there are sometimes other direct expenses that are easy to identify with particular products. Such expenses are relatively rare.

5 *Prime cost*. The total of direct material costs, direct labour costs and other direct expenses is known as prime cost.

6 *Manufacturing overhead*. Overhead is the collective term given to represent the total of all indirect costs, so any manufacturing costs that are not easy to identify with specific products will be classified separately under this heading.

7 *Indirect material cost, indirect labour cost and other indirect expenses*. Manufacturing overhead will probably be shown separately under these three headings.

8 *Total manufacturing overhead incurred*. This item represents the total of indirect material cost, indirect labour cost and other indirect expenses.

9 *Total manufacturing costs incurred*. The total of prime cost and the total of total manufacturing overhead incurred equals the total manufacturing costs incurred.

10 *Work-in-progress*. Work-in-progress represents the estimated cost of incomplete work that is not yet ready to be transferred to finished stock. There will usually be some opening and closing work-in-progress.

11 *Manufacturing cost of goods produced*. The manufacturing cost of goods produced equals the total manufacturing costs incurred plus (or minus) the difference between the opening and closing work-in-progress.

12 *Manufacturing profit*. The manufacturing cost of goods produced is sometimes transferred to the finished goods stock account without any addition for manufacturing profit. If this is the case the double-entry effect is as follows:

Debit: Finished goods stock account *Credit:* Manufacturing account with the manufacturing cost of goods produced.

The finished goods stock account is the equivalent of the purchases account in a trading organization.

Sometimes, however, a manufacturing profit is added to the manufacturing cost of goods produced before it is transferred to the trading account. The main purpose of this adjustment is to enable management to compare more fairly the company's total manufacturing cost inclusive of profit with outside prices (since such prices will also be normally inclusive of profit). The profit added to the manufacturing cost of goods produced may simply be an appropriate percentage, or it may represent the level of profit that the industry generally expects to earn. Any profit element added to the manufacturing cost (irrespective of how it is calculated) is an internal book-keeping arrangement, as the profit has not been *realized* or earned outside the business. The double-entry is effected as follows:

Debit: Manufacturing account *Credit:* Profit and loss account with the manufacturing profit.

13 *Market value of goods produced*. The market value of goods produced is the amount which will be transferred (that is, debited) to the trading account. The market value (if a profit loading is added) or the manufacturing cost (if no profit loading is added) is equivalent to the cost of purchasing the goods from an outside supplier.

You are now recommended to study again Exhibit 5.1 most carefully, along with the accompanying tutorial notes. Once you are clear about the basic structure of a manufacturing account, you can move on to the next section where how to construct such an account is explained.

Construction

The construction of a manufacturing account can best be observed by reference to a simple example. This is given in Exhibit 5.2.

Exhibit 5.2

The following balances, *inter alia*, have been extracted from the books of the Wren Manufacturing Company as at 31 March 19X5:

	Dr £
Carriage inwards (on raw materials)	6,000
Direct expenses	3,000
Direct wages	25,000
Factory administration	6,000
Factory heat and light	500
Factory power	1,500
Factory rent and rates	2,000
Factory supervisory costs	5,000
Purchase of raw materials	56,000
Raw materials stock (at 1 April 19X4)	4,000
Work-in-progress (at 1 April 19X4)	5,000

Additional information:

1 *The stock of raw materials at 31 March 19X5 was valued at £6,000.*
2 *The work-in-progress at 31 March 19X5 was valued at £8,000.*
3 *A profit loading of 50% is added to the total cost of manufacture.*

Required:
Prepare Wren's manufacturing account for the year to 31 March 19X5.

The answer to the exhibit is shown below. You are recommended to work through it very slowly, paying particular attention to its format. To help you understand how it has been constructed, some tutorial notes have been added to the solution.

Answer to Exhibit 5.2

Wren Manufacturing Company
Manufacturing account for the year to 31 March 19X5

	£	£	£
Direct materials			
Raw material stock at 1 April 19X4		4,000	
Purchases	56,000		
Carriage inwards (1)	6,000	62,000	
		66,000	
Less: Raw material stock at 31 March 19X5		6,000	
Cost of materials consumed			60,000
Direct wages			25,000
Direct expenses			3,000
Prime cost			88,000
Other manufacturing costs (2)			
Administration		6,000	
Heat and light		500	
Power		1,500	
Rent and rates		2,000	
Supervisory		5,000	
Total manufacturing overhead expenses			15,000
Total manufacturing costs incurred			103,000
Work-in-progress			
Add: Work-in-progress at 1 April 19X4		5,000	
Less: Work-in-progress at 31 March 19X5		(8,000)	(3,000)
Manufacturing cost of goods produced			100,000
Manufacturing profit (50%) (3)			50,000
Market value of goods produced (4)			£150,000

Tutorial Notes

1 Carriage inwards (i.e. the cost of transporting goods to the factory) is normally regarded as being part of the cost of purchases.

2 Other manufacturing costs include the factory overhead expenses. In practice, there would be a considerable number of other manufacturing (or factory) costs.
3 A profit loading of 50% has been added to the manufacturing cost (see Note 3 of the question). The manufacturing profit is a debit entry in the manufacturing account. The corresponding credit entry will eventually be made in the profit and loss account.
4 The market value of goods produced will be transferred to the finished goods stock account.

You are now recommended to work through Exhibit 5.2 again, but this time without reference to the answer.

A comprehensive example

In Exhibit 5.2, the manufacturing account was dealt with in isolation. In order to understand how the manufacturing account complements the trading account, the profit and loss account and the balance sheet, it is necessary for us to work through a comprehensive example. This is done in Exhibit 5.3. Once again, you are recommended to work through the solution most carefully with the guidance of the tutorial notes which follow the answer.

Exhibit 5.3

The following trial balance has been extracted from the books of account of the Knight Manufacturing Company as at 31 December 19X3:

	Dr	Cr
	£	£
Bank overdraft		2,500
Capital		24,000
Direct wages	75,000	
Discounts allowed	3,000	
Discounts received		1,000
Drawings	8,000	
Finished goods stock (at 1 January 19X3)	15,000	
Long-term loan		5,000
Long-term loan interest	500	
Manufacturing expenses (administration and supervisory)	35,000	
Motor van at cost	5,000	
Motor van: depreciation (at 1 January 19X3)		2,000
Motor van expenses	850	
Office expenses	1,650	
Plant and equipment at cost	28,000	
Plant and equipment: depreciation (at 1 January 19X3)		14,000
Purchases of raw materials	50,000	
c/fwd	222,000	48,500

	Dr £	Cr £
b/fwd	222,000	48,500
Raw material stock (at 1 January 19X3)	6,000	
Sales		250,000
Salaries (administration)	29,000	
Salaries (selling and distribution)	14,000	
Trade creditors		12,500
Trade debtors	30,000	
Work-in-progress (at 1 January 19X3)	10,000	
	£311,000	£311,000

Additional information:

1 Stocks at 31 December 19X3 were valued as follows:

	£
Raw materials	7,000
Work-in-progress	12,000
Finished goods	18,000

2 Depreciation is to be charged on the motor van at a rate of 20% on cost, and on the plant and equipment at a rate of 25% on cost.

3 There were no accruals or prepayments at the end of the year.

4 A manufacturing profit of 20% should be added to the manufacturing cost of goods produced.

5 The motor van is used entirely for the delivery of goods to customers.

Required:

(a) Prepare Knight's manufacturing, trading and profit and loss account for the year to 31 December 19X3; and

(b) a balance sheet as at that date.

This looks to be a formidable question, but remember that you have dealt with most of the items in the previous chapter. Only the manufacturing account details are new.

Now here is the solution. Take your time in working through it.

Answer to Exhibit 5.3

(a) Knight Manufacturing Company
Manufacturing, trading and profit and loss account for the year to 31 December 19X3

	£	£	£	£
Sales (1)				250,000
Less. Cost of goods sold:				
Finished stock at 1 January 19X3			15,000	
Market value of finished goods produced (2):				
Direct materials				
Raw material stock at 1 January 19X3		6,000		
Purchases of raw materials		50,000		
		56,000		
Less: Raw material stock at 31 December 19X3		7,000		
Cost of materials consumed		49,000		
Direct wages		75,000		
Prime cost		124,000		
Other manufacturing costs:				
Administration and supervisory	35,000			
Plant and equipment depreciation	7,000			
		42,000		
Total manufacturing costs incurred		166,000		
Work-in-progress:				
Add: Work-in-progress at 1 January 19X3	10,000			
Less: Work-in-progress at 31 December 19X3	(12,000)	(2,000)		
Manufacturing costs of goods produced		164,000		
Manufacturing profit (20%)		32,800	196,800	
			211,800	
Less: Finished stock at 31 December 19X3			18,000	193,800
Gross profit (3)				56,200
Add: Other incomes (4):				
Manufacturing profit			32,800	
Discounts received			1,000	
				33,800
			c/fwd	90,000

b/fwd			90,000
Less: Other expenses (4):			
Administration			
Office expenses	1,650		
Salaries	29,000	30,650	
Selling and distribution:			
Motor van depreciation	1,000		
Motor van expenses	850		
Salaries	14,000	15,850	
Finance			
Discounts allowed	3,000		
Loan interest	500	3,500	50,000
Net profit for the year			£40,000

(b) Knight Manufacturing Company
Balance sheet at 31 December 19X3

	£	£	£
Fixed assets (5)	*Cost*	*Accumulated depreciation*	*Net book value*
Plant and equipment (6)	28,000	21,000	7,000
Motor van (7)	5,000	3,000	2,000
(8)	£33,000	£24,000	9,000
	£	£	
Current assets			
Stocks: Raw materials (9)	7,000		
Work-in-progress (9)	12,000		
Finished goods (9)	18,000	37,000	
Trade debtors		30,000	
		67,000	
Less: Current liabilities:			
Trade creditors	12,500		
Bank overdraft	2,500	15,000	52,000
			£61,000
Financed by:			£
Capital			
Balance at 1 January 19X3			24,000
Add: Net profit for the year		40,000	
Less: Drawings		8,000	32,000
Proprietor's capital (10)			56,000
Loan (11)			5,000
			£61,000

Tutorial notes

1 Notice that with the vertical format the account begins with sales.
2 A detailed explanation is then given of how the manufacturing cost of goods produced has been arrived at. This part of the manufacturing account is similar to the one used in Exhibit 5.2.
3 At the gross profit stage both the manufacturing account and the trading account have been effectively completed.
4 If the information permits, it is customary to sectionalize other incomes and expenses into appropriate categories. Thus in this example the other expenses have been classified into administration, selling and distribution, and finance expenses.
5 As explained in the last chapter, the fixed assets should be analysed into different classes of assets. The cost, accumulated depreciation, and the net book value for each group of fixed asset should also be shown.
6 The accumulated depreciation of £21,000 for plant and equipment has been obtained from the trial balance by taking the accumulated depreciation of £14,000 as at 1 January 19X3 and adding the £7,000 depreciation charge for the year to 31 December 19X3 to it. The question states that depreciation is to be charged for that year at a rate of 25% on the cost of the machinery (i.e. 25% × £28,000).
7 The accumulated depreciation charge on the motor van has been calculated by taking the accumulated depreciation balance of £2,000 as at 1 January 19X3 from the trial balance, and adding it to the £1,000 depreciation charge for the year. The question states that depreciation is to be charged on the motor van at a rate of 20% of its cost (i.e. 20% × £5,000).
8 The total net book value for all classes of fixed assets is required for balancing purposes.
9 Details for the different categories of stock should be disclosed.
10 It is useful to show a separate total for the total amount of capital that the proprietor has got invested in the business.
11 The question states that the loan is a long-term loan. It should, therefore, be shown separately as part of the capital section, and not as part of the proprietor's capital.

Exhibit 5.3 is quite a complicated example. You should now work through it again, but without reference to the solution.

Conclusion

A manufacturing account needs to be prepared for those business entities that undertake further work on goods purchased before they are ready to be sold to customers. Manufacturing accounts are normally prepared annually along with all the other basic financial statements.

Some entities may try to prepare a manufacturing account more frequently than once a year, but the traditional double-entry book-keeping system is not really designed to cope with very frequent reporting requirements. Consequently, as we explained in Chapter 1, to cope with more frequent reporting we have seen the development of cost and management accounting. This important branch of accounting helps to overcome some of the disadvantages of financial accounting. Those entities who operate a cost and management accounting system will not normally find it necessary to prepare a manufacturing account.

Cost and management accounting will be dealt with in Part 3 of this book. In the meantime, some important aspects of financial accounting have still to be covered in the next three chapters.

Questions

5.1 The following information relates to Megg for the year to 31 January 19X1:

	£000
Stocks at 1 February 19X0:	
Raw material	10
Work-in-progress	17
Direct wages	65
Factory: Administration	27
Heat and light	9
Indirect wages	13
Purchases of raw materials	34
Stocks at 31 January 19X1:	
Raw material	12
Work-in-progress	14

Required:
Prepare Megg's manufacturing account for the year to 31 January 19X1.

5.2 The following balances have been extracted from the books of account of Moor for the year to 28 February 19X2:

	£
Administration expenses	33,000
Direct wages	50,000
Factory indirect wages	27,700
Purchase of raw materials	127,500
Sales	250,000
Selling and distribution expenses	10,200
Stocks at 1 March 19X1:	
Raw materials	13,000
Work-in-progress	8,400
Finished goods	24,000
Stocks at 28 February 19X2:	
Raw materials	15,500
Work-in-progress	6,300
Finished goods	30,000

Required:
Prepare Moor's manufacturing, trading, and profit and loss account for the year to 28 February 19X2.

5.3 The following balances have been extracted from the books of Stuart for the year to 31 March 19X3:

	Dr £000	Cr £000
Administration: Factory	230	
General	112	
Bank	7	
Capital at 1 April 19X2		264
Creditors		335
Debtors	184	
Direct wages	330	
Miscellaneous expenses	16	
Plant and machinery: At cost	594	
Accumulated depreciation at 31 March 19X3		199
Purchases of raw materials	1,123	
Sales		1,932
Stock at 1 April 19X2:		
Raw material	38	
Work-in-progress	29	
Finished goods	67	
	£2,730	£2,730

Additional information.

Stocks at 31 March 19X3:	£000
Raw materials	44
Work-in-progress	42
Finished goods	65

Required:
Prepare Stuart's manufacturing, trading, and profit and loss account for the year to 31 March 19X3, and a balance sheet as at that date.

5.4 The following balances have been extracted from the books of the David and Peter Manufacturing Company as at 30 April 19X4.

	Dr £000	Cr £000
Administration salaries	76	
Capital at 1 May 19X3		218
Cash	18	
Creditors		102
Debtors	116	
Direct wages	70	
Drawings	26	
c/fwd	£306	£320

	Dr £000	Cr £000
b/fwd	306	320
Factory equipment: At cost	360	
Accumulated depreciation at 1 May 19X3		180
General factory expenses	13	
General office expenses	9	
Heat and light (factory 3/4; general 1/4)	52	
Purchase of raw material	100	
Sales		420
Stocks at 1 May 19X3:		
Raw materials	12	
Work-in-progress	18	
Finished goods	8	
Rent and rates (factory 2/3; general 1/3)	42	
	£920	£920

Additional information:

1 Stocks at 30 April 19X4:

	£000
Raw material	14
Work-in-progress	16
Finished goods	22

2 The factory equipment is to be depreciated at a rate of 15% per annum on cost.

Required:
Prepare the David and Peter Manufacturing Company's manufacturing, trading, and profit and loss account for the year to 30 April 19X4, and a balance sheet as at that date.

5.5 Jeffrey is in business as a manufacturer. He has extracted the following trial balance from his books of account as at 31 May 19X5:

	Dr £000	Cr £000
Bank	6	
Capital		58
Creditors		156
Debtors	89	
Drawings	15	
Factory expenses:		
Direct wages	200	
General expenses	60	
c/fwd	£370	£214

		Dr	Cr
		£000	£000
	b/fwd	£370	£214
Office equipment:			
At cost		30	
Accumulated depreciation at 1 June 19X4			9
Office expenses		127	
Plant:			
At cost		160	
Accumulated depreciation at 1 June 19X4			70
Purchases of finished goods		55	
Purchases of raw materials		180	
Sales			693
Stocks at 1 June 19X4:			
Raw materials		17	
Work-in-progress		21	
Finished goods		26	
		£986	£986

Additional information:

1 Stocks at 31 May 19X5:

	£000
Raw materials	20
Work-in-progress	30
Finished goods	29

2 Goods manufactured by Jeffrey are transferred to finished stock at the cost of manufacture plus 20%.

3 Office equipment is to be depreciated at a rate of 10% per annum on cost, and plant at a rate of 20% per annum on cost.

Required:

Prepare Jeffrey's manufacturing, trading, and profit and loss account for the year to 31 May 19X5, and a balance sheet as at that date.

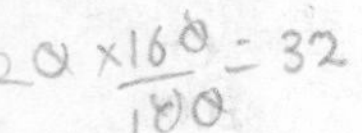

5.6 Clarico is a small manufacturing company. The following trial balance has been extracted from the books of account as at 30 June 19X6:

		Dr	Cr
		£000	£000
Administration expenses		39	
Capital			252
Carriage inwards		22	
Cash		7	
Delivery vans:			
At cost		36	
Accumulated depreciation at 1 July 19X5			18
Delivery van expenses		12	
	c/fwd	£116	£270

	Dr £000	Cr £000
b/fwd	116	270
Drawings	110	
Electricity	16	
Plant:		
At cost:	110	
Accumulated depreciation at 1 July 19X5		40
Provision for doubtful debts (at 1 July 19X5)		55
Purchases:		
Raw materials	450	
Finished goods	30	
Rent and rates	70	
Sales		1,570
Sales expenses	56	
Stocks at 1 July 19X5:		
Raw materials	120	
Work-in-progress	40	
Finished goods	48	
Trade creditors		265
Trade debtors	800	
Wages:		
Factory direct	142	
Factory indirect	48	
Administration	26	
Sales	18	
	£2,200	£2,200

Additional information:

1 Stocks at 30 June 19X6

	£000
Raw materials	102
Work-in-progress	74
Finished goods	76

2 Manufactured goods are transferred to finished goods stock at cost plus 10%.

3 Provision is to be made for the following amounts owing at 30 June 19X6:

	£000
Electricity	4
Rent	15
Delivery van expenses	3

4 The following expenses had been paid in advance at 30 June 19X6:

	£000
Rates	25
Delivery van licences	2

5 The bad debts provision is to be made equal to 10% of outstanding trade debtors as at 30 June 19X6.

6 Depreciation for the year is to be charged as follows:

Plant:	20% on cost
Delivery vans:	25% on cost

7 Expenses are to be apportioned as follows:

	Factory %	*Administration* %
Electricity	80	20
Rent and rates	60	40

Required:
Prepare Clarico's manufacturing, trading, and profit and loss account for the year to 30 June 19X6, and a balance sheet as at that date.

6 Partnership and company accounts

The last three chapters have dealt mainly with the sole trader type of entity. As argued earlier, this term is not to be taken too literally. The term *sole* trader does not necessarily mean that the trader is working entirely on his own, because he may have staff to help him. What it means is that the entity is *owned* by one individual. The entity could, in fact, be a very large one, and many hundreds of employees may work for it. The term *trader* is also misleading. It is not restricted to trading entities, that is those entities that buy and sell goods. It may be a manufacturing entity, or a business that offers a service, such as an accountant, a doctor or a solicitor.

Sole trader entities are quite common, especially amongst small businesses, but there are two other main types of entities that are perhaps just as common. These are partnerships and limited liability companies, and they form the subject of this chapter.

In order to form either a partnership or a company, at least two people are required. Almost any type of entity can be operated as a partnership. A partnership may simply involve two or more people getting together to form a business. A company may also be similarly formed, but the formation of a *limited liability company* is bound by some fairly severe legal restrictions.

As a result of its unique legal position, the accounts of limited liability companies present particular difficulties. Before examining such accounts in some detail, however, the partnership type of entity will be briefly examined in the next section.

Partnerships

A partnership entity is similar to that of a sole trader, except that a *partnership* is presumed to exist when two or more people get together in business with the objective of making a profit. This common form of business entity is considered in more detail in the following subsections.

Management

The law limits the total number of people who may get together to form a partnership. Apart from a few exceptions (such as firms of accountants and solicitors) a partnership may not consist of more than twenty partners. It is not necessary for an individual to contribute any capital for him to be considered a partner of the business. If he is regarded as being a partner, then it is assumed that he is a partner.

The management of the partnership will be by agreement amongst the partners, but if there is no apparent agreement (either formal or informal), then it is presumed that the partnership will operate in accordance with the 1890 Partnership Act. This Act lays down arrangements for dealing with such matters as the amount of capital to be contributed, the management of the business, and how the profits or losses are to be shared amongst the partners.

If the partners have come to an agreement amongst themselves, then partnerships (like sole traders) may operate without the detailed intervention of the law.

Accounts

Partnership accounts are very similar to those of sole traders. There are just three essential differences.

1 The net profit for the year (as per the profit and loss account) is transferred to what is called the profit and loss *appropriation* account. This account shows how the profit is divided amongst the partners.
2 Details concerning the partners' share of profits and their drawings are usually kept in *current* accounts. Current accounts enable such details to be kept separate from the partners' capital accounts, thereby ensuring that amounts contributed as capital are not obscured by day-to-day transactions. However, not all partnerships keep separate capital and current accounts.
3 The capital section on the balance sheet shows the respective partners' capital and current accounts balances.

An example of partnership accounts is shown in Exhibit 6.1.

Exhibit 6.1: Illustration of partnership accounts

Duke and Luke
Profit and loss appropriation account for the year to 31 March 19X9

	£	£
Net profit (1)		20,000
Appropriation (2):		
Duke (70%)	14,000	
Luke (30%)	6,000	20,000
		—

Duke & Luke
Balance sheet (extract) at 31 March 19X9

	£	£
Net assets (3)		24,500
Financed by:		
Capital accounts (4)		
Duke		10,000
Luke		5,000
		15,000
Current accounts (5)		
Duke	6,000	
Luke	3,500	9,500
		£24,500

Tutorial notes

1 Profit is calculated in exactly the same way as for sole trader entities.
2 The exhibit assumes that the partners have agreed to share out the profit in the ratio 70: 30, the double-entry effect being as follows:

Dr Profit and loss appropriation account with £20,000
Cr Duke's current account with £14,000
Cr Luke's current account with £6,000

By making these transfers to the partners' current accounts, no balance remains in the profit and loss account.
3 It is assumed that the net assets of the partnership are £24,500.
4 The partners have contributed £15,000 in capital (Duke £10,000 and Luke £5,000). It should be noted that the profit is not necessarily apportioned in their capital sharing ratio; this is a matter for the partners to agree amongst themselves.
5 The partners' current accounts represent their respective net balances as at the end of the year (after allowing for the balance brought forward, the partner's share of the profit and any drawings that he may have made during the year).
6 The total of the capital account and the current account balances represent the total amount of capital invested in the business by the partners. The current account balances are, however, usually just a short-term source of finance, since the partnership agreement would probably allow the partners to withdraw from their current accounts at any time. By using current accounts, the balances on the capital accounts will remain at their original levels, unless more capital is contributed or some withdrawn.

It should be noted that no matter what arrangements the partners make for the apportionment of profit amongst themselves (for example to draw a salary, to pay themselves interest on their capital and current accounts, or for that matter to charge each other interest on their drawings), such arrangements are all dealt with in the appropriation account. Such matters should *not* be entered in the profit and loss account, no matter how they are described. There is just one exception to this rule. Where a partner makes a specific *loan* to the partnership, and that loan lies outside the partnership agreement, then the interest on the loan *may* be charged to the profit and loss account.

The preparation of partnership accounts is a fairly routine accounting exercise which, as a non-accountant, you almost certainly will not be involved in. As a result this book need not consider them in any further detail.

The most important type of business entity will now be examined: the limited liability company.

Limited liability companies

There is a great personal risk in operating a business as a sole trader or as a partnership. If the business runs short of funds, the proprietors may be called upon to settle the business's debts out of their own private resources. This type of risk can have an inhibiting effect on the development of new businesses. Hence the need for a different type of entity which will neither make the owners bankrupt nor inhibit the growth of new businesses. This need became apparent in the nineteenth century as a consequence of the industrial revolution.

In order to finance the new and rapidly expanding industries (such as the iron and steel industry and in railway development), enormous amounts of capital were required. These sorts of ventures were undertaken at great risk. By agreeing to become involved in them, investors were often risking bankruptcy if (as seemed likely) the ventures were unsuccessful. It became apparent that the development of industry would be severely restricted unless some means could be devised of restricting the liability of prospective investors.

Hence the need for a form of limited liability. In fact, the concept of limited liability was not a new idea developed in the nineteenth century, but it received legal recognition for the first time in the 1855 Limited Liability Act. The Act only remained in force for a few months before it was repealed and incorporated into the 1856 Joint Stock Companies Act.

In accepting the concept of limited liability the 1855 Act, in effect, recognized the entity concept. By recognizing that there could be a distinction between the private and public affairs of business proprietors, it created a new form of entity. Since that time, parliament has passed a number of other companies acts (the most recent being the 1985 Companies Act). All of them have continued to give legal recognition to the concept of limited liability.

The important point about a limited liability company is that it does not require its members to contribute more than a certain amount of capital, no matter what financial difficulties the company may get into. Thus the risk of members being called upon to contribute unlimited amounts of capital is removed, and they are less likely to find themselves being forced into bankruptcy.

The concept of limited liability is often very difficult for business proprietors to understand, especially if they have formed a limited liability company out of what was originally a sole trader or a partnership entity. Unlike such entities, companies are bound by some fairly severe legal restrictions about their operations. Thus in return for the privilege of limited liability, there are some restrictions on the owners' freedom to manage the company as they might wish.

The legal restrictions can be somewhat burdensome, but they are necessary for the protection of all those parties who might have dealings with the company such as creditors and employees. If the company runs short of funds and its liability is limited, the creditors and employees might not get paid. It is only fair, therefore, to warn all those people who might have dealings with the company that its liability is limited, and there is a danger that their debts may not be settled. Consequently, the company has to be more open about its affairs than it would have to be if it operated as a non-limited liability entity.

Structure and operation

In this section, the structure and operation of limited liability companies will be briefly examined. For convenience the examination has been broken down into a number of subsections.

Share capital

Although the law recognizes that limited liability companies are separate beings (that is, separate from those individuals who collectively own the company), it also accepts that someone has to take responsibility for *promoting* the company, i.e. bringing it into being. Only two members are required to form a company. They agree to contribute to its capital by subscribing to shares in it. The capital of a company is known as its *share capital*. Although £1 shares are very common, the share capital may be divided into a number of shares of any monetary denomination. Depending upon the share capital of the company and the number of shares he wishes to hold, a member may just have one share, or he may purchase many thousands.

When a company is formed, it must state its maximum amount of share capital. In other words, it must place a limit on the total amount of share capital that it wishes to issue. This is known as its *authorized* share capital.

Although a company has to state its authorized share capital, this does not mean that it will necessarily issue shares up to that amount. It will probably only issue sufficient capital to meet its immediate requirements. The amount of share capital that it has actually issued is known as the *issued* share capital. Sometimes when the capital is issued, the prospective shareholders are only required to contribute in instalments. If a share capital is described as being *fully paid*, it means that it has received all of the capital that was due to be paid.

There are two main types of shares: *ordinary* shares and *preference* shares. Ordinary shares do not usually entitle the shareholder to any specific level of dividend (see pp. 110-111), and the rights of other parties always take precedence over the rights of the ordinary shareholders, for example on disposing of the assets when the company is wound up. Preference shareholders are normally entitled to a fixed level of dividend, and they may take priority over the ordinary shareholders if the company is wound up. Sometimes the preference shares are classed as *cumulative*. This means that if the company cannot pay its preference dividend in one year, the amount due accrues until such time as the company has the profits to pay the accumulated dividend.

There are many other different types of shares, but for the purpose of this chapter, only ordinary and preference shares need be considered.

Types of Companies

A prospective shareholder may invest in either a public company or a private company. A public company must have an authorized share capital of at least £50,000, and it must make its share capital available to the general public. This normally means that the shares will be listed on a stock exchange where the public can buy and sell the company's shares relatively easily.

As a warning to those parties who might have dealings with them, public limited liability companies must describe themselves as such, and include that term, or its abbreviation 'plc', after their name.

Any company which does not make its shares available to the public is regarded as being a private company. Like public companies, private companies must also have an authorized share capital, although no minimum amount is prescribed. Otherwise, as far as their share capital requirements are concerned, they are very similar to public companies.

Private companies also have to warn the public that their liability is limited. They must do so by describing themselves as 'limited liability companies', and by using that term or its abbreviation 'ltd' after their name.

Loans

Besides obtaining finance from their shareholders, companies often borrow money in the form of *debentures*. A company may invite the public to loan it some money for a certain period of time (although the period can be unspecified) at a fixed rate of interest. The loans may be secured on specific assets of the company, or on its assets generally, or they might not be secured at all. If they are secured and the company cannot repay the loans on their due date, the debentureholders may sell the secured assets and settle the amount due to themselves out of the proceeds.

Debentures may be bought and sold freely on the stock exchange, exactly like shares. The nearer the redemption date for the repayment of the debentures, the closer the market price will be to their nominal value. Indeed, if they are to be redeemed at a premium, the market price may exceed the nominal value.

Debenture holders are not shareholders of the company. They do not have voting rights, and for tax purposes, debenture interest is an allowable expense. Consequently, the issue of debentures is a favourite method of raising extra funds.

Disclosure of information

It is necessary for both public and private companies to supply a minimum amount of information to their members. The detailed requirements are dealt with in Part 4 of this book. It might be surprising to find that shareholders do not have a right of access to the company's premises or a right to receive any information that they demand. It would clearly be impractical to give all shareholders these rights, especially in large public companies where there might be hundreds of thousands of individual shareholders.

Instead, both private and public companies have to submit an annual report to their members (containing at least the minimum amount of information laid down by the 1985 Companies Act), and to file the report with the Registrar of Companies at Companies House in Cardiff or in Edinburgh. This means that on payment of a small fee, the report is open for inspection to any member of the public who wants to consult it. Some companies (defined as small or medium) are permitted to file abbreviated accounts with the Registrar, although they must still supply the more detailed report to their members.

Company accounts

The preparation of company accounts is very similar to that adopted for sole trader and partnership entities. Some modifications do, of course, have to be made because of the legal position that a company enjoys. Company accounts will be dealt with in more detail a little later on in the chapter.

Directors

A limited liability company is regarded as being a separate entity, that is, separate from those shareholders who own it collectively, and separate from anyone who is employed by it. This means that all those who work for it (no matter how senior) are employees. However, someone has to take responsibility for the management of the company on behalf of the shareholders. To look after their interests, shareholders usually appoint a number of *directors*.

Directors are the most senior level of management. They are responsible for the day-to-day running of the company on behalf of the shareholders. Directors are employees of the company, and any remuneration paid to them as directors is charged as an expense of the business. Directors may also be shareholders, but any remuneration paid to them as a shareholder is regarded as being a private matter and they will be treated like any other shareholder.

The distinction between employees and shareholder-employees is an important one, although it is one that is not always understood, especially in small companies where both employees and shareholders may be identical. As we have seen, in law the company is regarded as being a separate entity. Even if there are just two shareholders who both work full-time for the company, the company is still treated as distinct from the two individuals who manage and own it.

They may take decisions which appear to affect no one else except themselves, but because they are operating the company protected by the privilege of limited liability, they have certain obligations as well as rights. Consequently, they are not as free to operate the company as they might if they operated as a partnership.

Dividends

Profits are usually distributed to shareholders in the form of a *dividend*. A dividend may be calculated either as a percentage of the share capital, or as so many pence per share. The actual dividend will depend upon the amount of net profit earned during the year and how much profit it is considered necessary to retain for future investment within the company.

A dividend may have been *paid* during the year as an *interim* dividend. In effect, an interim dividend is a payment on account. The actual profit for the year will only be known once the year is over, so the directors have to allow for a *proposed* dividend when preparing the annual accounts. The proposed dividend is usually referred to as the *final* dividend. The payment of the final dividend has to be approved by the shareholders at their annual general meeting.

Taxation

Taxation is another feature which distinguishes a limited liability company from that of a sole trader or partnership entity.

Sole trader and partnership entities do not have tax levied on them as entities. Tax is charged on the profit which the proprietors or partners have earned in the business. The tax that they pay is a private matter, and in accordance with the entity rule, it is not the concern of the entity. Any tax that appears to have been paid by the entity on the proprietors' behalf is treated as part of their drawings.

Companies are treated quite differently. The law recognizes them as being distinct entities in their own right. They are, therefore, charged with their own form of taxation known as *corporation tax*. Corporation tax was introduced in 1965. All companies are eligible to pay corporation tax, but the payment dates are different for companies that existed before 1965. Such companies are permitted to pay their tax on dates laid down under the rules that were applicable at that time. Companies formed since 1965 are expected to pay their corporation tax nine months after their year end.

Corporation tax is based on a company's accounting profits, but the accounting profit has to be adjusted for certain items that are treated differently for tax purposes.

The corporation tax based on the accounting profits for the year will normally appear as a current liability on the balance sheet, since it will not be due for payment until some time after the end of the financial year.

Some corporation tax, however, may have to be paid in advance. This is known as *advance corporation tax (ACT)*. ACT is payable if a company pays a dividend. The amount is based on the dividend, but any ACT paid goes to reduce the total amount of corporation tax eventually payable on the profits for the year. The net amount of corporation tax payable (the total amount due less any ACT paid) is known as *mainstream* corporation tax.

Now that the basic structure and operation of limited liability companies has been outlined, company accounts can be examined in some detail, starting with the profit and loss account.

The profit and loss account

As suggested earlier, the preparation of a company's manufacturing, trading, and profit and loss account is basically no different from those applicable to sole trader entities. Almost an identical format may be adopted, and it is only after the net profit stage that some differences become apparent.

Like partnership accounts, company accounts also include a profit and loss appropriation account (although no clear distinction is drawn between where the profit and loss account ends and the appropriation account begins). Exhibit 6.2 illustrates a company's profit and loss appropriation account.

Exhibit 6.2: Example of a company's profit and loss appropriation account

	£
Net profit for the year before taxation	X
Taxation	(X)
Profit for the year after taxation	X
Dividends	(X)
Retained profit for the year	X
Retained profits brought forward	X
Retained profits carried forward	£X

As can be seen from Exhibit 6.2, the company's net profit for the year is used in three ways:

1 to pay tax;
2 to pay dividends; and
3 for retention within the business.

The balance sheet

The structure of a limited liability company's balance sheet is also very similar to that of a sole trader or of a partnership. The main differences arise because of the company's share capital structure, although there are some other features that are not usually found in non-company balance sheets.

The main features of a company's balance sheet are illustrated in Exhibit 6.3. Study this exhibit carefully, but note that the information has been kept to a minimum. The full details have not been given where there are no significant differences between a company's balance sheet and those for other entities.

Exhibit 6.3: Example of a company's balance sheet

Exhibitor Limited
Balance sheet at 31 March 19X1

	£	£	£
Fixed assets			X
Investments (1)			X
Current assets		X	
Less: Current liabilities			
Trade creditors	X		
Accruals	X		
Corporation tax (2)	X		
Proposed dividend (3)	X	X	X
			£X

Financed by:

Capital and reserves (4)	*Authorized*	*Issued and fully paid*
	£	£
Ordinary shares of £X each (5)	X	X
Preference shares of £X each (5)	X	X
	X	X
Capital reserves (6)		X
Revenue reserves (7)		X
Shareholders' funds (8)		X
Loans (9)		X
		£X

Note: The number shown after each narration refers to the tutorial notes below.

Tutorial notes

1 *Investments*. This item usually represents long-term investments in the shares of other companies. Short-term investments (such as money invested in bank deposit accounts) would be included in current assets. The shares may be either in public limited liability companies or in private limited companies.

It is obviously more difficult to buy shares in unlisted companies and to obtain current market prices for them. The market price of the investments should be stated, or where this cannot be obtained, a directors' valuation should be disclosed.

2 *Corporation tax*. Corporation tax represents the tax due on the company's profits for the year. As we explained earlier, companies incorporated after 1965 are due to pay the tax nine months after the year end, so in these cases it will always be a current liability. Some companies incorporated before 1965 may not have to pay the tax for at least twelve months, in which case the amount due would not be shown under current liabilities. It should be shown as a

separate item in the balance sheet after loans (see Note 9 below).

3 *Proposed dividend*. A proposed dividend will probably be due for payment very shortly after the year end, so it will usually be shown as a current liability.

4 *Capital and reserves*. Details of the authorized, issued and fully paid-up share capital should be shown.

5 *Ordinary shares and preference shares*. Details about the different types of shares that the company has issued should be shown.

6 This section may include several different reserve accounts of a capital nature, that is, amounts that are not available for distribution to the shareholders as dividend. It might include, for example, a *share premium account*, i.e. the extra amount paid by shareholders in excess of the nominal value of the shares. This extra amount does not rank for dividend, but sometimes shareholders are willing to pay a premium if they think that the shares are particularly attractive. Another example of a capital reserve account is a *revaluation* reserve account. A fixed asset may have been revalued, and the difference between the original cost and the revalued amount will be credited to this account.

7 *Revenue reserves*. Revenue reserve accounts are amounts which are available for distribution to the shareholders. Sometimes profits which could be distributed to shareholders are put into general reserve accounts, although no real purpose is served in classifying them in this way.

8 *Shareholders' funds*. The total amount available to shareholders at the balance sheet date is equal to the share capital originally subscribed, plus all the capital reserve and revenue reserve account balances.

9 *Loans*. The loans section of the balance sheet will include all the long-term loans obtained by the company, i.e. those loans which do not have to be repaid for at least twelve months such as debentures and long-term bank loans.

A comprehensive example

In this section the structure of company accounts will be examined in more detail. In Exhibit 6.4 it is assumed that the accounts are being prepared for internal management purposes. Accounts prepared for external-user purposes are dealt with in Part 4.

Exhibit 6.4

The following information has been extracted from the books of Handy Limited as at 31 March 19X5:

	Dr £	Cr £
Bank	2,000	
Capital: 100,000 issued and fully paid ordinary shares of £1 each		100,000
50,000 issued and fully paid 8% preference shares of £1 each		50,000
Debenture loan stock (10%: repayable 1999)		30,000
Debenture loan stock interest	3,000	
Discounts allowed	2,000	
Discounts received		5,000
c/fwd	7,000	185,000

	Dr £	Cr £
b/fwd	7,000	185,000
Dividends received		700
Dividends paid: Ordinary interim	5,000	
Preference	4,000	
Freehold land at cost	200,000	
Investments (listed: market value at 31 March 19X5 was £11,000)	10,000	
Office expenses	15,000	
Office salaries	35,000	
Motor van at cost	15,000	
Motor van: accumulated depreciation at 1 April 19X4		6,000
Motor van expenses	2,700	
Purchases	220,000	
Retained profits at 1 April 19X4		9,000
Sales		300,000
Share premium account		10,000
Stocks at cost (at 1 April 19X4)	20,000	
Trade creditors		50,000
Trade debtors	27,000	
	£560,700	£560,700

Additional information

1. The stocks at 31 March 19X5 were valued at cost at £40,000.
2. Depreciation is to be charged on the motor van at a rate of 20% per annum on cost. No depreciation is to be charged on the freehold land.
3. Corporation tax (based on profits for the year at a rate of 35%) has been estimated at £10,000.
4. The directors propose a final ordinary dividend of 10p per share.
5. The authorized share capital of the company is as follows:
   - 150,000 ordinary shares of £1 each; and
   - 75,000 preference shares of £1 each.

Required:

(a) Prepare Handy Limited's trading, profit and loss account for the year to 31 March 19X5; and

(b) a balance sheet as at that date.

The answer to the exhibit now follows. Work through it carefully making sure that you understand each step in its construction.

Answer to Exhibit 6.4

(a)

Handy Limited
Trading, profit and loss account for the year to 31 March 19X5

	£	£	£
Sales			300,000
Less: Cost of goods sold:			
Opening stocks		20,000	
Purchases		220,000	
		240,000	
Less: Closing stocks		40,000	200,000
Gross profit			100,000
Add: Incomes:			
Discounts received		5,000	
Dividends received		700	5,700
			105,700
Less: Expenditure:			
Debenture loan stock interest		3,000	
Discounts allowed		2,000	
Motor van depreciation (1)	3,000		
Motor van expenses	2,700	5,700	
Office expenses		15,000	
Office salaries		35,000	60,700
Net profit for the year			45,000
Less: Corporation tax (based on the profits for the year at a rate of 35%) (2)			10,000
			35,000
Less: Dividends (3):			
Preference dividend paid (10%)		4,000	
Interim ordinary paid (5p per share)		5,000	
Proposed final ordinary dividend (10p per share)		10,000	19,000
Retained profit for the year			16,000
Retained profits brought forward			9,000
Retained profits carried forward (4)			£25,000

(b) **Handy Limited**
Balance sheet at 31 March 19X5

	£	£	£
Fixed assets	*Cost*	*Accumulated depreciation*	*Net book value*
Freehold land (5)	200,000	—	200,000
Motor van (6)	15,000	9,000	6,000
	£215,000	£9,000	206,000
Investments			
At cost (market value at 31 March 19X5: £11,000) (7)			10,000
Current assets			
Stocks at cost		40,000	
Trade debtors		27,000	
Bank		2,000	
		69,000	
Less: Current liabilities			
Trade creditors	50,000		
Corporation tax (due for payment on 1 January 19X6) (8)	10,000		
Proposed ordinary dividend (9)	10,000	70,000	(1,000)
			£215,000
Financed by:			
Capital and reserves		*Authorized*	*Issued and fully paid*
Ordinary shares of £1 each (10)		150,000	100,000
Preference shares of £1 each (10)		75,000	50,000
		£225,000	150,000
Share premium account (11)			10,000
Retained profits (12)			25,000
Shareholders' funds (13)			185,000
Loans (14)			
10% debenture stock (repayable 1999)			30,000
			£215,000

Note: The number shown after each narration refers to the tutorial notes.

Tutorial notes

1 Depreciation has been charged on the motor van at a rate of 20% per annum on cost as instructed in question note 2.

2 Question note 3 requires £10,000 to be charged as corporation tax. Note that

the corporation tax rate of 35% is applied to the taxable profit (not given), and not the accounting profit of £45,000.

3 A proposed ordinary dividend of 10p has been included as instructed in question note 4.

4 The total retained profit of £25,000 is carried forward to the balance sheet (see tutorial note 12 below).

5 Question note 2 states that no depreciation is to be charged on the freehold land.

6 The accumulated depreciation for the motor van of £9,000 is the total of the accumulated depreciation brought forward at 1 April 19X4 of £6,000 plus the £3,000 written off to the profit and loss account for the current year (see tutorial note 1 above).

7 Note that the market value of the investments has been disclosed on the face of the balance sheet.

8 The corporation tax charged against profit (question note 3) will be due for payment on 1 January 19X6 (to be precise, nine months plus one day after the year end). It is, therefore, a current liability.

9 The proposed ordinary dividend will be due for payment shortly after the year end, so it is also a current liability. The interim dividend and the preference dividend have already been paid, so they are not current liabilities.

10 Details of the authorized, issued and fully paid share capital should be disclosed.

11 The share premium is a capital account; it cannot be used for the payment of dividends. This account will, therefore, tend to remain unchanged on successive balance sheets, although there are a few highly restricted purposes for which it may be used.

12 The retained profits become part of a revenue account balance that the company could use for the payment of dividends. The total retained profits of £25,000 is the amount brought in to the balance sheet from the profit and loss account.

13 The total amount of shareholders' funds should always be shown.

14 The loans are long-term loans. Loans are not part of shareholders' funds, and they should be shown in the balance sheet as a separate item.

You are now recommended to work through Exhibit 6.4 again without reference to the solution.

Conclusion

This chapter began with a brief outline of a partnership entity. It then briefly examined the background to company account legislation. This was followed by an explanation of how company accounts are prepared for *internal* purposes. The preparation of company accounts for *external* purposes will be examined in Part 4.

Although a great deal of information can be obtained from studying the financial accounts of a company, it is difficult to extract the most relevant and significant features. You require some guidance, therefore, in how to make the best of the accounting information presented to you as a non-accountant. That guidance is provided in the next two chapters.

Questions

6.1 The following balances have been extracted from the books of Margo Limited for the year to 31 January 19X1:

	Dr £000	Cr £000
Cash at bank and in hand	5	
Plant and equipment:		
At cost	70	
Accumulated depreciation (at 31.1.X1)		25
Profit and loss account (at 1.2.X0)		15
Profit for the financial year (to 31.1.X1)		10
Share capital (issued and fully paid)		50
Stocks (at 31.1.X1)	17	
Trade creditors		12
Trade debtors	20	
	£112	£112

Additional information:

1 Corporation tax based on the profits for the year is estimated at £3,000.
2 The company was formed in 1975.
3 Margo Limited's authorized share capital is £75,000 of £1 ordinary shares.
4 A dividend of 10p per share is proposed (ignore advance corporation tax).

Required:
Prepare Margo Limited's profit and loss account for the year to 31 January 19X1 (in so far as the information permits), and a balance sheet as at that date.

6.2 Harry Limited was formed in 1980. The following balances as at 28 February 19X2 have been extracted from the books of account after the trading account has been compiled:

	Dr £000	Cr £000
Administration expenses	65	
Cash at bank and in hand	10	
Distribution costs	15	
Dividend paid (on preference shares)	6	
Furniture and equipment:		
At cost	60	
Accumulated depreciation at 1.3.X1		36
Gross profit for the year		150
Ordinary share capital (shares of £1 each)		100
Preference shares (cumulative 15% of £1 shares)		40
Profit and loss account (at 1.3.X1)		50
Share premium account		20
Stocks (at 28.2.X2)	130	
c/fwd	£286	£396

	Dr £000	Cr £000
b/fwd	286	396
Trade creditors		25
Trade debtors	135	
	£421	£421

Additional information:

1 Corporation tax based on the profits for the year is estimated at £24,000.

2 Furniture and equipment is depreciated at an annual rate of 10% of cost and it is all charged against administration expenses.

3 A dividend of 20p per ordinary share is proposed (ignore advance corporation tax).

4 All of the authorized share capital has been issued and is fully paid.

Required:

Prepare Harry Limited's profit and loss account for the year to 28 February 19X2, and a balance sheet as at that date.

6.3 The following balances have been extracted from the books of Jim Limited as at 31 March 19X3:

	Dr £000	Cr £000
Advertising	3	
Bank	11	
Creditors		12
Debtors	118	
Furniture and fittings:		
At cost	20	
Accumulated depreciation (at 1.4.X2)		9
Directors' fees	6	
Profit and loss account (at 1.4.X2)		8
Purchases	124	
Rent and rates	10	
Sales		270
Share capital (issued and fully paid)		70
Stock (at 1.4.X2)	16	
Telephone and stationery	5	
Travelling expenses	2	
Vehicles:		
At cost	40	
Accumulated depreciation (at 1.4.X2)		10
Wages and salaries	24	
	£379	£379

Additional information:

1. Stock at 31 March 19X3 was valued at £14,000.
2. Furniture and fittings and the vehicles are depreciated at a rate of 15% and 25% respectively on cost.
3. Corporation tax based on the year's profits is estimated at £25,000.
4. A dividend of 40p per share is proposed (ignore advance corporation tax).
5. The company's authorized share capital is £100,000 of £1 ordinary shares.

Required:
Prepare Jim Limited's trading, and profit and loss account for the year to 31 March 19X3, and a balance sheet as at that date.

6.4 The following trial balance has been extracted from Cyril Limited as at 30 April 19X4:

	Dr £000	Cr £000
Advertising	2	
Bank overdraft		20
Bank interest paid	4	
Creditors		80
Debtors	143	
Directors' remuneration	30	
Freehold land and buildings:		
At cost	800	
Accumulated depreciation at 1.5.X3		102
General expenses	15	
Investments at cost	30	
Investment income		5
Motor vehicles:		
At cost	36	
Accumulated depreciation (at 1.5.X3)		18
Preference dividend paid	15	
Preference shares (cumulative 10% shares of £1 each)		150
Profit and loss account (at 1.5.X3)		100
Purchases	480	
Repairs and renewals	4	
Sales		900
Share capital (authorized, issued and fully paid ordinary shares of £1 each)		500
Share premium account		25
Stock (at 1.5.X3)	120	
Wages and salaries	221	
	£1,900	£1,900

Additional information:

1. Stock at 30 April 19X4 was valued at £140,000.

2 Depreciation for the year of £28,000 is to be provided on buildings and £9,000 for motor vehicles.
3 A provision of £6,000 is required for the auditors' remuneration.
4 £2,000 had been paid in advance for renewals.
5 Corporation tax based on the year's profits is estimated at £60,000.
6 The directors propose an ordinary dividend of 10p per share.
7 The market value of the investments at 30 April 19X4 was £35,000.
8 Ignore advance corporation tax.

Required:
Prepare Cyril Limited's trading, and profit and loss account for the year to 30 April 19X4, and a balance sheet as at that date.

6.5 Nelson Limited was incorporated in 1980 with an authorized share capital of 500,000 £1 ordinary shares, and 200,000 15% cumulative preference shares of £1 each. The following trial balance was extracted at 31 May 19X5:

	Dr £000	Cr £000
Administration expenses	257	
Auditor's fees	10	
Cash at bank and in hand	5	
Creditors		85
Debentures (12%)		100
Debenture interest paid	6	
Debtors	225	
Directors' remuneration	60	
Dividends paid:		
Ordinary interim	20	
Preference	5	
Furniture fittings and equipment:		
At cost	200	
Accumulated depreciation at 1.6.X4		48
Investments at cost (market value at 31.5.X5: £340,000)	335	
Investment income		22
Ordinary share capital (issued and fully paid)		400
Preference share capital		200
Profit and loss account (at 1.6.X4)		17
Purchases	400	
Sales		800
Share premium account		50
Stock at 1.6.X4	155	
Wages and salaries	44	
	£1,722	£1,722

Additional information:
1 Stock at 31 May 19X5 was valued at £195,000.
2 Administration expenses owing at 31 May 19X5 amounted to £13,000.

3 Depreciation is to be charged on the furniture and fittings at a rate of 12½% on cost.
4 Salaries paid in advance amounted to £4,000.
5 Corporation tax based on the profit for the year is estimated at £8,000.
6 Provision is to be made for a final ordinary dividend of 1.25p per share.
7 Ignore advance corporation tax.

Required:
Prepare Nelson Limited's trading, and profit and loss account for the year to 31 May 19X5, and a balance sheet as at that date.

6.6 The following trial balance has been extracted from the books of Keith Limited as at 30 June 19X6:

	Dr £000	Cr £000
Advertising	30	
Bank	7	
Creditors		69
Debentures (10%)		70
Debtors (all trade)	300	
Directors' remuneration	55	
Electricity	28	
Insurance	17	
Investments (quoted)	28	
Investment income		4
Machinery:		
At cost	420	
Accumulated depreciation at 1.7.X5		152
Office expenses	49	
Ordinary share capital (issued and fully paid)		200
Preference shares		50
Preference share dividend	4	
Profit and loss account (at 1 July 19X5)		132
Provision for doubtful debts		8
Purchases	1,240	
Rent and rates	75	
Sales		2,100
Stock (at 1.7.X5)	134	
Vehicles:		
At cost	80	
Accumulated depreciation (at 1.7.X5)		40
Wages and salaries	358	
	£2,825	£2,825

Additional information:
1 Stock at 30 June 19X6 valued at cost amounted to £155,000.
2 Depreciation is to be provided on machinery and vehicles at a rate of 20%

and 25% respectively on cost.

3 Provision is to be made for auditor's remuneration of £12,000.
4 Insurance paid in advance at 30 June 19X6 amounted to £3,000.
5 The provision for doubtful debts is to be made equal to 5% of outstanding trade debtors as at 30 June 19X6.
6 Corporation tax based on the profits for the year of £60,000 is to be provided.
7 An ordinary dividend of 10p per share is proposed.
8 The investments had a market value of £30,000 at 30 June 19X6.
9 The company has an authorized share capital of 600,000 ordinary shares of £0.50 each and of 50,000 8% cumulative preference shares of £1 each.
10 Ignore advance corporation tax.

Required:
Prepare Keith Limited's trading and profit and loss account for the year to 30 June 19X6, and a balance sheet as at that date.

7 Source and application of funds

The preparation of manufacturing, trading, and profit and loss accounts and balance sheets in previous chapters has been within the accounting rules laid down in Chapter 2. The accounts that have been prepared provide some basic information about profitability, although they are less concerned with *liquidity*, that is they do not tell the user very much about the entity's the cash position.

Information about liquidity is vital, because an entity is technically insolvent if it cannot settle its debts as they fall due. It is unlawful to carry on trading if the management knows that it is in this position. The entity's cash balances can always be checked, of course, by examining its balance sheet, but this only gives the user the opening and closing cash position.

It is for these reasons that all entities are now encouraged to produce what is known as a *statement of source and application of funds* (or, in short, a funds statement), as well as the traditional profit and loss account and balance sheet. The encouragement is so strong that it is mandatory for professional accountants to produce a funds statement for all those entities whose turnover is in excess of £25,000 per annum.

Funds statements are a link between the profit and loss account and the balance sheet, and they form the subject of this chapter.

Accounting profit and liquidity

Experience has taught accountants that it is unwise to rely entirely upon the profit and loss account and the balance sheet to monitor an entity's liquidity position. The opening and closing cash and bank balances can be obtained from the balance sheet, but they do not relay any information about the movement of cash during the year. A great deal more information is needed if we are to monitor how successful the entity has been in handling its cash. This is especially important when proprietors regard an increase in profit as the same as an increase in cash.

If this is the view of the proprietor, then as long as the entity's accounting profit appears acceptable, very little attention may be paid to the cash position. In the long-run, of course, the profit should materialize in the form of cash, but in the short-run, cash generated by profit might well have been invested in fixed assets and stocks. Furthermore, it might even be the case that much of the profit has been earned by selling on credit terms, and very few of the debtors have settled their debts in cash.

Indeed, it is not uncommon for an entity to be experiencing a boom in sales, but to go suddenly into liquidation. This rather paradoxical situation is known as *overtrading*. It arises because too much attention has been given to selling goods and making a profit, and not enough attention to managing cash resources.

It was suggested in an earlier chapter that proprietors want to know the answers to three basic questions, viz.:

1 What profit has the business made?
2 How much does the business owe?
3 How much is owed to it?

There ought, perhaps, to be a fourth question:

4 What is my cash position?

The answer might be to look at the cash and bank balances, but as has been suggested, the information from such sources does not enable us to see in detail where the cash has come from during a particular period and where it has gone to.

If you have worked through the questions in the earlier chapters of this book, you will appreciate that accounting profit does not necessarily lead to an automatic increase in cash. This arises because in preparing the traditional accounting statements, the realization and matching rules are adopted. These rules require the adjustment of the cash received and the cash paid to reflect the trading *activity* of a particular accounting period. It follows, therefore, that neither sales (and other incomes) nor purchases (and other expenses) will necessarily cause an immediate increase or decrease in the cash position. Furthermore, non-profit and loss items (such as the purchase of fixed assets and the issue of shares and debentures for cash) are, of course, not included in the calculation of accounting profit.

For these reasons it is very difficult to assess the entity's cash position from the information normally disclosed in the traditional financial accounting statements. We need another type of statement that will give us much more information about what has happened to the cash during an accounting period. A statement of source and application of funds is designed for that very purpose. The format and contents of such a statement is examined in the next section.

Format and contents

Statements of source and application of funds can usually be summarized fairly briefly, but the non-accountant should be warned that they are not easy to construct. In fact, to be able to do so, it is probably necessary to have good grasp of double-entry book-keeping. Chapters 3 and 4 of this book provided you with the necessary knowledge, and if you understand how funds statements are constructed, you will understand a great deal more about what they are trying to tell you. In this section, the format and contents of a simple funds statement will be looked at, whilst in the next section, how it is constructed will be explained.

For the moment, you should assume that when the term 'funds' is used we are really talking about cash and bank balances. With this assumption in mind, the modern funds statement can be further explained.

Exhibit 7.1 illustrates a statement of source and application of funds.

Exhibit 7.1: Example of a statement of source and application of funds

	£	£
Source of funds:		
Profit		X
Cash from issue of shares		X
Cash from sale of fixed assets		X
		X
Application of funds:		
Dividends paid	(X)	
Tax paid	(X)	
Purchase of fixed assets	(X)	
		(X)
		X
Increase/decrease in working capital:		
Increase in stocks	X	
Increase in debtors	X	
Decrease in creditors	X	
Increase in cash	X	X

You will see from Exhibit 7.1 that a funds statement comprises three main sections, viz.:

1 a section showing the source of funds;
2 a section showing the application of funds; and
3 a summary of the working capital movements.

The *sources* section lists the various sources from which the funds have come during a particular accounting period, for example from profits, from sales of fixed assets, and from the issue of shares for cash.

The *applications* section explains what has happened to those funds. In other words, it lists all the ways in which the funds have been used during that same period.

If the sources section is in excess of the applications section, then there will have been a net increase in funds during the period. Alternatively, there will have been a decrease in funds if the total applications are in excess of the total sources.

The working capital section explains where that increase (or decrease) has gone. It might have been used to buy more stocks, for example, or it might simply have been left in the bank account.

It is at this point that difficulties begin. You were asked to assume that funds were the same as cash and bank balances. It seems sensible to make such an assumption; after all, the main purpose of a funds statement is to give us more information about the cash position. Unfortunately, Statement of Standard Accounting Practice 10 (which deals with funds statements) defines the term 'funds' as being virtually the same as working capital. It is a pity that the standard defines funds in this way, because it only causes greater confusion. A statement presented in the recommended format is not really telling us about the movement of cash, but about the movement of working capital. Since the main purpose of a funds statement is to inform the proprietor about the source and application of *cash*, it is a mystery why the profession recommends a statement showing the source and application of working capital.

However, it is advisable to accept the recommended definition of funds, because that is the one you are likely to meet. In the next section, however, how to construct a funds statement will be explained.

Construction

The easiest way to explain how a funds statement is constructed is to work through a question that requires the preparation of such a statement. Exhibit 7.2 contains the details.

Exhibit 7.2

Ande forms a business on 1 June 19X1 with £10,000 in cash. During the year to 31 May 19X2, he bought some goods for cash costing £50,000. All of these goods were sold on cash terms during the year for £100,000. A few days after starting the business, he paid £8,000 for some machinery in cash. Ande did not keep a bank account.

Required:

Prepare Ande's statement of source and application of funds for the year to 31 May 19X2.

Answer to Exhibit 7.2

ANDE
Statement of source and application of funds for the year to 31 May 19X2 (1)

		£
Source of funds		
Profit (2)		50,000
Application of funds		
Purchase of machinery (3)		(8,000)
	(4)	42,000
Increase/decrease in working capital		
Increase in cash balance (5)		£42,000

Tutorial notes

1 The funds statement is prepared for a period of time like a profit and loss account.
2 Ande's cash profit amounted to £50,000 (£100,000 − £50,000), so his cash position ought to have increased by that amount if he has not spent cash on anything else.
3 In fact, Ande purchased some machinery for cash. This is an application of funds.
4 The net source (or application) is the difference between the total sources and the total applications.
5 The working capital section measures the difference between the opening working capital and the closing working capital. In Ande's case, the only working capital that he had was cash. The movement in his cash position can be reconciled as follows:

	£
Cash at 1 June 19X1	10,000
Add: Cash profit	50,000
	60,000
Less: Purchase of machinery	8,000
Cash at 31 May 19X2	£52,000

∴ The movement in cash during the year = £52,000 − £10,000 = £42,000.

Ande's statement of source and application of funds was a very simple one. All the transactions that took place during the year were for cash, and there were not many of them. What would happen if Ande had bought and sold goods on credit terms now needs to be examined. Exhibit 7.3 illustrates this situation.

Exhibit 7.3

Ande formed a business on 1 June 19X1 with £10,000 which he paid immediately into a business bank account. A few days after starting the business, he drew a cheque for £8,000 to pay for some machinery for use within the business.

During the year to 31 May 19X2, he bought some goods on credit for £50,000, and at the end of the year he still owed his creditors for this amount. By the end of the year he had sold all of the goods on credit for £100,000 and he was still owed for this amount at 31 May 19X2.

Required:
Prepare Ande's statement of source and application of funds for the year to 31 May 19X2.

Answer to Exhibit 7.3

ANDE
Statement of source and application of funds for the year to 31 May 19X2

	£	£
Source of funds:		
Profit (1)		50,000
Application of funds:		
Purchase of machinery		8,000
		(2) 42,000
Increase/decrease in working capital:		
Increase in debtors (3)	100,000	
(Increase) in creditors (4)	(50,000)	
(Decrease) in bank balance (5)	(8,000)	£42,000

Tutorial notes

1 Ande's profit is still £50,000 (£100,000 − £50,000), even though he has not paid for his purchases, and none of his customers have settled their accounts.
2 His net source of funds remains at £42,000.
3 Ande's increase in debtors is £100,000 (from £0 at the beginning of the year, to £100,000 at the end).
4 His creditors have increased by £50,000 (from £0 at the beginning of the year to £50,000 at the end). Note that an *increase* in creditors reduces working capital, whereas a *decrease* in creditors increases working capital. If this point is not clear, remember:

Working capital = (Debtors + Stocks + Cash) − Creditors

5 By the end of the year his bank balance has gone down by £8,000 (from £10,000 at the beginning of the year to £2,000 at the end of the year, a movement of £8,000).

By comparing Exhibits 7.2 and 7.3 it can be seen that in both cases, Ande has made an accounting profit of £50,000. When he traded on cash terms (as in Exhibit 7.2), his cash position had improved by £42,000 by the end of the year. However, when he traded on credit terms (as in Exhibit 7.3), his cash position had deteriorated by £8,000.

It is now possible to see why it is necessary to supplement the traditional financial statements with a statement of source and application of funds. Although Exhibits 7.2 and 7.3 are very simple, they do make the point.

If Ande had relied on his profit and loss account and balance sheet, he would normally have been quite justified in withdrawing the £50,000 accounting profit that he had made. In Exhibit 7.2 there would have been no problem, because the profit had been realized in cash. In Exhibit 7.3 however, it would have been most unwise of him to try to withdraw the profit, because his profit had not been realized in the form of cash. In more realistic circumstances, where there were constant changes in the creditor and debtor position during the year, he could have been misled by the apparent high level of trading activity into believing that he could withdraw his profit in the form of cash.

Before moving on to look at a more realistic example of a source and application of funds statement the recommended format must first be examined.

The recommended format

The basic structure and format of a simple statement of source and application of funds has now been covered. In this section, the format recommended in SSAP 10 for the preparation of a funds statement relating to a single entity will be examined (more complicated structures are covered in Chapter 19).

It should be noted that the format is not mandatory, but as it is the one that you are most likely to meet, it will be adopted even though it is perhaps not the best way of presenting information about liquidity.

Exhibit 7.4 presents a slightly simplified version of the recommended format.

Exhibit 7.4: Recommended format of statement of source and application of funds

SINGLE COMPANY LIMITED

Statement of source and application of funds for the year to XX

	£	£	£
Source of funds			
Profit before tax (1)			X
Adjustments for items not involving the movement of funds (2):			
Depreciation			X
Total generated from operations (3)			X
Funds from other sources (4):			
Issue of shares for cash			X
			X
Application of funds (5):			
Dividends paid		(X)	
Tax paid		(X)	
Purchase of fixed assets		(X)	(X)
			X
Increase/decrease in working capital (6):			
Increase in stocks (7)		X	
Increase in debtors (7)		X	
(Increase) in creditors-excluding taxation and proposed dividends (7)		X	
c/fwd		X	X

	£	£	£
b/fwd		X	X
Movement in net liquid funds (8):			
Increase (decrease) in:			
Cash balances	X		
Short-term investments	X	X	X

Note: The statement would also show details of previous year's results.

Tutorial notes

1 Notice that this is the profit *before* tax. This means that any appropriations of profit (such as tax and dividends) are ignored. In fact, as will be seen, only tax and dividends that have been *paid* are brought into a funds statement. Other tax and dividend adjustments (such as tax due and proposed dividends) are excluded altogether.
2 Adjustments for items not involving the movement of funds include such items as depreciation, and under- or over-depreciation on the sale of fixed assets. These items have to be added back (or deducted as the case may be) to accounting profit because they are what accountants call 'book entries'. Although they are a legitimate charge to the profit and loss account, they do not affect the movement of funds, i.e. cash does not either go up or go down as a result of making these entries, so a funds statement has to be adjusted to allow for them.
3 Funds obtained from operational activities (mainly from profit) should be shown separately from funds obtained from other sources.
4 Funds from other sources will include *cash* received from the sale of shares and debentures, and from the sale of fixed assets.
5 The application of funds section should only include amounts actually paid in cash. Thus tax due to be paid and any proposed dividend must *not* be included as an application of funds (see also tutorial note 1 above).
6 The working capital section illustrates the movement (i.e. the change) in working capital during the period. The movement is calculated simply by deducting the respective closing balances from the respective opening balances. Working capital is basically the difference between current assets and current liabilities, except that current liabilities do not include any tax payable or any proposed dividend. This definition of working capital is what SSAP 10 means by 'funds'.
7 It should be noted that changes in stocks, debtors and creditors *do* affect the movement of funds.
8 Movements in net liquid funds include cash and bank balances and those investments which could be turned into cash very quickly, such as cash invested in over-night deposit accounts.

Students usually find it very difficult to understand how a funds statement is constructed. There is usually particular difficulty in understanding how changes in working capital affect the movement of funds. Exhibit 7.5, therefore, summarizes the effect of working capital changes on cash flow.

Exhibit 7.5: Working capital movements: effect on cash flow

Item	*Movement (Closing balance – opening balance)*	*Effect on cash*
Stocks	(i) Increase	(i) Down (more cash has been spent on stock)
	(ii) Decrease	(ii) Up (less cash has been spent on stock)
Debtors and prepayments	(i) Increase	(i) Down (less cash has been received)
	(ii) Decrease	(ii) Up (more cash has been received)
Creditors and accruals	(i) Increase	(i) Up (less cash has been spent)
	(ii) Decrease	(ii) Down (more creditors have been paid)

As a non-accountant, it is unlikely that you will ever have to construct a funds flow statement. However, if you are able to work through a fairly straightforward example, it is more likely that you will understand what such statements are trying to tell you and you should thus find them much more useful. The next section, therefore, contains a comprehensive example which you are recommended to work through most carefully.

A comprehensive example

The example illustrated in this section is very much more complicated than those given earlier. You will probably, however, need to keep referring back to the previous exhibits as you work through Exhibit 7.6.

Exhibit 7.6

You are presented with the following summarized information for Martin Limited for the year to 31 March 19X8:

MARTIN LIMITED

Profit and loss account (extract) for the year to 31 March 19X8

		19X7 £000	19X8 £000
Net profit for the year before taxation		65	85
Taxation		30	35
Net profit after taxation	c/fwd	35	50

	19X7	19X8
	£000	£000
b/fwd	35	50
Proposed dividend	20	30
	15	20
Retained profits brought forward	10	25
Retained profits carried forward	£25	£45

MARTIN LIMITED
Balance sheet (extract) at 31 March 19X8

	19X7		19X8	
	£000	£000	£000	£000
Fixed assets				
Plant at cost		45		95
Less: Accumulated depreciation		18		25
		27		70
Current assets				
Stocks	51		67	
Debtors	110		170	
Bank	2		1	
	163		238	
Less: Current liabilities				
Creditors	15		28	
Taxation	30		35	
Dividends	20		30	
	65		93	
		98		145
		£125		£215
Financed by:				
Capital and reserves				
Ordinary shares of £1 each		100		150
Retained profits		25		45
Shareholders' funds		125		195
Loans				
Debenture stock		–		20
		£125		£215

Additional information:

1 There were no sales of fixed assets during the year.
2 During the year to 31 March 19X8, 50,000 ordinary shares of £1 each and £20,000 of debenture stock were issued for cash.

Required:
Prepare a statement of source and application of funds for the year to 31 March 19X8.

Answer to Exhibit 7.6

MARTIN LIMITED
Statement of source and application of funds for the year to 31 March 19X8

	£000	£000
Source of funds:		
Profit before tax (1)		85
Adjustment for items not involving the movement of funds:		
Depreciation (2)		7
Total generated from operations		92
Funds from other sources:		
Issue of shares for cash (3)	50	
Issue of debentures for cash (3)	20	70
		162
Application of funds:		
Dividends paid (4)	(20)	
Tax paid (4)	(30)	
Purchase of fixed assets (5)	(50)	(100)
		62
Increase/decrease in working capital (7):		
Increase in stocks	16	
Increase in debtors	60	
(Increase) in creditors	(13)	
Movement in net liquid funds:		
(Decrease) in cash balances (8)	(1)	£62

Tutorial notes

1 The funds statement normally begins with the profit *before* tax. This is the direct link that a funds statement makes with the profit and loss account.

2 Depreciation for the year has been calculated as follows:

	£000
Accumulated depreciation at 31 March 19X8 (as per the balance sheet)	25
Less: Accumulated depreciation at 31 March 19X7 (as per the balance sheet)	18
∴ Depreciation for the year	£7

It is possible to calculate the depreciation in this way because there were no sales of fixed assets during the year. The depreciation charge for the year would normally be obtained from the profit and loss account.

3 The question states that £50,000 of shares and £20,000 of debenture stock were issued for cash during the year.

4 Both the dividends paid and the tax paid relate to the items that were outstanding at 31 March 19X7. The 19X8 proposed dividend and the tax on the profits for the year will be paid during the year to 31 March 19X9, so they do not affect the 19X8's cash position.

5 The question states that there were no sales of fixed assets during the year. However, there were obviously some purchases of fixed assets because the plant at cost has increased from £45,000 in 19X7 to £95,000 in 19X8, an increase of £50,000.

6 Since the beginning of the year, the company has increased its funds by a net amount of £62,000 (£162,000 − £100,000). The working capital section shows where it has invested these funds.

7 The £62,000 of increased funds available to the business have been invested as follows:

Working capital at:	31.3.X7	31.3.X8	*Movement*
	£000	£000	£000
Stocks	51	67	16
Debtors	110	170	60
Bank	2	1	(1)
	163	238	75
Less: Creditors	15	28	13
Net working capital	£148	£210	£62

8 The net decrease in the closing bank balance can be reconciled as follows:

	£000	£000
Opening bank balance at 1 April 19X7		2
Add: Net sources of funds for the year		62
Reductions in amounts paid to creditors		13
		77
Less: Investment in stocks	16	
Reduction in receipts from debtors	60	76
Closing bank balance at 31 March 19X8		£1

You are now recommended to work through Exhibit 7.6 without reference to the solution.

Conclusion

The preparation of a statement of source and application of funds is a complex operation. As a non-accountant it is most unlikely that you will ever have to prepare your own funds statement, but it is considered that in order to make the best possible use of such a statement it is necessary to know something about its construction. In this chapter you have been given sufficient information to begin constructing your own funds statements, and in the process learn more about them.

A funds statement links the profit and loss account and the balance sheet, and the changes which have taken place in the amount of funds available to the business during a particular accounting period. Such information is extremely valuable, because unlike the traditional financial statements, a funds statement shows where the funds have come from and where they have gone to. Funds may be generated from operational sources or they may be raised outside the business. Funds may be disposed of either by spending them outside the business or by investing them in working capital.

This chapter is closely linked with the next which deals with the interpretation of accounts. The purpose of both chapters is threefold:

1 to enable the non-accountant to use the traditional financial statements to much greater effect;
2 to foster an awareness of their weaknesses; and
3 to impart sufficient understanding to be able to extract information which might be useful in taking more informed decisions.

Questions

7.1 You are presented with the following information:

DENNIS LIMITED
Balance sheet at 31 January 19X2

	31 January 19X1		31 January 19X2	
	£000	£000	£000	£000
Fixed assets:				
Land at cost		600		700
Current assets:				
Stock	100		120	
Debtors	200		250	
Cash	6		10	
	306		380	
Less: Current liabilities:				
Creditors	180	126	220	160
		£726		£860
Capital and reserves:				
Ordinary share capital		700		800
Profit and loss account		26		60
		£726		£860

Required:
Prepare Dennis Limited's statement of source and application of funds for the year to 31 January 19X2.

7.2 The following balance sheets have been prepared for Frank Limited:

Balance sheets at:	28.2.X1		28.2.X2	
	£000	£000	£000	£000
Fixed assets:				
Plant and machinery at cost		300		300
Less: Depreciation		80		100
		220		200
Investments at cost		—		100
Current assets:				
Stocks	160		190	
Debtors	220		110	
Bank	—		10	
	380		310	
Less: Current liabilities				
Creditors	200		160	
Bank overdraft	20		—	
	220	160	160	150
		£380		£450
Capital and reserves:				
Ordinary share capital		300		300
Share premium account		50		50
Profit and loss account		30		40
		380		390
Shareholders' funds				
Loans:				
Debentures		—		60
		£380		£450

Additional information:
There were no purchases or sales of plant and machinery during the year.

Required:
Prepare Frank Limited's statement of source and application of funds for the year to 28 February 19X2.

7.3 You are presented with the following information:

STARTER

Profit and loss account for the year to 31 March 19X3

	£	£
Sales		10,000
Less: Cost of goods sold:		
Purchases	5,000	
Less: Closing stock	1,000	4,000
Gross profit		6,000
Less: Depreciation		2,000
Net profit for the year		£4,000

Balance Sheet at 31 March 19X3

	£	£
Van		10,000
Less: Depreciation		2,000
		8,000
Stock	1,000	
Trade debtors	5,000	
Bank	12,500	
	18,500	
Less: Trade creditors	2,500	16,000
		£24,000
Capital		20,000
Add: Net profit for the year		4,000
N.B. Starter commenced business on 1 April 19X2.		£24,000

Required:
Compile Starter's statement of source and application of funds for the year to 31 March 19X3.

7.4 The following is a summary of Gregory Limited's accounts for the year to 30 April 19X4.

Profit and loss account for the year to 30 April 19X4

	£000
Net profit before tax	75
Taxation	25
	50
Dividend (proposed)	40
Retained profit for the year	£10

Balance sheet at 30 April 19X4

	30.4.X3		30.4.X4	
	£000	£000	£000	£000
Fixed assets:				
Plant at cost		400		550
Less: Depreciation		100		180
		300		370
Current assets:				
Stocks	50		90	
Debtors	70		50	
Bank	10		2	
	130		142	
Less: Current liabilities:				
Creditors	45		55	
Taxation	18		25	
Proposed dividend	35		40	
	98	32	120	22
		£332		£392
Capital and reserves:				
Ordinary share capital		200		200
Profit and loss account		132		142
		332		342
Loans		—		50
		£332		£392

Additional information:
There were no sales of fixed assets during the year to 30 April 19X4.

Required:
Prepare Gregory Limited's statement of source and application of funds for the year to 30 April 19X4.

7.5 The following summarized accounts have been prepared for Pill Limited:

Profit and loss account for the year to 31 May 19X5

	19X4	19X5
	£000	£000
Sales	2,400	3,000
Less: Cost of goods sold	1,600	2,000
Gross profit	800	1,000
c/fwd	800	1,000

		£000	£000
Gross profit	b/fwd	800	1,000
Less: Expenses:			
Administration expenses		310	320
Depreciation: Vehicles		55	60
Furniture		35	40
		400	420
Net profit		400	580
Taxation		120	150
		280	430
Dividends		200	250
Retained profits for the year		£80	£180

Balance sheet at 31 May 19X5

	31.5.X4		31.5.X5	
	£000	£000	£000	£000
Fixed assets:				
Vehicles at cost	600		800	
Less: Depreciation	200	400	260	540
Furniture	200		250	
Less: Depreciation	100	100	140	110
		500		650
Current assets:				
Stocks	400		540	
Debtors	180		200	
Cash	320		120	
	900		860	
Less: Current liabilities:				
Creditors	270		300	
Corporation tax	170		220	
Proposed dividends	150		100	
	590	310	620	240
		£810		£890
Capital and reserves:				
Ordinary share capital		500		550
Profit and loss account		120		300
Shareholders' funds		620		850
Loans:				
Debentures (8%)		190		40
		£810		£890

Additional information:
There were no sales of fixed assets during the year to 31 May 19X5.

Required:
Compile Pill Limited's statement of source and application of funds for the year to 31 May 19X5.

7.6 The following information relates to Brian Limited for the year to 30 June 19X6.

Profit and loss account for the year to 30 June 19X6

	£000	£000
Gross profit		230
Administration expenses	76	
Loss on sale of vehicle	3	
Increase in provision for doubtful debts	1	
Depreciation on vehicles	35	115
Net profit		115
Taxation		65
		50
Dividends		25
Retained profit for the year		£25

Balance sheet at 30 June 19X6

	19X5		19X6	
	£000	£000	£000	£000
Fixed assets:				
Vehicle at cost		150		200
Less: Depreciation		75		100
		75		100
Current assets:				
Stocks		60		50
Trade debtors	80		100	
Less: Provision for doubtful debts	4	76	5	95
Cash		6		8
		142		153
Less: Current liabilities:				
Trade creditors	60		53	
Taxation	52		65	
Proposed dividend	20	132	25	143
Net current assets c/fwd		10		10

		19X5		19X6	
		£000	£000	£000	£000
Net current assets	b/fwd		10		10
			85		110
Capital and reserves:					
Ordinary share capital			75		75
Profit and loss account			10		35
			£85		£110

Additional information:

1 The company purchased some new vehicles during the year for £75,000.

2 During the year the company sold a vehicle for £12,000 in cash. The vehicle had originally cost £25,000, and £10,000 had been set aside for depreciation.

Required:

Prepare a statement of source and application of funds for Brian Limited for the year to 30 June 19X6.

8 Interpretation of accounts

This chapter shows how the non-accountant can convert basic accounting data into a more meaningful form. This is done by using what is known as *ratio analysis*.

Data are extracted from the traditional accounting statements and converted into statistics which can be used to compare the entity's results either with previous periods or with similar entities in the same industry. Such comparisons can be done on a percentage basis or by using simple factors, but for convenience we will refer to such data as *ratios*.

Ratios are not usually very important when viewed in isolation, but they can be useful when they are used to *interpret* a set of accounts. Students often believe that if they calculate a great many ratios they have 'interpreted' the accounts. In fact, the calculation of a number of ratios is only a beginning. What must follow is a detailed investigation into the entity's results for the period, including a comparison with previous periods and with other similar entities.

By using ratio analysis in the interpretation of accounts we are able to put the information into context. This chapter is very important, therefore, because it will enable you as a non-accountant to get far more out of a set of accounts than by simply looking at the figures in isolation.

The need for ratios

It was suggested in Chapter 1 that a business proprietor wants to know the answers to three basic questions. These questions keep recurring, but will be repeated once again as they are very important. They are as follows:

1 How much profit has the business made?
2 How much does the business owe?
3 How much is owed to the business?

In Chapters 3 to 6 how an accountant would go about trying to answer these questions was outlined, but as has been seen the method is far from satisfactory. It has been possible to calculate only the *absolute* amount of profit, and the total amount of respective indebtedness. Even then, some highly arguable assumptions have been used in trying to arrive at the answers.

If such results are used in isolation, the proprietor could be misled by the current liquidity position and by the apparent long-term trend of the profits. The debtor and creditor balances do not tell very much, for example, are they too high or too low? It is not really possible to know until they have been put into context. An outstanding debtors' balance of £200,000 would appear to be a very large amount for a small business, but it might be a very small one for a large international company (although we cannot be sure until the matter has been gone into in much greater detail).

Ratio analysis is one way to do this. In practice, it is possible to produce hundreds of ratios, but for the purposes of this book it will be sufficient to outline a small number of key ones. This is so, partly because it is difficult to handle a great many ratios, and partly because it is not necessary to use a large number to demonstrate the basic principles of ratio analysis.

For convenience, the main ratios may be examined under four main headings: profitability ratios, liquidity ratios, efficiency ratios and investment ratios. Each classification is covered in the following sections.

Profitability ratios

Users of accounts will want to know how much profit a business has made, so that they can compare it either with previous periods or with other entities. Unfortunately, it is difficult to compare meaningfully the absolute level of profit unless it is related to the size of the entity and the amount of capital invested in it.

Return on capital employed ratio

The best way of doing this is to compare the profit with the capital invested in the form of a ratio. We can do so by using a ratio known as the *return on capital employed* (ROCE) ratio. It can be expressed quite simply as follows:

$$\text{ROCE} = \frac{\text{Profit} \times 100}{\text{Capital}}$$

This ratio (like most other ratios) is expressed as a percentage.

As far as ROCE is concerned, there is, unfortunately, no common agreement about the definition of either profit or of capital. As a result, different ROCE ratios can be produced by changing the definitions of both terms. Thus when comparing one ROCE ratio with another, it is important to make sure that the same definitions have been used.

If profit is considered from the point of view of how successful the entity has been in using its assets, profit should mean the net profit before tax and dividends. The profit (as defined) must then be related to the amount of capital needed to finance it. It would seem appropriate, therefore, to relate profit to the amount of capital needed to finance that level of profit, i.e. the shareholders' funds.

It must be appreciated, however, that there are several quite acceptable measures of ROCE, and the choice will depend upon the use to which it is to be put. It could be argued, for example, that ordinary shareholders will only be interested in the profit *after* tax and preference dividends, because their dividend will be based on what profit the company has available after setting aside a sufficient amount for tax and for paying the preference dividend.

Since you may need to calculate ROCE for different purposes, summarized below are the main methods of calculating this important ratio:

1 $\dfrac{\text{Net profit before tax}}{\text{Shareholders' funds}} \times 100$

2 $\dfrac{\text{Net profit after tax and preference dividend but before extraordinary items}}{\text{Shareholders' funds less preference shares}} \times 100$

3 $\dfrac{\text{Profit before tax and interest}}{\text{Shareholders' funds plus long-term loans}} \times 100$

4 $\dfrac{\text{Profit after tax and before extraordinary items}}{\text{Shareholders' funds}} \times 100$

Note: Extraordinary items are items that are material in amount. They are not considered to be part of the ordinary activities of the business, and it is not to be expected that they will recur frequently or regularly. Extraordinary items are considered further again in Chapter 19.

By calculating the return on capital employed ratio, a far better measure of the entity's profitability can be achieved than by merely viewing the level of profit in isolation. By using ROCE, sweeping assertions can be avoided about (say) a profit of £500 million being high (it might be thought relatively low if the capital employed was £10,000 million), or a profit of £500 being low (it might be acceptable if the capital invested was £2,000). High and low in this context can only be viewed in an absolute sense.

Gross profit ratio

There are a number of other important profitability ratios which ought to be considered. The *gross profit ratio*, for example, enables the *trading* profitability of the entity to be established. It is calculated as follows:

$$\text{Gross profit ratio} = \frac{\text{Gross profit}}{\text{Total sales revenue}} \times 100$$

The gross profit ratio measures how much profit the entity is earning in relation to the amount of sales that it is making. The definition of gross profit does not usually cause any problems. Most entities adopt the definition which has been used in this book, namely sales less the cost of goods sold, so meaningful comparisons can usually be made between different entities.

Mark-up ratio

The gross profit ratio complements another main trading ratio which for convenience may be termed the *mark-up ratio*, calculated as follows:

$$\text{Mark-up ratio} = \frac{\text{Gross profit}}{\text{Cost of goods sold}} \times 100$$

Mark-up measures the amount of profit added to the cost of goods sold (i.e. (Opening stock + Purchases) − Closing stock) to arrive at the selling price. The mark-up may be reduced to stimulate extra sales activity, but this will have the effect of reducing the gross profit. However, if extra goods are sold, the greater volume of sales compensates for the reduction in the mark-up on each unit.

Net profit ratio

Proprietors sometimes like to compare the net profit with the sales revenue. This can be expressed in the form of the *net profit ratio*, calculated as follows:

$$\text{Net profit ratio} = \frac{\text{Net profit before tax}}{\text{Total sales revenue}} \times 100$$

It is difficult to make a fair comparison between the net profit ratio calculated for different companies. Individual circumstances vary so much that companies are bound to have different levels of expenditure, no matter how efficient one company is compared with another. Thus it may only be practicable to use a net profit ratio in making comparisons between different periods within the same entity. Over a period of time a pattern will emerge, and it might then be possible to draw some conclusions by establishing a trend.

Liquidity ratios

Liquidity ratios measure the overall state of indebtedness of the entity. The total amount of trade debtors and trade creditors can be ascertained quite easily from the balance sheet, but whether they are high or low cannot be ascertained in isolation. Liquidity ratios, therefore, help put them into context. There are two main liquidity ratios: the *current assets ratio* and the *acid test ratio*.

Current assets ratio

This ratio is not usually expressed in the form of a percentage, but is calculated as follows:

$$\text{Current assets ratio} = \frac{\text{Current assets}}{\text{Current liabilities}}$$

In most circumstances it can be expected that current assets will be in excess of current liabilities (in which case, the current assets ratio will be at least 1 to 1). If this is not the case, the entity may not have sufficient liquid resources to meet its immediate financial commitments.

As the term *current* means receivable or payable within the next twelve months, the company may not always have to settle all of its current debts within the next week or even the next month. Its corporation tax, for example, may not have to be paid for at least nine months, and in the meantime, cash may be received from its debtors. Some entities, such as supermarkets, do not do much trade on credit terms, and it is not uncommon for them, therefore, to have a current assets ratio of less than 1 to 1. This is not usually a problem because they are receiving cash over the counter daily which should enable them to meet any immediate liability.

Nonetheless, in many circumstances, a current assets ratio of less than 1 to 1 can signify a serious financial position, especially if the current assets comprise a high proportion of stocks which the company would not want to be forced to sell.

Acid test ratio

The second main liquidity ratio is known as the acid test (or quick) ratio. It is calculated as follows:

$$\text{Acid test ratio} = \frac{\text{Current assets} - \text{stocks}}{\text{Current liabilities}}$$

The acid test ratio is probably a better measure of the entity's real liquidity than is the current assets ratio. If the acid test ratio measures a relationship of less than 1 to 1, it will be particularly important to investigate the detailed make-up of both current assets (less stock) and current liabilities. A ratio of less than 1 to 1 does not necessarily mean that the entity's liquidity position is immediately critical, but depending upon the circumstances, it could mean that the entity may shortly find it difficult to finance its future activities.

Efficiency ratios

Traditional accounting statements do not measure the *efficiency* of an entity, that is they do not tell us how successful the management has been in using the resources of the entity. As argued above, even the net profit does not give any real measure of efficiency when it is viewed in isolation. As a result, a number of efficiency ratios must be calculated which will help to put the results into context. There are many different types of efficiency ratios, but only the more common ones will be covered. These are examined below.

Stock turnover ratio

$$\text{Stock turnover ratio} = \frac{\text{Cost of goods sold}}{\text{Average stock}}$$

The average stock can be calculated as follows:

$$\frac{\text{Opening stock} + \text{Closing stock}}{2}$$

The sales revenue may be substituted for the cost of goods sold if the accounts do not disclose the cost of goods sold. Sales revenue should not be used if it can be avoided, however, since it contains a profit loading which can cause the ratio to be distorted. Many accountants also prefer to substitute a more accurate average stock level, particularly if goods are purchased irregularly. Sometimes it is also useful to compare the closing stock with the cost of sales in order to gain a clearer idea of what the stock position is like at the end of the year, although this can be misleading if the company's trade is seasonal and the year-end falls during the peak period.

The greater the stock turnover (it is not usually expressed as a percentage), the more efficient the entity would appear to be in purchasing goods and selling them quickly to its customers. A stock turnover of 2 for example, would suggest that the entity has about six months of sales in stock which (in most circumstances) would appear to be high, whereas a stock turnover of (say) 12 would mean that the entity only kept about a month's normal sales in stock.

Fixed assets turnover ratio

Another important area to examine from the point of view of efficiency relates to fixed assets. Fixed assets enable the business to function more efficiently, so an investment in fixed assets ought eventually to generate more sales. We can check this by calculating a ratio known as the *fixed assets turnover* ratio. It is calculated as follows:

$$\text{Fixed assets turnover ratio} = \frac{\text{Total sales revenue}}{\text{Fixed assets at net book value}}$$

This ratio may also be expressed as a percentage.

The fixed assets turnover ratio is really only useful if it is calculated as part of a trend; in isolation, it does not mean very much. For example, is a turnover of 5 good, and 4 poor? All we can suggest is that if the trend is upwards, then the investment in fixed assets is beginning to pay off, at least in terms of increased sales.

Average trade debtor collection period ratio

Generating extra sales revenue is not going to be very helpful, however, if the entity's trade debtors do not settle their debts very promptly. It might be possible to generate extra sales by a combination of lowering selling prices and by offering generous credit terms. In the meantime, the entity has to finance its operational activities, and if it is slow at turning its sales into cash, it might easily run into a short-term liquidity problem. It is important, therefore, for it to have tight control over its trade debtors.

How successful it is may be checked by calculating an *average trade debtor collection period* ratio as follows:

$$\text{Average trade debtor collection period} = \frac{\text{Average trade debtors}}{\text{Total credit sales}} \times 365$$

The average trade debtors are usually a simple average of opening and closing trade debtors, i.e. ½ (Opening trade debtors + Closing trade debtors). The closing trade debtors are sometimes substituted for the average trade debtors. This is acceptable provided that the closing trade debtors are representative of the period as a whole.

It is important to relate trade debtors to *credit* sales, and not to include any cash sales in the calculation. The method shown above for calculating the ratio would relate the average trade debtors to so many *days'* sales, but it would be possible to substitute weeks or months. It is not customary to express the ratio as a percentage.

It is not possible to suggest a typical debtor collection period, as much depends upon the type of trade in which the company is engaged. Some companies expect settlement within 28 days of delivery of the goods or receipt of the invoice. Other companies might expect settlement within 28 days following the end of the month in which the goods were delivered. On average, therefore, this adds another 14 days (half a month) to the overall period of 28 days. In these circumstances, therefore, a company would appear to be highly efficient in collecting its debts if the average debtor collection period was about 42 days.

Like most of the other ratios, however, it is important to establish a trend, and if the trend is upwards, then it might suggest that the company's credit control was beginning to weaken.

Average trade creditor payment period ratio

A similar ratio can be calculated for the average trade creditor payment period. The formula is as follows:

$$\text{Average trade creditor payment period} = \frac{\text{Average trade creditors}}{\text{Total credit purchases}} \times 365$$

The average trade creditors would again be a simple average of the opening and closing balances, although it is quite customary to substitute the closing trade creditors. The trade creditors must be related to *credit* purchases, and weeks or months may be substituted for the number of days. Like the trade debtor collection period ratio, it is not usual to express the average trade creditor payment period ratio as a percentage.

An upward trend in the average level of trade creditors would suggest that the entity is having some difficulty in finding the cash to pay its creditors. Indeed, it might be a warning that it is running into financial difficulties.

Investment ratios

The various ratios examined in the previous sections are probably of interest to all users of accounts, such as shareholders, managers, creditors or employees. There are, however, some other ratios which are primarily (athough not exclusively) of interest to investors. These are known as *investment* ratios, and the main ones are outlined below.

Dividend yield

The first investment ratio which might be found useful is the *dividend yield*. It may be calculated as follows:

$$\text{Dividend yield} = \frac{\text{Nominal value per share}}{\text{Market price per share}} \times \begin{array}{c}\text{Declared}\\ \text{dividend rate}\end{array}$$

The dividend yield measures the rate of return an investor would get by purchasing the shares at the current market rate on the basis of a declared dividend rate. If an investor buys 100 £1 ordinary shares, for example, at a market rate of £2 per share, and the next declared dividend rate was 10%, his yield would be 5% (£1/2 × 10%). As far as the company is concerned, although he has invested £200 (100 × £2 per share), he will be registered as holding a nominal amount of £100 (100 shares × £1). He is, therefore, entitled to a dividend of £10, but from the shareholder's point of view, however, he will be getting a return of £10 on £200 (or 5%). It should be noted that this method ignores any tax credit that may be attached to the dividend.

Dividend cover

Another investment ratio which it is useful to calculate is the *dividend cover*:

$$\text{Dividend cover} = \frac{\text{Net profit after tax and preference dividend}}{\text{Paid and proposed ordinary dividends}}$$

This ratio gives some idea of the proportion that the ordinary dividends bear to the earnings available for distribution to the ordinary shareholders. The dividend is usually described as being so many times covered by the profits. Thus if the dividend is covered twice, the company would be distributing half of its available earnings for that year as dividend.

Earnings per share

Another important investment ratio is that known as *earnings per share* (EPS). This ratio makes it possible to put the profit into context and to avoid looking at it purely in absolute terms. It may be calculated as follows:

$$\text{Earnings per share} = \frac{\text{Net profit after tax and preference dividend but before extraordinary items}}{\text{Number of ordinary shares in issue during the year}}$$

It is customary to calculate this ratio by taking the net profit after tax (although there is no reason why it could not be taken before tax). Preference dividends are deducted because they have to be paid before ordinary shareholders can receive a dividend out of the available earnings. Extraordinary items are excluded because, by definition, they cannot be expected to recur, and so their inclusion would distort the year's earnings.

This ratio makes a fair comparison possible between one year's earnings and another, and at the same time relates the earnings to something meaningful, i.e. the number of shares in issue.

Price/earnings ratio

Another common investment ratio is the *price/earnings* ratio (or P/E ratio). It is calculated as follows:

$$\text{Price/earnings ratio} = \frac{\text{Market price per share}}{\text{Earnings per share}}$$

The P/E ratio makes a comparison possible between the earnings per share (as defined above) and the market price. Effectively, it means that the market price is a multiple of the earnings. In theory, the higher the P/E ratio, the greater the demand for the shares (presumably because of the earnings), but a low P/E ratio could also mean that there was little demand for the company's shares even though its earnings were high.

Capital gearing ratio

Capital gearing refers to the proportion that the preference share capital and long-term loans bear to the shareholders' funds plus long-term loans. It may be calculated as follows:

$$\text{Capital gearing ratio} = \frac{\text{Preference shares} + \text{Long-term loans}}{\text{Shareholders' funds} + \text{Long-term loans}} \times 100$$

It should be noted that there are alternative ways of calculating the gearing ratio.

A company that has financed itself by a high proportion of borrowing (whether in the form of preference shares or long-term loans) is known as a high geared company. Conversely, a company with a low level of borrowing is regarded as being low geared. A high geared company is potentially a higher risk investment, because before the company can pay any ordinary dividend, it has to earn sufficient profit to cover the interest payments and the preference dividend. This should not be a problem when profits are rising, but if they are falling, then the earnings may not be sufficient to pay an ordinary dividend.

Summary of the main ratios

A considerable number of accounting ratios have now been examined. They are summarized below for convenience.

Profitability ratios

$$\text{ROCE} = \frac{\text{Net profit before tax} \times 100}{\text{Shareholders' funds}}$$ - all money invested

$$\text{ROCE} = \frac{\text{Net profit after tax and preference dividend but before extraordinary items}}{\text{Shareholders' funds less preference shares}} \times 100$$

$$\text{ROCE} = \frac{\text{Profit before tax and interest}}{\text{Shareholders' funds + Long-term loans}} \times 100$$

$$\text{ROCE} = \frac{\text{Profit after tax and before extraordinary items}}{\text{Shareholders' funds}} \times 100$$

$$\text{Gross profit ratio} = \frac{\text{Gross profit}}{\text{Total sales revenue}} \times 100$$

$$\text{Mark up} = \frac{\text{Gross profit}}{\text{Cost of goods sold}} \times 100$$

$$\text{Net profit ratio} = \frac{\text{Net profit before tax}}{\text{Total sales revenue}} \times 100$$

Liquidity ratios

$$\text{Current assets ratio} = \frac{\text{Current assets}}{\text{Current liabilities}}$$

$$\text{Acid test ratio} = \frac{\text{Current assets} - \text{Stocks}}{\text{Current liabilities}}$$

Efficiency ratios

$$\text{Stock turnover} = \frac{\text{Cost of goods sold}}{\text{Average stock}}$$

$$\text{Fixed assets turnover} = \frac{\text{Total sales revenue}}{\text{Fixed assets at net book value}}$$

$$\text{Trade debtor collection period} = \frac{\text{Average trade debtors}}{\text{Total credit sales}} \times 365 \text{ days}$$

$$\text{Trade creditor payment period} = \frac{\text{Average trade creditors}}{\text{Total credit purchases}} \times 365 \text{ days}$$

Investment ratios

$$\text{Dividend yield} = \frac{\text{Nominal value per share} \times \text{Declared dividend rate}}{\text{Market price per share}}$$

$$\text{Dividend cover} = \frac{\text{Net profit after tax and preference dividend}}{\text{Paid and proposed ordinary dividends}}$$

$$\text{Earnings per share} = \frac{\text{Net profit after tax and preference dividend but before extraordinary items}}{\text{Number of ordinary shares in issue during the year}}$$

$$\text{Price/earnings ratio} = \frac{\text{Market price per share}}{\text{Earnings per share}}$$

$$\text{Capital gearing} = \frac{\text{Preference sharees} + \text{Long-term loans} \times 100}{\text{Shareholders' funds} + \text{Long-term loans}}$$

The 18 ratios listed above form only a small sample of the total number of ratios that could be produced. Used in isolation, they are not particularly helpful. However, when they form part of a detailed analysis, they give a much greater understanding of the company's results than can be obtained from referring simply to the financial accounts.

An illustrative example

In this section the use of these ratios is illustrated in Exhibit 8.1 in interpreting a set of accounts. In order to establish a reasonable trend, the results of a company really need to be analysed over something like a five year period, and it is also useful to compare them with similar companies over the same period (there are commercial organizations that provide such comparative data).

However, in this example it would be impracticable to do this as it would obscure the basic procedures that are being illustrated. Consequently, data is limited to a single company for a two year period. Exhibit 8.1, therefore, explains how to go about interpreting a set of accounts.

Exhibit 8.1

You are provided with the following summarized information relating to Gill Limited for the year to 31 March 19X3:

Gill Limited

Trading, profit and loss account for the year to 31 March 19X3

	19X2		19X3	
	£000	£000	£000	£000
Sales		160		180
Less: Cost of goods sold:				
Opening stock	10		14	
Purchases	100		130	
	110		144	
Less: Closing stock	14	96	24	120
Gross profit	c/fwd	64		60

		19X2		19X3	
		£000	£000	£000	£000
Gross Profit	b/fwd		64		60
Less: Expenses:					
Administration		18		24	
Loan interest		1		1	
Selling and distribution		12	31	16	41
Net profit before taxation			33		19
Taxation			15		6
Net profit after taxation			18		13
Dividends: preference (paid)		2		2	
ordinary (proposed)		8		5	
			10		7
Retained profit for the year			8		6
Retained profits brought forward			4		12
Retained profits carried forward			£12		£18

GILL LIMITED
Balance sheet at 31 March 19X3

	19X2			19X3		
	£000 Cost	£000 Depreciation	£000 Net book value	£000 Cost	£000 Depreciation	£000 Net book value
Fixed assets						
Freehold property	60	—	60	60	—	60
Vehicles	42	14	28	48	22	26
	£102	£14	88	£108	£22	86
Current assets						
Stocks		14			24	
Trade debtors		20			60	
Bank		3			1	
		37			85	
Less: current liabilities						
Trade creditors	10			62		
Taxation	15			6		
Proposed dividend	8	33	4	5	73	12
			£92			£98

	19X2	19X3
	£000	£000
Financed by:		
Capital and reserves		
Authorized, issued and fully paid ordinary shares of £1 each	40	40
Preference shares (10%)	20	20
Profit and loss account	12	18
Shareholders' funds	72	78
Loans		
Debenture stock (5%)	20	20
	£92	£98

Additional information:

1. Purchases and sales are made evenly throughout the year.
2. All purchases and all sales are made on credit terms.
3. You may assume that price levels are stable.
4. The company only sells one product: in 19X2 it sold 40,000 units and in 19X3 60,000 units.
5. There were no sales of fixed assets during the year.
6. The market value of the ordinary shares was estimated to be worth £2.30 per share at 31 March 19X2 and £1.80 per share at 31 March 19X3.

Required:

(a) Compute significant ratios for the two years to 31 March 19X2 and 19X3 respectively; and

(b) using the ratios which you have calculated in part (a) of the question, comment upon the results for the year to 31 March 19X3.

Answer to Exhibit 8.1

(a) Significant ratios GILL LIMITED

	19X2	19X3
Profitability ratios:		
Return on capital employed (ROCE)		
$\frac{\text{Net profit before tax} \times 100}{\text{Shareholders' funds}}$	$= \frac{33{,}000 \times 100}{72{,}000}$ = 45.83%	$= \frac{19{,}000 \times 100}{78{,}000}$ = 24.36%
Gross profit		
$\frac{\text{Gross profit}}{\text{Total sales revenue}} \times 100$	$= \frac{64{,}000 \times 100}{160{,}000}$ = 40.00%	$= \frac{60{,}000 \times 100}{180{,}000}$ = 33.33%
Mark up		
$\frac{\text{Gross profit}}{\text{Cost of goods sold}} \times 100$	$= \frac{64{,}000 \times 100}{96{,}000}$ = 66.67%	$= \frac{60{,}000 \times 100}{120{,}000}$ = 50.00%

		19X2		19X3
Net profit				
$\dfrac{\text{Net profit before tax} \times 100}{\text{Total sales revenue}}$	=	$\dfrac{33{,}000 \times 100}{160{,}000}$	=	$\dfrac{19{,}000 \times 100}{180{,}000}$
	=	20.63%	=	10.56%

Liquidity ratios:

		19X2		19X3
Current assets				
$\dfrac{\text{Current assets}}{\text{Current liabilities}}$	=	$\dfrac{37{,}000}{33{,}000}$	=	$\dfrac{85{,}000}{73{,}000}$
	=	1.12 to 1	=	1.16 to 1
Acid test				
$\dfrac{\text{Current assets} - \text{Stocks}}{\text{Current liabilities}}$	=	$\dfrac{37{,}000 - 14{,}000}{33{,}000}$	=	$\dfrac{85{,}000 - 24{,}000}{73{,}000}$
	=	0.70 to 1	=	0.84 to 1

Efficiency ratios:

		19X2		19X3
Stock turnover				
$\dfrac{\text{Cost of goods sold}}{\text{Average stock*}}$	=	$\dfrac{96{,}000}{½(10{,}000 + 14{,}000)}$	=	$\dfrac{120{,}000}{½(14{,}000 + 24{,}000)}$
	=	8.0 times	=	6.3 times

* ½ (Opening stocks + Closing stocks)

		19X2		19X3
Fixed assets turnover				
$\dfrac{\text{Total sales revenue}}{\text{Fixed assets at net book value}}$	=	$\dfrac{160{,}000}{88{,}000}$	=	$\dfrac{180{,}000}{86{,}000}$
	=	1.82 times	=	2.09 times
Trade debtor collection period				
$\dfrac{\text{Closing trade debtors*}}{\text{Total credit sales}}$	=	$\dfrac{20{,}000 \times 365}{160{,}000}$	=	$\dfrac{60{,}000 \times 365}{180{,}000}$
	=	46 days	=	122 days

*Opening trade debtors have not been given for 19X2, so closing trade debtors have been used.

		19X2		19X3
Trade creditor collection period				
$\dfrac{\text{Closing trade creditors*} \times 365}{\text{Total credit purchases}}$	=	$\dfrac{10{,}000 \times 365}{100{,}000}$	=	$\dfrac{62{,}000 \times 365}{130{,}000}$
	=	37 days	=	174 days

*Opening trade creditors have not been given for 19X2, so closing trade creditors have been used.

Investment ratios:

		19X2		19X3
Dividend yield				
$\dfrac{\text{Nominal value per share}}{\text{Market price per share}} \times \text{Declared dividend rate}$	=	$\dfrac{1.00}{2.30} \times 20\%$*	=	$\dfrac{1.00}{1.80} \times 12.5\%$**
	=	8.70%		6.94%

* $\dfrac{8{,}000 \times 100}{40{,}000}$		** $\dfrac{5{,}000 \times 100}{40{,}000}$
= 20%	=	12.5%

		19X2		19X3
Dividend cover				
Net profit after tax and preference dividend / **Paid and proposed ordinary dividends**	=	18,000 − 2,000 / 8,000	=	13,000 − 2,000 / 5,000
	=	2.00 times	=	2.20 times
Earnings per share (EPS)				
Net profit after tax and preference dividend / **Number of ordinary shares in issue during the year**	=	18,000 − 2,000 / 40,000	=	13,000 − 2,000 / 40,000
	=	40.00p		27.50p
Price/earnings (P/E) ratio				
Market price per share / **Earnings per share***	=	2.30 / 0.40	=	1.80 / 0.275
	=	5.75	=	6.55
Capital gearing				
Preference share + Long-term loans × 100 / **Shareholders' funds + Long-term loans**	=	20,000 + 20,000 × 100 / 72,000 + 20,000	=	20,000 + 20,000 × 100 / 78,000 + 20,000
	=	43.48%	=	40.82%

(b) Comments on the ratios

Profitability

1 The selling price of the product in 19X2 must have been £4.00 per unit since the company sold 40,000 units and its total sales revenue was £160,000 (£160,000 ÷ 40,000). In 19X3 the company sold 60,000 units and its total sales revenue was £180,000. The selling price per unit must, therefore, have been £3.00. It would appear that Gill Limited deliberately reduced its selling price per unit by 25% (£1.00 × 100/£4.00 = 25%). There was thus a 50% increase in sales volume (from 40,000 units to 60,000), but its total sales revenue only increased by £20,000 (or 12.5%).

2 The relatively modest increase in sales revenue did not help to increase the gross profit (down from £64,000 to £60,000), largely because the reduction in mark-up (down from 66.67% to 50%) did not generate sufficient extra sales.

3 The large increase in sales volume also affected overall profitability. The net profit on sales was reduced from 20.63% to 10.56%, partly because of the reduction in gross profit and partly because other expenses increased by £10,000. Consequently, the return on capital employed was much reduced: from 45.83% to 24.36%. This is still a favourable rate of return when compared with alternative forms of investment, but the company's management must view the downward trend with some concern.

Liquidity

1 Gill's current assets position does not appear to have been greatly affected by the overall decline in profitability. In fact the current assets ratio has increased

slightly, from 1.12 to 1 to 1.16 to 1. The current assets are in excess of current liabilities in both years, so provided that receipts from trade debtors can be kept in step with payments to trade creditors, the company would appear not to have an immediate liquidity problem.

2 If stocks are excluded from current assets, however, the position is a little more worrying. The acid test ratio was 0.71 to 1 in 19X2, and 0.84 to 1 in 19X3, so there has been an improvement in Gill's immediate liquidity position. Even so, by the end of 19X3 the company did not have sufficient cash to pay its proposed dividend, so it was dependent on either being able to obtain overdraft facilities from the bank, or on cash receipts from its trade debtors (note that there was a similar situation in 19X2). Fortunately, the tax would probably not have to be paid until 1 January 19X4 (i.e. nine months after the year end).

Efficiency

1 Gill was not as efficient in trading in 19X3 as it had been in 19X2. Its stock turnover was down from 8.0 to 6.3, which means that it was not turning over its stocks as quickly in 19X3 as it did in 19X2.

2 The company's investment in fixed assets (as measured by its sales activity) has improved from 1.82 times in 19X2 to 2.09 times in 19X3. This arose largely because the purchase of new assets only increased the gross book value of its fixed assets by £6,000, whereas the depreciation charge for the year reduced the total net book value by £8,000, a net difference of £2,000.

3 The extra sales generated during 19X3 were made at some cost to its potential liquidity position. At the end of 19X2 its outstanding trade debtors represented 46 days' sales, but at the end of 19X3, they represented 122 days' sales. This suggests that Gill encouraged a greater sales volume by reducing both its selling prices and by offering more generous credit terms. It is also possible that the company was so busy coping with the increased operational activity that it did not have time to control its debtor position.

4 Gill appears to have been fortunate in 19X3 in not having to pay its trade creditors as promptly as it did in 19X2. At the end of 19X2, its trade creditors represented about 37 days' purchases, but at the end of 19X3 they represented 174 days' purchases (or nearly six months' purchases). If Gill had had to pay its creditors as quickly in 19X3 as it had done in 19X2, its total trade creditors at the end of 19X3 would have amounted to about £13,000 (£130,000 × 37/365), instead of the £62,000 actually owing at that date. By paying its trade creditors more quickly, Gill would probably have had a bank overdraft of some £48,000 ((£62,000 − £13,000) = £49,000 − £1,000), instead of the favourable balance of £1,000.

Investment

1 Gill Limited is a private company, so its shares would not be freely available on a recognized stock exchange. The market price of the shares given in the question is bound to be rather a questionable one, and it probably does not reflect the earnings' potential of the company.

2 The dividend yield has fallen from 8.7% in 19X2 to 6.94% in 19X3. Compared with the yield currently available from other investments, these yields are about average, although the reduction in the dividend for 19X3 could be the start of a downwards trend.

3 Whilst the reduction in the dividend from 20% in 19X2 to 12.5% in 19X3 is worrying, the dividend is well covered by the earnings. Indeed, the company could have paid the same dividend in 19X3 as it did in 19X2, and the dividend would still have been covered 1.38 times (£13,000 − 2,000/8,000). It would appear that

the company's policy is to pay less than half of its earnings as dividend, even if it means reducing the dividend. This would not matter as much to a private company as it would to a public one. In a public company a reduction in dividend can result in a fall in the market value of its shares, thus reflecting the reduction in confidence that the market has in the company.

4 No new shares were issued during the year. Thus as a result of the reduction in profits, the earnings per share declined from 40.00p to 27.50p.

5 The increase in the price earnings ratio (up from 5.75 to 6.55) is surprising. It was probably caused by the market's view (albeit a rather restricted one) that the company's future is a reasonably good one, notwithstanding the reduction in the company's profit. However, this company is a private one, so we cannot be certain how the market price of its shares has been determined.

6 Gill Limited is a fairly high geared company. In 19X2, nearly 44% of its financing had been raised in the form of fixed interest stock, but in 19X3 this was reduced to just under 41%. By financing itself in this way, the company is committed to making annual payments of £3,000 (£2,000 of preference dividend + £1,000 of debenture interest). In absolute terms, this amount is not large, and so although it is a relatively high geared company, its earnings should be sufficient to cover its interest commitments.

Summary

1 In 19X3 Gill Limited achieved its presumed objective of increasing its sales. It did this partly by reducing its unit selling price, and partly by offering extended credit terms to its customers. The effect of this policy has been to reduce gross profit by £4,000 and its net profit by £14,000.

2 The new policy did not affect its liquidity position, largely because the extended credit terms (leading to delays in the settlement of its trade debts) were offset by similar delays in paying its trade creditors.

3 As a result of the reduction in its profits for 19X3, the company reduced its dividend, although its earnings were still sufficient for it to maintain the same dividend as in 19X2.

4 The market (such as it is) does not seem to agree that the reduction in the profit or of the dividend is serious. Indeed, it can be argued the company's future is healthy provided that it can persuade its trade debtors to pay their debts more promptly.

You are now recommended to study Exhibit 8.1 most carefully. Make sure that you know how to calculate the ratios, and that you know what they mean. Then try and list your own views on Gill Limited's progress during 19X3. The comments listed above are only brief ones, and much more could have been written about the company. However, it is hoped that it has been demonstrated that by using ratios a great deal more information can be extracted from the traditional profit and loss account and balance sheet than is sometimes appreciated.

Ratios help to put the information into context, but it must be emphasized that they must then be used as part of a detailed overall analysis. Ratios are like sign posts: they point you in the right direction, but you still have to make the effort to get there.

In the next section, how you would carry out a detailed investigation will be outlined in broad terms.

Analysing the accounts

As explained earlier, a considerable number of people will be interested in the affairs of a company. Analysts, creditors, employees, central and local government, investors, journalists, management, shareholders, trade unions and the general public will all have some interest to a greater or a lesser degree in the performance of a particular company. Some of these people may want to know everything that there is to know about the company, whilst others may be only interested in a fairly limited amount of information.

If you are asked to analyse a set of accounts, therefore, the amount of work you undertake will depend upon the reasons for your investigation. If you are asked to examine a company's accounts because your own company is considering making a take-over bid for another company, for example, you will probably need all the information that you can get. However, if you are a creditor, your main interest will probably be in finding out whether the company is in a position to pay its debts.

Nonetheless, it is possible to recommend a general procedure which can be followed irrespective of the reasons for the investigation. In the following subsections, how to conduct a general investigation into the affairs of a company is explained.

Obtaining information

You are recommended to find out as much about the company as you can and how it compares with similar companies in the same industry. It would also be useful to examine its future and that of the industry in a national and international context.

It is not usually difficult to obtain information if you search for it. You can start with the company's annual accounts (how to use these are explained in Part 4). Even the company's own public relations' department may be willing to supply you with a great deal of data about the company. There are also a number of commercial agencies that specialize in obtaining company information, and much information is published in journals, magazines and newspapers.

Assimilating such information about the company from a wide range of sources will help you interpret the company's accounts much more meaningfully.

Calculating trends and ratios

It has been explained earlier that it is desirable to examine a company's accounts over a number of years. As a general rule, it is suggested that you choose a period of some three to five years. Too short a period will not enable you to establish much of a trend, and too long a period could mean that you are using information that is somewhat out-of-date.

Once you have collected a set of accounts, the next step is to calculate a number of representative trends and ratios. The exact number and type will depend upon the purpose of your investigation, and in addition to the ones which have been examined in earlier sections, you may need to calculate some specialist ratios. If you were examining the accounts for a hotel, for example, you might want to calculate the rooms occupied as a proportion of the rooms in the hotel, or in the case of a retailing organization, the selling staff salaries as a proportion of sales revenue.

You can begin to assess the trends and calculate the ratios by using a number of different techniques. We summarize the four main techniques briefly below:

1 *Horizontal analysis*. This technique requires a line-by-line comparison to be made between the company's annual accounts over the period chosen for the investigation.
2 *Trend analysis*. Trend analysis is similar to horizontal analysis, except that the first accounts in the series are given a weighting of 100, subsequent accounts in the series then being related to the base of 100.
3 *Vertical analysis*. This technique requires both the profit and loss account and balance sheet items respectively to be expressed as a percentage of the total items.
4 *Ratio analysis*. The calculation of ratios have already been dealt with in some detail. As has been emphasized, it is possible to produce a great many ratios, so depending upon your purpose, you may want to convert each item in the accounts into a ratio and compare it with similar ratios for previous periods.

If you had adopted all of these techniques, you would by now have collected a great deal of data, and you would be in a position to compare each year's accounts on a similar basis. However, it is unlikely that the accounts you have obtained will have been adjusted for inflation, so to make a fairer comparison between them you should make some allowance for this factor. This subject is covered further in Chapter 20, but as a rough guide, remember that with an inflation rate of 5% per annum, prices double over a period of 15 years or increase by about 30% over a five year period.

Besides calculating trends and ratios specifically for the company that you are investigating you might also have been able to obtain similar statistics for other companies in the same industry. You are now, therefore, in a position to try to work out what all the information means.

Interpreting the accounts

You have now collected a considerable amount of information about the company. You know about its history, its operations, its management, its competitors, and how it relates to the national and international context. You have calculated a number of trends and ratios over a three to five year period, and you have similar information about other companies in the same industry.

The last and most difficult step, therefore, is to explain or to interpret the data. What guides are available to help you come to a decision about the company? Much, of course, depends upon the reason for your investigation, but in general it is suggested that you ask the following questions:

1 *The market for the company's products*. Has this expanded or contracted in recent years, and how has the company coped with the changes in market conditions? What will the market be like over (say) the next five years? How will it be affected by general demographic, economic, political and social factors? Does the company seem attuned to these possible changes?

2 *Sales and profits*. Have these increased or decreased over the period? If there has been any growth, has it been because of internal expansion or because of acquisition? Does the management seem keen enough to pursue growth or is the company stagnating?

3 *Capital investment*. What capital investment has there been and what is planned? How would future investment be financed? What retained reserves has the company built up?

4 *Management*. What is the record of its management? Are the senior managers near retirement? Are they young enough to seek change? Are they ambitious? How well do they seem to have managed the company's resources? Is its liquidity position secure? How good are they at portraying a favourable public image of the company?

5 *Employees and industrial relations*. Does the company appear to have a stable work-force? Has it had any industrial disputes? What is its attitude and relationship like to the trade unions? How does the output and profit record per employee compare with other companies?

6 *Generally*. Having found out a great deal about the company, does it inspire you with some confidence about its future? Is it likely to survive and expand both in the short term and in the long term?

The above questions are not exhaustive, but there is no doubt that having extensively researched a company's history and examined its future, you will already have formed a provisional view before you come to make your recommendations. All that remains for you to do is to set them down on paper. At that stage you may well find that you are expected to produce a brief report, so you have the difficult task of summarizing the main features of the company in just a few pages. You may well find that producing such a summary is almost as difficult as carrying out the initial investigation!

Conclusion

This chapter concludes the first main part of the book. By now, you should know something about the nature of accounting information, where it comes from, and how it is used.

As has been argued throughout this book, the techniques adopted by accountants are open to some criticism, so it is only right that some reservations should be made about the reliability of accounting information. However, no one has yet devised a better method of accounting, and until they do, we have to make the best of the present one. It could be argued that by being fully aware of the deficiencies of financial accounting, the non-accountant can make allowances for them when using that information.

The next part of the book deals with cost and management accounting. This is a most important branch of accounting which is of especial interest to non-accountants working in industry, although its techniques can be applied in other entities. However, it can only be fully appreciated if it is first preceded by a study of financial accounting. If you are in any doubt, therefore, about your understanding of the last six chapters, you are recommended to go back and have another attempt at some of the exhibits and questions.

Questions

8.1 The following information has been extracted from the books of account of Betty for the year to 31 January 19X1.

Trading and profit and loss account for the year to 31 January 19X2

	£000	£000
Sales (all credit)		100
Less: Cost of goods sold:		
Opening stock	15	
Purchases	65	
	80	
Less: Closing stock	10	70
Gross profit		30
Administration expenses		16
Net profit		£14

Balance sheet at 31 January 19X1

	£000	£000
Fixed assets (net book value)		29
Current assets:		
Stock	10	
Trade debtors	12	
Cash	3	
	25	
Less: Current liabilities		
Trade creditors	6	19
		£48
Financed by:		
Capital at 1 February 19X0		40
Add: Net profit	14	
Less: Drawings	6	8
		£48

Required:
Calculate the following accounting ratios:
1 gross profit;
2 net profit;
3 return on capital employed;
4 current ratio;
5 acid test;
6 stock turnover; and
7 debtor collection period.

8.2 You are presented with the following summarized accounts:

JAMES LIMITED
Profit and loss account for the year to 28 February 19X2

	£000
Sales (all credit)	1,200
Cost of sales	600
Gross profit	600
Administration expenses	(500)
Debenture interest payable	(10)
Profit on ordinary activities	90
Taxation	(30)
	60
Dividends	(40)
Retained profit for the year	£20

JAMES LIMITED
Balance sheet at 28 February 19X2

	£000	£000	£000
Fixed assets (net book value)			685
Current assets:			
Stock		75	
Trade debtors		200	
		275	
Less: Current liabilities			
Trade creditors	160		
Bank overdraft	10		
Taxation	30		
Proposed dividend	40	240	35
			£720
Capital and reserves			
Ordinary share capital			600
Profit and loss account			20
Shareholders' funds			620
Loans:			
10% debentures			100
			£720

Required:
Calculate the following accounting ratios:
1 return on capital employed;
2 gross profit;
3 mark-up;
4 net profit;
5 acid test;
6 fixed asset turnover;
7 debtor collection period; and
8 capital gearing.

8.3 You are presented with the following information for each of three companies:

Profit and loss accounts for the year to 31 March 19X3

	Mark Limited £000	*Luke Limited* £000	*John Limited* £000
Profit before tax	£64	£22	£55

Balance sheet (extracts) at 31 March 19X3

	Mark Limited	*Luke Limited*	*John Limited*
	£000	£000	£000
Capital and reserves			
Ordinary share capital of £1 each	100	177	60
Cumulative 15% preference shares of £1 each	—	20	10
Share premium account	—	70	20
Profit and loss account	150	60	200
Shareholders' funds	250	327	290
Loans			
10% debentures	—	—	100
	£250	£327	£390

Required:
Calculate the following accounting ratios:
1 return on capital employed; and
2 capital gearing.

8.4 The following information relates to Helena Limited:

Trading account year to 30 April

	19X1	19X2	19X3	19X4	19X5	19X6
	£000	£000	£000	£000	£000	£000
Sales (all credit)	—	130	150	190	210	320
Less: Cost of goods sold:						
Opening stock	—	20	30	30	35	40
Purchases (all in credit terms)	—	110	110	135	145	305
	—	130	140	165	180	345
Less: Closing stock	—	30	30	35	40	100
	—	100	110	130	140	245
Gross profit	—	£30	£40	£60	£70	£75
Trade debtors at 30 April	£40	£45	£40	£70	£100	£150
Trade creditors at 30 April	£20	£20	£25	£25	£30	£60

Required:
Calculate the following account ratios for each of the five years to 30 April 19X2 to 19X6 inclusive:
1 gross profit;
2 mark-up;
3 stock turnover;
4 trade debtor collection period; and
5 trade creditor payment period.

8.5 You are presented with the following information relating to Hedge Public Limited Company for the year to 31 May 19X5:

(a) The company has an issued and fully paid share capital of £500,000 ordinary shares of £1 each. There are no preference shares.
(b) The market price of the shares at 31 May 19X5 was £3.50.
(c) The net profit after taxation for the year to 31 May 19X5 was £70,000.
(d) The directors are proposing a dividend of 7p per share for the year to 31 May 19X5.

Required:
Calculate the following accounting ratios:
1 dividend yield;
2 dividend cover;
3 earnings per share; and
4 price/earnings ratio.

8.6 The following information relates to Style Limited for the two years to 30 June 19X5 and 19X6 respectively:

Trading, profit and loss accounts for the year

	19X5		19X6	
	£000	£000	£000	£000
Sales (all credit)		1,500		1,900
Less: Cost of goods sold:				
Opening stock	80		100	
Purchases (all on credit terms)	995		1,400	
	1,075		1,500	
	100	975	200	1,300
Gross profit		525		600
Less: Expenses		250		350
Net profit		£275		£250

Balance sheet at 30 June

	19X5		*19X6*	
	£000	*£000*	*£000*	*£000*
Fixed assets (net book value)		580		460
Current assets:				
Stock	100		200	
Trade debtors	375		800	
Bank	25		—	
	500		1,000	
c/fwd	500	580	1,000	460

	£000	£000	£000	£000
b/fwd	500	580	1,000	460
Less: Current liabilities				
Bank overdraft	—		10	
Trade creditors	80		200	
	80	420	210	790
		£1,000		£1,250
Capital and reserves:				
Ordinary share capital		900		900
Profit and loss account		100		350
Shareholders' funds		£1,000		£1,250

Required:

(a) Calculate the following accounting ratios for the two years 19X5 and 19X6 respectively:

1 gross profit;
2 mark-up;
3 net profit;
4 return on capital employed;
5 stock turnover;
6 current ratio;
7 acid test;
8 trade debtor collection period; and
9 trade creditor payment period.

(b) Comment upon the company's performance for the year to 30 June 19X6.

PART 3

Cost and management accounting

9 Basic costing principles

Part 2 of this book was concerned with *financial* accounting. The other main branch of accounting - *cost and management accounting* - will now be considered. For convenience, it will be referred to as *costing*, although as explained in Chapter 1, there are some technical differences in definition between costing (or cost accounting) and management accounting.

Costing is a routine procedure concerned with establishing the detailed costs of individual products and processes. Accountants need costing information in order to help them make recommendations to management for use in decision-making. This part of the accounting process should strictly be referred to as management accounting. Accountants, however, do not adhere rigidly to any of these terms, and they are often interchangeable.

The distinction between costing and management accounting is similar to the one between book-keeping and financial accounting. Book-keeping is concerned with the recording of basic accounting information. Financial accounting summarizes that information for the benefit of those parties who have a need or a use for it. Such parties may include analysts, creditors, employees, central and local government, journalists, management, shareholders, and the general public.

Costing information is similar to financial accounting information in that it has also to be collected, recorded, stored, and eventually extracted. It then needs to be summarized in a format which will help management in decision-making.

In this chapter the background to costing is examined. In Chapters 10 and 11 absorption costing is covered which is one of the main techniques used in costing, and Chapter 12 looks briefly at the subject of cost book-keeping. In Chapter 13 marginal costing, a most important technique used in short-term decision-making, is investigated. In Chapters 14 and 15 the subjects of budgeting and standard costing are introduced, whilst Chapter 16 examines capital investment appraisal.

Historical review

As explained in earlier chapters, accounting evolved out of a need for information about how well a business was doing, how much it owed, and how much was owing to it. As businesses became more complex, and as ownership gradually became separated from managerial control, some documentary information became essential both for owners and management. Over the last 150 years, the law has increasingly protected the rights of company shareholders by insisting that a minimum amount of information be supplied to them annually.

The information supplied is usually extracted from company records kept specially for that purpose. These records may also be used to supply the management of the company with information in order to help it plan and control the day-to-day activities of the company. Indeed, sometimes the records that are kept mainly for external reporting purposes may be the only major documentary source of information for management.

In these circumstances, management will only be supplied with any detailed information when the company's annual accounts are prepared. If this is the case, then it may be the only time that the management appreciates that urgent action needs to be taken, for example over an impending liquidity crisis. The management ought to know, of course, from their specialist knowledge of the business and their daily contact with it that some problems are beginning to build up. However, they can sometimes be so involved in dealing with routine matters that, unless advised, they are not aware of long-term trends. By the time that they do become aware of them, it might be too late to do much about them. In any case, the annual accounts are not designed for management reporting purposes.

It is not surprising, therefore, to find that with increasing industrialization and specialism, management began to demand more information. In particular, they wanted it designed especially for them, and for it to be supplied to them much more frequently than once a year.

In responding to this demand, accountants initially set up a different set of records from those required for financial reporting purposes (even though much of the data were common to both systems). A costing system which is kept quite separate from a financial recording system is known as an *interlocking* system. Nowadays, it is much more common to find that both systems are kept within one single system. If this is the case, it is known as a *integral* system of costing.

The collection of information specifically for management accounting purposes and its separation from the financial records gradually evolved over a long period of time. Indeed, costing as a major branch of accounting is a relatively recent development. It was not practised very widely in the United Kingdom before 1914, and whilst the increased industrial activity caused by the two world wars of 1914–18 and 1939–45 encouraged the demand for more information, it was not until about

1960 onwards that costing began to grow on any scale. Even in the late 1980s, there is some evidence that management in many companies still rely on inadequate information for decision-making purposes. It can be argued very strongly that better information should be supplied to management so that managers can both plan and control the company's activities more effectively. This is the subject of the next section.

Planning and control

If an entity is to be run efficiently, management must know what is expected of it. It is important, therefore, that the entity lays down its basic objectives. These might be quite straightforward, for example to achieve the maximum return on its capital employed, to provide a service that the public wants, or to provide a healthy environment in which employees can work.

Once the objectives have been established, management has then to work out how best to achieve them. In other words, it has to do some planning, following which it has to put the plans into action. Thereafter, it must ensure that the plans are being carried out by detailed control of the actual events.

Costing information can play a most important part in this process. Unlike financial accounting information, a costing system has been specially designed to help management to plan and to control. Costing has, therefore, the following advantages over financial accounting:

1 it can be produced regularly and frequently;
2 it is very detailed;
3 it is as up-to-date as any information can possibly be;
4 it does not depend entirely on historical information; and
5 it encourages a forward looking approach.

These are substantial claims which will be proved in subsequent chapters. In the meantime, how a costing system would be implemented is explained in the next section.

Implementation procedure

In order to operate a costing system, a clear organizational structure must be established and that sufficient information is available in some documentary form must be ensured. It will be easier to see why if these two requirements are considered separately.

Organizational structure

Planning and control can best be achieved by establishing clear lines of managerial responsibility. This may require a careful examination of the way in which the entity is structured and what responsibility is given to individuals within it.

In large organizations this may involve setting up a considerable number of interrelated departments and subdepartments which range from production departments at the lowest level of the structure to the board of directors at the highest level in the form of a pyramid. This can be shown in a diagrammatic format as in Exhibit 9.1.

Exhibit 9.1: Organizational structure: the pyramid format

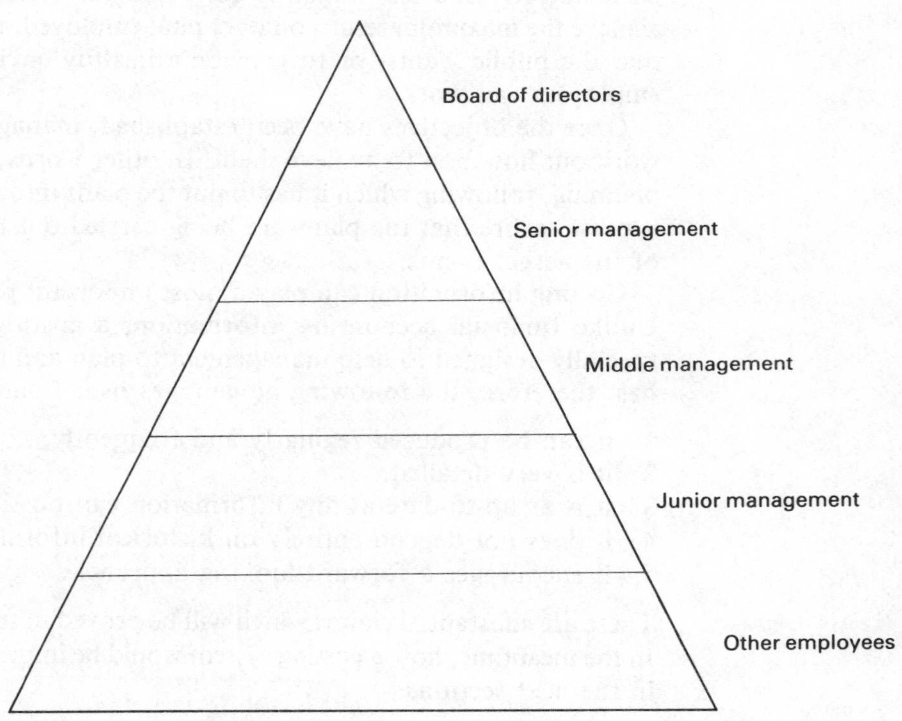

In large companies it is not uncommon for the organizational structure to be of a divisional nature, perhaps based on products or geographical areas in which the company operates. Within each division there may be a number of factories (or works). Each factory may be divided into functions (for example, administration, distribution and production), and each function into departments (for example, machine shop, stores control and wages). The organizational structure of a typical manufacturing company is shown in Exhibit 9.2.

Exhibit 9.2: Organizational structure of a manufacturing company

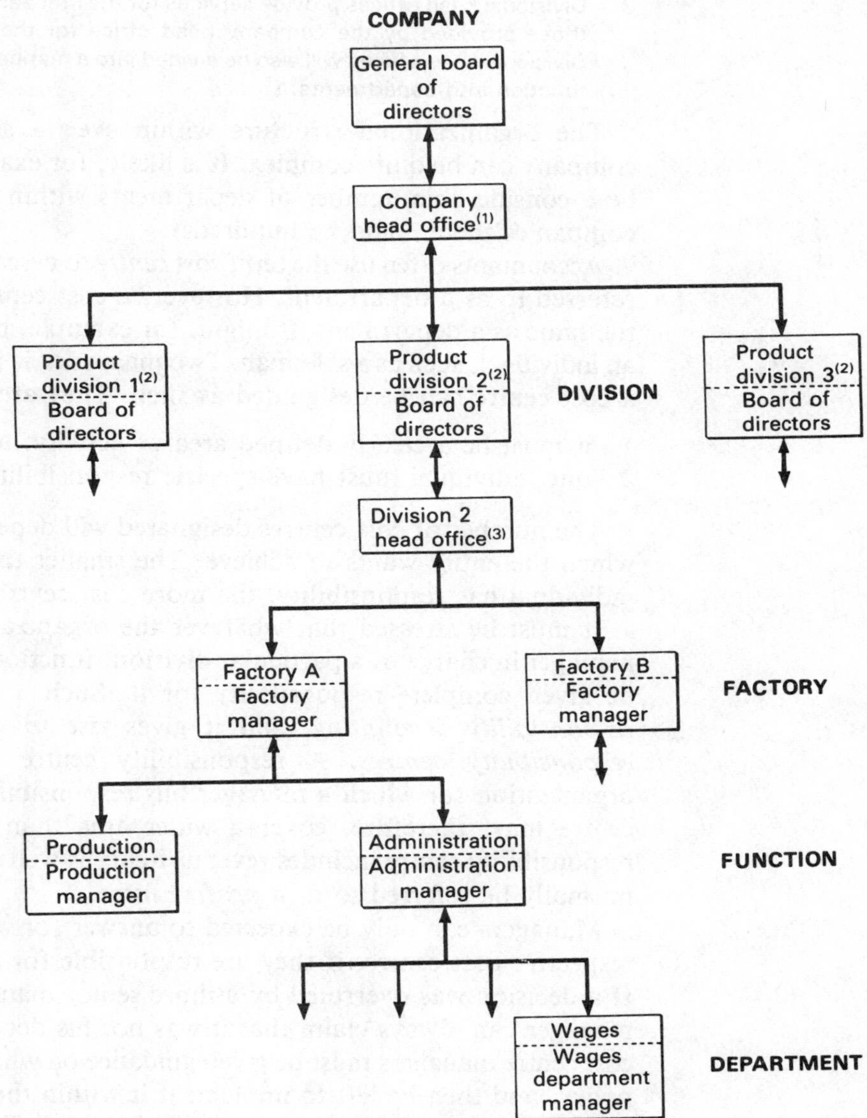

Notes:

1 The company's head office co-ordinates overall company policy. It also provides assistance and guidance generally throughout the company. The head office itself will be divided into a number of functions, such as accounting, marketing and personnel. Within each function there will probably be a number of departments, such as cash, taxation and salaries.

2 Divisions will usually be managed by a divisional board of directors, the board

being answerable to the general board. Divisions often operate as separate limited liability companies in their own right (although all their shares may be owned by the main company).

3 Divisional head offices provide services for their respective divisions, similar to those provided by the company head office for the company as a whole. Divisional head offices will also be divided into a number of functions, and each function into departments.

The organizational structure within even a small manufacturing company can be quite complex. It is likely, for example, that there will be a considerable number of departments within a function (in large companies there could be hundreds).

Accountants often use the term *cost centre* to describe what is ordinarily referred to as a department. However, a cost centre is not necessarily the same as a department. It might, for example, be a machine or even an individual, such as a salesman. Two main criteria have to be met before a cost centre can be designated as such. They are:

1 it must be a clearly defined area of activity; and
2 one individual must have specific responsibility for it.

The number of cost centres designated will depend upon the control which the entity wants to achieve. The smaller the area for which an individual has responsibility, the more cost centres there will be.

It must be stressed that whatever the organizational structure, the manager in charge of a particular division, function or cost centre must be given complete responsibility for it. Such a system is known as *responsibility accounting*, and it gives rise to what are known as *responsibility centres*. A responsibility centre is any part of an organization for which a manager has responsibility. A responsibility centre may, therefore, cover a wider area than a cost centre. If a responsibility centre includes revenue items as well as expenses, it would normally be referred to as a *profit centre*.

Managers can only be expected to answer for what goes on in their respective cost centres if they are responsible for any decisions taken. If a decision was overruled by a more senior manager, the cost centre manager can always claim that it was not his decision. Consequently, cost centre managers must be given guidance on what is overall company policy, and then be left to implement it within their own cost centres. The theory (and practice) suggests that if individual units are all autonomously managed, they will be better managed, because individuals work better if they are left to work on their own. It can then be argued that if each individual unit is well managed there will be a collective benefit for the entity as a whole.

Documentation

The type of organizational structure described above is clearly highly complex. By instituting a considerable number of largely autonomous cost centres there are formidable problems in managing it as a co-ordinated unit. The charging of costs to cost centres, for example, becomes a major exercise. It is not only necessary to report to each cost centre manager in some detail, but to do so frequently and regularly.

It is essential, therefore, to ensure that all the relevant accounting information is carefully documented, and that the cost of each transaction is charged to the correct cost centre. If this is not done, an incorrect decision may eventually be taken by the manager because he has based his decision on inaccurate or incomplete data.

In operating a costing system, the following procedure should be implemented:

1 All transactions should be documented.
2 Verbal instructions (for example, orders placed over the telephone) should not be accepted unless they are later confirmed in writing.
3 All documents should be specially designed to suit the particular transaction.
4 There should be a separate document for each type of transaction.
5 Designated documents should only be supplied to authorized users.
6 All transactions should be approved and signed by authorized personnel.

A costing system usually involves so much documentation that if each transaction is to be charged to the correct cost centre, it is usually necessary to have a coding system. This is almost certainly the case if the entity uses a computerized system of accounting. Unfortunately, codes can become very cumbersome, and it is very easy to make a mistake in coding a document (just as it is when dialling a telephone number). Furthermore, coding may be done by relatively junior members of staff who often do not understand the importance of coding documents correctly.

In a large organization, where the accounting may be done centrally by computer and a common code has been adopted, each document may need to be coded with a code of many digits if the transaction is to be charged to the correct cost centre. Such a code might be built-up as follows:

Responsibility centre	*Number of digits required*
Division	000
Factory	000
Cost centre	000
Type of expense	0000
Total digits required	13

Suppose, for example, that the Glasgow factory (code 123), which is part of the fibres division (code 015), has a maintenance department (code 666). During a particular period it purchases some raw materials (code 5432). When the invoice is eventually received from the supplier, it will be coded as follows:

015/123/666/5432

It would obviously be possible to reduce the number of digits depending upon the number of responsibility centres and the degree of analysis required. If possible, codes with few digits should be introduced, although even codes of less than six digits lend themselves very easily to errors.

A costing system will not work properly unless its purpose has been explained to the staff, and they understand its importance. Operating a costing system is expensive. There is no point in operating one if the information that it provides is not accepted, either because it is considered inaccurate or because it is regarded as being irrelevant. Indeed, costing systems that are imposed without any consultation or agreement are usually not effective.

The costing procedure will now be examined in some detail.

Costing procedure

In practice, it is not always easy to decide where the responsibility of one manager should end and the responsibility of another manager should begin. It follows, therefore, that it is sometimes difficult to decide which manager should be responsible for a certain cost.

Consider rates as an example. Rates are a form of local authority taxation levied on property located in a particular local authority area. No one cost centre manager is responsible for the rates charged on the building as a whole (presumably the general or divisional board of directors originally approved the purchase or construction of the building), so which cost centre should be responsible for the rates charge? In such circumstances, it is tempting to charge the rates to a general or miscellaneous cost centre for which no one manager is directly responsible. It has to be accepted that even the factory manager does not have any real control over rates, because he has probably not got the authority to close the factory down and hence avoid the rates charge. This would appear to be an argument in favour of using a sundry cost centre.

Accountants do not, however, recommend the use of sundry cost centres. The use of such centres tends to defeat one of the main objectives of responsibility accounting, that is to make sure that *all* costs are controlled by designated managers. In practice, sundry cost centres tend to attract more and more costs, because by using that cost centre, managers do not have to take a difficult decision. The best advice that can be given is to suggest that the most appropriate cost centre should be chosen, no matter how remote the real control a manager has over a particular cost. Thus rates might be charged to a legal department cost centre, since that department is probably best placed to negotiate with the local authority if there is any dispute about the charge. However, it must be recognized that the legal department manager does not have any formal control over the rates charge, and this must be taken into account when requiring the manager to answer for his departmental costs.

If it is possible to charge all costs to specific cost centres without having too much difficulty in deciding which cost centre to choose, such costs may be described as *direct* costs. This term was examined in Chapter 5. Thus a direct cost in this context is a cost which is easy to identify with a particular cost centre. Of course, if a sundry cost centre has been used, any cost charged to it must be an *indirect* cost, because it has not been possible to identify it with a specific cost centre. All such costs will eventually have to be apportioned to those cost centres which benefit indirectly from the service that they provide. Such an apportionment needs to be undertaken because ultimately all costs will need to be charged to individual products.

Once all the costs have been charged to specific cost centres, some of them may then become *indirect* costs. For example, all the factory canteen costs may have been collected in one cost centre. As far as the canteen cost centre is concerned, those costs are direct. However, they will not be easy to identify with the products that are being manufactured in the factory, so they will be indirect costs as far as the *products* are concerned.

Similarly, in a production department manufacturing specific production units, all costs charged to that department will be classified as direct costs, but some of the costs may be difficult to identify with the actual production units. Thus as far as those units are concerned, they will be classified as indirect costs. The total of indirect costs is often referred to as *overhead*.

Cost centres that deal directly with the actual manufacturing and production of units (or processes) are known as *production* cost centres. Those cost centres which provide support services for the production cost centres are known as *service* cost centres.

From the above analysis, it can be ascertained that the cost of a particular unit (for convenience it will be referred to as a unit cost, but the same applies to industries where there is no identifiable single unit) is comprised of three main elements:

1 direct production costs;
2 indirect production costs; and
3 service costs.

By building up the cost of a unit in this way, it is possible to calculate the total cost of producing a specific unit. If a percentage is added on to the cost in order to allow something for profit, it should be possible then to determine its selling price. In practice, however, it may not be possible to fix selling prices using this method because selling prices will also have to bear some relationship to the competitors'.

The cost structure of a specific unit is shown in more detail in Exhibit 9.3.

Exhibit 9.3: Unit cost structure: the elements of cost (1)

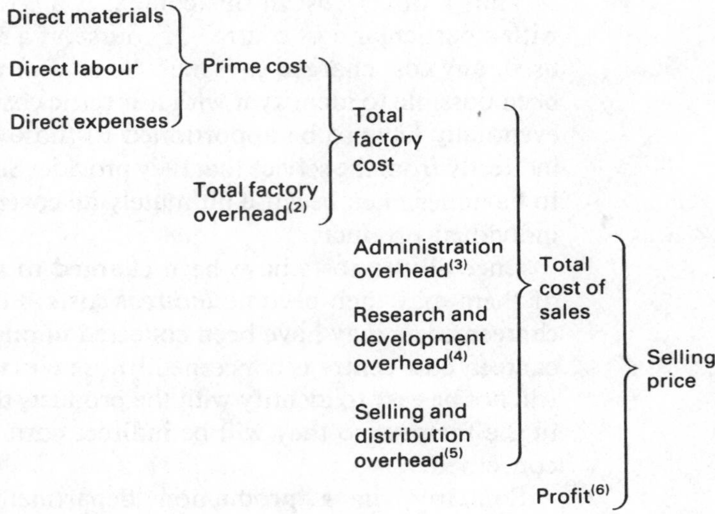

Notes:

1 The structure of the elements of cost is very similar to the structure which was used in Chapter 5 when preparing manufacturing accounts.

2 Factory overhead includes indirect production costs and other factory costs that are not easy to identify with production.

3 Administrative overhead will include the non-factory cost of operating the company.

4 Research expenditure will include the cost of working on new products and processes. Development costs relate to costs incurred in developing existing products and processes.

5 Selling and distribution overhead includes the cost of promoting the company's product and the cost of distributing them to its customers.

6 A profit loading may be added to the total cost of sales in order to arrive at the unit's selling price.

Exhibit 9.3 would suggest that the company should base its selling prices on the unit cost structure as shown in the exhibit. In some industries it may be able to do so. In the construction industry, for example, tender prices are built up on the basis of costs similar to the structure shown in Exhibit 9.3. However, as argued above, in many industries there is so much competition that a company is not free to fix its selling prices on a cost-plus basis (that is, on the basis of taking the total unit cost and adding something on for profit). The company has to charge a price similar to that of its competitors, but at the same time, try to ensure that its total costs will not be in excess of its total sales revenue.

In summary, therefore, the detailed costing procedure described above is important for two main reasons:

1 it is necessary in those industries where selling prices are fixed on a cost-plus basis; and
2 where the company is restrained in fixing its own selling prices, it enables it to control its total costs so that they are not in excess of its total sales revenue.

The method which has been described above to explain how to arrive at the total cost of a unit is known as *total absorption costing*. This method is the one most commonly adopted, and it will be considered again in more detail in Chapter 11.

It is sufficient for the present purpose merely to note that there are considerable problems to be overcome in building up the total cost of a unit in the way that has been described. By definition, direct costs should be easy to *allocate* (allocation is the process of charging whole costs to cost centres or units) to respective cost centres or units, but as has been seen, this is not always the case. Direct costs will be considered in the next chapter.

The treatment of indirect costs poses even more problems, especially those costs that are not incurred at the factory level. For this reason, some companies adopt an *absorption costing* system, which means that they do not try to absorb non-factory overhead into product costs. This can cause problems if their selling prices are based on total cost, but the absorption of non-factory overhead is not strictly necessary for control purposes, since it is largely an arithmetical procedure that is undertaken mainly (if at all) for pricing purposes.

One other problem arises in dealing with absorption costing. Some costs, for example rent and rates, tend to remain unchanged irrespective of the level of activity in the factory. Such costs are known as *fixed* costs. Those costs that *do* change with activity are known as *variable* costs, such as materials used directly in production. If the fixed costs are shared out on the basis of activity, then the more units that the factory produces, the lower the fixed costs per unit. Conversely, the fewer units that the factory produces, the higher the fixed costs per unit. It follows, therefore, that if the unit selling price is based on cost, the selling price will vary, depending upon how active the factory has been. This could result in widely fluctuating selling prices, and selling prices that change frequently are not likely to help the competitive position of the company.

The problem of fixed costs has given rise to the important costing technique of *marginal costing*, which will be dealt with in Chapter 12.

Conclusion

Cost and management accounting (referred to for convenience as costing) is now a very important branch of accounting. It assists management to achieve better planning and more efficient control of resources. Costing has evolved out of financial accounting, and its language and basic methods are similar to those found in financial accounting.

Essentially, costing provides management with a great deal more information than can be obtained from a financial accounting system. In order to introduce a costing system into an entity, a clear organizational structure needs to be established that gives management specific responsibilities within carefully defined limits. Such limits are usually designated as cost centres. A cost centre is usually similar to a department, but it can be extended to a sub-unit within a department, or even to an individual. Once delineated, such cost centres will be charged with those costs for which their respective managers are responsible. Responsibility centres are those areas for which responsibility has been given to specific managers, and profit centres are those responsibility centres that may have revenues charged to them. In order to ensure that costs are charged correctly to cost centres, all information of an accounting nature should be documented. To assist the charging of costs to cost centres, a coding system may have to be adopted.

The most common method of costing is absorption costing, a technique which attempts to share out the total costs of the entity amongst those units which it has manufactured. This method is useful for planning and control purposes, but it is also necessary when selling prices are based on total cost. However, the technique can give rise to some problems when the entity's total cost contains an element of fixed costs. For this reason, marginal costing has evolved for use in those circumstances where absorption costing would be inappropriate.

Both of these techniques are considered further in the following chapters.

Questions

1 Briefly describe the differences between financial accounting and management accounting.
2 List the categories into which costs may be classified.
3 Into what main categories might the organizational structure of a manufacturing entity be classified?
4 What is a cost centre?

10 Direct costs

In the last chapter it was suggested that the principle objectives of costing are to help management plan and control an entity's operations. It is possible to achieve these objectives by laying down a clear organizational structure of responsibility, and then leaving the respective managers to operate within that structure with as much autonomy as possible. Overall control is achieved by regular monitoring of each department's progress. In production departments, this may extend to details about the cost of producing each unit in that particular department.

As outlined in Chapter 9, the total cost of a specific unit is comprised of two main elements: direct costs and indirect costs. Direct costs are those costs that are easily identified with that unit, whilst indirect costs are those costs that are not easy to identify with it.

The definition of a direct cost is fairly imprecise, so that if any difficulty is experienced in deciding whether a cost is a direct cost or not, then by definition it must be an indirect cost. Classifying costs into direct costs and indirect costs is not easy, so that if the definition was taken too literally, hardly any cost at all would be classified as a direct cost. In practice, there are some costs that are generally recognized as being direct because they are *relatively* easy to identify with specific units.

It follows that the charging out of direct costs involves some subjectivity, because even direct costs are only relatively easy to classify. As will be seen in the next chapter, there is even more subjectivity in dealing with indirect costs. Consequently, the entire process of trying to build up the total cost of a particular unit has to be based on a number of arguable assumptions. This means that normally there is no possibility of ever being able to calculate the *exact* cost of any one unit, because the cost of that unit will depend upon the assumptions that the accountant makes in determining it.

In this chapter, the problems involved in dealing with *direct* costs will be examined.

Direct materials

Direct materials comprise raw materials and component parts that can be easily and readily identified with particular units of production. If a table was being made, for example, the wood and metal parts used in making it would be treated as direct materials, because it would normally be easy to identify them with that particular table. However, the screws needed to hold the parts together would probably not be treated as a direct material cost (even though they are used directly in production). This is because it may be both difficult and impracticable to isolate the cost of a few screws. They would, therefore, be treated as an indirect material cost.

In practice, even if it is relatively easy to identify the physical quantity of goods used in manufacturing a particular unit, it is not always easy to determine the exact cost of that material. Those products that contain liquids, for example, are often quite difficult to cost precisely and hence charge to production, because liquids are usually stored in containers. The containers will contain stock purchased at various times. As the liquid is gradually issued to production, it will be replaced with new stock. The new stock may have been purchased at a different price from the old stock, but by keeping all of the liquid in one container, there is no means of determining the *actual* price of the liquid being issued to production. Inevitably, therefore, the material being issued will have been purchased at a variety of prices. Thus although it may be relatively easy to calculate the actual quantity of material issued to production, it is not necessarily easy to cost it very accurately.

In these circumstances, the accountant may even have to estimate the actual cost of direct materials. If the actual cost of direct materials used in production is known, the accountant will, of course, use that cost, otherwise one of a number of recognized stock valuation methods must be chosen. Some of the main methods of pricing the issue of goods to production are outlined in the following subsections.

Specific identification

It has already been suggested that if the actual price of material is known, the accountant will use that price in charging out the cost of direct materials to production. This is known as the *specific identification* method, and it is, of course, the most obvious one to adopt. In practice, it is often quite difficult to keep separate and to identify material purchased at various dates at varying prices, and so other pricing methods may have to be adopted.

First in, first out (FIFO)

It is good practice to issue the oldest stock to production first, followed by the next oldest and so on, and this should be done wherever possible.

This method of storekeeping means that old stock is not kept in store for very long, thus avoiding the possibility of deterioration or obsolescence. However, as above, some material may be stored in such a way that it is a mixture of old and new stock, and it is often not possible to identify each separate purchase. Even so, as far as pricing is concerned, it would still seem logical to charge production with the oldest prices first, followed by the next oldest and so on, as this method would probably be adopted if it were possible to identify specific receipts with specific issues.

FIFO is a very common method used in charging the cost of materials to production. Starting with the price paid for the oldest material in stock, any issues to production are charged at that price. Once the quantity of goods originally purchased at that price has been issued to production, the next oldest price is used. All further issues are then charged out at that price until the same quantity of goods purchased at the second oldest price has been issued. The third oldest price will be next used, and so on.

It follows, of course, that the prices attached to the physical issue of goods to production are not necessarily the same as those paid for the actual purchases of those goods. Indeed, if it had been possible to identify specific receipts with specific issues, it would have been possible to use the specific identification method.

An example of the FIFO pricing method is shown in Exhibit 10.1.

Exhibit 10.1: The FIFO pricing method

The following information relates to the receipt and issue of material X into stock during January 19X1:

Date	*Receipts into stores*			*Issues to production*
	Quantity	*Price*	*Value*	*Quantity*
	Units	£	£	*Units*
1.1.X1	100	10	1,000	
10.1.X1	150	11	1,650	
15.1.X1				125
20.1.X1	50	12	600	
31.1.X1				150

Required:
Using FIFO (first in, first out) method of pricing the issue of goods to production, calculate the following:

(a) the issue prices at which goods will be charged to production; and
(b) the closing stock value at 31 January 19X1.

Answer to Exhibit 10.1

(a) The issue price of goods to production:

Date of issue	*Tutorial note*	*Calculation*	£
5.1.X1	(1)	100 units × £10 =	1,000
	(2)	25 units × £11 =	275
		125	£1,275
31.1.X1	(3)	125 units × £11 =	1,375
	(4)	25 units × £12 =	300
		150	£1,675

(b) Closing stock:
25 units × £12 = £300

Check:

Total receipts (£1,000 + £1,650 + £600) =	3,250
Total issues (£1,275 + £1,675) =	2,950
Closing stock =	£300

Tutorial notes

1 The goods received on 1 January 19X1 are now assumed to have all been issued.
2 This leaves 125 units in stock out of the goods received on 10 January 19X1.
3 All the goods purchased on 10 January 19X1 are now assumed to have been issued.
4 There are now 25 units left in stock out of the goods purchased on 20 January 19X1.

Exhibit 10.1 is a simple example, but it can be seen that the FIFO method may involve using a considerable number of different prices if the amount issued to production comprises a whole series of different purchases.

Last in, first out (LIFO)

An alternative method to FIFO is to adopt LIFO, whereby the *latest* prices are used to charge the issue of goods out to production. The physical quantity of the issue is identified, and the latest price paid for the last receipt of goods is determined. The goods are then charged out at that price. If more goods are being issued than were received at that price, the next oldest price will be used, and so on. Consequently, if there has been a large issue of goods to production, the total value of the issue could comprise a large number of prices.

How the method works is illustrated in Exhibit 10.2.

Exhibit 10.2: The LIFO pricing method

Use the same data as in Exhibit 10.1.

Required:
Using LIFO (last in, first out) method of pricing the issue of goods to production, calculate the following:
(a) the issue prices at which goods will be issued to production; and
(b) the value of closing stock at 31 January 19X1.

Answer to Exhibit 10.2

(a) The issue price of goods to production:

Date of issue	*Tutorial notes*	*Calculation*	£
15.1.X1	(1)	125 units × £11 =	£1,375
31.1.X1	(2)	50 units × £12 =	600
		25 units × £11 =	275
		75 units × £10 =	750
		150	£1,625

(b) Closing stock value:

25 units × £10 =	£250

Check:

Total receipts (£1,000 + £1,650 + £600) =	3,250
Total payments (£1,375 + £1,625) =	3,000
Closing stock =	£250

Tutorial Notes

1 This was the latest price at 15 January 19X1.
2 The latest price at 31 January 19X1 was £12, but only 50 units were purchased. The next oldest price, therefore, is used, but only 25 units are left at £11, because 125 units were priced out at £11 on 15 January 19X1. The balance is made up of goods purchased for £10 per unit, which also leaves 25 units in stock at that price.

The LIFO method (like FIFO) can be extremely complicated to use in practice, but there is a certain logic to it. By using the latest prices, production is being charged with current economic prices. However, the closing stock will be valued at much older prices. Thus by using LIFO in times of rising prices, the gross profit tends to be lower than it does under FIFO. The lower profit arises because of a combination of a greater charge to production, and a lower value placed on closing stock (a lower closing stock figure reduces the cost of goods sold, because a smaller amount is being deducted from opening stock + purchases). The reverse applies, of course, when prices are falling.

In the United Kingdom, FIFO is an acceptable method of valuing stock for taxation purposes. LIFO is not acceptable, and it is, therefore, an unpopular method. The adoption of LIFO means extra work, because in computing the company's tax charge, it is necessary to re-calculate the company's profit if a stock valuation method has been adopted which is not allowable for tax purposes.

Weighted average

In order to avoid the detailed arithmetical calculations which are involved in using both the FIFO and LIFO methods of pricing the issue of goods to production, it is possible to substitute an average pricing method. There are two main types of weighted average methods:

1 periodic weighted average; and
2 continuous weighted average method.

The *periodic* weighted average method involves calculating an average issue price based on all the prices paid for materials purchased during a particular *period*. The goods issued to production during that particular period are all then charged out at that average price. By using this method, it is not possible to charge out goods to production until after the period end, because the issue price cannot be calculated until all the purchase prices for the period are known.

The periodic weighted average method is illustrated in Exhibit 10.3.

Exhibit 10.3: The periodic weighted average pricing method

Use the same data as in Exhibit 10.1.

Required:
Using the periodic weighted average method of pricing the issue of goods to production, you are required to calculate the following:
(a) the issue price for January 19X1; and
(b) the closing stock value as at 31 January 19X1.

Answer to Exhibit 10.3

(a) The issue price of goods to production:

Total value of receipts (£1,000 + £1,650 + £600) =	£3,250
Total number of units received (100 + 150 + 50) =	300
∴ Periodic weighted average price =	£10.83
∴ Issue on 15.1.X1: 125 units × £10.83 =	£1,354
∴ Issue on 31.1.X1: 150 units × £10.83 =	£1,625

(b) Value of closing stock:

	£	£
Total receipts		3,250
Less: Issues - 15.1.X1	1,354	
- 25.1.X1	1,625	2,979
∴ Closing stock value =		£271

The *continuous* weighted average method, on the other hand, necessitates frequent changes to be made to the issue price of goods charged to production. Although this method appears very complicated, it is the easiest one to adopt in practice, especially if receipts and issues are recorded in a stores ledger account. Such an account would show both the quantity and value of stock in store at any particular moment. By dividing the total value of the stock by the total quantity, the continuous weighted average price may be obtained. A new average will need to be calculated each time additional receipts are taken into stock at different purchase prices. Unlike the periodic weighted average price, therefore, the continuous weighted average price may change frequently.

The continuous weighted average method is illustrated in Exhibit 10.4. The data are the same that we have used in the previous three exhibits, but the opportunity is taken to present a little more information so that the continuous weighted average price can be explained more clearly.

Exhibit 10.4: The continuous weighted average price method

You are presented with the following information relating to the receipt and issue of material X into stock during January 19X1:

Date	*Receipts into stores*			*Issues to production*			*Stock balance*	
	Quantity	*Price*	*Value*	*Quantity*	*Price*	*Value*	*Quantity*	*Value*
	Units	£	£	*Units*	£	£	*Units*	£
1.1.X1	100	10	1,000				100	1,000
10.1.X1	150	11	1,650				250	2,650
15.1.X1				125	10.60	1,325	125	1,325
20.1.X1	50	12	600				175	1,925
25.1.X1				150	11.00	1,650	25	275
31.1.X1							25	275

Note:
The company uses the continuous weighted average method of pricing the issue of goods to production.

Required:
Show how the price of goods issued to production during January 19X1 has been calculated.

Answer to Exhibit 10.4

The issue prices of goods to production during January 19X1 using the continuous weighted average method have been calculated as follows:

15.1.X1	Total stock value at 10.1.X1 =	£2,650	= £10.60
	Total quantity in stock at 10.1.X1 =	250	
25.1.X1	Total stock value at 20.1.X1 =	£1,925	= £11.00
	Total quantity in stock at 20.1.X1	175	

Other methods

There are a considerable number of other methods that may be considered suitable for determining the pricing of material issues to production. Most of them are examined in accounting textbooks, but they have little importance in practice. However, there is one other method which ought to be mentioned at this stage. This is the *standard cost method* which will be encountered in detail in Chapter 15.

The standard cost method involves estimating the cost of materials to be purchased during a particular future period of time. This is known as the *planned* price, and it would then be used in charging out the cost of materials during the period in question. The actual price of materials would be ignored in charging out materials to production during that period, although it would be necessary to investigate any difference between the actual prices and the planned prices.

The standard cost method is usually adopted as part of a *standard costing system*. Such systems adopt standard (or planned) costs for all elements of cost. Frequent comparisons have to be made with actual costs and immediate action taken if there are any discrepancies between them.

Choice of pricing method

It would be helpful at this stage if the advantages and disadvantages of each of the above pricing methods were summarized so that you can come to a decision about which you think is the most appropriate to use. This is done in the following table.

Method	*Advantages*	*Disadvantages*
1 FIFO	1 It is logical	1 It is arithmetically cumbersome.
	2 It matches the physical issue of goods.	2 The cost of production relates to out-of-date prices.

Method	*Advantages*	*Disadvantages*
1 FIFO contd	3 The closing stock is closer to the current economic value. 4 The stores ledger account is self-balancing: there are no balancing adjustments to be written-off to the profit and loss account. 5 It is acceptable for tax purposes.	
2 LIFO	1 Production is charged with costs that are close to current economic values. 2 The stores ledger account is self-balancing: there are no balancing adjustments to be written-off to the profit and loss account.	1 It is arithmetically cumbersome. 2 The closing stock is valued at much older prices that may bear little relationship to current economic prices. 3 This method is not acceptable for tax purposes.
3 Periodic weighted average	1 It is simple to calculate. 2 The issue price relates both to quantities purchased and to changing prices. 3 It is highly accurate because the price is not calculated until the period has ended. 4 It achieves a compromise between the lowest and highest prices. 5 It is not distorted by the quantities purchased.	1 The price cannot be calculated until the period has ended. 2 Prices in previous periods are ignored. 3 It lags behind current economic prices. 4 It may not relate to any price actually paid. 5 It may be necessary to write-off balancing adjustments to the profit and loss account.
4 Continuous weighted average	1 Previous period prices are taken into account. 2 It is easy to calculate. 3 It relates the price of goods purchased to quantities purchased. 4 It produces a price that is not distorted either by low or high prices paid, or by small or large quantities purchased.	1 It lags behind current economic prices. 2 It may not relate to prices actually paid. 3 It may be necessary to write off balancing adjustments to the profit and loss account.

Method	*Advantages*	*Disadvantages*
4 Continuous weighted average contd	5 A new price is calculated on each receipt of goods, so the price is constantly being updated.	

Precise rules cannot be laid down for the choice of a pricing method. LIFO is largely unsuitable because of its tax disadvantages, and the periodic weighted average method is somewhat impracticable as it can only be used after the period end. FIFO matches the attempt to issue the goods in the order in which they were received. This is a theoretical advantage, however, because where the specific identification method cannot be used, there is no certainty that the goods being issued relate to the order in which they were purchased. Wherever possible, the specific identification method would be adopted. In those circumstances where issues of goods cannot be identified with specific purchase prices, the continuous weighted average method would appear to be the one that is most suitable: it is easy to calculate, and it does not result in the use of an extreme range of prices. In those cases where a company operates a standard costing system, a standard cost will be used for all issue prices. This can lead to many problems which will be explored in Chapter 15.

As seen, the charging of direct material cost to production is not a straightforward exercise. It is usually clear what quantity of direct material has been transferred to production (if this is not the case, the material would have to be treated as an indirect cost), but in many circumstances it is by no means easy to price the issue of goods to production. This arises because it is not possible to distinguish between different purchases of goods, since it may be impractical to store them separately or because they cannot be physically separated.

The need to use an estimated price (irrespective of the method adopted) means that the total cost of the unit must also, at least in part, be an estimated cost. As will be seen shortly, before arriving at the total cost of producing a unit, even more estimates have to be made. Thus it follows that it is possible to argue that there is no such thing as the *true* cost of a specific unit. Costs can only be accurate in an arithmetical sense, as a result of the varying assumptions used in calculating them. This point will be argued in more detail in the next chapter.

Direct labour

Labour costs include the cost of employees' remuneration plus other costs associated with the employment of labour, such as the employers' national insurance and pension fund contributions. Labour costs that can be easily identified with specific units of production will be charged directly to production. Other labour costs that are difficult to identify directly with production will be charged as part of overheads.

Once the total labour cost has been analysed between direct and indirect labour (although this will not always be an easy task), the charging of the direct labour cost to production is a relatively straightforward exercise. Unlike the charging of direct material cost, there is no need to devise elaborate charging methods.

Employees engaged directly on production activities will be required to keep timesheets so that the amount of time that they spend working on each unit can be charged to that unit. Thus the hours worked on that unit by each grade of labour will be multiplied by the respective hourly rates of pay, and a percentage added for the employers' other direct employment costs, such as national insurance, pension fund contributions and holiday pay. The total amount is then charged directly against the specific unit.

It must not be assumed that it is always easy to distinguish between direct and indirect labour costs. Supervisory wages at the factory level, for example, are undoubtedly a direct production cost, but they may not be easy to identify with specific units of production, in which case they would be treated as an indirect cost. The definition should not be interpreted too widely because, as was suggested earlier, *all* costs will eventually tend to get charged as an indirect cost if each time that management is faced with a difficult decision about classifying a particular cost it decides to treat it as an indirect cost. If a high proportion of cost is classified as an indirect cost, a further problem will subsequently arise when the indirect costs are charged out to production. This problem is examined in the next chapter.

Labour costs are usually an important constituent element of total unit cost, especially in manufacturing industry. It is important, therefore, that a careful distinction is made between direct and indirect labour costs, and that they are charged out accurately. Management must explain to their employees the purpose of keeping an accurate record of how much time they spend on each job. It may be rather an irksome task for employees to keep an accurate time record, but its importance in unit pricing cannot be overemphasized. In this respect it is a vital task of *supervisory* management to ensure that timesheets are accurate, and that they are kept up to date.

Direct expenses

Apart from direct material and direct labour costs, there may be other types of direct expenses. These are, however, relatively rare as it is difficult to identify other expenses very easily with specific units. There may be some special cases. For example when the company hires special plant or equipment for work on one specific unit the hire charge will then be charged out directly to that particular unit.

Although it is rare to come across other direct expenses, it is important that apparently indirect expenses are carefully examined to see whether it is possible to classify some of them as direct expenses. The smaller the proportion of indirect costs, the less difficult the problem in making a charge to production for such costs.

Conclusion

This chapter has dealt specifically with *direct* costs: by definition a direct cost is one which is easy to identify with a specific cost centre or with a specific unit. It must be emphasized that the identification of even direct costs (as defined) is not easy. In establishing the level of direct material cost, for example, it has been argued that in many circumstances it is necessary to estimate its cost. Consequently, it is possible to argue that there is no one true cost. A cost may only be accurate in the arithmetical sense, since normally it has to be estimated on the basis of a number of arguable assumptions.

As far as direct *labour* costs are concerned, it has been argued that it is not usually too difficult to attach a meaningful cost to direct labour provided that accurate records are kept of the time spent on each job.

In some cases, there may be other types of direct expenses. They are, however, usually quite rare and they do not normally cause any problems in charging them directly to production.

Questions

10.1 The following stocks were taken into stores as follows:

1.1.X1 1,000 units @ £20 per unit.
15.1.X1 500 units @ £25 per unit.
There were no opening stocks.
On 31.1.X1 1,250 units were issued to production.

Required:
Calculate the amount which would be charged to production on 31 January 19X1 for the issue of material on that date using each of the following methods of material pricing:

1 FIFO (first in, first out);
2 LIFO (last in, first out); and
3 periodic weighted average.

10.2 The following information relates to material ST 2:

		Units	Unit price £	Value £
1.2.X2	Opening stock	500	1.00	500
10.2.X2	Receipts	200	1.10	220
12.2.X2	Receipts	100	1.12	112
17.2.X2	Issues	400	—	
25.2.X2	Receipts	300	1.15	345
27.2.X2	Issues	250	—	

Required:
Calculate the value of closing stock at 28 February 19X2 assuming that the continuous weighted average method of pricing materials to production has been adopted.

10.3 You are presented with the following information for Trusty Limited:

19X3	*Purchases (units)*	*Unit cost* £	*Issues to production (units)*
1 January	2,000	10	
31 January			1,600
1 February	2,400	11	
28 February			2,600
1 March	1,600	12	
31 March			1,000

Note: There was no opening stock.

Required:
Calculate the value of closing stock at 31 March 19X3 using each of the following methods of pricing the issue of materials to production.

1 FIFO (first in, first out);
2 LIFO (last in, first out); and
3 continuous weighted average.

10.4 The following information relates to a certain raw material taken into stock:

	Receipts		*Issues to production*
	Units	*Value*	*Units*
1.4.X4	50	350	
3.4.X4	30	213	
5.4.X4			60
9.4.X4	20	139	
11.4.X4			25
14.4.X4			10
18.4.X4	35	252	
23.4.X4	60	423	
26.4.X4			100
30.4.X4	45	315	

The opening stock was 20 units at a total value of £120.

Required:
Using the periodic weighted average method of pricing the issue of materials to production, calculate the value of the closing stock as at 30 April 19X4.

10.5 The following information relates to Steed Limited for the years to 31 May 19X5:

	£
Sales	500,000
Purchases	440,000
Opening stock	40,000
Closing stock value using the following pricing methods:	
1 FIFO (first in, first out)	90,000
2 LIFO (last in, first out)	65,000
3 Periodic weighted average	67,500
4 Continuous weighted average	79,950

Required:
Prepare Steed Limited's gross profit for the year to 31 May 19X5 using each of the above four closing stock values.

10.6 Iron Limited is a small manufacturing company. During the year to 31 December 19X2 it has taken into stock and issued to production the following items of raw material, known as XY1:

Date 19X2	*Receipts into stock*			*Issues to production*
	Quantity (Litres)	*Price per unit* £	*Total value* £	*Quantity (Litres)*
January	200	2.00	400	
February				100
April	500	3.00	1,500	
May				300
June	800	4.00	3,200	
July				400
October	900	5.00	4,500	
December				1,400

Notes:
1 There were no opening stocks of raw materials XY1.
2 The other costs involved in converting raw material XY1 into the finished product (marketed as *Carcleen*) amounted to £7,000.
3 Sales of *Carcleen* for the year to 31 December 19X2 amounted to £20,000.
4 For the purpose of this question, an accounting period is defined as the calendar year.

Required:
(a) Illustrate the following methods of pricing the issue of materials to production:

1 **first in, first out (FIFO);**
2 **last in, first out (LIFO);**
3 **periodic weighted average;**
4 **continuous weighted average.**

(b) Calculate the gross profit for the year using each of the above methods of pricing the issue of materials to production.

11 Indirect costs

In the last two chapters it was emphasized that the calculation of total unit cost involves two broad stages of cost classification: first, the identification of direct costs; and secondly, the apportionment of indirect costs. For convenience, we have referred to specific units, although the same procedure may be applied to other forms of production. In the last chapter the identification problems associated with direct costs were dealt with. In this chapter the treatment of indirect costs will be examined.

Indirect costs comprise indirect material cost, indirect labour cost and other expenses which are not easy to identify with specific units. The total of indirect cost is usually referred to as *overhead*. Overhead arises from two main sources:

1 those costs originally allocated to production cost centres but which thereafter cannot be easily identified with specific units; and
2 those costs allocated to service costs centres, which must, therefore, be indirect costs as far as specific units are concerned.

There is no obvious way of identifying indirect costs with specific units (if there was, then there would not be any indirect costs), so if we want to calculate the total cost of producing a particular unit, we have to share out indirect costs using some equitable method.

In subsequent sections, how to share out indirect costs will be explained.

Factory overhead

In Chapter 9 it was argued that for control purposes it is necessary for all costs within an entity to become the direct responsibility of a designated cost centre manager. In this section how the total factory overhead eventually gets charged to specific units will be examined. It is quite a complicated procedure, so for convenience it is divided into stages.

Stage 1: Allocate all costs to specific cost centres

It cannot be emphasized too strongly the importance of allocating all costs to specific cost centres. You will recall that allocation is the process of charging out of whole items of cost either to cost centres or cost units, that is, it is possible to make such a charge without having to apportion it between a number of cost centres. The allocation of costs to specific units was dealt with in the last chapter. This chapter is concerned with *indirect* costs.

As has been seen, it is not always easy to allocate costs to particular cost centres. Sometimes it is necessary to charge a cost to a particular cost centre, even though the manager of that centre may only be remotely responsible for that cost.

If some costs are left unallocated, then they will have to be apportioned (i.e. shared out using some arithmetical basis) amongst those cost centres that benefit from their services. Factory rates, for example, would probably be apportioned on the basis of floor space. Thus if the rates for the factory amounted to £5,000 and the factory had just two cost centres, one occupying 60% of the total floor space and the other cost centre occupying 40% of the remaining floor space, the first cost centre would be charged with £3,000 of the rates and the second cost centre with £2,000. Once all costs have either been allocated or apportioned to appropriate cost centres, the next stage is to share out the factory service centre costs.

Stage 2: Share out the factory service cost centre costs

Factory service centre costs will consist mainly of allocated costs, but they could also include some apportioned costs. By definition, service cost centre costs are not directly related to the production of specific units, and they must all be indirect costs as far as the production units are concerned.

The next stage in unit costing, therefore, is to share out the total service centre costs amongst the *production* cost centres. This is usually done by apportioning each service centre's total cost amongst those production cost centres which benefit from the service. The method used to apportion the service cost centre costs may be very simple. A few of the more common methods are as follows:

1 *Numbers of employees*. This method would be used for those service cost centres which provide a service to individual employees, for example the canteen, the personnel department and the wages office. Such cost centres may have their costs apportioned on the basis of the number of employees working in a particular production department compared to the total number of employees in all production cost centres.

2 *Floor area*. This method would be used for such cost centres as cleaning and building maintenance.

3 *Activity*. Examples of where this method might be used include the drawings office (on the basis of drawings made), materials handling (based

on the number of requisitions processed) and the transport department (on the basis of vehicle operating hours).

A problem arises in dealing with the apportionment of service cost centre costs when service cost centres provide services for each other. The wages office will presumably provide a service for the canteen staff, and in turn, staff employed in the wages office presumably use the canteen. Before the service cost centre costs can be apportioned amongst the production cost centres, therefore, it would appear necessary to make sure that each service cost centre is charged with its share of the other service cost centre costs.

The problem, however, becomes a circular one, because it is not possible to charge some of the canteen costs to the wages office until the canteen has been charged with some of the wages office costs. Equally, it is not possible to charge out the wages office costs until part of the canteen costs have been charged to the wages office. The treatment of reciprocal service costs can become an involved and time-consuming process unless a clear policy decision is taken about their treatment. There are three main possibilities:

1 *Ignore interdepartmental service costs*. If this method is adopted, the respective service cost centre costs are only apportioned amongst the production cost centres. Any servicing that the service cost centres provide for each other is ignored.

2 *Specified order of closure*. This method requires the service cost centre costs to be closed off in some specified order and apportioned out amongst the production cost centres and the remaining service cost centres. Eventually, as the service cost centres are gradually closed off, there will be only one service cost centre left. The remaining service cost centre's costs will then be apportioned amongst the production cost centres. Some order of closure has to be specified, and this may be quite arbitrary. It may be based, for example, on those centres which provide a service for the largest number of other service cost centres, or it could be based on the cost centres with the highest or the lowest cost in them prior to any interdepartmental servicing. It could also be based on an estimate of the benefit received by other centres.

3 *Mathematical apportionment*. By using this method, the respective service cost centre costs are apportioned amongst the production cost centres and the other service cost centres on the basis of the estimated benefit provided by the respective service cost centre to all other cost centres. What happens, however, is that additional amounts keep being charged back to a particular service cost centre as further apportionment takes place. It can take a very long time before eventually there is no more cost to charge out to any of the service cost centres, but when it is reached, all of the service cost centre costs will then have been charged

to the production cost centres. This method involves a great deal of exhaustive arithmetical apportionment, and it is also very time-consuming, especially where there are a great many service cost centres. Although it is possible to carry out the calculations arithmetically, it is more easily done by computer program.

In choosing one of the above methods, it should be remembered that they all depend upon an estimate of how much benefit one department receives from another. Such an estimate amounts to not much more than an informed guess. It seems unnecessary, therefore, to build an involved arithmetical exercise on the basis of some highly questionable data. It is suggested that in most circumstances interdepartmental servicing charging may be ignored.

Some fairly complicated procedures have been examined in dealing with stages 1 and 2, so before moving on to stage 3, what has been covered so far will be illustrated in Exhibit 11.1.

Exhibit 11.1

You are provided with the following indirect cost information relating to the New Manufacturing Company Limited for the year to 31 March 19X5:

Cost centre	£
Production 1: indirect expenses (to units)	24,000
Production 2: indirect expenses (to units)	15,000
Service cost centre A: allocated expenses	20,000
Service cost centre B: allocated expenses	8,000
Service cost centre C: allocated expenses	3,000

Additional information:
The estimated benefit provided by the three service cost centres to other cost centres is as follows:

Service cost centre A:	Production 1 50%; Production 2 30%; Service cost centre B 10%; Service cost centre C 10%.
Service cost centre B:	Production 1 70%; Production 2 20%; Service cost centre C 10%.
Service cost centre C:	Production 1 50%; Production 2 50%.

Required:
Calculate the total amount of overhead to be charged to cost centre units for both Production cost centre 1 and Production cost centre 2 for the year to 31 March 19X5.

Answer to Exhibit 11.1

New Manufacturing Company Limited
Overhead distribution schedule for the year to 31 March 19X5

Cost centre	*Production*		*Service*		
	1	2	A	B	C
	£	£	£	£	£
Allocated indirect expenses	24,000	15,000	20,000	8,000	3,000
Apportion service cost centre costs:					
A (50:30:10:10)	10,000	6,000	(20,000)	2,000	2,000
B (70:20:0:10)	7,000	2,000	–	(10,000)	1,000
C (50:50:0:0)	3,000	3,000	–	–	(6,000)
Total overhead to be absorbed by specific units	£44,000	£26,000	–	–	–

Tutorial notes

1 Units passing through Production cost centre 1 will have to share total overhead expenditure amounting to £44,000. Units passing through Production cost centre 2 will have to share total overhead expenditure amounting to £26,000. Units passing through both departments may be identical: for example, they might be assembled in cost centre 1 and packed in cost centre 2.

2 The total amount of overhead to be shared amongst the units is £70,000 (£44,000 + £26,000 = £24,000 + £15,000 + £20,000 + £8,000 + £3,000). The total amount of overhead originally collected in each of the five cost centres does not change.

3 This exhibit does involve some interdepartmental re-apportionment of service cost centre costs. However, no problem arises because of the basis upon which the question requires us to apportion the respective service cost centre costs.

4 The objective of apportioning service centre costs is to charge them out to the production cost centres so that they can be charged to specific units.

Stage 3: Absorption of factory overhead

Once all of the indirect costs have been collected in the production cost centres, the next step is to charge it out to specific units. This procedure is known as *absorption.*

The method of absorbing overhead into units is normally a simple one. Accountants recommend a single factor, preferably one that relates as closely as possible to the movement of *overhead*. In other words, an attempt is made to choose a factor which directly correlates to the amount of overhead expenditure incurred. Needless to say, like so much else in accounting, there is no obvious factor to choose. Indeed, if there was a close correlation between overhead expenditure and an appropriate factor, it is doubtful whether it would be necessary to designate any expenditure as an overhead expense.

On the whole it is believed that overheads tend to move with time.

Thus the longer a unit stays in production, the more likely it is that there will be more expenditure incurred on overheads. In fact, there are six main methods that could be used for absorbing factory overhead, although only three of them are based on relating overhead to the time that each unit spends in production. Each will be discussed in turn, but they all depend upon the following basic equation:

$$\text{Cost centre overhead absorption rate (OAR)} = \frac{\text{Total cost centre overhead (TCCO)}}{\text{Total cost centre activity}}$$

A different absorption rate will have to be calculated for each production cost centre, so by the time that the total cost of the unit has been calculated, it will have been charged with a share of overhead for each of the production cost centres that it has been through.

Each of the six main absorption methods will now be examined in the following subsections.

Specific units

This method is the simplest to operate. It is calculated as follows:

$$\text{Absorption rate} = \frac{\text{Total cost centre overhead}}{\text{Number of units processed in the cost centre}}$$

The same rate would be applied to each unit, thus it is only a suitable method if the units are identical.

Direct material cost

$$\text{Absorption rate} = \frac{\text{Total cost centre overhead}}{\text{Cost centre total direct material cost}} \times 100$$

The direct material cost of each unit is then multiplied by the absorption rate in order to determine the amount of overhead to be charged to that unit.

It is unlikely that there will normally be a strong correlation between the direct material cost and the level of overheads. There might be special cases, but they are probably quite unusual, such as where a company uses a high level of precious metals and its overhead costs strongly reflect the cost of safely protecting those materials.

Direct labour cost

$$\text{Absorption rate} = \frac{\text{Total cost centre overhead}}{\text{Cost centre total direct labour cost}} \times 100$$

The direct labour cost of each unit is then multiplied by the absorption rate in order to determine the amount of overhead to be charged to that unit.

If it is true that overhead expenditure tends to increase the more time that a unit spends in production, then this method may be suitable, since the direct labour cost is a combination of hours worked and rates paid. It may not be suitable, however, where the total direct labour cost consists of a relatively low level of hours worked and of a high labour rate per hour, because the total direct labour cost will not then correlate closely with the time that the unit spends in production.

Prime cost

$$\text{Absorption rate} = \frac{\text{Total cost centre overhead}}{\text{Prime cost}} \times 100$$

The prime cost of each unit is then multiplied by the absorption rate in order to determine the amount of overhead to be charged to that unit.

This method assumes that there is a close correlation between prime cost and overhead incurred. However, it is believed that in most cases this is unlikely to be true. It could also be argued that if there is no close correlation between either direct materials or direct labour and overheads, then it is unlikely that there will be much of a correlation between prime cost and overhead. Hence the prime cost method tends to combine the disadvantages of both the direct materials and the direct labour cost methods without having any real advantages of its own.

Direct labour hours

$$\text{Absorption rate} = \frac{\text{Total cost centre overhead}}{\text{Cost centre total direct labour hours}}$$

The direct labour hours of each unit are then multiplied by the absorption rate in order to determine the amount of overhead to be charged to that unit.

This method is highly acceptable, especially in those cost centres that are labour intensive, because it does relate time spent in production to the cost of overhead incurred.

Machine hours

$$\text{Absorption rate} = \frac{\text{Total cost centre overhead}}{\text{Cost centre total machine hours}}$$

The number of machine hours that each unit took to produce are then multiplied by the absorption rate in order to determine the amount of overhead to be charged to that unit.

This is the most appropriate method to use in those departments that are machine intensive. There is probably quite a strong correlation between the amount of machine-time that a unit takes to produce and the amount of overhead incurred.

It is difficult to appreciate what these absorption methods mean until they are put into context. This is achieved in Exhibit 11.2.

Exhibit 11.2

Old Limited is a manufacturing company. The following information relates to the assembling department for the year to 30 June 19X8:

	Assembling department total
	£000
Direct material cost incurred	**400**
Direct labour cost incurred	**200**
Total factory overhead incurred	**100**
Number of units produced	**10,000**
Direct labour hours worked	**50,000**
Machine hours used	**80,000**

Required;

Calculate the overhead absorption rates for the assembling department using each of the following methods:

1 specific units;
2 direct material cost;
3 direct labour cost
4 prime cost;
5 direct labour hours; and
6 machine hours.

Answer to Exhibit 11.2

1 Specific units:

$$\text{OAR} = \frac{\text{TCCO}}{\text{Number of units}} = \frac{£100{,}000}{10{,}000} = \underline{\underline{£10.00 \text{ per unit}}}$$

2 Direct material cost:

$$\text{OAR} = \frac{\text{TCCO}}{\text{Direct material cost}} \times 100 = \frac{£100{,}000}{400{,}000} \times 100 = \underline{\underline{25\%}}$$

3 Direct labour cost:

$$\text{OAR} = \frac{\text{TCCO}}{\text{Direct labour cost}} \times 100 = \frac{£100{,}000}{200{,}000} \times 100 = \underline{\underline{50\%}}$$

4 Prime cost:

$$\text{OAR} = \frac{\text{TCCO}}{\text{Prime cost}} \times 100 = \frac{£100{,}000}{400{,}000 + 200{,}000} \times 100 = \underline{\underline{16.67\%}}$$

5 Direct labour hours:

$$\text{OAR} = \frac{\text{TCCO}}{\text{Direct labour hours}} = \frac{£100{,}000}{50{,}000} = \underline{\underline{£2.00 \text{ per direct labour hour}}}$$

6 Machine hours:

$$\text{OAR} = \frac{\text{TCCO}}{\text{Machine hours}} = \frac{£100{,}000}{80{,}000} = \underline{\underline{£1.25 \text{ per machine hour}}}$$

Exhibit 11.2 illustrates the six absorption methods which were covered in the text. It will be appreciated, of course, that in practice only one absorption method would be chosen for each production cost centre. The most appropriate absorption rate method to adopt will depend upon individual circumstances. A careful study would have to be made of the correlation between (a) direct materials, direct labour, other direct expenses, direct labour hours, and machine hours; and (b) total overhead expenditure. In most circumstances, as has been argued, it is generally accepted that overhead tends to move with time. Consequently, the longer a unit spends in production, the more overhead that particular unit will incur. As a result, each individual unit ought to be charged with its share of overhead based on the time that it spends in production.

This argument suggests that labour intensive cost centres should use the direct labour hour method of absorbing overhead, and machine intensive departments the machine hour rate.

A comprehensive example

At this stage it would be useful to illustrate overhead absorption in the form of a comprehensive example. It would clearly be impracticable to use an example that involved hundreds of cost centres, since the purpose of the example is to demonstrate the *principles* of absorption costing, and too much data would obscure those principles. Thus Exhibit 11.3 has been designed to outline the main principles involved in calculating the cost of a specific unit using the minimum amount of data.

Exhibit 11.3

Oldham Limited is a small manufacturing company producing a variety of pumps for the oil industry. It operates from one factory which is geographically separated from its head office. The components for the pumps are assembled in the assembling department, and they are then passed through to the finishing department where they are painted and packed. There are three service cost centres: administration, stores and work study.

The following costs were collected for the year to 30 June 19X6:

	£000
Allocated cost centre overhead costs:	
Administration	70
Assembling	25
Finishing	9
Stores	8
Work study	18

Additional information:

1 The allocated cost centre costs are all considered to be indirect costs as far as specific units are concerned.

2 During the year to 30 June 19X6, 35,000 machine hours were worked in the assembling department, and 60,000 direct labour hours in the finishing department.

3 The number of employees working in each department was as follows:

Administration	15
Assembling	25
Finishing	40
Stores	2
Work study	3
	85

4 During the year to 30 June 19X6, the stores received 15,000 requisitions from the assembling department, and 10,000 requisitions from the finishing department. The stores department did not provide a service for any other department.

5 The work study department carried out 2,000 chargeable hours for the assembling department, and 1,000 chargeable hours for the finishing department.

6 One special pump (code named MEA 6) was produced during the year to 30 June 19X6. It took 10 machine hours of assembling time, and 15 direct labour hours were worked on it in the finishing department. Its total direct costs (material and labour) amounted to £100.

Required:

(a) Calculate an appropriate absorption rate for:
  1 the assembling department; and
  2 the finishing department.

(b) Calculate the total factory cost of the special pump.

Answer to Exhibit 11.3

(a) OLDHAM LIMITED

Overhead distribution schedule for the year to 30 June 19X6

Cost centre	*Production*		*Service*		
	Assembling	*Finishing*	*Administ-ration*	*Stores*	*Work study*
	£000	£000	£000	£000	£000
Allocated costs (1)	25	9	70	8	18
Apportion administration (2): 25:40:3:2	25	40	(70)	2	3
Apportion stores (3): 3:2	6	4	—	(10)	—
Apportion work study: 2:1	14	7	—	—	(21)
Total overhead to be absorbed	£70	£60	—	—	—

Tutorial notes

1 The allocated costs were given in the question.
2 Administration costs have been apportioned on the basis of employees. Details were given in the question. There were 85 employees in the factory, but 15 of them were employed in the administration department. Administration costs have, therefore, been apportioned on a total of 70 employees, or £1,000 per employee. The administration department is the only service department to provide a service for the other service departments, so no problem of interdepartmental servicing arises.
3 The stores costs have been apportioned on the number of requisitions made by the two production cost centres, that is 15,000 + 10,000 = 25,000, or 3 to 2.
4 The work study costs have been apportioned on the basis of chargeable hours i.e. 2,000 + 1,000 = 3,000, or 2 to 1.

Calculation of chargeable rates:

1 Assembling department:

$$\frac{\text{TCCO}}{\text{Total machine hours}} = \frac{£70{,}000}{35{,}000} = \underline{\underline{£2.00 \text{ per machine hour}}}$$

2 Finishing department:

$$\frac{\text{TCCO}}{\text{Total direct labour hours}} = \frac{£60{,}000}{60{,}000} = \underline{\underline{£1.00 \text{ per direct labour hour}}}$$

It would seem appropriate to absorb the assembling department's overhead on the basis of machine hours because it appears to be a machine intensive department. The finishing department appears more labour intensive, so its overhead will be absorbed on that basis.

(b) MEA 6: Calculation of total factory cost

	£	£
Direct costs (as given)		100
Add: Factory overhead:		
Assembling department (10 machine hours × £2.00 per MH)	20	
Finishing department (15 direct labour hours × £1.00 per DLH)	15	35
Total factory cost		£135

You are now recommended to work through Exhibit 11.3 again without reference to the answer.

Non-factory overhead

So far this chapter has concentrated on the apportionment and absorption of factory overhead expenditure. Most companies will, however, incur expenditure in areas that are not directly connected with factory activities. There will, for example, be the cost of operating the company's head office, the cost of research and development, and the cost of selling and distributing the product.

As argued in previous chapters, the overall objective in setting up a costing system is to help in planning and controlling the company's costs more effectively. It follows that non-factory overhead cannot be ignored in achieving overall control of the company's costs. It will be necessary to set up a cost centre structure for this type of overhead, and to give managers autonomy for clearly defined areas of responsibility.

If the company's selling prices are based on cost, it will also be necessary to share out non-factory overhead amongst specific units of production. For pricing purposes, therefore, the factory cost of the unit will have to have an amount added to it in order to recover the cost of administration, research and development, and selling and distribution overhead. Unfortunately, there is no satisfactory way of absorbing such overhead, because it is difficult to correlate general overhead with any appropriate level of activity.

Sometimes an estimated percentage is simply applied to the total factory cost. This is bound to be a somewhat arbitrary method, and the effect on tendering or selling prices will have to be examined very carefully. The main methods by which non-factory overhead could be absorbed into unit costs are outlined below.

Administration overhead

The absorption rate for administration overhead can be calculated by relating the total cost of overhead to the total cost of production. The formula is as follows:

$$\text{Absorption rate} = \frac{\text{Total administration overhead}}{\text{Total production cost}} \times 100$$

The absorption rate is then applied to the total factory cost of each unit.

If the sales revenues are known (i.e. selling prices are not based on cost), administration overhead is sometimes apportioned on the basis of sales revenue. The formula is as follows:

$$\text{Absorption rate} = \frac{\text{Total administration overhead}}{\text{Total sales revenue}} \times 100$$

The absorption rate is then applied to the selling price (on the assumption that it is known) of each unit.

Research and development overhead

Like administration overhead, a research and development overhead absorption rate may be calculated on the basis of total production cost, i.e.

$$\text{Absorption rate} = \frac{\text{Total research and development overhead}}{\text{Total production cost}} \times 100$$

The rate is then applied to the total factory cost of each unit.

Selling and distribution overhead

The absorption rate for selling and distribution overhead can again be calculated by reference to the total cost of production:

$$\text{Absorption rate} = \frac{\text{Total selling and distribution overhead}}{\text{Total cost of production}} \times 100$$

The rate is then applied to the total factory cost of each unit.

It may also be possible to absorb this type of overhead on the basis of sales revenue if the company does not operate a cost-plus pricing policy. The formula would then be as follows:

$$\text{Absorption rate} = \frac{\text{Total selling and distribution overhead}}{\text{Total sales revenue}} \times 100$$

The absorption rate would then be applied to the selling price of each unit.

It must be emphasized that the absorption of non-factory overhead amongst specific units does not help to control the total cost of such units. It is largely an arithmetical exercise. Its real value lies only in trying to work out a more accurate selling or tendering price, or in enabling a comparison to be made between the total cost of the company's own products and those of its competitors.

As mentioned in Chapter 9, the absorption of all types of overhead into product cost is known as *total absorption costing*. The absorption of factory overhead only is known simply as *absorption costing*. Absorption costing is more common than total absorption costing, partly because of the difficulty of relating non-factory overhead to specific units, and partly because it is not particularly useful in controlling costs.

A further problem arises in trying to work out an appropriate absorption rate. It must be decided whether to calculate the absorption rate on an historical basis, or whether to try to work one out in advance. This problem is discussed in the next section.

Pre-determined rates

It has been emphasized throughout this chapter that there is no close correlation between overhead and any particular measure of activity: overhead can only be shared out on some reasonable basis. However, if the total actual overhead incurred is known, it is possible to make sure that it is all charged to specific units, even if it is not clear what relationship it has with any activity level.

To do so, of course, an absorption rate cannot be calculated until the actual overhead cost and the actual activity (whether this is measured in machine hours, direct labour hours or some other measure) are known. In other words, the calculation can only be made on an historical basis.

The adoption of historical absorption rates is not usually very practicable. It is necessary to wait until the actual period is over before it is possible to calculate an absorption rate, cost the products and invoice customers. It would, therefore, normally be desirable to calculate an absorption rate in advance. This is known as a *pre-determined rate*.

In order to calculate a pre-determined absorption rate, it is necessary to estimate both the overhead which it is thought the company will incur, and the hours that are going to be worked (if hours are to be used as the method of absorbing overhead). If one or other of these estimates turns out to be inaccurate, then the customers could have been either undercharged (if the rate was too low), or overcharged (if the rate was too high).

This situation could be very serious for the company. Low selling prices caused by using a low absorption rate could have made the company's products very competitive, but there is not much point in selling a great many units if the company's total sales revenue is not covering its total costs. Similarly, on a cost-plus pricing basis, a high absorption rate may have resulted in a high selling price. The units may not then be competitive, because whilst the profit on each unit may be high, not enough units may be sold for the company to be able to recoup its total costs out of its total sales revenue.

The use of pre-determined absorption rates may, therefore, result in an under- or over-recovery of overhead. Overhead may be under- or over-absorbed if the company has under- or over-estimated the actual cost of the overhead or the actual level of activity (irrespective of how activity is measured). The difference between the actual overhead incurred and the total overhead that the company has charged to production (calculated on a pre-determined basis) gives rise to what is known as a *variance*. If the actual overhead incurred is in excess of the amount charged out, the variance will be *adverse*, that is, the profit will be that much less. However, if the total overhead charged to production was less than was estimated, then the variance will be *favourable*. Other things being equal, a favourable variance gives rise to higher profits, and an adverse variance results in lower profits.

It is a cardinal rule in costing that variances should be written off to the profit and loss account at the end of the costing period in which they were incurred in order not to burden the next period's accounts with the previous period's mistakes.

Conclusion

Absorption costing aims to help management plan and control the entity's operations more effectively, but it may also be useful in determining selling prices.

The technique is a highly questionable one, because it is necessary to make a number of arguable assumptions, for example costs have to be classified into direct and indirect categories. In practice, it is not always easy to charge out direct costs, but it is even more difficult to deal with indirect costs.

The technique is carried out in a number of stages. The first stage is to allocate indirect factory costs to appropriate cost centres. The second stage is to apportion service centre costs amongst the relevant production cost centres. The third stage is to absorb the total overhead collected in each production cost centre into specific units.

The apportionment and the absorption stages both depend upon a relationship being established between the overhead cost and an appropriate measure of activity, even though such relationships are likely to be somewhat distant. Non-factory overhead is also sometimes absorbed into unit costs, but the relationship between this type of expenditure and production activity is even more distant. For control purposes it is not particularly helpful, although it may sometimes have to be done if selling prices are fixed on a cost-plus pricing basis.

Overhead absorption rates have usually to be pre-determined, because it is impracticable to wait until the period has ended before goods are charged out to production (and hence ultimately to customers). This means that some overhead may be over- or under-absorbed at the period end, and, as a result, a favourable or an adverse variance will arise. The variance will be favourable or adverse depending upon whether the estimated cost or estimated level of activity has been over- or underestimated. Such variances should be written off to the profit and loss account for that particular period. They should not be carried forward and charged to the next period's accounts.

Such variances may be very serious in the long run. They suggest that the company could be either under- or over-pricing its products. Under-pricing may lead to an under-recovery of total cost, whilst over-pricing could result in a reduction in sales volume. In both cases there will ultimately be a reduction in profitability.

Absorption costing is a technique which must be used with caution. However, as long as managers are aware of its limitations it can be useful in helping to control the company's total costs.

Questions

11.1 Scar Limited has two production departments and one service department. The following information relates to January 19X1:

	£
Allocated expenses	
Production department: A	65,000
B	35,000
Service department	50,000

The allocated expenses shown above are all indirect expenses as far as individual units are concerned.

The benefit provided by the service department is shared amongst the production departments A and B in the proportion 60 : 40.

Required:
Calculate the amount of overhead to be charged to specific units for both production department A and production department B.

11.2 Bank Limited has several production departments. In the assembly department it has been estimated that £250,000 of overhead should be charged to that particular department. It now wants to charge a customer for a specific order. The data relevant are:

	Assembly department	*Specific unit*
Number of units	50,000	—
Direct material cost	£500,000	£8.00
Direct labour cost	£1,000,000	£30.00

	Assembly department	*Specific unit*
Prime cost	£1,530,000	£40.00
Direct labour hours	100,000	3.5
Machine hours	25,000	0.75

The accountant is not sure which overhead absorption rate to adopt.

Required:
Calculate the overhead to be absorbed by a specific unit passing though the assembly department using each of the following overhead absorption rate methods:

1 specific units;
2 percentage of direct material cost;
3 percentage of direct labour cost;
4 percentage of prime cost;
5 direct labour hours; and
6 machine hours.

11.3 The following information relates to the activities of the production department of Clough Limited for the month of March 19X3:

	Production department	*Order Number 123*
Direct materials consumed	£120,000	£20
Direct wages	£180,000	£25
Overhead chargeable	£150,000	
Direct labour hours worked	30,000	5
Machine hours operated	10,000	2

The company adds a margin of 50% to the total production cost of specific units in order to cover administration expenses and to provide a profit.

Required:
(a) Calculate the total selling price of order number 123 if overhead is absorbed using each of the following methods of overhead absorption:
1 direct labour hours;
2 machine hours.
(b) State which of the two methods you would recommend for the production department.

11.4 Burns Limited has three production departments (processing, assembly and finishing) and two service departments (administration and work study). The following information relates to April 19X4.

	£
Direct material:	
Processing	100,000
Assembling	30,000
Finishing	20,000

	£
Direct labour:	
Processing (£4 × 100,000 hours)	400,000
Assembling (£5 × 30,000 hours)	150,000
Finishing (£7 × 10,000 hours + (£5 × 10,000 hours)	120,000
Administration	65,000
Work study	33,000
Other allocated costs:	
Processing	15,000
Assembling	20,000
Finishing	10,000
Administration	35,000
Work study	12,000

Appointment of costs:

	Process	*Assembling*	*Finishing*	*Work study*
	%	%	%	%
Administration	50	30	15	5
Work study	70	20	10	—

Total machine hours: Processing 25,000

All units produced in the factory pass through the three production departments before they are put into stock. Overhead is absorbed in the processing department on the basis of machine hours, on the basis of direct labour hours in the assembling department and on the basis of the direct labour cost in the finishing department.

The following details relate to unit XP6:

	£	£
Direct materials:		
Processing	15	
Assembling	6	
Finishing	1	22
Direct labour:		
Processing (2 hours)	8	
Assembling (1 hour)	5	
Finishing (1 hour × £7 + 1 hour × £5)	12	25
Prime cost		£47

XP6: Number of machine hours in the processing department - 6

Required:
Calculate the total cost of producing unit XP6.

11.5 Outlane Limited's overhead budget for a certain period is as follows:

	£000
Administration	100
Depreciation of machinery	80
Employer's national insurance	10
Heating and lighting	15
Holiday pay	20
Indirect labour cost	10
Insurance: machinery	40
property	11
Machine maintenance	42
Power	230
Rent and rates	55
Supervision	50
	£663

The company has four production departments: L, M, N and O. The following information relates to each department.

Department	L	M	N	O
Total number of employees	400	300	200	100
Number of indirect workers	20	15	10	5
Floor space (square metres)	2,000	1,500	1,000	1,000
Kilowatt hours	30,000	50,000	90,000	60,000
Machine maintenance hours	500	400	300	200
Machine running hours	92,000	38,000	165,000	27,000
Capital cost of machines (£)	110,000	40,000	50,000	200,000
Depreciation rate of machines (on cost)	20%	20%	20%	20%
Cubic capacity	60,000	30,000	10,000	50,000

Previously the company has absorbed overhead on the basis of 100% of the direct labour cost. It has now decided to change to a separate machine hour rate for each department.

The company has been involved in two main contracts during the period, the details of which are as follows:

Department	Contract 1: Direct labour hours and machine hours	Contract 2: Direct labour hours and machine hours
L	60	20
M	30	10
N	10	10
O	–	60
	100	100

Direct labour cost per hour in both departments was £3.00.

Required:

(a) Calculate the overhead to be absorbed by both contract 1 and 2 using the direct labour cost method; and

(b) calculate the overhead to be absorbed using a machine hour rate for each department.

11.6 Sarah Limited has two production cost centres (D and P) and three service cost centres (1, 2, and 3). The following information relates to June 19X6.

Allocated costs	£000
Production cost centres:	
D	45
P	35
Service cost centres:	
1	160
2	71
3	34

All of the above costs are indirect as far as individual production units are concerned.

The service cost centres provide a service both for the production cost centres and for each other. The estimated benefit provided by each service cost to the other cost centres is as follows:

	Production		*Service*		
	D	P	1	2	3
	%	%	%	%	%
Service: 1	55	20	—	15	10
2	45	40	5	—	10
3	50	10	20	20	—

Required:

Calculate the total amount of overhead to be absorbed by production cost centre D and production cost centre P.

12 Recording cost data

In previous chapters, it has been assumed that it is possible to arrive at the cost of a *specific* unit. The discussion has been limited to unit costing, because it is easier to think of costing in these terms. In practice, however, it is not always possible to cost individual units, so the costing system has to be adapted in order to cope with different manufacturing systems.

This chapter first examines how absorption costing is incorporated into the cost book-keeping system. The main costing methods applied in specific industries are then outlined. However, cost book-keeping will not be examined in great detail since it is only necessary for non-accountants to have a general understanding of the procedures that are involved.

Cost book-keeping

As explained in Chapter 9, it is possible for a costing system to be kept quite separate from a financial accounting system. Such systems are known as an interlocking system. Interlocking cost book-keeping systems are rather an unnecessary waste of time and money, because they duplicate a great deal of information that is already contained within the financial accounting system.

In order to avoid as much duplication as possible, it is now quite common to find that cost and financial systems are operated jointly. This type of joint system is known as an integral or an integrated system and is particularly appropriate where the book-keeping is computerized. Since this is the most common form of cost book-keeping, it will be adopted in this chapter in order to explain how such a system works.

Costing information is still subject to the same basic accounting rules that were outlined in Chapter 2, irrespective of whether an interlocking or an integral system of costing is operated. However, the application of the dual aspect rule does require some modification in order to cope with the much more detailed information which is recorded in a costing system.

Books of account (or ledgers) are still used with each entry being entered in a separate account in a double-entry format. Expenditure continues to be debited to an account and incomes to be credited. The essential difference lies in the number and the type of accounts that are needed in order to provide management with detailed and up-to-date information.

The cost accounts will, in fact, be grouped according to elements of cost, namely:

1 material;
2 labour; and
3 overheads.

In addition, other accounts will record the incomes, such as sales revenue, dividends receivable and rents receivable. A simplified version of a financial accounting system is shown in Exhibit 12.1.

Exhibit 12.1: A simplified financial accounting system

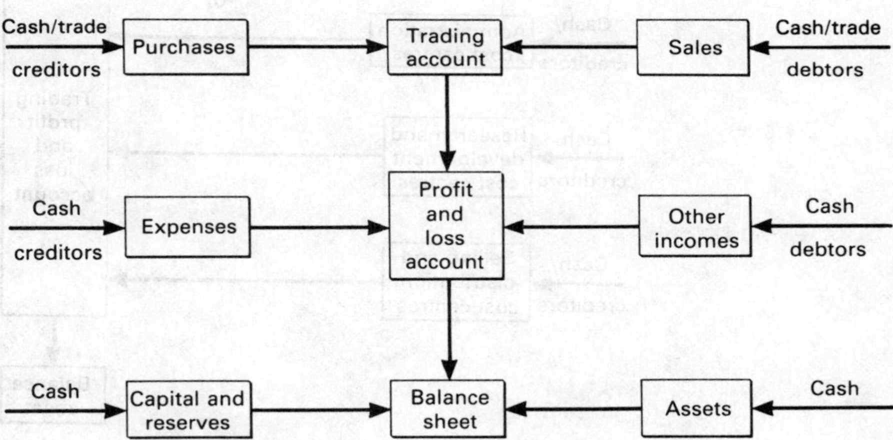

Exhibit 12.1 should be contrasted with the similarly simplified version of an integral cost book-keeping system shown in Exhibit 12.2. To help you understand Exhibit 12.2, some detailed tutorial notes have been included which you should consult as you are following through the recording of the costs in the system.

Exhibit 12.2: A simplified cost book-keeping system

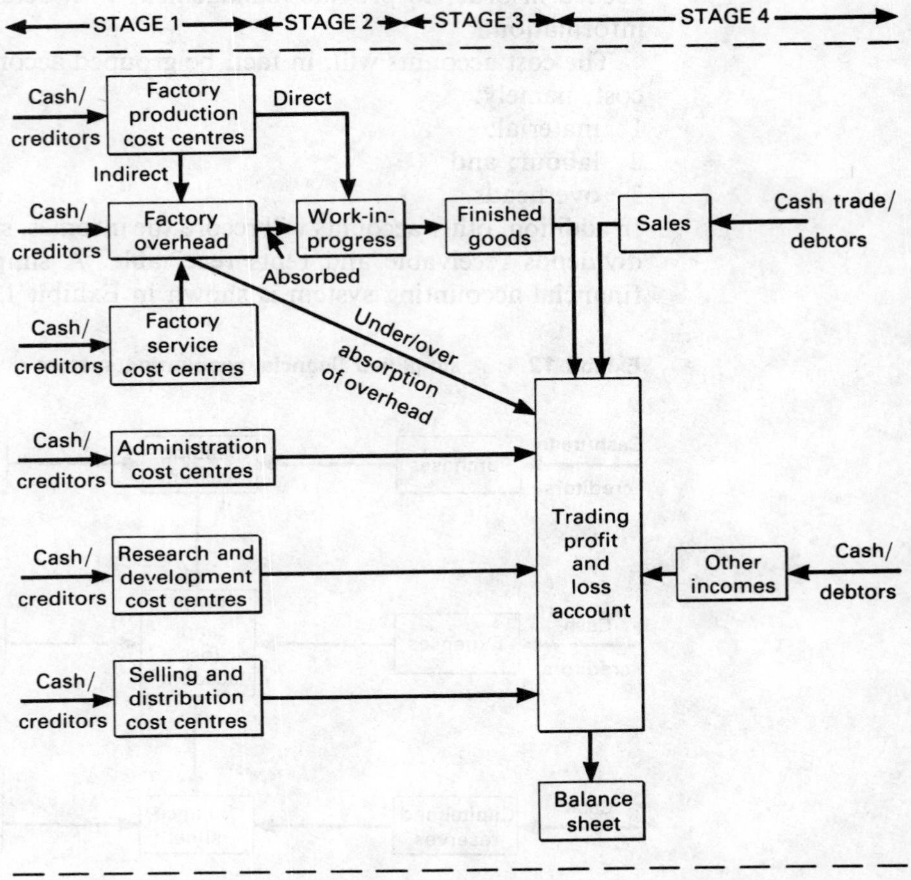

Tutorial notes

Stage 1: The exhibit looks at the system as a whole. Thus each main block of cost centres (factory production, factory service, administration, research and development, and selling and distribution) will be comprised of a considerable number of cost centres.

Stage 2: As a particular unit begins its manufacturing process, a separate work-in-progress account will be opened for each specific unit being manufactured. The work-in-progress account will be debited with (a) the unit's direct costs obtained from the production cost centres, and (b) a share of absorbed factory overhead.

Stage 3: When the unit is completed, it will be transferred at its total factory cost to the finished goods stock account.

Stage 4: (a) The total cost of finished goods sold will be transferred to the trading account and matched with the total sales revenue.

(b) Administration, research and development, and selling and distribution overhead will be transferred to the profit and loss account (assuming that it is not absorbed into product costs).

(c) Other incomes (such as dividends received, rents received and interest received) will be credited to the profit and loss account. The net profit along with all the other remaining balances within the system (for example, raw material stocks, work-in-progress, finished goods stock, debtors, cash and creditors) will then be transferred to the balance sheet.

Basic costing methods

As explained earlier, for the purposes of illustration it has been assumed that separate units of production can be recognized at an early stage in the production process. Consequently, it has been possible to explain how to begin to build up the cost of each specific unit. In fact, this is not always possible.

In producing milk, for example, it is not usually possible to think in terms of specific units until the milk has been bottled. For costing purposes, the amount of milk transferred from the farm to the dairy has to be treated as a bulk amount which is treated as a whole until such times as it is bottled in recognizable units. If the milk was treated in any other way, it would probably be necessary to set up a separate work-in-progress account for each bottle of milk. This would, of course, be impracticable.

The type of input/output problem described above gives rise to two main types of costing methods: specific order costing and operation costing. Both methods are capable of sub-classification, so it is appropriate to discuss each separately.

Specific order costing

This type of costing is possible where specific units can be identified at an early stage in the manufacturing process. In practice, it may be impossible literally to cost each *unit* separately, especially when the units are very small, so it may be necessary to cost them in batches. Specific order costing falls into three broad groupings:

1 *Job costing*. This method is used when specific units are produced, such as in an engineering works, or in maintenance or servicing-type jobs, such as decorating, joinery, or plumbing.

2 *Batch costing*. This method is used when the specific units are too small to cost individually. It may be used, for example, in factories producing nuts and bolts, or boots and shoes.

3 *Contract costing*. Here, the specific unit may be very large, such as the construction of a motorway, or of a school.

In specific order costing, each particular method gives rise to its own problems. The basic costing principles will still apply, but the procedure will probably need some amendment in order to cope with different manufacturing systems.

Operation costing

Operation costing methods are found in those industries where specific units are difficult to identify until a very late stage in the production or assembling process. There are two broad groupings:

1 *Process costing*. Process costing is frequently found in those industries that convert raw materials into a finished product using a process which often requires a chemical change, such as in iron and steel making, and in the chemical and glass industries.
2 *Service costing*. Service costing is found in those industries whose basic objective is to provide a service, such as in local government and in transport undertakings.

Process costing, in particular, gives rise to some very special costing problems. In those processing-type industries, for example, where a chemical change takes place during the manufacturing process, it is quite customary to transfer a larger quantity of raw material into the process and to get out a smaller quantity of processed goods. The loss in production arises as a result of the chemical change that has taken place during manufacture. This loss in production is known as a *normal* loss and it can usually be allowed for in costing the product. However, it is not uncommon to find that there is sometimes an *abnormal* gain or loss. It is usual to write off abnormal gains and losses to the profit and loss account, and not to charge them against the cost of specific products.

Besides different methods of costing, there are also a number of *techniques*. We discuss these in the next section.

Costing techniques

The nature of production will determine what type of costing method it will be necessary to adopt. Thereafter there are a number of costing techniques which can be used in most industries, irrespective of the costing method. The main costing techniques are outlined below.

Absorption costing

Absorption costing has been covered in some detail in earlier chapters. Despite some of the difficulties which were outlined, of all the costing techniques, absorption costing is still the most widely adopted, and most cost book-keeping systems are usually based upon it.

Marginal costing

Marginal costing requires costs to be classified into two broad categories: fixed costs and variable costs. Fixed costs are those costs which tend to remain constant irrespective of the level of activity. Variable costs are those costs which vary in direct proportion to activity.

The costing books may be kept on the basis of marginal costing, but it is more customary to adopt the technique when dealing with specific decisions. Marginal costing will be covered in more detail in the next chapter.

Superimposed techniques

Both absorption costing and marginal costing are capable of having other techniques *superimposed* upon them. This means that they can be operated independently of any other technique, but it is possible for them to be used in conjunction with the other techniques.

There are two main superimposed techniques. They are outlined briefly below, but will be encountered again in later chapters.

1 *Budgetary control*. This technique involves preparing detailed plans of future costs and incomes. The plans (or budgets, as they are known) are then compared frequently and regularly with actual results. If necessary, action is then taken to bring the actual results into line with the budgeted results.
2 *Standard costing*. This technique is very similar to budgetary control, except that detailed budgets (or standards) are drawn up for each unit or process. The standards are then compared with the actual result (again, like the budgetary control technique on a frequent and regular basis), and any necessary corrective action taken.

Standard costing is used in conjunction with *variance accounting*, a technique that allows detailed arithmetical comparisons to be made between actual results and budgeted results. The comparisons are made not only in terms of total cost, but also on the basis of each element of cost.

Conclusion

This chapter has explained briefly how costs are recorded within an absorption costing system. It has also outlined some basic costing methods and techniques.

It has been argued that the costing principles examined in earlier chapters are relevant even in those industries where specific unit costing is not possible. Consequently, a basic foundation in costing techniques has been provided for all non-accountants irrespective of the type of

industry in which they work. However, some of those techniques need to be examined in a little more detail because of their widespread application. This is done in the next three chapters.

Questions

1 **What is an integral cost book-keeping system?**
2 **What is an interlocking cost book-keeping system?**
3 **What is meant by the term 'basic costing methods'?**
4 **What is meant by the term 'costing techniques'?**

13 Marginal costing

As has been argued in previous chapters, absorption costing can provide some misleading information, especially if it is used for short-term decision-making. The main problems arise because absorption costing requires that *all* costs be shared out amongst specific units, irrespective of whether some of those costs are increased or decreased as a result of producing more or less units. The technique that has been devised to cope with this problem is known as *marginal costing*, and it forms the subject of this chapter.

The problem of fixed costs

In absorption costing the distinction between fixed costs and variable costs is not recognized. These costs were defined in an earlier chapter, but as a reminder: fixed costs are those costs which tend not to change regardless of the level of activity, whilst variable costs are those costs which tend to vary in direct proportion to activity.

In absorption costing the fact that some costs (i.e. the fixed costs) will not be affected by making a particular unit is disregarded, and some of those costs are charged to that unit even though there is no relationship between them. This questionable assumption can best be illustrated by an example.

Suppose that an attempt is being made to estimate the cost of a particular car journey by someone who already owns a car that is fully taxed and insured. If the car is to be used for the journey, the main cost arising will be that spent on petrol (although there will be a slight increase in its servicing requirements, and it may depreciate a little more quickly). The tax and insurance costs will not be affected by this particular journey: they are fixed costs, no matter how many extra journeys are undertaken. Thus as far as that specific journey is concerned, we are only interested in the extra cost, i.e. the cost of the petrol. The decision to estimate only the *extra* cost of the journey (or for that matter, the extra cost of producing one more unit) gives rise to the technique of marginal costing.

If absorption costing was used in estimating the cost of the journey, all the costs of running the car over (say) a year would be added up and the total cost would be divided by its annual mileage. The average (or absorbed) cost per mile would then be applied to the mileage expected to be incurred on any particular journey. Clearly, it would be absurd to cost a specific journey in this way: the total cost of running the car is not being affected by the journey. What must be calculated is the marginal (or the extra) cost of the journey, and this is then perhaps contrasted with the cost of optional forms of transport, such as travelling by train or by aircraft. Even then, cost may not be the sole criterion in deciding to use the car instead of travelling by train or going by air, because such non-quantifiable factors as comfort and convenience would also need to be taken into account.

In costing the extra cost of a car journey, the *fixed* costs of owning a car are effectively being ignored. They do form part of the overall cost of car ownership, of course, and they do have to be taken into account when deciding how much it costs to run a car. Once purchased, however, the fixed costs can be ignored when calculating the cost of a specific journey.

Managers in industry face similar costing decisions. These decisions can also best be solved by using the marginal cost technique. An absorbed cost is not very helpful in deciding upon the outcome of a specific event, for example in reducing selling prices or in contracting for new work. In taking such specific decisions, the company's fixed costs may not be immediately affected, although in the long run, of course, even the fixed costs may change if the company expands (or contracts) on any scale.

Nonetheless, the marginal cost technique is useful for short-term specific decision-making. In the next section, how it works will be explained.

The marginal cost technique

As was stated in earlier chapters, costing records are usually kept on the basis of absorption costing. It would be possible to keep them on a marginal costing basis, but this means that in extracting data from such records there is a danger that the fixed costs will be completely ignored in taking decisions. In the long run, of course, the company has to recover all of its costs, even though in the short run, the fixed costs may be ignored in dealing with a specific decision. Consequently, most companies prefer to use absorption costing for book-keeping purposes, but to reconstitute the data when information for specific decisions is needed.

In theory the marginal costing technique is very easy to adopt, although in practice there are some considerable problems to overcome. These problems largely arise because of the assumptions which have to be made in using the technique. These assumptions are summarized below.

1 Total cost can be analysed into fixed costs and variable costs.

2 Fixed costs tend to remain constant in the short term irrespective of the level of activity.
3 Fixed costs do not bear any relationship whatsoever to the specific units (or processes) being produced, and it is impossible to apportion them amongst specific units because no relationship exists between them.
4 Variable costs tend to vary in *direct* proportion to activity.
5 Some costs are semi-variable, that is they contain an element of both fixed and variable costs (electricity costs and telephone charges, for example, both contain a fixed rental element, but the variable charge depends upon the use made of the service).

Whilst these assumptions are somewhat simplistic, they are useful in helping to arrive at decisions in cases where some costs are not likely to be affected by the decision being taken.

In marginal costing, all that is done basically is to classify total cost into its fixed and variable elements instead of classifying it into direct and indirect categories as in absorption costing. Exhibit 13.1 shows a cost statement presented on a marginal cost basis.

Exhibit 13.1: A typical marginal cost statement

	Product			
	A	B	C	Total
Sales revenue (1)	X	X	X	X
Less: Variable cost of sales (2)	X	X	X	X
Contribution (3)	X	X	X	X
Less: Fixed costs (4)				X
Profit/(Loss) (5)				£X

Tutorial notes

1 The total sales revenue would be analysed into different product groupings (in this example for products A, B and C).
2 The variable costs include direct materials, direct labour costs, other direct expenses and variable overhead. In most cases, direct costs are the same as variable costs, but there can be some instances of where they are not the same, for example, a machine operator's salary which is fixed under a guaranteed annual wage agreement.
3 The term *contribution* is used to describe the difference between the sales revenue and the variable cost of those sales. A positive contribution helps to pay for the fixed costs.
4 The fixed costs include all the other costs that do not vary in direct proportion to the sales revenue. Fixed costs are assumed to remain constant over a period of time. They do not bear any relationship to the units produced or the sales achieved, and therefore it is not possible to apportion them amongst the individual products. The total of the fixed costs can *only* be deducted from

the total contribution.

5 Total contribution less the fixed costs gives the profit (if the balance is positive) or a loss (if the balance is negative).

From Exhibit 13.1 it can be seen that it is possible to arrange the information in the form of a series of equations:

Let S = sales revenue
V = variable costs
C = contribution
F = fixed costs
P = profit

Therefore:

$$S - V = C$$
$$C - F = P$$

or

$$C = F + P$$
$$\therefore\ S - V = F + P$$

The equation S − V = F + P is known as the marginal cost equation, and it captures the essence of the marginal cost technique. How it is used is explained in the next section.

The application of marginal costing

By using the marginal cost equation it is possible to cost extremely quickly any specific decision which management is thinking of taking. Indeed, even if a decision might affect the basic marginal costing assumptions, it is still possible to change the data used in the equation relatively easily, for example if a decision does, in fact, appear to affect the level of fixed costs.

The marginal cost equation can be rapidly adapted for two main reasons.

1 It can normally be assumed that fixed costs will remain constant and that they will not be affected by a particular decision.
2 It is possible to calculate the contribution at any level of sales activity, since the variable costs are assumed to vary in direct proportion to the sales revenue.

Exhibit 13.2 illustrates these reasons more clearly.

Exhibit 13.2: Examples of changes in variable cost and contribution

	Product			
	One unit	*100 units*	*1,000 units*	%
	£	£	£	
Selling price	10	1,000	10,000	100
Less: Variable costs	6	600	6,000	60
Contribution	£4	£400	£4,000	40%

Tutorial notes

1 The variable cost per unit is 60%, and the contribution 40% of the sales revenue.
2 This relationship is assumed to hold good no matter how many units are sold.
3 For every unit sold, the company makes a contribution of £4.
4 The fixed costs are ignored, because they are assumed not to change irrespective of the level of activity.

Once all the fixed costs have been covered by the total contribution each extra unit sold results in an extra amount of profit equal to the contribution earned by that unit. Note, however, that profit is not necessarily the same as contribution. This will only be the case once the total contribution has covered the fixed costs. It is only at that stage that any further contribution will be the same as an increase in profit. The point is illustrated in Exhibit 13.3.

Exhibit 13.3: Effect on profit at varying levels of activity

Activity in units:	1,000	2,000	3,000	4,000	5,000
	£	£	£	£	£
Sales	10,000	20,000	30,000	40,000	50,000
Less: Variable costs	5,000	10,000	15,000	20,000	25,000
Contribution	5,000	10,000	15,000	20,000	25,000
Less: Fixed costs	10,000	10,000	10,000	10,000	10,000
Profit/loss	£(5,000)	–	£5,000	£10,000	£15,000

Tutorial notes

1 The exhibit illustrates five levels of activity: from 1,000 units to 5,000 units.
2 At each level of activity, the fixed costs remain constant.
3 At each level of activity, the variable costs remain in direct proportion to the sales revenue, i.e. 50%. This means that the relationship of contribution to sales is also 50%.

We can see from Exhibit 13.3 that only when the fixed costs have been covered by the contribution (at an activity level of 2,000 units), does the increase in contribution thereafter equal the increase in profit. At an activity level of 2,000 units the company's sales revenue is just sufficient to cover its total costs, and at this level it neither makes a profit nor a loss. This is known as its *break-even* position.

The relationship of contribution to sales is known (rather confusingly) as the *profit/volume* (or P/V) *ratio*. Note that it does not mean *profit* in relation to sales, but the *contribution* in relation to sales.

The P/V ratio is extremely useful. Once it has been calculated, it can be applied to any level of sales, the fixed costs deducted and the new profit on the amended level of sales arrived at. Sometimes, of course, the fixed costs will be affected by a change in activity, but again if the fixed costs do change, only a minor amendment is necessary to the basic marginal equation in order to allow for the change in the fixed costs.

The relationships which have been described above are sometimes presented in the form of a chart known as a *break-even graph* (or chart). Accountants believe that it is sometimes much easier to make the point about the relationship between sales, variable costs and fixed costs if it is presented diagrammatically. Exhibit 13.4 is based on the same data as used in Exhibit 13.3 and illustrates a break-even graph.

Exhibit 13.4: A break-even chart

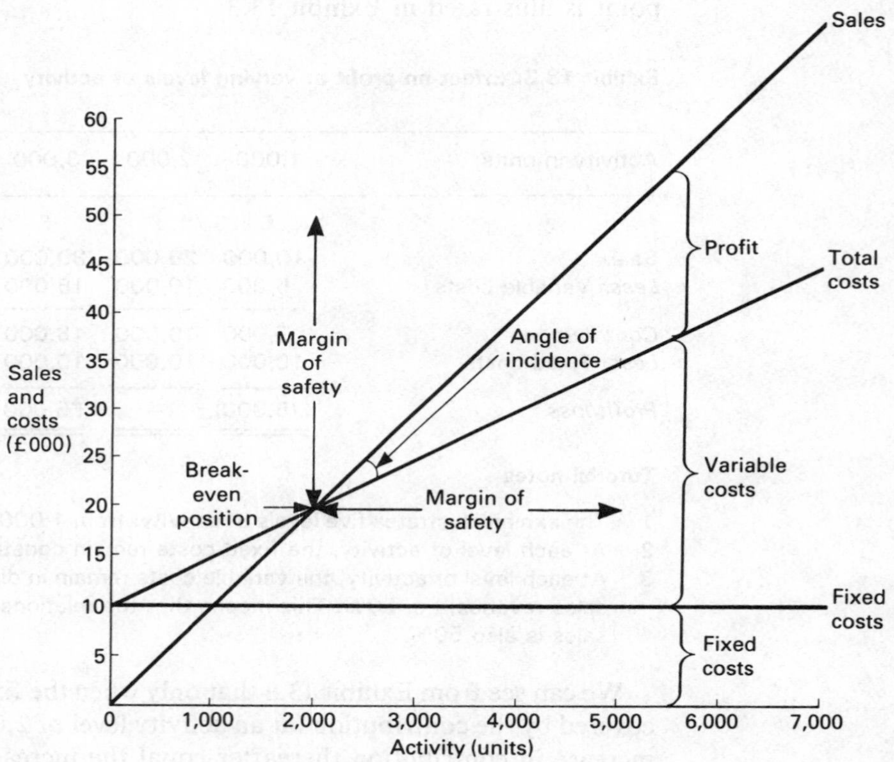

Tutorial notes

1 The total cost line is a combination of the fixed costs and the variable costs. It thus ranges from a total cost of £10,000 (fixed costs only) at a nil level of activity, to £35,000 when the activity level is 5,000 units (fixed costs of £10,000 + variable costs of £25,000).

2 The angle of incidence is the angle formed between the sales line and the total cost line. The wider the angle, the greater the amount of profit.
3 The margin of safety is the distance between the sales achieved and the sales level needed to break-even. It can be measured either in units (along the *x* axis) or in sales revenue terms (along the *y* axis).
4 Activity (measured along the *x* axis) may be measured in units, as a percentage of the theoretical maximum level of activity, or in terms of sales revenue.

Exhibit 13.4 shows quite clearly the relationships that are assumed to exist when the marginal cost technique is adopted. Thus the sales revenue, the variable costs and the fixed costs are all assumed to be linear, i.e. they can all be represented by straight lines from a point where there is no activity right through to infinity.

In practice, these relationships are not likely to remain linear over such a wide range of activity. The basic marginal cost assumptions may only be valid, in fact, over a narrow range of activity. Whilst this point may appear to create some difficulty in adopting the marginal cost technique, it should be appreciated that wide fluctuations in activity are not normally experienced. Companies usually operate over a fairly narrow range of activity, and over such a range the relationships between sales revenue and fixed and variable costs may be fairly linear. The information prepared is only a guide to management. It must not be taken too literally, and in any case there are, of course, many other factors also to be taken into account.

Nonetheless, it would be useful to summarize the criticisms of marginal costing so that you can take them into account when assessing the value of costing information prepared on marginal cost lines. This is the subject of the next section.

Criticisms of marginal costing

The assumptions adopted in preparing marginal cost statements lead to a number of criticisms of the technique:

1 Costs cannot be easily divided into fixed and variable categories.
2 Variable costs do not vary in direct proportion to activity at all levels of activity, for example direct materials may increase or decrease in cost because of shortages in supply or because of bulk buying, whilst the direct labour costs may be fixed in the short run because of the need to give a minimum period of notice to staff before they can be dismissed.
3 The fixed costs will change (at least to some extent) as activity increases or decreases.
4 It is difficult to decide over what period of time costs do remain fixed: in the long run all costs become variable in the sense that the company can avoid them altogether by going into liquidation.
5 A specific decision affecting one product may in turn affect other

products, especially if they are complementary, such as a garage that sells oil and petrol.
6 Fixed costs cannot be entirely ignored, because if the company is to survive in the long run, its total sales revenue must cover all of its costs.
7 Non-cost factors (such as the security of supplies and the availability of finance) cannot be ignored in arriving at a specific decision.

These are all very severe criticisms of the marginal cost technique. Even so, in practice it is still a very useful technique to adopt, provided that it is used with caution, that the information is only treated as a *guide* to decision-making, and that other non-cost factors are taken into account.

Marginal costing formulae

The marginal cost technique requires cost to be classified into fixed and variable categories, and it has been demonstrated that the respective relationships can be put in the form of an equation. It is possible to extract a number of other equations from the marginal cost equation, and these other equations can be quite useful in examining specific problems. For convenience these equations are summarized below:

1 Sales − variable cost of sales = contribution: $S - V = C$

2 Contribution − fixed costs = profit/(loss): $C - F = P$

3 Break-even (B/E) position = contribution − fixed costs: $C - F$

4 B/E in sales value terms = $\frac{\text{Fixed costs} \times \text{sales}}{\text{Contribution}}$: $\frac{F \times S}{C}$

5 B/E in units = $\frac{\text{Fixed costs}}{\text{Contribution per unit}}$: $\frac{F}{C \text{ per unit}}$

6 Margin of safety (M/S) in value terms = $\frac{\text{Profit} \times \text{sales}}{\text{Contribution}}$: $\frac{P \times S}{C}$

7 M/S in units = $\frac{\text{Profit}}{\text{Contribution per unit}}$: $\frac{P}{C \text{ per unit}}$

The application of some of these formulae is illustrated in Exhibit 13.5.

Exhibit 13.5: Use of marginal cost formulae

The following information relates to Happy Limited for the year to 30 June 19X8:

Number of units sold		10,000
	Per unit	*Total*
	£	£000
Sales	30	300
Less: Variable costs	18	180
Contribution	12	120
Less: Fixed costs		24
Profit		£96

Required:
In value and unit terms calculate the following:

1 the break-even position; and
2 the margin of safety.

Answer to Exhibit 13.5

1 Break-even position in value terms:

$$\frac{F \times S}{C} = \frac{£24{,}000 \times £300{,}000}{120{,}000} = £60{,}000$$

Break-even in units:

$$\frac{F}{C \text{ per unit}} = \frac{£24{,}000}{12} = 2{,}000 \text{ units}$$

2 Margin of safety in value terms:

$$\frac{P \times S}{C} = \frac{£96{,}000 \times 300{,}000}{120{,}000} = £240{,}000$$

Margin of safety in units:

$$\frac{P}{C \text{ per unit}} = \frac{£96{,}000}{12} = 8{,}000 \text{ units}$$

Check that you understand the significance of the above solutions. You could also use the data to prepare a break-even chart.

An illustrative example

It would now be helpful to examine the technique of marginal costing in the context of a simple example. Exhibit 13.6 summarizes a typical problem with which a board of directors might be faced.

Exhibit 13.6

Looking ahead to the financial year ending 31 March 19X5, the directors of Problems Limited are faced with a budgeted loss of £10,000. This is based on the following data:

Budgeted number of units	10,000
	£000
Sales revenue	100
Less: Variable costs	80
Contribution	20
Less: Fixed costs	30
Budgeted loss	£(10)

The directors would like to aim for a profit of £20,000 for the year to 31 March 19X5. Various proposals have been put forward, none of which require a change in the budgeted level of fixed costs. These proposals are as follows:

1 Reduce the selling price of each unit by 10%.
2 Increase the selling price of each unit by 10%.
3 Stimulate sales by improving the quality of the product; this would increase the variable cost of the unit by £1.50 per unit.

Required:

(a) For each proposal calculate:
  (i) the break-even position in units and in value terms;
  (ii) the number of units required to be sold in order to meet the profit target.

(b) State which proposal you think should be adopted.

Answer to Exhibit 13.6

Problems Limited
(a) (i) and (ii):

Workings:	£
Profit target	20,000
Fixed costs	30,000
Total contribution required	£50,000

The budgeted selling price per unit is £10 (£100,000/10,000).

The budgeted outlook compared with each proposal may be summarized as follows:

Per unit:	*Budgeted position*	*Proposal 1*	*Proposal 2*	*Proposal 3*
	£	£	£	£
Selling price	10	9	11	10.00
Less: Variable costs	8	8	8	9.50
(a) Unit contribution	£2	£1	£3	£0.50
(b) Total contribution required to break-even (= fixed costs)	£30,000	£30,000	£30,000	£30,000
(c) Total contribution required to meet the profit target	£50,000	£50,000	£50,000	£50,000

	Budgeted position	Proposal 1	Proposal 2	Proposal 3
	£	£	£	£
∴ no. of units to break-even ((b)/(a))	15,000	30,000	10,000	60,000
∴ no. of units to meet the profit target ((c)/(a))	25,000	50,000	16,667	100,000

(b)

Comments:

1. By continuing with the present budget proposals, the company would need to sell 15,000 units to break-even or 25,000 units to meet the profit target. In order to break-even the company needs to increase its sales by 50%, or by 250% to meet the profit target.
2. A reduction in selling price of 10% per unit would require sales to increase by 300% in order to break-even, or by 500% to meet the profit target.
3. By increasing the selling price of each unit by 10%, the company would only have to sell at the budgeted level to break-even, but its unit sales would have to increase by two-thirds to meet the profit target.
4. By improving the product at an increased variable cost of £1.50 per unit, the company would require a six-fold increase to break-even, or ten-fold to meet the profit target.

Conclusion

It would appear that increasing the selling price by 10% would be a more practical solution for the company to adopt. In the short run, at least it will break-even, and there is the possibility that sales could be sufficient to make a small profit. In the long run it has a much better chance of meeting the profit target than do the other proposals. Some extra stimulus would be needed, however, to lift sales to this level over such a relatively short period of time. In any case, it is not clear why an increase in price should increase sales, unless the product is one which only sells at a comparatively high price, such as cosmetics and patent medicines. It must also be questioned whether the cost relationships will remain as indicated in the exhibit over such a large increase in activity. In particular, it is unlikely that the fixed costs will remain entirely fixed if there is such a large increase in sales.

Limiting factors

As was seen in Exhibit 13.6, when optional decisions are considered, the aim will always be to maximize contribution, because the greater the contribution, the more chance there is of covering the fixed costs and hence of making a profit. When managers are faced with a choice, therefore, between (say) producing product A at a contribution of £10 per unit, or of producing product B at a contribution of £20 per unit, they would normally choose product B. Sometimes, however, it may not be possible to produce unlimited quantities of product B because there could be a limit on how many units of B could either be sold or produced.

Such limits are known as *limiting factors* (or *key factors*). They may arise for a number of reasons; for example, it may not be possible to sell more than a certain number of units, or there may be production restraints (such as shortages of raw materials, skilled labour, or factory space), or the company may not be able to finance the anticipated rate of expansion in the immediate future.

If there is a product that cannot be produced and sold in unlimited quantities, then it is necessary to follow a simple rule in order to decide which product to concentrate on producing. The rule can be summarized as follows:

> Choose that work which provides the maximum contribution per unit of limiting factor employed.

This sounds very complicated but in fact it is quite simple. Suppose that direct materials are a limiting factor, and that only a certain quantity is available. The contribution each unit makes would then be converted into (say) the contribution per kilogram. If the number of direct labour hours are a limiting factor, and a choice had to be made between two jobs, the respective contributions would be converted into the amount of contribution earned for every direct labour hour worked on each job. The choice would then be for that job which earned the most contribution for each direct labour worked on it.

The application of key factors is illustrated in Exhibit 13.7.

Exhibit 13.7

Quays Limited manufactures a product for which there is a shortage of raw materials PX. During the year to 31 March 19X7, only 1,000 kilograms of PX will be available. PX is used in manufacturing both product 8 and product 9. The following information is relevant:

Per unit	*Product 8*	*Product 9*
	£	£
Selling price	300	150
Less: Variable costs	200	100
Contribution	£100	£50
P/V ratio	33⅓	33⅓
Kilograms required	5	2

Required:
State which product Quays Limited should concentrate on producing.

Answer to Exhibit 13.7

	Product 8	*Product 9*
	£	£
Contribution per unit	100	50
Limiting factor per unit	5	2
∴ contribution per kilogram	£20	£25

Choice:
Product 9 because it gives the highest contribution per unit of limiting factor.

Check:
Maximum contribution of product 8:
200 units (1,000/5) × contribution per unit = 200 × £100 = £20,000

Maximum contribution of product 9:
500 units (1,000/2) × contribution per unit = 500 × £50 = £25,000

In Exhibit 13.7 we have assumed that there is only one limiting factor. There could, of course, be many more limiting factors; for example, it might not be possible to sell 500 units of product 9. If this is the case, as many units of product 9 would be sold as possible, and then what remains of the scarce raw material would be used to produce units of product 8.

Conclusion

Marginal costing is a most important technique. It is particularly useful in short-term decision-making, but it is of less value when decisions have to be viewed over the long term.

The technique depends upon two main assumptions:

1 some costs remain fixed, irrespective of the level of activity; and
2 other costs vary in direct proportion to sales.

These assumptions are not valid over the long term, but they can be usefully adopted in the short term as long as they are used with caution.

It should also be remembered that the marginal costing technique is only a *guide* to decision-making, and that other non-cost factors have to be taken into account.

This concludes our study of the basic structure of cost and management accounting. In the next two chapters budgetary control and standard costing will be examined. These are two further techniques which can be operated in conjunction with a basic costing system.

Questions

13.1 The following information relates to Pole Limited for the year to 31 January 19X2.

	£000
Administration expenses:	
Fixed	30
Variable	7
Semi-variable (fixed 80%, variable 20%)	20

	£000
Materials:	
Direct	60
Indirect	5
Production overhead (all fixed)	40
Research and development expenditure:	
Fixed	60
Variable	15
Semi-variable (fixed 50%, variable 50%)	10
Sales	450
Selling and distribution expenditure:	
Fixed	80
Variable	4
Semi-variable (fixed 70%, variable 30%)	30
Wages:	
Direct	26
Indirect	13

Required:
Using the above data, compile a marginal cost statement for Pole Limited for the year to 31 January 19X2.

13.2 **You are presented with the following information for Giles Limited for the year to 28 February 19X2.**

	£000
Fixed costs	150
Variable costs	300
Sales (50,000 units)	500

Required:
(a) Calculate the following:
(i) the break-even point in value terms and in units;
(ii) the margin of safety in value terms and in units.
(b) Prepare a break-even chart.

13.3 **The following information applies to Ayre Limited for the two years to 31 March 19X2 and 19X3 respectively:**

Year	*Sales* £000	*Profits* £000
31.3.19X2	750	100
31.3.19X3	1,000	250

Required:
Assuming that the cost relationships had remained as given in the question, calculate the company's profit if the sales for the year to 31 March 19X3 had reached the budget level of £1,200,000.

13.4 The following information relates to Carter Limited for the year to 30 April 19X3:

Units sold	50,000
Selling price per unit	£40
Net profit per unit	£9
Profit/volume ratio	40%

During 19X4 the company would like to increase its sales substantially, but to do so it would have to reduce the selling price per unit by 20%. The variable cost per unit will not change, but because of the increased activity, the company will have to invest in new machinery which will increase the fixed costs by £30,000 per annum.

Required:
Given the new conditions, calculate how many units the company will need to sell in 19X4 in order to make the same amount of profit as it did in 19X3.

13.5 Puzzled Limited would like to increase its sales during the year to 31 May 19X5. To do so, it has several mutually exclusive options open to it as follows:

1 reduce the selling price per unit by 15%;
2 improve the product resulting in an increase in the variable cost per unit of £1.30;
3 spend £15,000 on an advertising campaign;
4 improve factory efficiency by purchasing more machinery at a fixed extra annual cost of £22,500.

During the year to 31 May 19X4, the company sold 20,000 units. The cost details were as follows:

	£000
Sales	200
Variable costs	150
Contribution	50
Fixed costs	40
Profit	£10

These cost relationships are expected to hold in 19X5.

Required:
State which option you would recommend and why.

13.6 Micro Limited has some surplus capacity. It is now considering whether it should accept a special contract to use some of its spare capacity. However, this contract will use some specialist direct labour which is in short supply.

The following details relate to the proposed contract:

	£
Contract price	50,000
Variable costs:	
Direct materials	10,000
Direct labour	30,000

4,000 direct labour hours would be required in order to complete the contract.

The company's budget for the year during which the contract would be undertaken is as follows:

	£000
Sales	750
Less: Variable costs	500
Contribution	250
Less: Fixed costs	230
Profit	£20

Direct labour hours: 50,000 maximum available during the year.

Required:
State, giving your reasons, whether the special contract should be accepted.

14 Budgetary control

The last five chapters have examined the basic principles of cost and management accounting. It has been assumed, for the sake of convenience, that most of the costing information has been prepared on an historical basis. However, as was pointed out in Chapter 9, one of the major disadvantages of *financial* accounting is that it is almost entirely concerned with looking back to what has happened. Management are probably more concerned with looking to the future to what *might* happen.

If the maximum benefits are to be obtained from a cost and management accounting system it also ought to be able to provide management with information which deals with the future, as well as with the past. This can be achieved by incorporating into the cost and management accounting system a technique known as *budgetary control*. Budgetary control is the subject of this chapter.

Budgetary control is known as a *superimposed* technique, that is it supplements an already existing costing system. Thus it is possible to operate a costing system without budgetary control, but it is particularly advantageous to incorporate budgetary control into it. In this chapter, budgetary control is examined from the point of view of a non-accountant. As will be seen, the preparation of budgets (and their use for control purposes), involves some fairly detailed exercises. Such exercises are usually undertaken by a team of accountants specially employed for the purpose, although the team does, of course, need the assistance of other personnel. Indeed, if the budgetary control system is to work successfully, most employees will need to be heavily involved in the entire exercise.

The preparation of budgets involves considerable detail beyond the scope of this book. Here, we will be concerned primarily with those aspects of budgeting that are of particular relevance to the non-accountant, and will begin by examining what is meant by budgeting.

The nature of budgeting

The term 'budget' is well understood. In private life, many individuals often prepare their own personal budget. Even in an informal sense, everyone does some budgeting at some time or other, for example by working out what one expects to earn over (say) the next twelve months, and comparing it with what one expects to spend during the same period. Such a budget may not be very precise, and it may not be formally written down. Nonetheless, it contains all the ingredients of what accountants mean by a budget.

The essential features of a budget are summarized below.

1 It lays down policies which are expected to be pursued in order to meet the overall objectives of the entity.
2 It contains both quantitative and financial data.
3 The data is usually formally documented.
4 It is prepared for a future period of time.
5 It covers a defined period of time.

In practice, a considerable number of budgets will be prepared, for example for sales, production and administration. These detailed budgets will then be combined into what is known as a *master* budget.

Once the master budget has been prepared, it will be examined in great detail in order to see whether the overall plan can be accommodated. It could be the case, for example, that the sales budget suggests that a large increase in sales will occur. As a result, the production budgets will have been prepared to meet the extra sales demand. However, the cash budget might suggest that the entity cannot meet the extra activity required. In those circumstances, it is likely that additional financing arrangements will be made, because obviously no organization would normally turn down the opportunity of increasing its sales revenue if it was going to result in an increase in profit.

The detailed preparation of individual budgets is a valuable exercise in its own right, because it forces management to look ahead. It is a natural human tendency always to be looking to the past, but past experience may not always help us prepare for the future. If a manager is asked to produce a budget it does at least encourage him to examine what he *has* been doing in relation to what he *could* do.

Nonetheless, the full benefits of a budgeting system are only realized when it is also used for day-to-day control purposes. When budgets are used as a form of control, the technique is known as *budgetary control*.

Budgetary control has several important features which may be summarized as follows:

1 Each manager's responsibilities have to be clearly defined.
2 Each manager's budget lays down the policies for his or her own sphere of responsibility.
3 The manager has a responsibility to follow his or her budget once it has been approved.
4 The manager's actual performance is constantly compared with the planned (or budgeted) results.

5 Corrective action is taken if the actual results differ from the budgeted results.
6 Departures from budget are only permitted if they have been approved by senior management.
7 Variances that are unaccounted for will be subject to individual investigation.

Budgetary control is, therefore, basically a control technique whereby actual results are continuously checked against planned results. If there are any variances, then these are carefully investigated. If it is judged necessary, the immediate actual performance will be changed so that it can be brought into line with the budgeted results, or the budget will be amended to take account of new developments.

Now that the nature of budgeting and budgetary control has been briefly examined it is possible to look into how it is operated. This is covered in the next section.

Budget procedure

In practice, the budget procedure may be very detailed and extremely time-consuming. The procedure starts with a determination of the entity's objectives. These may be very simple. There may, for example, be an overall wish to maximize profits, to foster better relations with its customers, or to improve the working conditions of its employees. Once the entity has decided what it is aiming to achieve over the budget period, it will then need to make a forecast of what is likely to happen.

There is a technical difference between a forecast and a budget. A forecast is a prediction of what is *likely* to happen. A budget is a formal written statement of what *should* happen.

For clarity the budgeting process will be considered in various stages in the following subsections.

The budget period

The main budget period is usually based on a calendar year. A calendar year fits in with the time-scale necessary for the preparation of the financial accounts. However, the choice of an appropriate budget period may also depend upon the type of product that the entity produces. In the fashion industry, for example, product changes occur extremely frequently, so it may be difficult to plan in detail for a full twelve month period. By contrast, in the construction industry where projects may take many years to complete, the main budget period could be well in excess of twelve months.

Besides determining the main budget period, it is also necessary to prepare sub-period budgets. Sub-period budgets are required, because for budgetary control purposes, actual results are compared with budgeted results, and this has to be done regularly if it is to be effective. The sub-budget periods for some functions may need to be very short if tight control is to be exercised over them. The cash budget, for example, may need to be prepared on a weekly basis, whereas the administration budget may only need to be prepared monthly.

Administration

The budget procedure may be administered by a special budget committee, or it may be supervised by the accounting function. It will be necessary for the budget committee to lay down general guidelines in accordance with the entity's objectives, and to ensure that individual departments do not operate completely independently. The production department needs to know, for example, what the entity is budgeting to sell so that it can prepare its own budget on the basis of the budgeted level of sales, but the detailed production budget must be left to the production manager to decide.

This principle is in line with the concept of responsibility accounting which was outlined in an earlier chapter. If the control procedure is to work properly, managers must be given responsibility for a clearly defined area of activity, such as a cost centre. Thereafter, they are expected to be fully answerable for all that goes on in their own cost centre. Unless managers are given responsibility they cannot be expected to be answerable for something which is outside their control. This means that as far as budgets are concerned, managers must help prepare, amend and *approve* their own department's budget, otherwise the budgetary control system will not work.

The budgeting process

The budgeting process is illustrated in Exhibit 14.1. Study the exhibit very carefully noting how the various budgets all fit together.

Later on in the chapter a quantitative example will illustrate how the budgeting process actually works in practice, but for the moment a brief description will be sufficient.

In commercial organizations the first budget to be prepared is usually the sales budget. Once the sales for the budget period (and for each sub-budget period) have been determined, the next stage is to calculate the effect on production. This will then enable an agreed *level of activity* to be determined. The level of activity may be expressed in so many units or as a percentage of the theoretical productive capacity of the entity. Once it has been established, departmental managers can be instructed to prepare their budgets on the basis of the required level of activity.

Exhibit 14.1: The budgeting process

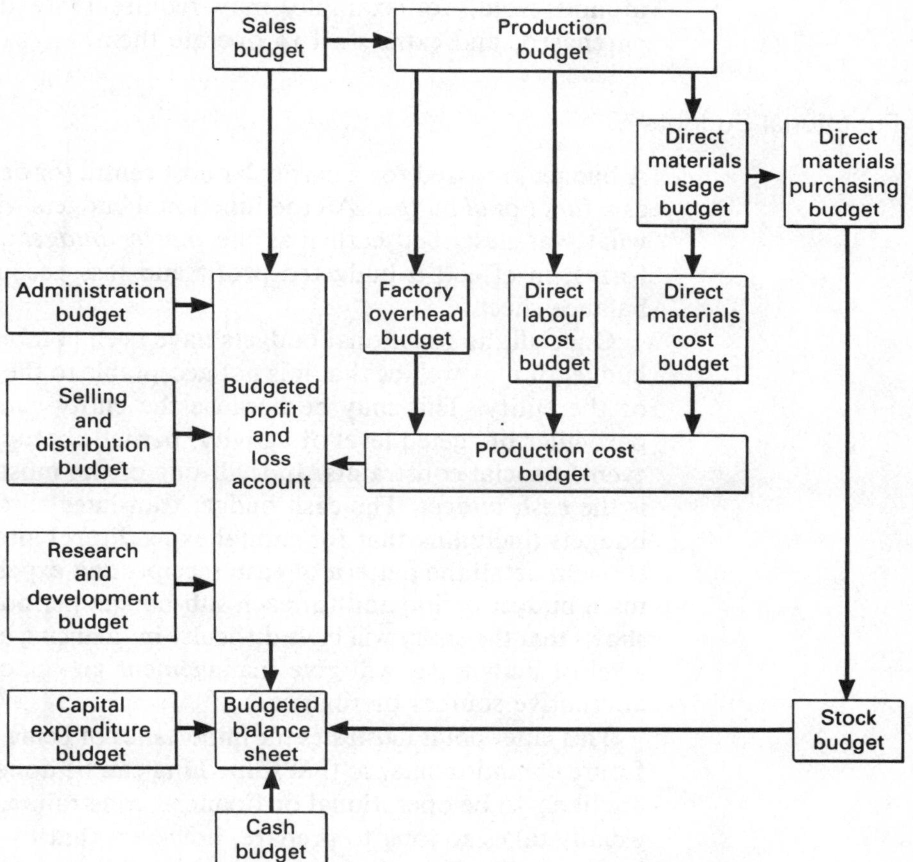

Assume, for example, that it has been agreed that 1,000 units can be sold during a particular budget period. The production department manager will need this information in order to prepare his budget. This does not necessarily mean that he will budget for a production level of 1,000 units, because he will need to allow for any units he expects to have in stock at the beginning of the budget period, and for the number of units he wants to have in stock at the end of the budget period.

The budgeted production level will then be translated into how much material and labour will be required to meet that particular budgeted level. Similarly, it will be necessary to prepare overhead budgets. Much of the general overhead expenditure of the entity (such as factory administration, general administration, and research and development expenditure) will tend to be fixed expenditure and will not be directly affected by production levels. However, in some instances, a marked change in activity may lead to changes having to be made to the overhead budgets.

The sales and distribution overhead budget may be one overhead budget that will not be entirely fixed in nature. An increase in the number of units sold, for example, may require more delivery vans to be purchased, and extra staff to operate them.

Functional budgets

A budget prepared for a particular cost centre (or department) is known as a *functional budget*. All the functional budgets will be combined into what was described earlier as the *master budget*. The master budget forms, in effect, a budgeted profit and loss account and a budgeted balance sheet.

Once all the functional budgets have been combined into the master budget, it may well be that it is not acceptable to the senior management of the entity. This may be because the entity cannot cope with that particular budgeted level of activity, perhaps because of production or even financial constraints. Indeed, one of the most important budgets is the *cash budget*. The cash budget translates all the other functional budgets (including that for capital expenditure) into cash terms. It will show in detail the pattern of cash receipts and expenditure both for the main budget period and for each sub-budget period. If the cash budget shows that the entity will have difficulty in financing a particular budgeted level of activity, it will give management an opportunity to seek out alternative sources of finance.

This latter point illustrates the importance of being aware of the entity's future commitments, so that something can be done in advance if there are likely to be operational or financial constraints. The master budget usually takes so long to prepare, however, that by the time that it has been completed, it will be almost impossible to make major alterations to it. It is then tempting for senior management to make changes to the functional budgets without reference to the individual cost centre managers. It is most unwise to do so without consultation with the managers concerned, because it is difficult to use such budgets for control purposes if they have not agreed to the changes. As argued earlier, they can hardly take responsibility for budgets which have been imposed upon them.

As it is difficult to see how all the functional budgets fit together, it would be helpful to demonstrate how they are prepared in an illustrative example. This follows in the next section.

Functional budgets: an illustrative example

It would obviously be very difficult to observe the basic procedures involved in the preparation of the functional budgets if a detailed example were used. Exhibit 14.2 has therefore been especially devised to illustrate the *main* procedures. In practice there would, of course, be very many more steps involved.

Exhibit 14.2

Sefton Limited manufactures one product known as EC2. The following information relates to the preparation of the budget for the year to 31 March 19X9:

1 Sales budget details for product EC2:
   Expected selling price per unit: £100.
   Expected sales in units: 10,000.
   All sales are on credit terms.
2 EC2 requires 5 units of raw material E and 10 units of raw material C. E is expected to cost £3 per unit, and C £4 per unit. All goods are purchased on credit terms.
3 Two departments are involved in producing EC2, machining and assembly. The following information is relevant:

	Direct labour per unit of product	*Direct labour rate per hour*
	(hours)	£
Machining	1.00	6
Assembling	0.50	8

4 The finished production overhead costs are expected to amount to £100,000.
5 At 1 April 19X8, 800 units of EC2 are expected to be in stock at a value of £52,000, 4,500 units of raw material E at a value of £13,500, and 12,000 units of raw material C at a value of £48,000. Stocks of both finished goods and raw materials are planned to be 10% above the expected opening stock levels as at 1 April 19X8.
6 Administration, selling and distribution overhead is expected to amount to £150,000.
7 Other relevant information:
   (a) Opening trade debtors are expected to be £80,000. Closing trade debtors are expected to amount to 15% of the total sales for the year.
   (b) Opening trade creditors are expected to be £28,000. Closing trade creditors are expected to amount to 10% of the purchases for the year.
   (c) All other expenses will be paid in cash during the year.
   (d) Other balances at 1 April 19X8 are expected to be as follows:

	£	£
(i) Share capital: ordinary shares		225,000
(ii) Retained profits		17,500
(iii) Proposed dividend		75,000
(iv) Fixed assets at cost	250,000	
Less: Accumulated depreciation	100,000	
		150,000
(v) Cash at bank and in hand		2,000

8 Capital expenditure will amount to £50,000 payable in cash on 1 April 19X8.
9 Fixed assets are depreciated on a straight-line basis at a rate of 20% per annum on cost.

Required:
In so far as the information permits, prepare all the relevant budgets for Sefton Limited for the year to 31 March 19X9.

Answer to Exhibit 14.2

Even with a much simplified budgeting exercise, there is clearly a great deal of work involved in preparing the budgets. To make it easier for you to understand what is happening, the procedure will be outlined step by step.

Step 1: Prepare the sales budget

Units of EC2	*Selling price per unit*	*Total sales value*
	£	£
10,000	100	1,000,000

Step 2: Prepare the production budget

	Units
Sales of EC2	10,000
Less: Opening stock	800
	9,200
Add: Desired closing stock (opening stock + 10%)	880
Production required	10,080

Step 3: Prepare the direct materials usage budget

Direct material:	
E: 5 units × 10,080	50,400 units
C: 10 units × 10,080	100,800 units

Step 4: Prepare the direct materials purchase budget

Direct material	E *(Units)*	C *(Units)*
Usage (as per Step 3)	50,400	100,800
Less: Opening stock	4,500	12,000
	45,900	88,800
Add: Desired closing stock (opening stock + 10%)	4,950	13,200
	50,850	102,000
	× £3	× £4
∴ Total value of purchase	£152,550	£408,000

Step 5: Prepare the direct labour budget

	Machining	*Assembling*
Production units (as per Step 2)	10,080	10,080

contd

	Machining	*Assembling*
× direct labour hours required	× 1 DLH	× 0.50 DLH
	10,080 DLH	5,040 DLH
× direct labour rate per hour	× £6	× £8
	£60,480	£40,320

Step 6: Prepare the fixed production overhead budget

Given £100,000

Step 7: Calculate the value of the closing raw material stock

Raw material	*Closing stock** *(units)*	*Cost per unit* £	*Total value* £
E	4,950	3	14,850
C	13,200	4	52,800
			£67,650

*Step 4

Step 8: Calculate the value of the closing finished stock

		£	£
Unit cost:			
Direct materials:	E - 5 units × £3 per unit	15	
	C - 10 units × £4 per unit	40	55
Direct labour:	Machining - 1 hour × £6 per DLH	6	
	Assembling - 0.50 hours × £8 per DLH	4	10
Total direct cost			£65
× units in stock			× 880
			£57,200

Step 9: Prepare the administration, selling and distribution budget

Given £150,000

Step 10: Prepare the capital expenditure budget

Given £50,000

Step 11: Calculate the cost of goods sold

	£
Opening stock (given)	52,000
Manufacturing cost:	
Production units (Step 2) × Total direct cost (Step 3) = 10,080 × £65	655,200
	707,200
Less: Closing stock (Step 8: 880 units × £65)	57,200
Cost of goods sold (10,000 units)	£650,000

Step 12: Prepare the cash budget

	£
Receipts	
Opening debtors	80,000
Sales (£1,000,000 × 85%)	850,000
	930,000
Payments	
Opening creditors	28,000
Purchases (Step 4: (£152,550 + 408,000) × 90%)	504,495
Wages (Step 5: £60,480 + 40,320)	100,800
Fixed production overhead	100,000
Administration, selling and distribution overhead	150,000
Capital expenditure	50,000
Proposed dividend (19X8)	75,000
	1,008,295
Net receipts	(78,295)
Add: Opening cash	2,000
Budgeted closing cash balance (overdrawn)	£(76,295)

Step 13: Prepare the budgeted profit and loss account

	£	£
Sales (Step 1)		1,000,000
Less: Variable cost of sales (Step 8: 10,000 × £65)		650,000
Gross margin		350,000
Less: Fixed production overhead (Step 6)	100,000	
Depreciation (£250,000 + 50,000) × 20%))	60,000	
		160,000
Production margin		190,000
Less: Administration, selling and distribution overhead (Step 9)		150,000
Budgeted net profit		£40,000

Step 14: Prepare the budgeted balance sheet

	£	£	£
Fixed assets (at cost)			300,000
Less: Accumulated depreciation			160,000
			140,000
Current assets			
Raw materials (Step 7)		67,650	
Finished stock (Step 8)		57,200	
Trade debtors (15% × £1,000,000)		150,000	
c/fwd		274,850	

	£	£	£
b/fwd		274,850	140,000
Less: Current liabilities			
Trade creditors (Step 4: 10% × (£152,550 + 408,000))	56,055		
Bank overdraft (Step 12)	76,295	132,350	142,500
			£282,500
Financed by:			
Share capital			
Ordinary shares			225,000
Retained profits (£17,500 + 40,000)			57,500
			£282,500

Exhibit 14.2 is a fairly complicated example, although too much detail has been avoided. For example, it was assumed that the company produces only one product, and that the value of the opening stocks at 1 April 19X8 will be the same as the budgeted costs of manufacture in the year to 31 March 19X9.

You are now recommended to work through Exhibit 14.2 once more. Use as your guide the budgeting process shown in diagrammatic format in Exhibit 14.1. It would then be advisable to have another go at Exhibit 14.2, but this time without reference to the solution.

Fixed and flexible budgets

Once the master budget has been agreed, all personnel in the entity are expected to ensure that they work as close to it as possible. However, some entities only use the budgeting process as a planning exercise. Once it has been agreed, there may be no attempt to use it as a control technique. Thus the actual results will not be frequently compared with the budgeted results, and the budget may be virtually ignored. If this is the case, the entity is not getting the best out of the budgeting system.

As suggested earlier, budgets are particularly useful if they are also used as a means of control. The control is achieved if the actual performance is constantly compared with the budgeted results, any variance investigated, and corrective action taken if this proves necessary. The constant comparison of the actual results with the budgeted results may be done either on a *fixed* budget basis or a *flexible* budget basis. If we operate a fixed budget system, then the actual results for a particular period will be compared with the original budgets. A flexible budget system allows for changes which may have taken place since the budgets were prepared. Thus, in certain circumstances, the original budgets will be changed (or in accounting terminology, *flexed*) before they are compared with the actual results.

It may seem a little strange to suggest that in certain circumstances the budget may be changed. A budget is a form of measure; to consider changing it, therefore, would seem to be like having an elastic ruler. If measurements are to be consistent, the ruler has to stay the same length, and it would appear that the same requirement should apply to budgets.

This argument is a very attractive one, but if it is accepted for budgetary control purposes, some quite misleading variances may well be produced.

It was explained earlier that in order to prepare their budgets, managers (especially those directly involved in production) will need to be given the budgeted level of activity. Consequently, their budgets will be based on that level of activity. Managers will have to allow for more expenditure on direct materials, direct labour and other expenses the higher the level of activity.

Suppose, for example, that a manager has prepared a cost centre budget on the basis of an anticipated level of activity of 70% of the maximum number of units that the plant is capable of producing. During the actual period, the company is much busier than it expected, and the actual level of activity turns out to be 80%. Almost certainly, those cost centres which have been affected by the increased activity will have spent more on materials and labour than they had budgeted for.

If the actual performance is then compared with the original budget on a fixed budget basis, it will appear as though the manager has greatly exceeded the budget. There is then a tendency to argue that the variances have been caused by the unexpected increase in activity (which may be outside the control of the manager concerned). Whilst this may be true in part, the increased activity may hide variances which the manager should have been able to control.

This problem may be overcome by *flexing* the budget, that is revising it on the basis of what it would have been if the manager had budgeted for an activity level of 80% instead of 70%. The other assumptions and calculations made at the time the budget was prepared (such as material prices and wage rates) will not be amended.

If the entity operates a flexible budget system, the original budgets may be prepared on the basis of a wide range of possible activity levels. This method, however, is very time-consuming, and the entity will be very lucky to prepare one that is exactly identical to the actual level of activity. The best method is to wait until the actual level of activity is known, and then take the original budget data and flex (or amend) it accordingly.

The procedure is illustrated in Exhibit 14.3.

Exhibit 14.3: Flexible budget procedure

The following information had been prepared for Carp Limited for the year to 30 June 19X6:

	Budget	*Actual*
Level of activity	**50%**	**60%**
	£	**£**
Costs:		
Direct materials	**50,000**	**61,000**
Direct labour	**100,000**	**118,000**
Variable overhead	**10,000**	**14,000**
Total variable cost	**160,000**	**193,000**
Fixed overhead	**40,000**	**42,000**
Total costs	**£200,000**	**£235,000**

Required:
Prepare a flexed budget operating statement for Carp Limited for the year to 30 June 19X6.

Answer to Exhibit 14.3

Carp Limited
Flexed budget operating statement for the year to 30 June 19X6

	Flexed budget	*Actual costs*	*Variance: favourable/ (adverse)*
	£	£	£
Direct materials (1)	60,000	61,000	(1,000)
Direct labour (1)	120,000	118,000	2,000
Variable overhead (1)	12,000	14,000	(2,000)
Total variable costs	192,000	193,000	(1,000)
Fixed overhead (2)	40,000	42,000	(2,000)
Total costs (3)	£232,000	£235,000	£(3,000)

Tutorial notes

1. All the budgeted variable costs have been flexed by 20% because the actual activity was 60% compared with a budgeted level of 50% (i.e. a 20% increase).
2. The budgeted fixed costs are not flexed because by definition they ought not to change with activity.
3. Instead of using the total fixed budget cost of £200,000 (as per the question), the total flexed budget costs of £232,000 can be compared more fairly with the total actual cost of £235,000.
4. Note that the terms 'favourable' and 'adverse' (as applied to variances) mean favourable or adverse to profit. In other words, profit will be either greater or less than the budgeted profit.

5 The reasons for the variances between the actual costs and the flexed budget will need to be investigated. The flexed budget shows that even allowing for the increased activity, the actual costs were in excess of the budget allowance.
6 Similarly, it will be necessary to investigate why the actual activity was higher than the budgeted activity. It could have been caused by inefficient budgeting, or by quite an unexpected increase in sales activity. Whilst this would normally be welcome, it might have placed a strain on the productive and financial resources of the entity. Consequently, if the increase is likely to be permanent, management will need to make immediate arrangements to accommodate the new level of activity.

It should be emphasized that the primary purpose of a budgetary control system is to control as closely as possible the activities of the entity. There will invariably be variances between the actual and the budgeted results no matter how carefully the budgets are prepared. This does not matter unduly, as long as it is possible to find out why the variances occurred and to take action before it is too late to do anything about them.

Conclusion

This chapter has argued that the full benefits of a cost and management accounting system can best be gained if a budgetary control system is superimposed upon it. The preparation of budgets is a valuable exercise in itself. It forces management to look ahead to what might happen rather than to look back to what did happen. However, it is even more valuable if it is also used as a form of control.

Budgetary control enables actual results to be frequently measured against an agreed plan. Departures from that plan can be quickly spotted, and steps taken to correct any unwelcome trends. However, the comparison of actual results with a fixed budget may not be particularly helpful if the company has operated at a different level of activity from the budgeted level. It is preferable, therefore, to compare actual results with a flexed budget.

It will, of course, be necessary for the variance between the actual level of activity and the budgeted level to be carefully investigated. As so many of the functional budgets are based upon the budgeted level of activity, it is vital that it be calculated as accurately as possible, since an error in estimating the level of activity will affect all of the company's financial and operational activities.

The next chapter deals with standard costing. Standard costing is a technique which is very similar to budgetary control, although it involves much more detail.

Questions

14.1 You are presented with the following information for Moray Limited.

Budgeted sales units for the six months to 30 June 19X1

January	200
February	250
March	370
April	400
May	500
June	550

Additional information:

1 Opening stock at 1 January 19X1 was expected to be 320 units.
2 Desired closing stock level at 30 June 19X1 was 450 units.

Required:
Calculate the minimum number of units to be produced each month if an even production flow is to be established.

14.2 You have been presented with the following budgeted information relating to Jordan Limited for the six months to 31 December 19X2:

	July	*August*	*September*	*October*	*November*	*December*
Sales (units)	70	140	350	190	150	120
Closing stock (units)	230	370	200	190	180	100

Additional information:
Opening stock at 1 July 19X2 is expected to be 100 units.

Required:
Calculate the monthly production levels required to meet the above budgeted data.

14.3 The directors of Dalton Limited have been presented with the following budgeted information for the six months to 30 June 19X3:

	January	*February*	*March*	*April*	*May*	*June*
Sales (units)	90	150	450	150	130	120

Additional information:

1 The opening stock at 1 January 19X3 is expected to be 100 units.
2 Units are only available for sale in the period following the month in which they were manufactured.

Required:
Calculate the minimum number of units to be produced each month in order to meet the budgeted monthly sales figures assuming that the directors wish to adopt the minimum possible production flow.

14.4 The following information has been prepared for Tom Limited for the six months to 30 September 19X4:

Budgeted production levels Product X	
	Units
April	140
May	280
June	700
July	380
August	300
September	240

Product X uses two units of component A6 and three units of component B9. At 1 April 19X4 there were expected to be 100 units of A6 in stock, and 200 units of B9. The desired closing stock levels of each component were as follows:

Month end 19X4	*A6 (units)*	*B9 (units)*
30 April	110	250
31 May	220	630
30 June	560	340
31 July	300	300
31 August	240	200
30 September	200	180

During the six months to 30 September 19X4, component A6 was expected to be purchased at a cost of £5 per unit and component B9 at a cost of £10 per unit.

Required:
Prepare the following budgets for each of the six months to 30 September 19X4:

1 direct materials usage budget; and
2 direct materials purchase budget.

14.5 Don Limited has one major product which requires two types of direct labour to produce it. The following data refer to certain budget proposals for the three months to 31 August 19X5:

Month	*Production units*
30.6.X5	600
31.7.X5	700
31.8.X5	650

Direct labour hours required per unit:

	Hours	*Budgeted rate per hour* £
Production	3	4
Finishing	2	8

Required:
Prepare the direct labour cost budget for each of the three months to 31 August 19X5.

14.6 Gorse Limited manufactures one product. The budgeted sales for period 6 are for 10,000 units at a selling price of £100 per unit. Other details are as follows:

1 Two components are used in the manufacture of each unit:

Component	*Number*	*Unit cost of each component*
		£
XY	5	1
WZ	3	0.50

2 Stocks at the beginning of the period are expected to be as follows:
(a) 4,000 units of finished goods at a unit cost of £52.50 per unit.
(b) Component XY: 16,000 units at a unit cost of £1.
Component WZ: 9,600 units at a unit cost of £0.50.

3 Two grades of employees are used in the manufacture of each unit:

Employee	*Hours per unit*	*Labour rate per hour*
		£
Production	4	5
Finishing	2	7

4 Factory overhead is absorbed into units cost on the basis of direct labour hours. The budgeted factory overhead for the period is estimated to be £96,000.

5 The administration, selling and distribution overhead for the period has been budgeted at £275,000.

6 The company plans a reduction of 50% in the quantity of finished stock at the end of period 6, and an increase of 25% in the quantity of each component.

Required:
Prepare the following budgets for period 6:
1 sales;
2 production quantity;
3 materials usage;
4 materials purchase;
5 direct labour; and
6 the budgeted profit and loss account for period 6.

14.7 The following budget information relates to Flossy Limited for the three months to 31 March 19X7.

1 Budgeted profit and loss accounts:

Month	31.1.X7	28.2.X7	31.3.X7
	£000	£000	£000
Sales (all on credit)	2,000	3,000	2,500
Cost of sales	1,200	1,800	1,500
Gross profit	800	1,200	1,000

c/fwd

Month		31.1.X7	28.2.X7	31.3.X7
		£000	£000	£000
Gross profit	b/fwd	800	1,200	1,000
Depreciation		(100)	(100)	(100)
Other expenses		(450)	(500)	(600)
		(550)	(600)	(700)
Net profit		£250	£600	£300

2 Budgeted balance sheets:

Budgeted balances	31.12.X6	31.1.X7	28.2.X7	31.3.X7
	£000	£000	£000	£000
Current assets:				
Stocks	100	120	150	150
Debtors	200	300	350	400
Short-term investments	60	—	40	30
Current liabilities:				
Trade creditors	110	180	160	150
Other creditors	50	50	50	50
Taxation	150	—	—	—
Dividends	200	—	—	—

3 Capital expenditure to be incurred on 20 February 19X7 was expected to amount to £470,000.
4 Sales of plant and equipment on 15 March 19X7 are expected to raise £30,000 in cash.
5 The cash at bank and in hand on 1 January 19X7 was expected to be £15,000.

Required:
Prepare Flossy Limited's cash budget for each of the three months during the quarter ending 31 March 19X7.

14.8 Chimes Limited has prepared a flexible budget for one of its factories for the year to 30 June 19X8. The details are as follows:

Production capacity	30%	40%	50%	60%
	£000	£000	£000	£000
Direct materials	42	56	70	84
Direct labour	18	24	30	36
Factory overhead	22	26	30	34
Administration overhead	17	20	23	26
Selling and distribution overhead	12	14	16	18
	£111	£140	£169	£198

Additional information:
1 The company is only operating at 45% of its capacity, and an increase in capacity during the year to 30 June 19X8 is unlikely. At that capacity, the

sales revenue has been budgeted at a level of £135,500.

2 It would be possible to close the factory down for twelve months, and then re-open it again on 1 July 19X8 when trading conditions are beginning to improve. The costs of doing so are estimated to be as follows.

	£000
Redundancy and other closure costs	30
Property and plant maintenance during the year to 30 June 19X8	10
Re-opening costs	20

However, £30,000 would be saved as a result of a reduction in general company and factory fixed overheads.

Required:
Determine whether the factory should be closed during the year to 30 June 19X8.

15 Standard costing

Standard costing is an extension of budgetary control. In standard costing, however, instead of just preparing a budget for a particular department, an attempt is made to prepare a budget for each unit (or each process) that flows through that department. The budgeted unit (or process) cost is referred to as the *standard cost*. The system is also similar to budgetary control in that the standard cost of each unit is compared with the actual unit cost. Immediate action is then taken to correct any adverse trends.

Whilst there are close similarities between budgetary control and standard costing, much greater detail is required in standard costing. For example, not only is the total variance between the actual cost of a particular unit and the standard cost calculated, but it is also analysed into its constituent elements. The degree of analysis depends partly upon management requirements, and partly upon the type of product being produced. This type of detailed analysis is known as *variance analysis*.

The calculation of the variances is largely a routine arithmetical exercise, and the non-accountant is unlikely to be involved in it. You are more likely to be responsible for investigating the reasons why variances have arisen. It is much easier to investigate their causes, however, if you know where to look for the main variances. If you have been able to find out, for example, that a variance has arisen mainly because of overspending on direct materials, then you can begin to investigate whether it was caused by an increase in material prices or because more material was used.

Although budgetary control and standard costing adopt very similar principles, not all entities can incorporate standard costing into their control procedures. Standard costing is really only suitable where the company is producing a product. In order to produce standard costs it is necessary to prepare cost centre budgets. It follows, therefore, that it is possible to have a budgetary control system without having a standard costing system, but it is impossible to have a standard costing system without having a budgetary control system.

This chapter basically falls into two main parts. In the first part the background to standard costing is examined and in the second part variance analysis is considered at some length.

Administration

In the introduction to this chapter it was explained that standard costing is an extension of a budgetary control system. The responsibility for administering it will, therefore, either be that of the budget committee or of the accounting function. The detailed procedure is considered in the following subsections.

The standard costing period

The overall period for which the standards are prepared will normally conform with the main and sub-budget periods. It may also be necessary (as it sometimes is with budgeting) to adopt fairly short standard costing periods, for example where market and production conditions are subject to frequent changes or where it is difficult to plan ahead for very long periods of time. As the selling price charged to customers will usually be based on the standard cost of a particular unit, it would be unwise to fix the selling price based on out-of-date information simply because that was the standard cost for the period, no matter how long ago it was determined.

Types of standard

The preparation of standard costs requires great care and attention to detail. As each element of cost is subject to detailed arithmetical analysis and investigation, it is important that the initial information is accurate. Indeed, the information produced by a standard costing system will be virtually useless if subsequent analyses reveal that the main cause of any variance was inefficient budgeting and standard setting.

In preparing standard costs, management will need to be informed of the level of activity to be used in preparing the standard costs. An activity level should be chosen that is capable of being achieved. It would be possible to choose a standard that was *ideal*, that is one that represented a performance that could be achieved only under the most favourable of conditions. Such a standard, however, would be unrealistic, because it is rare for ideal conditions to be experienced.

A much more practical standard to adopt is an *expected* standard. An expected standard is one that the entity can expect to attain in reasonably efficient working conditions. In other words, it accepts that some delays and inefficiencies will occur, but it assumes that management will attempt to minimize them.

In the short run, it may be necessary to adopt the *current* standard. By accepting the current standard, the entity is accepting that it takes time to eliminate all the obvious inefficiencies, but it will plan on the basis of current conditions until it can move to a reasonably attainable standard. Hence entities should only plan to use current standards for a short time before they move to an expected standard.

Preparation

Standard costing is a sophisticated means of planning and controlling an entity's operations. The standard costs themselves are time-consuming to prepare, costly to produce and expensive to operate. The technique requires so much detailed information that most employees need to be convinced of its value if it is to work properly. Consequently, the preparation of standard costs calls for considerable team-work.

There is no point in having a standard costing system if those who are supposed to benefit from it regard it as having no value. If standard costing is to operate effectively its purpose has to be understood by the employees, because they will be responsible for preparing the basic information. If this is done ineffectively or inefficiently, then any decision based upon it will be questionable.

The type of information required to produce standard costs can be summarized as follows:

1 Direct materials: types, quantities and price.
2 Direct labour: grades, numbers and rates of pay.
3 Variable overhead: the total variable overhead cost analysed into various categories such as employee and general support costs.
4 Fixed overhead: the total fixed overhead analysed into various categories such as employee costs, building costs and general administration expenses.

From the above information, it can be seen that the standard cost of a particular unit comprises four main elements:

1 direct materials;
2 direct labour;
3 variable overhead; and
4 fixed overhead.

In turn, each element comprises two factors, namely quantity and price. Thus the total standard cost of a specific unit is built-up as follows:

		£
1	Direct materials:	
	Quantity × price	X
2	Direct labour:	
	Hours × hourly rate	X
3	Variable overhead:	
	Hours × variable overhead absorption rate per hour	X
	c/fwd	X

	£
b/fwd	X
4 Fixed overhead:	
Hours × fixed overhead absorption rate per hour	X
Total standard cost per unit	X

Note: The above summary assumes that the unit cost is calculated on the basis of standard *absorption* costing. This is the most common method of standard costing, although it is possible to adopt a system of standard *marginal* costing.

If the standard costs are prepared on the basis of absorption costing, overhead will be absorbed on the basis of standard hours (in a non-standard costing system, you will recall, overhead is absorbed on the basis of actual hours). A standard hour represents the amount of work that should be performed in an hour, given that it is produced in standard conditions, that is in *planned* conditions. Each unit is given a standard time of so many hours in which it should be produced, and it is against that standard that the actual hours will be compared.

In order to calculate the standard overhead cost of a unit the standard overhead absorption rate for the period is multiplied by the number of *standard* (not actual) hours that the unit should have taken to produce.

The absorption of overhead by multiplying the standard absorption rate by the standard hours is a significant departure from that adopted in a non-standard costing system. This is a most important point, and it will be returned to a little later on in the chapter.

Some companies also prepare standard costs for sales, although they are not as common as cost variances. If sales variances are to be prepared, the difference between the actual sales revenue and the standard revenue is analysed into a number of representative sales variances. A detailed analysis of the budgeted sales will be needed in order to obtain the following information:

1 the range and number of each product to be sold;
2 the selling price of each product;
3 the respective periods in which sales are to take place; and
4 the geographical areas in which they are to be sold.

Control ratios

In Chapter 8 the main financial accounting ratios were discussed. In a standard costing system it is also possible to extract a number of ratios. In particular, there are three important control ratios. These inform management about the level of efficiency that the entity has achieved and enable management to spot unfavourable trends so that immediate corrective action can be taken.

Before these three control ratios are examined yet again one most important point must be emphasized. In standard costing, actual costs are compared with the standard cost of the *actual* level of activity achieved. It is tempting to compare the actual costs with the budgeted cost, but it is not customary to do so in standard costing. By comparing the actual cost with the standard cost of the actual production, the budget is effectively being flexed. This means that any variances that do then arise can be more realistically assessed, because the same level of activity is then being used to measure the actual costs against the budgeted costs.

Bearing this point in mind, the three control ratios can now be introduced in the following subsections.

The productivity (or efficiency) ratio

This ratio compares the total standard (or allowed) hours of units produced with the total actual hours taken to produce those units. It is calculated as follows:

$$\frac{\text{Standard hours of production} \times 100}{\text{Actual hours worked}}$$

The productivity ratio enables management to check whether the company has produced the units in more or less time than it was allowed.

The capacity ratio

The capacity ratio compares the total actual hours worked with the total budgeted hours. It is calculated as follows:

$$\frac{\text{Actual hours worked} \times 100}{\text{Budgeted hours}}$$

This ratio enables management to ascertain whether all of the budgeted hours were used to produce actual units.

The production/volume ratio

This ratio compares the total allowed hours for the work actually produced with the total budgeted hours. It is calculated as follows:

$$\frac{\text{Standard hours of production} \times 100}{\text{Budgeted hours}}$$

The production/volume ratio enables management to compare the work produced (measured in terms of standard hours) with the budgeted hours of work. This ratio gives management some information about how effective the company has been in using the budgeted hours.

The productivity, capacity and production/volume ratios are illustrated in Exhibit 15.1.

Exhibit 15.1

The following information relates to the Frost Production Company Limited for the year to 31 March 19X4:

1 Budgeted direct labour hours: 1,000.
2 Budgeted units: 100.
3 Actual direct labour hours worked: 800.
4 Actual units produced: 90.

Required:
Calculate the following control ratios:
(a) the productivity ratio;
(b) the capacity ratio; and
(c) the production/volume ratio.

Answer to Exhibit 15.1

(a) The productivity ratio:

$$\frac{\text{Standard hours of production}}{\text{Actual hours worked}} \times 100 = \frac{900^*}{800} \times 100 = \underline{\underline{112.5\%}}$$

*Each unit is allowed 10 standard hours (1,000 hours/100 units), and since 90 units were produced, the total standard hours of production = 900.

It would appear that the company has been more efficient in producing the goods that it did. It was allowed 900 hours to do so, but it produced them in only 800 hours.

(b) The capacity ratio:

$$\frac{\text{Actual hours worked}}{\text{Budgeted hours}} \times 100 = \frac{800}{1{,}000} = \underline{\underline{80\%}}$$

In this case, all of the time planned to be available (the capacity) was not utilized, either because it was not possible to work 1,000 direct labour hours, or because the company did not undertake as much work as it could have done.

(c) The production/volume ratio:

$$\frac{\text{Standard hours of production}}{\text{Budgeted hours}} \times 100 = \frac{900^*}{1{,}000} \times 100 = \underline{\underline{90\%}}$$

*As calculated for the productivity ratio.

It appears that if the 90 units had been produced in standard conditions, another 100 hours would have been available (10 units × 10 hours). In fact, since the 90 units only took 800 hours to produce, at least another 20 units could have been produced in standard conditions

$$\frac{1{,}000 - 80}{10} = \underline{\underline{20 \text{ units}}}$$

Comment on the results

The budget allowed for 100 units to be produced and each unit was expected to take 10 direct labour hours to complete, a total budgeted activity of 1,000 direct labour hours. However, only 90 units were actually produced. If these units had been produced in standard time, they should have taken 900 hours (90 units × 10 direct labour hours). These are the standard hours of production. In fact, the 90 units were completed in 800 actual hours. It appears, therefore, that the units were produced more efficiently than had been expected. The management will still need, of course, to investigate why only 90 units were produced and not the 100 budgeted units.

Variance analysis

As outlined earlier, any difference between actual costs and standard costs is comprised of two main variances: price and quantity. As far as profit is concerned, these variances may either be favourable (F) to profit or adverse (A). This means that the actual prices paid or costs incurred can be either more than was anticipated (adverse to profit) or less than anticipated (favourable to profit).

Similarly, the quantities used in production can result in more being used (adverse to profit) or less than expected (favourable to profit).

It is possible to analyse each element of cost into price and quantity variances (although they are not always referred to as such). The main cost variances may be summarized as follows:

1 Direct material cost variance = Direct material price variance + Direct material usage variance.
2 Direct labour cost variance = Direct labour rate variance + Direct labour efficiency variance.
3 Variable production overhead variance: it is possible to analyse this variance into price and quantity (referred to as volume), but this is not usually done.
4 Fixed production overhead variance = Fixed production expenditure variance + Fixed production volume variance. (The Fixed production volume variance is usually subanalysed as follows: Fixed production volume variance = Fixed production capacity variance + Fixed production productivity variance.)

The main variances are shown in diagrammatic form in Exhibit 15.2.

Exhibit 15.2: Standard costing - analysis of variances

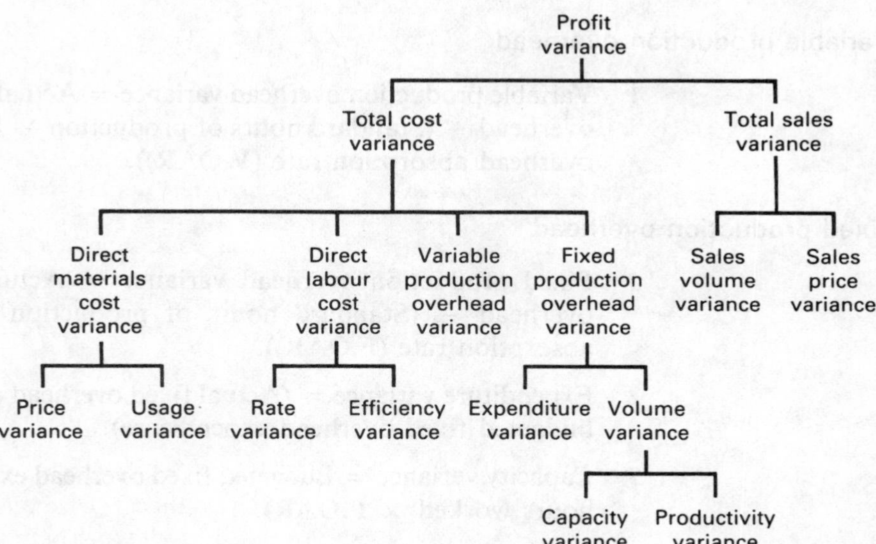

Variance analysis formulae

Before the calculation of cost variances is explained it would be useful at this stage if the basic formulae were summarized for convenient reference in later exhibits.

The formulae used in calculating the main standard cost variances are as in the following subsections.

Direct materials

1 Cost variance = (Actual price per unit × Actual quantity used) − (Standard price per unit × Standard quantity for actual production).

2 Price variance = (Actual price per unit − Standard price per unit) × Total actual quantity used.

3 Usage variance = (Total actual quantity used − Standard quantity for actual production) × Standard price.

Direct labour

1 Cost variance = (Actual hourly rate × Actual hours) − (Standard hourly rate × Standard hours for actual production).

2 Rate variance = (Actual hourly rate − Standard hourly rate) × Actual hours worked.

3 Efficiency variance = (Actual hours worked − Standard hours for actual production) × Standard hourly rate.

Variable production overhead

1 Variable production overhead variance = Actual variable production overhead − (Standard hours of production × Variable production overhead absorption rate (V.OAR)).

Fixed production overhead

1 Fixed production overhead variance = Actual fixed production overhead − (Standard hours of production × Fixed overhead absorption rate (F.OAR)).

2 Expenditure variance = (Actual fixed overhead expenditure − Total budgeted fixed overhead expenditure).

3 Capacity variance = Budgeted fixed overhead expenditure − (Actual hours worked × F.OAR).

4 Productivity variance = (Actual hours worked − Standard hours for actual production) × F.OAR.

5 Volume variance = Budgeted fixed overhead expenditure − (Standard hours for actual production × F.OAR).

NB: Capacity variance = Productivity variance + Volume variance.

An illustrative example

The calculation of the main cost variances will now be illustrated in Exhibit 15.3.

Exhibit 15.3

The following information has been extracted from the records of the Frost Production Company Limited for the year to 31 March 19X4:

Budgeted costs per unit:	£
Direct materials (15 kilograms × £2 per kilogram)	30
Direct labour (10 hours × £4 per direct labour hour)	40
Variable overhead (10 hours × £1 per direct labour hour)	10
Fixed overhead (10 hours × £2 per direct labour hour)	20
Total budgeted cost per unit	£100

The following budgeted data are also relevant:

1 The budgeted production level was 100 units.
2 The total standard direct labour hours amounted to 1,000.
3 The total budgeted variable overhead was estimated to be £1,000.

4 The total budgeted fixed overhead was £2,000.
5 The company absorbs both fixed and variable overhead on the basis of direct labour hours.

	£
Direct materials	2,100
Direct labour	4,000
Variable overhead	1,000
Fixed overhead	1,600
Total actual costs	£8,700

Note: 90 units were produced in 800 actual hours, and the total actual quantity of direct materials consumed was 1,400 kilograms.

Required:
Calculate the direct materials, direct labour, variable overhead and fixed overhead cost variances.

Answer to Exhibit 15.3

To begin the answer to this question first summarize the total variance for each element of cost:

Actual units produced	*Actual costs* (1)	*Total standard cost for actual production*		*Variance*	
	£	£		£	
Direct materials	2,100	2,700	(1)	600	(F)
Direct labour	4,000	3,600	(2)	(400)	(A)
Variable overhead	1,000	900	(3)	(100)	(A)
Fixed overhead	1,600	1,800	(4)	200	(F)
Total	£8,700	£9,000		£300	(F)

Notes:
(a) F = favourable to profit; A = adverse to profit.
(b) The numbers in brackets refer to the tutorial notes below.

Tutorial notes

1 The standard cost of direct materials for actual production = the actual units produced × the standard direct material cost per unit, i.e. 90 × £30 = £2,700.
2 The standard cost of direct labour for actual production = the actual units produced × standard direct labour cost per unit, i.e. 90 × £40 = £3,600.
3 The standard variable cost for actual performance = the actual units produced × variable overhead absorption rate per unit, i.e. 90 × £10 = £900.
4 The fixed overhead cost for the actual performance = the actual units produced × fixed overhead absorption rate, i.e. 90 × £20 = £1,800.

It can be seen from Exhibit 15.3 that the total actual cost of producing the 90 units was £300 less than the budget allowance. An investigation would need to be held in order to find out why only 90 units were produced when the company had budgeted for 100 units. In addition, although the 90 units have cost £300 less than might have been expected, a number of other variances have contributed to the overall variance. Assuming that these variances are considered significant, they would need to be carefully investigated in order to find out what caused them. Both the direct materials and the fixed overhead, for example, cost £600 and £200 respectively less than the budget allowance, whilst the direct labour cost £400 and the variable overhead £100 more than might have been expected.

As a result of calculating the variances for each element of cost, it would now be much easier for management to investigate why the actual production cost was £300 less than might have been expected. However, the accountant can provide even greater guidance by analysing the variances into their major causes. How this is achieved will be explained by examining each element of cost in turn. First the calculation of the respective variances is shown, and then a brief explanation of what might have caused them is given.

Direct materials

1 Direct materials price variance = (Actual price per unit − Standard price per unit) × Total actual quantity used.
∴ The price variance = (£1.50 − 2.00) × 1,400 kg
= £700 (F)

The actual price per unit was £1.50 (£2,100/1,400) and the standard price was £2.00 per unit. There was, therefore, a total saving (as far as the price of the materials is concerned) of £700 (£0.50 × 1,400).

2 Direct materials usage variance = (Total actual quantity used − Standard quantity for actual production) × Standard price.
∴ The usage variance = (1,400 − 1,350) × £2.00
= £100 (A)

Frost should have used 1,350 kilograms (90 × 15 kg) in producing 90 units, but 1,400 kilograms were used. If this extra usage is valued at the standard price (the difference between the actual price and the standard price has already been allowed for), there is an adverse usage variance of £100 (50 kg × £2).

3 Direct materials cost variance = Price variance + Usage
= £700 (F) + £100 (A)
= £600 (F)

The £600 favourable cost variance was shown earlier in the cost summary on page 271. This variance might have arisen because Frost purchased cheaper materials. If this was the case, then it probably resulted in a greater wastage of materials because the materials were of an inferior quality.

Direct labour

1 Direct labour rate variance = (Actual labour hourly rate − Standard labour hourly rate) × Actual hours worked.

∴ The rate variance = (£5.00 − 4.00) × 800 DLH
= £800 (A)

The actual hourly rate is £5.00 per DLH (£4,000/800). Every extra actual hour worked, therefore, results in an adverse variance of £1.00, or £800 in total (£1.00 × 800).

2 Direct labour efficiency variance = (Total actual hours worked − Total standard hours for actual production) × Standard hourly rate.

∴ The efficiency variance = (800 − 900) × £4 per hour
= £400 (F)

The actual hours worked were 800. However, 900 hours would have been allowed for the 90 units actually produced (90 × 10 DLH). If these hours are valued at the standard hourly rate (differences between the actual rate and the standard rate have already been allowed for when calculating the rate variance), a favourable variance of £400 arises. The favourable efficiency variance has arisen because the 90 units took less time to produce than the budget allowed.

3 Direct labour cost variance = Rate variance + Efficiency variance
= £800 (A) + £400 (F)
= £400 (A)

The £400 adverse variance was shown earlier in the cost summary on page 271. It arises because the company paid more per direct labour hour than had been budgeted, although this was offset to some extent by the units being produced in less time than the budgeted allowance. This variance could have been caused by using a higher grade of labour than had been intended, but the higher labour rate per hour was not completely offset by greater efficiency.

Variable production overhead

It is usually not considered necessary to analyse the variable production overhead variance into sub-variances (although it is possible to do so). The adverse variance, therefore, of £100 (A) (as shown earlier in the summary of variances on page 271) arises because the variable overhead absorption rate was calculated on the basis of a budgeted cost of £10 per unit. In fact the absorption rate ought to have been £11.11 per unit

(£1,000/90), because the total actual variable cost was £1,000. There would, of course, be no variable production overhead cost for the ten units that were not produced.

Fixed production overhead

1 Fixed overhead expenditure variance = Actual fixed overhead expenditure − Budgeted fixed overhead expenditure.
∴ Expenditure variance = £1,600 − £2,000
= £400 (F)

The budgeted expenditure was £400 in excess of the actual expenditure. This means that the fixed production overhead absorption rate (F.OAR) was £400 higher than it needed to have been assuming that there were no other fixed overhead variances.

2 Fixed production volume variance = Budgeted fixed overhead − (Standard hours of production × F.OAR).
∴ Volume variance = £2,000 − (900 × £2.00)
= £200 (A)

As a result of producing fewer units than the budget had anticipated, £200 *less* overhead has been absorbed into production.

3 Fixed production overhead capacity variance = Budgeted fixed overhead − (Actual hours worked × F.OAR).
∴ Capacity variance = £2.00 − (800 × £2.00)
= £400 (A)

The capacity variance shows that the actual hours worked were less than the budgeted hours. Other things being equal, therefore, not enough overhead would have been absorbed into production. It should be noted that the capacity variance will be *favourable* when the actual hours are in excess of the budgeted hours. This might seem odd, but it means that the company has been able to use more hours than it had originally budgeted. Consequently, it should have been able to produce more units, thereby absorbing more overhead into production. This variance links with the capacity ratio calculated earlier in the chapter. The capacity ratio showed that, in Frost's case, only 80% of the budgeted capacity had been utilized, and as a result, probably not as much overhead was absorbed into production as had been originally expected.

4 Fixed production overhead productivity variance = (Total actual hours worked − Total standard hours for actual production) × F.OAR.
∴ Productivity variance = (800 − 900) × £2,000
= £200 (F)

This variance shows the difference between the 900 standard hours that the work is worth (90 × 10 = 900 hours), compared with the amount of time that it took to produce those units (i.e. 800 hours). As explained earlier, in a standard costing system overhead is absorbed on the basis of standard hours. Assuming, therefore, that the budgeted fixed overhead expenditure had been equal to the actual fixed overhead expenditure, production would have been charged with £200 of extra overhead because the 90 units were produced in less time than the standard allowance. The factory has been *more* efficient in producing the goods than might have been expected. This variance complements the productivity (or efficiency) ratio of 112.5% which was illustrated earlier in the chapter.

Remember:

Capacity variance + Productivity variance = Volume variance.
∴ Volume variance = £400 (A) + £200 (F)
= £200 (A)
(See also 2 above.)

5 Fixed production overhead variance. This variance was calculated earlier (shown on the summary of variances on page 271). The simplified formula is as follows:

Overhead variance = Expenditure variance + Volume variance
= £400 (F) + £200 (A)
= £200(F)

The actual activity was less than the budgeted activity. Thus less fixed overhead was absorbed into production. However, the overhead expenditure was budgeted at a level of £2,000, but the actual expenditure was only £1,600. The overestimate of expenditure, therefore, compensated for the overestimate of activity. This means that the 90 units actually produced were charged £200 more of overhead than was necessary. If the selling price is based on standard costs, it is possible that this overestimate could make their eventual selling price less competitive. In this example, however, the variance would appear to be very small.

A considerable number of variances have now been worked through. Using the formulae listed on pp. 269–70, you are recommended to attempt Exhibit 15.2 again without reference to the solution.

Sales variances

It was suggested earlier that sales variances are not common in practice. If adopted, there is a choice between two different types: (1) variances based on sales value; and (2) variances based on sales margin. Sales value variances are based on actual and budgeted selling prices. Sales margin variances allow for the cost of selling the goods, the margin being defined as the difference between the sales revenue of units sold and the *standard* cost of those sales. The standard cost may be based either on absorption costing or marginal costing.

Assuming that it has been decided to use sales variances, it is recommended that the sales margin method be used whenever possible as this method highlights the effect on profit of sales. However, in this section both types of variances will be examined.

The formulae to be used in calculating sales variances are summarized in the subsections below. The summary is in two parts: the first part showing the formulae for sales value variances, and the second part the formulae for sales margin variances. (See Exhibit 15.4.)

Sales value variances

1 Sales value total variance:
Total variance = (Actual selling price per unit × Actual quantity) − (Standard selling price per unit × Budgeted quantity).

2 Sales value selling price variance:
Price variance = (Actual selling price per unit − Standard selling price per unit) × Total quantity of units sold.

3 Sales value volume variance:
Volume variance = (Total actual quantity of units sold − Total budgeted quantity) × Standard selling price.

4 Note that the Total variance (1) = Price (2) + Volume (3).

Sales margin variances

1 Sales margin operating profit due to sales variance:
Operating profit variance = [(Actual selling price per unit − standard cost per unit) × Actual quantity] − (Standard margin × Budgeted quantity).

2 Sales margin due to selling price variance:
Selling price variance = [(Actual selling price per unit − Standard cost per unit) × actual quantity] − (Standard margin per unit × Actual quantity).

3 Sales margin due to sales volume variance:
Sales volume variance = (Actual quantity − Budgeted quantity) × Standard margin.

4 Note that the Operating profit due to sales variance (1) = Due to selling price (2) + Due to sales volume (3).

The use of these formulae is illustrated in Exhibit 15.4.

Exhibit 15.4

The following data relate to Frozen Limited for the year to 31 July 19X9:

	Budget/standard	*Actual*
Sales	100 units	90 units
Selling price per unit	£10	£10.50
Standard absorption cost per unit	£7	—

Required:
Calculate the following sales variances:
1 sales value variances; and
2 sales margin variances.

Answer to Exhibit 15.4

1 *Sales value variances*

(a) Sales value selling price variance:
Price variance = (Actual selling price per unit − Standard selling price per unit) × Total actual quantity of units sold.
∴ Selling price variance = (£10.50 − 10.00) × 90
= £45 (F)

The actual selling price per unit was £0.50 more than the standard selling price, so an overall total favourable variance arises. Other things being equal, profit would have been £45 higher than had been anticipated.

(b) Sales value volume variance:
Volume variance = (Total actual quantity of units sold − Total budgeted quantity) × Standard selling price per unit.
∴ Volume variance = (90 − 100) × £10.00
= £100 (A)

Ten fewer units were sold than had been envisaged, and so the effect on sales revenue (ignoring any price variance) would be to reduce the total sales revenue by £100.

(c) Sales value total variance. We can calculate the sales value total variance either by adding together the price variance and the volume variance (£45 (F) + £100 (A) = £55 (A)), or by using the detailed formula:
Total variance = (Actual selling price per unit × Actual quantity) − (Standard selling price per unit × Budgeted quantity).
∴ Total variance = (£10.50 × 90) − (£10.00 × 100)
= £945 − £1,000
= £55 (A)

The £55 adverse variance arises partly because the number of units sold was only 90 compared with a budgeted quantity of 100 units. However, the reduction in volume (which caused an adverse variance) was compensated by an increase in the selling price of each unit. It is possible that the price increase caused the sales volume to drop, but this point would need to be carefully investigated.

2 *Sales margin variances*

(a) Sales margin variance due to selling price:
Price variance = [(Actual selling price per unit − Standard cost per unit) × Actual quantity] − (Standard margin per unit × Actual quantity).

∴ Price variance = [(£10.50 − 7.00) × 90] − [(£10.00 − 7.00) × 90]
= £315 − £270
= £45 (F)

The sales margin variance due to selling price should be exactly the same as that calculated by the sales value method.

(b) Sales margin variance due to sales volume:
Volume variance = (Actual quantity − Budgeted quantity) × Standard margin.
∴ Volume variance = (100 − 90) × (£10.00 − £7.00)
= £30 (A)

This margin variance arises because the number of units sold fell below the budgeted level, thereby affecting the overall amount of profit (or margin) achieved.

(c) Sales margin operating profit due to sales variance. This variance is the total of the selling price variance and the sales volume variance, i.e. £45 (F) + £30 (A) = £15 (F). It may also be calculated by formula:
Operating profit variance = [(Actual selling price per unit − Standard cost per unit) × Actual quantity] − (Standard margin × Budgeted quantity).
∴ Operating profit variance = [(£10.50 − £7.00) × 90] − (£3 × 100)
= £15 (F)

The favourable selling price variance of £45 (or £0.50 per unit) helped to offset the adverse volume variance of £30 caused by selling ten fewer units. It should be noted that the *standard* cost is used in calculating sales margin variances. Any variance between actual costs and standard costs will be extracted as part of the cost analysis.

You are now recommended to work through Exhibit 15.4 without reference to the answer, although you may need to refer to the sales variance formulae listed on page 276.

Operating statements

As seen, the calculation of standard cost variances is a complex arithmetical process. This process can become even more complicated if the variances outlined in the preceding sections are analysed into sub-variances. Fortunately for the non-accountant, it is unlikely that he or she will ever have to calculate such variances personally. However, it is important to have some knowledge of how they are calculated in order to be in a better position to investigate how they may have occurred. Indeed, the non-accountant's main role in variance analysis will probably be to carry out a detailed investigation of their causes, and then to take any necessary corrective action.

Once all the variances have been calculated, they may usefully be summarized in an operating statement. There is no standardized format for such statements, but the one shown in Exhibit 15.5 is reasonably representative.

Exhibit 15.5: Example of a standard cost operating statement

	Adverse	Favourable	
			£
Budgeted profit			X
Sales volume variance			X
			X
Standard margin of actual sales			X
Sales price variance			X
			X
Actual margin of actual sales			
Cost variances:	*Adverse*	*Favourable*	
	£	£	
Direct materials:			
Price			
Usage			
Direct labour:			
Rate			
Efficiency			
Variable production overhead			
Fixed production overhead			
Expenditure			
Capacity			
Productivity			
	X	X	X
Less: Actual non-production overhead:			
Administration		X	
Research and development		X	
Selling and distribution		X	
Actual profit			£X

The above format is particularly valuable because it shows in detail the link between the budgeted profit and the actual profit. Consequently, management can trace the main causes of sales and cost variances. In practice, the statement would also show the details for each product.

The operating profit statement will help management to decide where to begin an investigation into the causes of the respective variances. It is unlikely that they will all need to be investigated. It may be company policy, for example, to investigate only those variances which are particularly significant irrespective of whether they are favourable or adverse variances. In other words, only *exceptional* variances would be investigated, and a policy decision would have to be taken on how 'exceptional' should be defined.

Conclusion

This has been a long and complex chapter. You may have found that it has been difficult to understand just how standard cost variances are calculated. However, as stressed on several occasions throughout the chapter, it is unlikely that you personally will have to calculate them for yourself. It is sufficient for your purpose to understand their meaning and have *some* idea of the arithmetical foundation upon which they are built.

The non-accountant's main responsibility will be to investigate the causes of the variances, and to take action if there are any unwelcome trends. A standard costing system is supposed to help management plan and control the entity much more tightly than can be achieved in the absence of such a system. However, it can only be of real benefit if it is accepted by those managers whom it is supposed to help. It can hardly be of help to management if all it does is produce a lot of incomprehensible data. Comprehension comes with understanding and knowledge. It is hoped that this chapter has helped in that respect.

The next chapter deals with the problems of capital investment. Such problems may come to light, for example, as a result of trying to match the sales forecasts with the production capacity. Thus the budgeting and standard costing exercises may lead to a review of capital investment requirements.

Questions

15.1 You are presented with the following information for X Limited:

Standard price per unit: £10.
Standard quantity for actual production: 5 units.
Actual price per unit: £12.
Actual quantity: 6 units.

Required:
Calculate the following variances:
1 direct materials cost variance;
2 direct materials price variance; and
3 direct materials usage variance.

15.2 The following information relates to Malcolm Limited.

Budgeted production: 100 units.
Unit specification (direct materials): 50 Kilograms × £5 per kilogram = £250.
Actual production: 120 units.
Direct materials used: 5,400 kilograms at a total cost of £32,400.

Required:
Calculate the following variances:
1 direct materials cost;
2 direct materials price; and
3 direct materials usage.

15.3 The following information relates to Bruce Limited:

Actual hours: 1,000.
Actual wage rate per hour: £6.50.
Standard hours for actual production: 900.
Standard wage rate per hour: £6.00.

Required:
Calculate the following variances:
1 direct labour cost;
2 direct labour rate; and
3 direct labour efficiency.

15.4 You are presented with the following information for Duncan Limited:

Budgeted production: 1,000 units.
Actual production: 1,200 units.
Standard specification for one unit: 10 hours at £8 per direct labour hour.
Actual direct labour cost: £97,200 in 10,800 actual hours.

Required:
Calculate the following variances:
1 direct labour cost:
2 direct labour rate; and
3 direct labour efficiency.

15.5 The following overhead budget has been prepared for Anthea Limited:

Actual fixed overhead: £150,000.
Budgeted fixed overhead: £135,000.
Fixed overhead absorption rate per hour: £15.
Actual hours worked: 10,000.
Standard hours of production: 8,000.

Required:
Calculate the following fixed overhead variances:
1 fixed production overhead variance:
2 expenditure variance;
3 volume variance;
4 capacity variance; and
5 productivity variance.

15.6 Using the data contained in the previous question, calculate the following control ratios:

1 efficiency.
2 capacity; and
3 activity.

15.7 The following information relates to Osprey Limited:

Budgeted production: 500 units.

Standard hours per unit: 10.
Actual production: 600 units.
Budgeted fixed overhead: £125,000.
Actual fixed overhead: £120,000.
Actual hours worked: 4,900.

Required:
Calculate the following fixed overhead variances:
1 fixed production overhead;
2 expenditure;
3 volume;
4 capacity; and
5 productivity.

15.8 Using the data from the previous question, calculate the following control ratios:
1 efficiency;
2 capacity; and
3 activity.

15.9 Milton Limited has produced the following information:

Total actual sales: £99,000.
Actual quantity sold: 9,000 units.
Budgeted selling price per unit: £10.
Standard variable cost per unit: £7.
Total budgeted units: 10,000 units.

Required:
Calculate the following sales margin variances:
1 operating profit due to sales;
2 selling price; and
3 sales volume.

15.10 You are presented with the following information for Doe Limited:

Budget sales	100 units
Per unit:	
Budget selling price	£30
Less: Budget variable cost	£20
Contribution	£10
Actual sales	120 units
Actual selling price per unit	£28

Required:
Calculate the following sales variances:
(a) Sales margin variances:
1 operating profit variance due to sales;
2 selling price; and

3 sales volume

(b) Sales value variances:

1 total sales volume variance;
2 selling price; and
3 sales volume.

15.11 The following data relate to Judith Limited:

	Budget specification	
Production at sales budget		2,000 units
Per unit:	£	£
Selling price		150
Less: Variable costs:		
Direct materials (7 kilos × £10 per kilo)	70	
Direct wages (5 DLH × £5 per DLH)	25	
Fixed overhead (5 DLH × £6 F.OAR)	30	125
Budgeted profit per unit		£25
Actual production and sales		2,200 units
Actual selling price per unit		£145
Actual cost:		
Direct material (8 kilos × £9 per kilo)		£72 per unit
Direct wages (4 DLH × £6 per DLH)		£24 per unit
Total actual fixed overhead		£65,000

Required:

(a) Calculate the following control ratios:

1 efficiency.
2 capacity; and
3 activity

(b) Calculate the following variances:

1 sales margin operating profit due to sales;
2 sales margin selling price;
3 sales margin sales volume;
4 direct materials cost;
5 direct materials price;
6 direct materials usage;
7 direct labour cost;
8 direct labour rate variance;
9 direct labour efficiency;
10 fixed production overhead;
11 fixed production overhead expenditure;
12 fixed production overhead volume;
13 fixed production overhead capacity; and
14 fixed production overhead productivity.

(c) Prepare the standard cost operating statement for the period.

16 Capital investment

The preparation of budgets and standard costs may make it clearly apparent that the entity needs to provide for additional capital investment. The sales forecast, for example, may show that there is likely to be an increase in demand for the company's products. However, a review of the productive capacity may confirm that the company cannot meet that forecast unless there is further investment.

Given that the sales forecast is accurate, there should be every incentive to prepare the sales and production budgets to meet that particular forecast. This may be very difficult to achieve in the short term, although every opportunity should be taken to do so, perhaps by the introduction of overtime working. In the long term, the company may have to expand its productive capacity.

Two main problems arise in deciding whether to seek further capital investment:

1 how to assess the profitability of the prospective investment; and
2 how to finance it.

These problems are examined briefly in this chapter. Accountants now use some fairly sophisticated and mathematical techniques to assess project profitability, but as these are beyond the scope of this text the following sections are merely intended to give some idea of what is involved.

Project profitability

There is little point in seeking further capital investment if the project does not eventually make a profit. There are three basic methods accountants use in deciding whether a project is likely to be profitable. They are considered in the following subsections.

Payback

The payback method compares the cost of the investment with the time that it would take for the investment to pay for itself. The investment return is measured in terms of the net cash flow. Net cash flow is the difference between the total amount of cash received during a particular period and the total amount of cash paid out during the same period.

Exhibit 16.1: The payback method

Miln Limited is considering investing in some new machinery. The following information has been prepared to support the project:

	£000	£000
Cost of machinery		20
Expected net cash flow:		
Year 1	1	
2	4	
3	5	
4	10	
5	10	30
Net profitability		£10

Required:
Calculate the prospective investment's payback period.

Answer to Exhibit 16.1

The payback period is as follows:

	£000
Cumulative net cash flow:	
Year 1	1
2	5
3	10
4	20
5	30

Thus the investment will have paid for itself at the end of the fourth year. At that stage £20,000 will have been received back from the project in terms of net cash flow, and that sum would be equal to the original cost of the project.

As can be seen from Exhibit 16.1, the payback method is very simple to operate, but it does have several disadvantages:

1 It is difficult to calculate the net cash flows and to estimate the periods in which they will be received.
2 The project with the shortest payback period would normally be chosen, even though other projects with longer payback periods may eventually prove more profitable.
3 The total amount of the investment is ignored and therefore comparisons made between different projects may lead to a misleading conclusion. Thus a project with an initial investment of £10,000 may have a shorter payback period than one with an initial investment of £100,000, although in the long run, the bigger investment may prove more

profitable.

4 The timing of the cash flows is ignored. A project with a short payback period, for example, may recover most of its investment towards the end of its payback period, whilst another project with a longer payback period may recover most of the original investment in the very early stages. There is clearly less risk in accepting a project which recovers most of its cost very quickly than there is accepting one where the benefits are much more long term.

Notwithstanding these disadvantages, the payback method has something to recommend it. Whilst it may appear to be rather simplistic, it does help managers to compare projects, and to think in terms of how long it takes for a project to pay for itself.

Accounting rate of return

The accounting rate of return method assesses project profitability by relating the average net profit of the project to the cost of the original investment. The relationship is usually expressed in the form of a percentage. The method is illustrated in Exhibit 16.2.

Exhibit 16.2: The accounting rate of return method

Bridge Limited is considering investing in a new project, the details of which are as follows:

Project life		5 years
	£000	£000
Project cost		50
Estimated net profit:		
Year 1	12	
2	18	
3	30	
4	25	
5	5	
Total net profits	£90	

Required:
Calculate the accounting rate of return of the proposed new project.

Answer to Exhibit 16.2

The accounting rate of return would be calculated as follows:

$$\frac{\text{Average annual net profits} \times 100}{\text{Cost of the investment}}$$

Average annual net profits = £18,000 (£90,000/5)

$\therefore$ Accounting rate of return = $\frac{£18,000}{50,000} \times 100 = \underline{\underline{36\%}}$

The accounting rate of return method (like the payback method) also has several disadvantages:

1 *The definition of profit*. Net profit, for example, could mean either net profit before allowing for depreciation on the project, or net profit after allowing for the project's depreciation.
2 *The cost of the project*. There is some doubt whether the original cost of the investment should be used, or whether it is more appropriate to substitute an average for the amount of capital invested in the project.
3 *The rate of return*. The method gives no guidance on what is an acceptable rate of return.
4 *Timing of returns.*. The benefit of earning a high proportion of the total profit in the early years of the project is not taken into account.

The accounting rate of return method, however, may be suitable where very similar short-term projects are being considered.

Discounted cash flow

An increasingly common method of project appraisal is that known as discounted cash flow (DCF). There are two main methods of using DCF in project appraisal: (1) the net present value method (NPV); and (2) the internal rate of return method (IRR). Each of these methods is discussed separately below.

1 The net present value method

The NPV method recognizes that cash received today might be worth more than cash which is receivable in the future. A smaller sum might be available now, but if it is invested, its total value might eventually be in excess of any sum receivable in the future. Thus if £90.91 is available now, and it can be invested at a rate of interest of 10% per annum, it will be worth £100 in one year's time (£90.91 + £9.09). Clearly, in these circumstances, it is preferable to have £90.91 now, rather than to be offered less than £100 in a year's time.

This concept is known as the *time value of money*, and it can be incorporated into project appraisal. Since cash receivable in the future might not be worth as much when it is received as cash which is available now, it would be fairer if they were compared in terms of their present value. To do so, the future net cash flows must be estimated, and then brought back to their present value. Hence this method involves the use of *discounting*. It is also necessary to choose an appropriate rate of interest to use in bringing the future net cash flows back to their present value. The rate of interest chosen might be similar to that which can be obtained by opting for an alternative investment.

It should be noted that future net cash flows are not necessarily worth less because of the effect of inflation (although the declining purchasing power of the monetary unit will be taken into account in assessing future net cash flows). The point is that in DCF calculations, cash receivable in the future is considered to be worth less than cash received now, because cash that is available at present can be used, i.e. invested.

By adopting the NPV method, optional projects can be more fairly assessed, since the total of their respective net present values can be compared. The project with the highest NPV is likely to be the most profitable, although there are other factors to be taken into account, such as projects that are necessary for safety reasons.

To help with DCF calculations a discount table is included in Appendix 1. For example, to work out what the value of £100 receivable in twelve months' time is worth at the present time assuming that it is invested at a rate of return of 10% per annum simply consult the discount table. Look along the top line for the appropriate rate of interest: in this case it is 10%. Work down the 10% column until you come to the line opposite the year (shown in the left-hand column) in which the cash would be received. In this example, the cash is going to be received in one year's time, so it is only necessary to look down to the first line. The present value of £1 receivable in a year's time is, therefore, £0.9091, or £90.91 if £100 is to be received in a year's time. This calculation can be checked by adding 10% (£9.09) to the £90.91. It is correct, because £9.09 + £90.91 equals the £100 that is required to be received in a year's time.

An example of the NPV method is shown in Exhibit 16.3.

Exhibit 16.3: The net present value method

Rage Limited is considering two capital investment projects. The details are outlined below.

Project	1	2
Estimated life	3 years	5 years
Commencement date	1.1.X1	1.1.X1
	£000	£000
Project cost at 1.1.X1	100	100
Estimated net cash flows:		
Year to: 31.12.X1	20	10
31.12.X2	80	40
31.12.X3	40	40
31.12.X4	–	40
31.12.X5	–	20

The company expects a rate of return of 10% per annum on its capital employed.

Required:

Using the net present value method of project appraisal, assess which project would be more profitable.

Answer to Exhibit 16.3

RAGE LIMITED

Project appraisal:

Year	Project 1 Net cash flow	Project 1 Discount factor	Project 1 Present value	Project 2 Net cash flow	Project 2 Discount factor	Project 2 Present value
	£	10%	£	£	10%	£
31.12.X1	20,000	0.9091	18,182	10,000	0.9091	9,091
31.12.X2	80,000	0.8264	66,112	40,000	0.8264	33,056
31.12.X3	40,000	0.7513	30,052	40,000	0.7513	30,052
31.12.X4	—	—	—	40,000	0.6830	27,320
31.12.X5	—	—	—	20,000	0.6209	12,418
Total present value			114,346			111,937
Less: Initial cost			100,000			100,000
Net present value			£14,346			£11,937

Tutorial note

The discount factors have been obtained from the discount table shown in Appendix 1.

Although both projects have a positive NPV, project 1 should be chosen in preference to project 2 because its NPV is higher.

Two main problems arise in adopting the NPV method:

1 It is difficult to calculate the net cash flows for each year during the life of the project (a difficulty which is common to other methods of project appraisal).

2 It is not easy to select an appropriate rate of interest. One rate that could be chosen is that rate which the company could earn if it decided to invest the funds outside the business (the external rate of interest). Alternatively, an internal rate of interest could be chosen. This rate would be based on an estimate of what return the company expects to earn on its existing investments. In the long run if its internal rate of return is lower than the external rate, then it would appear more profitable to liquidate the company and invest the funds elsewhere.

Notwithstanding these problems, the NPV method does take into account the timing of the net cash flows, the project's profitability and the return of the original investment.

2 Internal rate of return method

An alternative method of investment appraisal based on discounted cash flow is the internal rate of return method (IRR). This method requires the calculation of a rate of return which would discount the future net cash flows back to a net present value equal to the original cost of the project. A project would be accepted if the IRR produced a total net present value which was equal to or in excess of the cost of the project. The project would not be accepted, however, if it produced a negative rate of return.

The method is illustrated in Exhibit 16.4.

Exhibit 16.4: The internal rate of return method

Bruce Limited is considering whether to invest £50,000 in a new project. The project's expected net cash flows would be as follows:

Year	£000
1	7
2	25
3	30
4	5

Required:
Calculate the internal rate of return for the proposed new project.

Answer to Exhibit 16.4

BRUCE LIMITED

Calculation of the internal rate of return:

Step 1: Select two discount rates
The first step is to select two discount rates and then using the two rates, calculate the net present value of the project. The two rates usually have to be chosen quite arbitrarily, although they should preferably cover a narrow range. One of the rates should produce a positive rate of return, and the other rate a negative rate of return. As far as this question is concerned rates of 10% and 15% respectively will be chosen to illustrate the method.

Year	*Net cash flow*	*Discount factors*		*Present value*	
		10%	15%	10%	15%
	£			£	£
1	7,000	0.9091	0.8696	6,364	6,087
2	25,000	0.8264	0.7561	20,660	18,903
3	30,000	0.7513	0.6575	22,539	19,725
4	5,000	0.6830	0.5718	3,415	2,859
Total present values				52,978	47,574
Initial cost				50,000	50,000
Net present value				£2,978	£(2,426)

The project is expected to cost £50,000. If the company expects a rate of return of 10%, the project will be accepted, because the NPV is positive. However, if the required rate of return is 15% it will not be accepted, because its NPV is negative. The maximum rate of return which will ensure a positive rate of return must, therefore, lie somewhere between 10% and 15%, so the next step is to calculate the rate of return at which the project would just pay for itself.

Step 2: Calculate the rate of return

In order to calculate an IRR that would enable the project to pay for itself, it is necessary to interpolate between the rates used in Step 1. This can be done by using the following formula:

$$\text{IRR} = \text{Positive rate} + \left(\frac{\text{Positive NPV}}{\text{Positive NPV} - \text{Negative NPV*}} \times \text{Range of rates} \right)$$

*The negative sign is ignored.

$$\begin{aligned} \text{Thus: IRR} &= 10\% + \left(\frac{2{,}978}{(2{,}978 + 2{,}426)} \times (15\% - 10\%) \right) \\ &= 10\% + (0.5511 \times 5\%) \\ &= 10\% + 2.76\% \\ &= \underline{\underline{12.76\%}} \end{aligned}$$

The project will be profitable, therefore, provided that the company does not require a rate of return in excess of about 13%. Note that the method of calculation used above does not give the precise rate of return (because the formula is only an approximation), but it is adequate enough for decision-making purposes.

We can see from Exhibit 16.4 that the IRR method is similar to the NPV method. Future net cash flows have to be estimated and then discounted to their net present value using discount tables. After calculating the net cash flows, the main problem in using the IRR method is to calculate the internal rate of return. However, as seen, an approximate rate can be calculated by trial and error.

A company would not necessarily go ahead with a project, of course, simply because a project appraisal suggested that it was likely to be profitable. Indeed, there will probably be so many competing projects that they will have to be ranked in order of profitability. In addition, there may well be other projects which have to be undertaken even though they are not revenue earning, for example projects involving health and safety such as the provision of car parks and sports grounds. These types of projects may only provide an indirect benefit to the company, but sometimes they have to be undertaken.

Once the company has decided which project to support, it is then necessary to decide how to finance it. This problem is considered briefly in the next section.

Source of funds

Another most important factor to consider is how the project is going to be financed. Basically, there are five main sources of funds available to a company:

1 *From retained profits*. This is probably the main source of funds for most companies.

2 *By issuing more shares for cash*. This can be an expensive administrative operation. If preference shares are issued the company is formally committing itself to paying a preference dividend. If it issues ordinary shares, its total ordinary dividend payable is likely to increase, even if it maintains the same rate of dividend. Thus if its profits do not match its expectations, the company may have difficulty in meeting a higher amount of dividend.

3 *By long-term borrowing*. The company could issue debentures to pay for its capital investment programme. The debenture interest would be allowable against corporation tax, but the company could become very high geared if it issued more long-term debt. This might cause a problem if profits began to decline, and it was committed to paying out a high proportion of its earnings in the form of debenture interest and preference dividend.

4 *By short-term borrowing*. This may be achieved by delaying payments to trade creditors, or by obtaining overdraft facilities at the bank. Capital investments financed by short-term borrowings are clearly very risky: the loan may be called in at short notice, and it may not be renewable.

5 *By leasing and hire purchase contracts*. In the last fifteen years, leasing has been a popular way of obtaining the use of fixed assets, probably because of the tax advantages which the method has attracted. These tax advantages have now been reduced, and leasing as a form of financing is not likely to be as popular. Hire purchase is also quite a popular form of financing, but it is an expensive method of financing the purchase of fixed assets because of the high rate of interest usually charged on such arrangements.

Capital investment appraisal is part of the budgeting process. The budget will have identified what projects need to be undertaken. Usually there are so many competing projects that the company has to rank them in order of priority, including those projects which are necessary on health, social or welfare grounds, although they do not contribute directly to profit. A capital expenditure programme will be matched with the available finance in order to ensure that sufficient funds are available at the implementation stage. In most circumstances, the company will finance its capital expenditure programme out of retained earnings, but with large projects it might have to issue either more shares or engage in long-term borrowing.

Conclusion

Capital investment appraisal is a complex and time-consuming exercise. It is not possible to be totally accurate in determining the profitability of individual projects, but it is possible to make a reasoned comparison between competing projects.

Managers tend to be very enthusiastic about their own sphere of responsibility. Thus the marketing manager may be *sure* that additional sales will be possible, the production director *certain* that a new machine will pay for itself, whilst the data processing manager is *convinced* that a new computer is essential.

In choosing between such competing projects, the accountant's role is to try to assess the cost of such projects and compare them with the possible benefits. Once a choice has been made, it is then necessary to ensure that the necessary finance will be available when the project is implemented. Capital investment appraisal should not be used as a means of blocking new projects. It is no different from all the other accounting techniques: it is meant to provide additional guidance to management. It is the responsibility of management to ensure that other factors are taken into account.

Capital investment appraisal concludes this part of the book. The two main branches of accounting – financial accounting and cost and management accounting have now been covered. Both the main parts of the book have concentrated on examining techniques for *internal* management purposes. The final part of the book will be looking at information prepared largely for *external* reporting purposes.

Questions

16.1 Prospect Limited is considering investing in a new project. The project would cost £100,000 to implement, it would last 5 years and it would then be sold for £50,000. The following are the relevant profit and loss accounts for each year during the life of the project:

Year to 31 March	19X1	19X2	19X3	19X4	19X5
	£000	£000	£000	£000	£000
Sales	2,000	2,400	2,800	2,900	2,000
Less: Cost of goods sold					
Opening stock	—	200	300	450	350
Purchases	1,600	1,790	2,220	1,960	1,110
	1,600	1,990	2,520	2,410	1,460
Less: Closing stock	200	300	550	350	50
	1,400	1,690	1,970	2,060	1,410
Gross profit	600	710	830	840	590
Less: Expenses	210	220	240	250	300
Depreciation	190	190	190	190	190
	400	410	430	440	490
Net profit	200	300	400	400	100
Taxation	40	70	100	100	10
Retained profits	£160	£230	£300	£300	£990

Additional information:

1 All sales are made and all purchases are obtained on credit terms.

2 Outstanding trade debtors and trade creditors at the end of each year are expected to be as follows:

Year 1	*Trade debtors*	*Trade creditors*
	£000	£000
1	200	250
2	240	270
3	300	330
4	320	300
5	400	150

3 Expenses would all be paid in cash during each year in question.

4 Taxation would be paid on 1 January following each year end.

5 Half of the project would be paid for in cash on 1 April 19X1, and the remaining half (also in cash) on 1 January 19X2. The resale value of £50,000 will be received in cash on 30 June 19X6.

Required:
Calculate the annual relevant net cash flows arising from this project.

16.2 Buchan Limited is considering investing in a new machine. The machine will be purchased on 1 January 19X1 and at a cost of £50,000. It is estimated that it would last for 5 years, and it will then be sold at the end of the year for £2,000 in cash. The respective net cash flows estimated to be received by the company as a result of purchasing the machine during each year of its life are as follows:

Year	£	
1	8,000	(excluding the initial cost)
2	16,000	
3	40,000	
4	45,000	
5	35,000	(exclusive of the project's sale proceeds)

Required:
Calculate the payback period for the project.

16.3 Lender Limited is considering investing in a new project. It is estimated that it will cost £100,000 to implement, and that the expected net profit after tax will be as follows:

Year	£
1	18,000
2	47,000
3	65,000
4	65,000
5	30,000

Required:
Calculate the accounting rate of return of the proposed project.

16.4 The following net cash flows relate to Lockhart Limited in connection with a certain project which has an initial cost of £2,500,000:

Year	*Net cash flow* £000	
1	800	(excluding the initial cost)
2	850	
3	830	
4	1,200	
5	700	

The company's required rate of return is 15%.

Required:
Calculate the net present value of the project.

16.5 Moffat Limited has calculated the following net cash flows for a proposed project costing £1,450,000:

Year	*Net cash flow* £000	
1	230	(excluding the initial cost)
2	370	
3	600	
4	650	
5	120	

Required;
Calculate the internal rate of return generated by the project.

16.6 Marsh Limited has investigated the possibility of investing in a new machine. The following data have been extracted from the report relating to the project:

Cost of machine on 1 January 19X6: £500,000.
Life: 4 years to 31 December 19X9.
Estimated scrap value: Nil.
Depreciation method: Straight-line.

Year	*Accounting profit after tax* £000	*Net cash flows* £000	
1	100	50	(excluding the
2	250	200	initial cost)
3	250	225	
4	200	225	
5	—	100	

The company's required rate of return is 15%.

Required:

Calculate the return the machine would make using the following investment appraisal methods:

1 payback;
2 accounting rate of return;
3 net present value; and
4 internal rate of return.

PART 4

Annual reports

17 Disclosure of information

In Chapter 6 it was explained how to construct a set of company accounts. The type of accounts that were considered in that chapter were to be compiled largely for the benefit of management. All limited liability companies, however, have to supply their shareholders with a copy of their annual accounts. Such accounts (often referred to as the *published* accounts) are an abbreviated version of those prepared for management purposes. It might seem strange that the owners of the company (i.e. the shareholders) are only supplied with a summary of the annual accounts. Indeed, by law they are only entitled to the *minimum* amount of information as laid down in the Companies Act 1985.

In this chapter, the legal position will be reviewed with regard to the disclosure of information, along with the additional requirements demanded by the various professional accountancy bodies and by the Stock Exchange. In later chapters the contents of an annual report will be considered in much greater detail.

Minimum disclosure requirements

During the last 40 years, there has been a gradual increase in the minimum amount of information that companies must disclose to their shareholders. As a result, even the minimum disclosure requirements now result in some very complex accounts being prepared for shareholders. Until 1981, Parliament had only laid down broad guidelines which had to be followed in disclosing information to shareholders. Up until that time, it had been left largely to each individual company to decide how and in what form it should be presented. The 1981 Companies Act, however, went much further than earlier Companies Acts and laid down precise formats for the presentation of the profit and loss account and the balance sheet. The 1981 Act was later consolidated into the Companies Act 1985 (along with the Companies Acts of 1948, 1967, 1976 and 1980), and the 1985 Act still retains the prescribed formats.

In addition to statutory requirements, the six major accountancy bodies also insist upon certain additional information being included in the published accounts. As explained earlier in this book, these requirements are contained within Statements of Standard Accounting Practice (SSAPs), the first statement having been issued in 1971. Altogether 23 SSAPs have been issued, although two have subsequently been withdrawn.

The statements do not lay down precise guidelines. It is recognized that individual circumstances vary considerably, and it would be impossible to insist upon a rigid interpretation of the methods advocated in the standards. However, professionally qualified accountants are supposed to adopt the recommendations when they are preparing published accounts. The standards do not apply exclusively to companies, since it is believed that the principles and methods can be applied to most entities. Nonetheless, some standards are fairly specialist, such as SSAP 21 which deals with leasing and hire purchase accounting.

Besides the 1985 Companies Act and professional accountancy requirements, listed companies have also to comply with a number of Stock Exchange disclosure requirements. Many of these have now been incorporated into the 1985 Act, and they are not quite as significant as they used to be.

As mentioned in Chapter 6, besides supplying a copy of their annual accounts to shareholders, all companies (irrespective of whether they are public or private companies) have to file a copy of their accounts with the Registrar of Companies at Companies House in Cardiff or in Edinburgh. This means that on payment of a small fee the accounts of limited liability companies are open to public inspection. Thus the same information that is available to shareholders is available to any member of the general public.

The 1985 Companies Act does, however, allow some concessions to private companies depending upon the size of the company. All public companies must file the same set of accounts that they submit to their shareholders. Private companies may file modified accounts if they meet two out of the three following criteria:

	Company	
Criteria	*Small*	*Medium*
	Not greater than:	Not greater than:
Turnover	£2.00 million	£8.00 million
Gross assets	£0.95 million	£3.90 million
Employees	50	250

Notwithstanding this concession, small and medium-sized companies must still supply a detailed set of accounts to their shareholders that comply with the minimum disclosure requirements of the 1985 Companies Act.

The only accounts that most employees of public companies are likely to see are the published accounts prepared for the shareholders. Sometimes, employees are supplied with a copy of the shareholders' accounts (although they have no legal right to such a copy), or they can obtain one by applying to the company secretary.

Employees of private companies may only have the option of inspecting the accounts at Companies House (there are various agencies that will make the inspection on behalf of an applicant), and if they are employed in small or medium-sized companies, they may only be able to inspect the modified version.

In recent years, there has been a tendency for both private and public companies to prepare accounts specially for their employees. Although successive governments have prepared legislation which has encouraged this trend, employees are still not as well provided for as are shareholders. Nonetheless, many companies do now supply some fairly detailed information to their employees, and it would appear that the practice is beginning to become much more common.

Although this part of the book is only concerned with the *minimum* disclosure requirements, it must be appreciated that an annual report is still a fairly long and complicated document. Shareholders who have no knowledge of accounting are probably quite mystified by the contents of such reports, but students who have worked through this book should not have too much difficulty in understanding them.

Contents of an annual report

The contents of an annual report extend now to much more than a summary of the internal profit and loss account and balance sheet of a company. Besides containing some promotional material, they also contain a number of detailed reports and statements that are either required by Statements of Standard Accounting Practice or by Stock Exchange regulations.

It is, however, possible to break down a fairly typical report into four main sections. These may be summarized as follows:

Promotional material

Companies usually take the opportunity to include in their annual report details of their products. Shareholders are consumers, of course, so it is beneficial to the company if it can persuade its shareholders to buy its products.

As this type of information does not form part of the accounting function, it is beyond the scope of this text.

Specialist reports

A report will usually be included from the following:

1 the chairman;
2 the directors; and
3 the auditors.

In this book, such reports will be referred to as the *principal* reports, and form the subject of the next chapter.

The main financial statements

The main financial statements consist of the following:

1 the profit and loss account;
2 the balance sheet; and
3 a statement of source and application of funds.

These statements will be examined further in Chapter 19.

Supplementary statements

A number of other reports and statements are usually included in an annual report. The exact number and type depend upon the company, but in Chapter 20 a number of typical examples will be considered that are sometimes found in annual reports.

Conclusion

As a non-accountant it is unlikely that you will be involved in the detailed preparation of your company's annual report, although you may, of course, have to provide information which might be used for that purpose. In fact, the only times that you are likely to see the published version of your company's accounts are if the company issues them to its employees or you own shares in a company.

It is most unlikely that an annual report will mean much unless you have had some specialist training in financial accounting, as found in this book. The remaining chapters will put that training into context.

Note: An assignment covering the material in this chapter will be found at the end of Chapter 20.

18 The principal reports

The annual accounts of a company have to be circulated to every shareholder at least 21 days before the general meeting at which those accounts are to be considered. This requirement also applies to both the auditors' report and the directors' report. It is also usual for the chairman to provide a report for the shareholders. It will be appropriate, therefore, to examine these three reports together in this chapter.

The chairman's report

There is no statutory or professional accounting requirement for the chairman to report to the shareholders, although most annual reports appear to contain a chairman's report. The chairman's report is usually presented in an early part of the annual report, often immediately after a list of the board of directors and a brief summary of some key statistics.

The report may be very long, although most chairmen manage to limit their comments to one or two pages. As there are no legal, professional or Stock Exchange requirements covering the contents of such a report, a chairman is quite free to include almost anything that he likes. Whilst the auditors may check the contents (especially those elements containing financial data), there is no obligation for them to make any comment about the report. Nonetheless, the chairman will be mindful of the effects that any remarks are likely to have on the company's share price, and a great deal of embarrassment could be caused if any comments were eventually proved to be unjustified.

A chairman's report may include the following items:

1 A review of the company's overall results for the year, including some information on divisional, product and sectional performance.
2 A very brief summary of the financial results for the year, especially a comment about the net profit for the year compared with the previous year.
3 A brief statement of the company's paid and proposed dividends for the year.
4 An explanation of what steps have been taken to improve the company's efficiency and productivity.

5 Details of major acquisitions and disposals of shares in which the company had a controlling interest.
6 Some information about the board of directors, for example about new members, resignations, retirements, achievements and honours.
7 Details about employees, such as those retiring after exceptionally long service.
8 The chairman's thanks to fellow directors, employees and other personnel involved in the company.
9 Some comments about the company's prospects.

The directors' report

The directors' report usually follows the chairman's report. It is a statutory requirement that the directors should *attach* a copy of their report to the set of accounts that are sent to the shareholders.

A directors' report now contains a great deal of information, so all that is possible in this section is to summarize the main contents.

Activities

This section may include details of the following:
1 principal activities of the company and any changes in them during the year;
2 a review of developments during the year and a statement of future ones;
3 research and development activities;
4 important events that have happened during the year;
5 the recommended dividend; and
6 the amount set aside or withdrawn from reserves.

Auditors

The auditors have to be re-appointed annually by the shareholders, so it is necessary to state in the report that the auditors are seeking election (or otherwise).

Directors

All the names of those individuals who have been directors during the year should be stated. The directors who are still directors at the end of the year must have their share and loan capital holdings listed. Any director not having any shares or debentures must disclose that fact.

Subject to the company's articles (i.e. its rules), the directors of public companies who are over the age of 70 have to retire or be re-appointed annually. The names of such directors should be stated and the fact that they are offering themselves for re-election has also to be mentioned.

Donations

If the company has made certain charitable and political donations during the year which *together* exceed £200, then the separate total for both the charitable and the political donations must be stated. If a particular political donation exceeds £200, both the amount and the name of the recipient must be reported.

Employment policy

It is necessary to state the company's employment policy towards disabled persons, their training and their career development.

Fixed assets

Any major changes in fixed assets or any significant difference between the market value and the book value of land and buildings should be mentioned.

Share capital

Information about changes in the company's share capital will be given in the accounts, but any such changes should be referred to in the directors' report.

The directors' report should end with the signature of the chairman (or one of the other directors) and stated as being signed 'on behalf of the board'. The signature should then be followed by the date when the report was agreed by the board. If the report is signed by anyone other than the chairman or one of the directors (such as the company secretary), he may sign it 'by order of the board'.

The auditors' report

The auditors' report will normally be quite short. Most auditors' reports will be fairly similar. A typical one would read as follows:

> Report of the auditors to the members of XXXX plc
> We have audited the financial statements on pages XX to XX in accordance with approved auditing standards.
> In our opinion the financial statements, which have been prepared under the historical cost convention give a true and fair view of the state of the company's affairs at XX XXXX 19XX and of its profit and source and application of funds for the year then ended and

comply with the Companies Act 1985.

XXXXXX & Co

Chartered Accountants

XX XXXX 19XX

An auditors' report such as the one outlined above, would be regarded as an *unqualified* audit report. This means that in the opinion of the auditors, the accounts give a true and fair view and that they have nothing further to say about them. A *qualified* audit report is supposed to draw the attention of the shareholders to certain aspects of the accounts which do not appear to give a true and fair view, for example because of the method used to value stocks. The qualification may arise only as a result of a minor point, but even a major qualification (such as that in certain respects the accounts do not represent a true and fair view) is supposed to be very serious.

There is some uncertainty about the importance and relevance of a qualified audit report, particularly if the qualification appears to be a minor one. It used to be rare for audit reports to be qualified, but in recent years it has become quite common. The effect of a qualified audit report ought, at the very least, to result in some searching questions being put to the directors at the general meeting. If the explanation appears unsatisfactory to the shareholders, then they should consider dismissing the directors. Such an event, however, is comparatively rare.

The auditors' report may come either before or after the main financial statements which will be considered in the next chapter.

Conclusion

This chapter has outlined the contents of the three main reports which are contained within a typical annual report. First the chairman's report, which is not a report required either by statute or by professional accounting requirements. Then the contents of a directors' report were summarized since it is now a major source of much statutory and professional accounting information. Finally, the contents of a typical auditors' report, one of the shortest reports to be found in the annual report, were outlined.

Note: An assignment covering the material in this chapter will be found at the end of Chapter 20.

19 The main financial statements

The main financial statements that will be considered in this chapter are the profit and loss account, the balance sheet, and a statement of source and application of funds. Annual reports usually contain other types of statements, and these will be examined in the next chapter.

The background to published accounts

The structure and format of profit and loss accounts, balance sheets and statements of source and application of funds have already been examined in previous chapters. In those chapters the primary concern was the preparation of accounts for internal management purposes. In practice, the contents of such statements can be extremely complex. The Companies Act 1985 recognizes that it would be impracticable to expect a company to supply the same amount of information to all its shareholders.

Consequently, only a certain minimum amount of information has to be disclosed to shareholders, but when additional professional accounting and Stock Exchange requirements are also included, the total amount is quite considerable.

Additional features

There are certain features of published financial statements which have not been encountered before. These are summarized below.

Group accounts

Most published annual accounts will contain the results for a *group* of companies. There are a few examples of public companies that are not part of a group, but they are comparatively rare.

A group is like a family. The company (say Company A) may buy shares in another company (say Company B). When Company A owns more than 50% of the voting shares in Company B, B becomes a *subsidiary* of A. If A owned more than 20% of the voting shares in B but less than 50%, B would be known as an *associated* (or *related*) company of A. In effect B is considered to be the off-spring of A, and in turn B might have children of its own (say Company C and Company D). C and D then become part of the family, i.e. they become part of the group structure.

The significance of these relationships is that the published accounts will be prepared for the group as a whole. Even though B, C and D are companies in their own right (and might therefore be expected to prepare accounts for themselves), the entity becomes part of the group, and any inter-group relationships between them are ignored when preparing the accounts.

Thus normally when inspecting a set of published accounts you can expect to see a *group* profit and loss account, a *group* balance sheet, and a *group* statement of source and application of funds. The 1985 Companies Act permits group accounts to be presented in several ways, but the most common method is to prepare a group profit and loss account, a group balance sheet, and a balance sheet for the *holding* company (Company A in our example). Statements of source and application of funds are not required by law, but normally a group funds statement would also be presented.

In order to prepare group accounts it is necessary to add together (or consolidate) all of the company accounts that form part of the group. As a result, the subsidiary company and associated company results are absorbed into the holding company's accounts (although some specific information about such companies has still to be disclosed). The preparation of group accounts can be an enormous and highly specialist task. Indeed, it is something of a specialism even amongst accountants.

Notes to the accounts

Another additional feature of group accounts is that they will probably be accompanied by many pages of notes. These notes provide even more information about the items disclosed in the accounts themselves. Such notes form an integral part of the accounts, but they usually contain so much information that it is sometimes difficult to find the information.

Comparative figures

The 1985 Companies Act requires the current year's accounts to be accompanied by comparisons with the previous year's results. This adds to the amount of information given in the accounts, although it is advantageous, of course, to be able to compare the current year with the previous year.

With this preliminary review of published accounts, it is now possible to begin a more detailed investigation of them.

The group profit and loss account

The 1985 Companies Act lays down a choice of two types of format for the presentation of the profit and loss account. These are as follows:

1 the horizontal format, whereby the expenditure is listed on the left-hand side of the page, and the income on the right-hand side; and
2 the vertical format, whereby the income and expenditure is displayed on a line-by-line basis.

In preparing accounts in this book the vertical format has almost exclusively been used. This format is a deliberate choice as it appears to be used by the majority of companies, and is therefore the one that is most likely to be met with in practice.

Besides permitting a choice of structural formats, the Act also permits the expenditure to be displayed according to its type. There are two types of format permitted by the Act:

1 the operational format; and
2 the type of expenditure format.

These formats are illustrated in Exhibit 19.1.

Exhibit 19.1: The vertical profit and loss account expenditure formats

1 *Operational format*	£	2 *Type of expenditure format*	£	£
Turnover	X	Turnover		X
Cost of sales	(X)	Changes in stocks of finished goods and work-in progress		X
Gross profit	X	Own work capitalized		X
		Other operating income		X
				X
Distribution costs	(X)	Raw materials and consumables	(X)	
Administration expenses	(X)	Other external charges	(X)	
		Staff costs	(X)	
		Depreciation and other amounts written off tangible and intangible fixed assets	(X)	
Other operating income	X	Other operating charges	(X)	(X)
Operating profit	£ X	*Operating profit*		£ X

Note: After the operating profit stage the two formats are identical.

As can be seen from Exhibit 19.1, the type of expenditure format is very much more detailed than the operational format. Both types are used in the United Kingdom, but it is possible that the operational format is more popular, probably because it is a little easier to follow. It is, in fact, basically the same format that was adopted in examples in earlier chapters.

You should now be in a position to examine a published profit and loss account in some detail. Such an account is given in Exhibit 19.2, accompanied by some comprehensive notes.

Exhibit 19.2: Example of a published profit and loss account

ENERGY PUBLIC LIMITED COMPANY
Group profit and loss account for the year to 31 March 19X2

	Notes to the accounts (1)	*19X2* £	*19X1* £
Turnover (2)	2	X	X
Cost of sales (3)		(X)	(X)
Gross profit (4)		X	X
Distribution costs (5)		(X)	(X)
Administrative expenses (5)		(X)	(X)
Other operating income (6)		X	X
Operating profit (7)		X	X
Share of profits less losses of related companies (8)		X	X
Income from other fixed asset investments (9)		X	X
Other interest receivable and other income (10)		X	X
Interest payable and similar charges (11)		(X)	(X)
Profit on ordinary activities before taxation (12)	2/3	X	X
Tax on profit on ordinary activities (13)	4	(X)	(X)
Profit on ordinary activities after taxation (14)		X	X
Minority interests (15)		(X)	(X)
Profit before extraordinary items attributable to members of the holding company (16)		X	X
Extraordinary items (17)	5	(X)	(X)
Profit for the financial year (18)	6	X	X
Dividends paid and proposed (19)	7	(X)	(X)
Retained profit for the year (20)		£ X	£ X
Earnings per share (21)	8	xxp	xxp

Note: The numbers in brackets shown after each narration relate to the tutorial notes given below.

Tutorial notes

1 The formal notes to the accounts have not been presented with this exhibit, as most of the items will be considered as part of these tutorial notes. It will

be noticed that Note 1 to the accounts is missing. This is because the first formal note to the accounts is often a statement of accounting policies that have been adopted in drawing up that particular set of accounts.

2 Turnover is usually defined as being sales to customers outside the group less returns by customers, exclusive of trade discounts and value added tax.
3 The detailed calculation for the cost of goods sold does not have to be disclosed.
4 The gross profit is identical to that shown in the internal accounts.
5 The 1985 Companies Act does not define what is meant by distribution costs or administrative expenses.
6 Other operating income will include income from rentals and royalties.
7 This is the point at which the operational and type of expenditure formats become identical.
8 Share of profits less losses of related (i.e. associated) companies will include the group's share of such profits or losses.
9 Income from other fixed asset investments will include dividends received from non-group companies.
10 Other interest receivable and similar income includes interest received on loans.
11 Interest payable and similar charges will include interest payable on bank and other short-term borrowings.
12 The profit on ordinary activities before taxation will require a detailed formal note to the accounts. It will include such information as the auditors' remuneration, directors' emoluments (as they are called), details of wages and salaries (in total), depreciation charges (in total), and social security and pension costs.
13 The tax on the profit on ordinary activities will be comprised largely of the company's corporation tax.
14 The amount shown for profit on ordinary activities after taxation is simply a sub-total. It illustrates what could be paid in dividends if all of the after-tax profit was to be distributed.
15 A proportion of the after-tax profits may be due to shareholders outside the group if the holding company has not purchased all of the shares in a subsidiary company. These outside shareholders must, of course, always be in a minority if the holding company owns more than 50% of the share capital of the other company.
16 The amount of profit available to group members before extraordinary items is a sub-total. It shows the amount of after-tax profit for the year that could be distributed to group members.
17 Extraordinary items are incomes (or expenditures) that (a) are material; (b) arise outside the ordinary course of business; and (c) are not expected to recur frequently or regularly. If such items were not separately disclosed they would distort the ordinary results.
18 The profit for the financial year is the total amount of net profit for the year that could be distributed to group members.
19 The dividends paid and proposed to be paid will include dividends paid or payable on all types of shares.
20 The retained profit for the year will be transferred to the revenue reserves shown in the balance sheet. It will be used to help finance the future expansion of the company.
21 How to calculate the earning per share was illustrated in Chapter 8.

As can be seen from Exhibit 19.2, even the minimum amount of information that it is necessary to disclose in a published profit and loss account is quite formidable. It should also be remembered that examples of the formal notes to the profit and loss account have not been reproduced. It is to be expected that for a large company such notes would probably require about six pages of closely printed material.

The group balance sheet

The 1985 Companies Act allows a choice of balance sheet format. The choice is as follows:

1 a horizontal format, whereby the assets are laid out on the left-hand side of the page, and the capital on the right-hand side; and
2 a vertical format, whereby the assets are listed before the liabilities.

In this book the vertical format has almost exclusively been adopted. In the United Kingdom vertical balance sheets are quite common, although some companies prefer a more traditional horizontal type.

A published balance sheet will not look very different from one prepared for internal purposes, although, as noted earlier, it will probably be prepared for a group, comparative figures will be given, and there will be many formal notes attached to it.

A typical published balance sheet is shown in Exhibit 19.3. The exhibit is followed by tutorial notes which give an explanation of each item.

Exhibit 19.3: Example of a published balance sheet

ENERGY PUBLIC LIMITED COMPANY
Group balance sheet at 31 March 19X2

	Notes to the accounts	*Group*		*Company*	
		19X2	*19X1*	*19X2*	*19X1*
	(1)	£	£	£	£
Fixed assets (2)					
Intangible assets (3)	9	X	X	X	X
Tangible assets (4)	10	X	X	X	X
Investments (5)	11	X	X	X	X
(6)		X	X	X	X
Current assets (7)					
Stocks (8)	12	X	X	X	X
Debtors (9)	13	X	X	X	X
Investments (10)	14	X	X	X	X
Cash at bank and in hand (11)		X	X	X	X
(12)		X	X	X	X

contd

	Notes to the accounts	Group 19X2	Group 19X1	Company 19X2	Company 19X1
	(1)	£	£	£	£
Creditors: Amounts falling due within one year (13)	15	(X)	(X)	(X)	(X)
Net current assets (14)		X	X	X	X
Total assets less current liabilities (15)		X	X	X	X
Creditors: Amounts falling due after more than one year (16)	16	(X)	(X)	(X)	(X)
(17)		£ X	£ X	£ X	£ X
Capital and reserves (18)					
Called-up share capital (19)	17	X	X	X	X
Share premium account (20)	18	X	X	X	X
Revaluation reserve (21)	19	X	X	X	X
Other reserves (22)	20	X	X	X	X
Profit and loss account (23)	21	X	X	X	X
(24)		X	X	X	X
Minority interests (25)		X	X	X	X
(26)		£ X	£ X	£ X	£ X

Approved by the board on XX June 19X2 (27)

. . . .
} Directors
. . . .

(28)

Note: The number in brackets after each narration relates to the tutorial notes.

Tutorial notes

1 Formal notes have not been attached to this exhibit as most of the items will be considered as part of these tutorial notes. The first formal balance sheet note begins at (9), because it is a continuation of the profit and loss account notes shown in the previous section. In order to comply with the 1985 Companies Act, both the group and the holding company's own balance sheets are shown.
2 The net book value must be shown under the three headings of (a) intangible assets, (b) tangible assets, and (c) investments.
3 Intangible assets are those assets that are not of a physical nature, such as goodwill, patents and development costs.
4 Tangible assets include land and buildings, plant and machinery, fixtures, fittings, tools and equipment.
5 Fixed asset investments are those that are intended to be held for the long term, i.e. in excess of twelve months.
6 This line is the total net book value of all the fixed assets.
7 Current assets have also to be analysed into a number of categories.

8 Stocks must be disclosed under a number of categories, e.g. raw materials and consumables, work-in-progress, finished goods and payments on account.

9 Debtors have also to be analysed under such headings as trade debtors, other debtors, prepayments and accrued income.

10 Current asset investments are those investments held for the short term, i.e. for normally less than twelve months.

11 Cash at bank and in hand. This will be the same amount that appears in the balance sheet prepared for internal purposes.

12 This line represents the total of current assets.

13 Creditors have to be analysed between short-term creditors (i.e. those payable within the next twelve months), and long-term creditors (i.e. those that do not have to be paid for at least twelve months). Both short- and long-term creditors have to be analysed into a number of categories, such as trade creditors, other creditors, and accruals and deferred income.

14 The net current assets line is a sub-total (Current assets (12) *less* Creditors: Amounts falling due within one year (13)).

15 This is another sub-total (Fixed assets (6) *plus* Net current assets (14)).

16 See tutorial note 13 above.

17 This line represents the balance sheet total.

18 The capital and reserves section is the other main part of the balance sheet. It explains how the net assets (17) have been financed.

19 The called-up share capital represents all of the shares that have been issued, details of which will be shown in a formal balance sheet note.

20 The share premium account records the extra amount on top of the nominal value of their shares which shareholders were willing to pay when they bought their shares. It does not attract a dividend, and there are very few uses to which it can be put.

21 Sometimes fixed assets, such as land and buildings, will be revalued. The difference between the revalued amount and the net book value will be credited to a revaluation reserve account. The balance cannot be distributed to shareholders.

22 Other reserves. This balance may include a number of other reserve accounts both of a capital nature (i.e. reserves that cannot be distributed to shareholders) and of a revenue nature (i.e. amounts that may be distributed to shareholders).

23 This is the total of all the profits that have not been distributed to shareholders, less those that have been put in special reserve accounts.

24 This is the total of the capital and reserves section of the balance sheet. It represents shareholders' funds.

25 The minority interests represent that proportion of the net assets of subsidiary companies which is owned by shareholders outside the group.

26 This line should balance with line 17.

27 The balance sheet should be signed by two directors.

28 It is possible that other formal notes will be attached to the balance sheet.

Study Exhibit 19.3 very carefully. Its basic layout should be reasonably familiar to you, although there is a lot more detail than you have been used to in earlier examples.

Group statements of source and application of funds

The construction of a statement of source and application of funds has already been considered in some detail in Chapter 7. Published funds statements differ little from the format that was used in that chapter, apart from reflecting the activities of the group of companies, and the inclusion of comparative figures.

Unlike the profit and loss account and the balance sheet, funds statements do not have any statutory backing. However, the accountancy profession consider them so important that they can be considered as one of the main financial statements. Indeed, SSAP 10 requires any entity with a turnover in excess of £25,000 per annum to prepare such a statement, but as argued earlier, there is some doubt whether they do mean a great deal to the layman.

Exhibit 19.4 gives an example of a statement of source and application of funds for a group of companies. You will see that apart from more detail, its format is reasonably familiar.

Exhibit 19.4: Example of a group statement of source and application of funds

ENERGY PUBLIC LIMITED COMPANY

Statement of source and application of funds for the year to 31 March 19X2

	19X2			*19X1*		
	£	£	£	£	£	£
Source of funds						
Profit before tax and extraordinary items, less minority interest (1)			X			X
Extraordinary items (2)			X			(X)
			X			X
Adjustments for items not involving the movement of funds:						
Minority interests in the retained profits for the year (3)			X			X
Depreciation			X			X
Profits retained in associated companies (4)			(X)			(X)
Total generated from operations			X			X
Funds from other sources (5)						
Shares issued in part consideration of the acquisition of a subsidiary			X			X
Capital raised under executive option scheme			X			X
			X			X
Application of funds						
Dividends paid		(X)			(X)	
Tax paid		(X)			(X)	
Purchase of fixed assets		(X)			(X)	
Purchase of goodwill on acquisition of a subsidiary (6)		(X)			(X)	
Debentures redeemed		(X)	(X)		(X)	(X)
			X			X

contd

	19X2			19X1		
	£	£	£	£	£	£
Increase/Decrease in working capital						
Increase in stocks		X			X	
Increase in debtors		X			X	
Decrease in creditors - excluding taxation and dividends		X			X	
Movement in net liquid funds:						
Increase (decrease) in cash balances	X			X		
Increase (decrease) in short-term investments	X	X	X	X	X	X

Note: The figures in brackets after some of the narrations refer to the tutorial notes given below.

Tutorial notes

1. This line links with the various items in the published profit and loss account.
2. Extraordinary items can either be a source of funds (as they were in 19X2) or an application of funds (as they were in 19X1).
3. The minority interests share of the retained profits do not belong to the group, but they are still a source of funds because they have not been paid out.
4. The group only receives dividends from associated companies, and not the whole of its profits. The associated company's profits have, therefore, to be added back because they are not a source of funds.
5. Funds from other sources are just illustrative examples.
6. The cost of purchasing goodwill in a subsidiary will be the difference between the total amount paid for the shares and the value of the investment.

The format of Exhibit 19.4 is based on the example given in the appendix to SSAP10. This format is not mandatory, and the student may well come across funds statements that are quite different from the examples used in this book.

Conclusion

You are now recommended to study very carefully the format of a published profit and loss account, a published balance sheet and a published statement of source and application of funds. The basic structures have been given in this chapter, but you should obtain copies of published accounts so that you can make comparisons between them.

Although the 1985 Companies Act has done much to standardize the format of published accounts, you will still find that different companies have their own style. However, in this chapter will be found an explanation of the basic features that will be common to most companies, and you should now be able to work your way through almost any set of published accounts.

Note: An assignment covering the material in this chapter will be found at the end of Chapter 20.

20 Supplementary statements and reports

Annual reports usually contain other statements and reports besides the ones which were examined in the previous two chapters. There are no legal or professional accounting requirements which make it necessary to produce additional statements, although at various times the Accounting Standards Committee has given much encouragement to the publication of more reports.

The amount, type and format of additional statements varies enormously. All that is possible in this chapter, therefore, is to outline some of the more common types of supplementary statements and reports. Four such statements will be covered:

1 inflation adjusted reports;
2 value added statements;
3 statistical summaries; and
4 employee reports.

Inflation adjusted reports

In recent years the accountancy profession has produced a number of proposals which would allow for the effect of inflation on accounts prepared on the basis of the historical cost convention. As yet in the United Kingdom, all of these proposals have been abandoned, largely because it is not easy to gain acceptance for any new method of accounting which would replace one that has been in existence for centuries. However, before examining these proposals, something about the nature of inflation must first be explained and what effect it has on accounts prepared under the *historical cost* convention.

Inflation and its effect

There is no satisfactory definition of inflation, but for the purposes of this text it can be regarded as either an upward movement in prices, or a downwards movement in the purchasing power of the monetary unit. In other words, during a period of inflation, £100 available in cash in 19X1 will purchase fewer goods in 19X2 than it did in 19X1. Thus in order to purchase the same amount of goods in 19X2 as in 19X1, more than £100 will have to be paid.

As far as accounting is concerned, the effect of inflation on the traditional historic cost accounts can be stated quite simply: it tends to overstate the amount of profit. By overstating profit, the proprietors may withdraw more profit, and as a result, the entity's liquid resources may begin to deteriorate. Eventually, the entity may find that it is difficult to replenish its stock with the same quantity that it has consumed in previous periods, and to replace its fixed assets as they become worn out. If it cannot find alternative sources of finance, then in the long run (depending upon the rate of inflation), the entity will have to contract its operating activities.

The main effects of inflation on historic cost accounts may be summarized as follows:

1 *Closing stock value*. The closing stock tends to have a higher value than goods purchased in earlier periods. A high closing stock figure tends to overstate the gross profit (because the closing stock is *deducted* from the opening stock + purchases). However, when the stock is eventually sold it will probably cost more to replace it than when it was purchased.
2 *Depreciation understated*. Depreciation is usually based on the historic cost of the asset. Assets will have to be replaced eventually at a greater cost, so not enough profit will have been set aside to replace them if the depreciation charge is based on the historic cost.
3 *Loss on loans*. If the entity has put some of its funds into short- or long-term loans (such as in a bank deposit account or into debenture stock), such loans will lose value in a period of inflation. The entity might have invested (say) £10,000 in debenture stock in 19X1 which will be repaid in 19X5. In 19X5 the entity will be repaid £10,000, but £10,000 received in 19X5 will not purchase the same amount of goods as £10,000 did in 19X1. Consequently, the entity loses by investing in an investment which is fixed in money terms.

It also loses by allowing credit to its customers. Such debts will be fixed in money terms, so that when the cash is eventually received it will purchase fewer goods.
4 *Gains on borrowings*. An entity does not always lose during a period of inflation. If it borrows money on a short-term or on a long-term basis it will benefit. Goods purchased on credit terms, for example, will be settled in *money* terms, but the monetary payment will then be worth less than it was when it was originally incurred. An entity also gains by borrowing on a long-term basis. By borrowing money through issuing debentures, for example, it will eventually have to pay back less money in purchasing power terms than it borrowed.

The accountancy profession's answer

In trying to cope with the effect of inflation on historic cost accounts, two main schools of thought have evolved. These are as follows:

The purchasing power school

This school of thought recommends that the historic cost accounts should be adjusted on the basis of some suitable inflation index. In the United Kingdom, the index that is usually recommended is that known as the *retail price index* (RPI). This index is well known and recognized. Whilst this is an advantage, it suffers from two main disadvantages:

1 it measures the effect of inflation on retail consumption; and
2 it does not necessarily measure the effect of inflation on a specific company.

Nonetheless, this method of allowing for inflation is relatively easy to adopt and the historic cost accounts are still retained. Each transaction (or collection of transactions) is then measured against the index at the time that it was purchased, and compared with the index at the end of the relevant accounting period. The historic cost of the transaction is thereby adjusted by multiplying it by the closing index and dividing it by the opening index. Take, for example, the following information:

	£	RPI
Fixed asset purchased on 1.1.X1:	1,000	100
Historic cost accounts prepared on 31.12.X1		120

∴ In the current purchasing power accounts the fixed asset would be shown as:

$$\frac{(£1,000 \times 120)}{100} = \underline{\underline{£1,200}}$$

You are likely to find that many tables and charts in an annual report have been adjusted on a current purchasing power (CPP) basis, although it is unlikely that the main financial statements have been indexed in this way.

The current value school

In the United Kingdom, the CPP school of thought was much in favour until about 1975, but since then it has lost ground to the current value school. There are several versions of current value accounting. Essentially, they require fixed assets and stocks to be included in the accounts at their current value, rather than at their historic cost.

The main version of current value accounting adopted in the United

Kingdom is known as *current cost accounting* (CCA). CCA became the subject of an accounting standard in 1980 (SSAP 16). Like all standards, it was supposed to be mandatory, but it became so unpopular that it was virtually abandoned at the end of 1985.

SSAP 16 was a very complicated statement (probably one reason for its unpopularity). Basically, what it tried to do was to reduce the level of the historic cost profit in order to allow for the effect of inflation. By so doing, the entity would always be able to retain sufficient funds in the business to be able to continue operating at the same level that it had done in the past. In the jargon of accounting, this is known as *maintaining its operating capability*.

The statement required four main adjustments to be made to the historic cost profit and loss account, and two to the balance sheet. Each of these adjustments will be considered separately, so that you may judge for yourself whether they meet the problems of accounting for inflation which were outlined earlier, starting with the profit and loss account adjustments.

1 *A cost of sales adjustment (COSA)*. This adjustment required both the opening and closing stock to be adjusted (normally by indexing using a method similar to that adopted in CPP accounting) to a value which represented the average value of stock for the period. Hence both the opening and the closing stock was put on the same price base as the purchases made during the period.

2 *An additional depreciation adjustment (ADA)*. This adjustment meant that the depreciation charge for the year was normally based on the *replacement* cost of the asset, rather than on its historic cost.

3 *A monetary working capital adjustment (MWCA)*. Monetary working capital is basically the difference between trade debtors and trade creditors. SSAP 16 required an adjustment to be made for monetary working capital for the reasons outlined earlier, i.e. in times of inflation, entities gain by borrowing and lose by lending. This adjustment made an allowance for such gains and losses. The adjustment was made by adjusting both the opening net monetary working capital and the closing net monetary working capital so that they were measured on the same price basis. The opening and closing values were usually indexed so that they both represented the average value for the year. The adjustment was very similar to that adopted for making the cost of sales adjustment.

4 *A gearing adjustment (GA)*. It is quite customary for a company to finance its operations partly from long-term borrowings, usually in the form of debentures. As argued earlier, if a company has borrowed money on a long-term basis during a period of inflation, it will benefit by being able to repay the loan in monetary terms, because by the time that the company comes to repay the loan, the purchasing power of the original loan will have declined.

The cost of sales adjustment, the additional depreciation adjustment, and the monetary working capital adjustment all normally reduce the profit available for distribution to the shareholders. It seems only fair, therefore, that if shareholders are also to benefit from inflation as a result of long-term borrowings, then their profit should be increased by a proportion of the inflationary gain.

The gearing adjustment tried to measure the extent of the shareholders' gain. It was a highly complex and controversial adjustment, but basically the total of the three other profit and loss adjustments (COSA, ADA and MWCA) were reduced by that proportion of the company financed by long-term borrowings. Suppose, for example, that the total of COSA + ADA + MWCA = £10,000, and that the gearing proportion was 20% (i.e. average long-term borrowings during the year = 20%), then £2,000 (£10,000 × 20%) would be credited to the profit and loss account. The net extra cost to the profit and loss account to allow for inflation would be £8,000 (£10,000 − £2,000).

The two balance sheet adjustments required under SSAP 16 were as follows:

1 *Fixed assets*. These were normally to be included at their net replacement cost (i.e. their gross replacement cost less the accumulated depreciation based on that replacement cost). In effect, the gross replacement cost would be what the company would have to pay for similar assets at the balance sheet date if the original assets were to have been replaced.

2 *Closing stocks*. The closing stocks were also to be included in the balance sheet at their replacement cost valued as at the date of the balance sheet.

It should be noted that these six adjustments (four in the profit and loss account and two in the balance sheet) would, of course, alter the balancing of the accounts. SSAP 16 enabled the doubling entry to be completed by the use of what was called the *current cost reserve account*. This account was nothing more than a balancing account.

The current position

As a result of the abandonment of SSAP 16, it is unlikely that many companies will in future include current cost accounts in their annual reports. Some companies, however, may still produce summaries of their historic cost accounts adjusted for inflation. They could do this in one of two ways:

1 they could either index some (if not all) of their historic cost results by adopting a CPP approach; or

2 they could adjust both their fixed assets and closing stocks on to a

value basis, even if they do not produce a full set of SSAP 16 adjusted accounts.

The non-accountant need not be unduly concerned with the technicalities of accounting for inflation. You should be aware, however, of the misleading results obtained by using summaries of accounting information (perhaps over a five year or a ten year period) which have not been adjusted to allow for the effects of inflation.

Ideally, you should also make some allowance for inflation. We would suggest that in the absence of any other information, you should use the retail price index to index the data.

Value added statements

In 1975 the Accounting Standards Steering Committee (now the Accounting Standards Committee) published a discussion paper called 'The Corporate Report'. The purpose of the study was to re-examine the aims and scope of published financial reports. In its report, the Committee suggested that there was a need for entities to publish a number of additional reports to complement the main financial statements. One of the reports recommended was a *statement of value added* (or a value added statement).

Value added was defined as 'the wealth created by the entity as a result of the collective efforts of capital, employees and management'. It was argued that the statement should show how the value was added (basically, sales revenue less materials and purchased services), and how that value was used (basically to pay employees, shareholders and the government).

As a result of 'The Corporate Report', many companies began to include a value added statement in their annual reports, but in recent years they have become less popular. To date, they have not received any statutory or professional accountancy backing. Nonetheless, they are a useful addition to an annual report. In format, they appear very similar to statements of source and application of funds: in the first part of the statement they explain where the *value* has come from, and in the second part of the statement they outline where it has gone to.

As there are no statutory or professional accountancy requirements supporting the inclusion of a value added statement in an annual report, there is little agreement about their precise format. In the absence of general agreement, therefore, the format of a value added statement will be illustrated by adopting the example used in 'The Corporate Report'. The details are shown in Exhibit 20.1.

Exhibit 20.1: Example of a value added statement

ENERGY PUBLIC LIMITED COMPANY

Group value added statement for the year to 31 March 19X2

	19X2		19X1	
	£	%	£	%
Turnover (1)	X		X	
Brought-in materials and services (2)	(X)		(X)	
	X		X	
Other incomes (3)	X		X	
Value added (4)	£ X		£ X	
Applied the following ways:				
To pay employees (5)				
Wages, pensions and fringe benefits	X	x	X	x
To pay providers of capital (5)				
Interest on loans	X		X	
Dividends to shareholders	X		X	
	X	x	X	x
To pay government (5)				
Corporation tax payable	X	x	X	x
To provide for maintenance and expansion of capital (5)				
Depreciation	X		X	
Retained profits	X		X	
	X	x	X	x
Value added (6)	£ X	100%	£ X	100%

Note: The numbers in brackets after some of the narrations refer to the tutorial notes given below.

Tutorial notes

1 Turnover represents sales to external customers, net of trade discounts, value added tax and other sales taxes.
2 Bought-in materials and services include, *inter alia*, the cost of sales, salaries, wages and other employment costs.
3 Other incomes include investment income.
4 Value added is the wealth created during the particular period in question.
5 The disposition of the wealth is shown under four main headings: (a) to pay employees; (b) to pay the providers of capital; (c) to pay the government; and (d) to provide for maintenance and expansion of the assets.
6 The total disposition should agree with the total value added (see tutorial note 4).

The information needed to compile a value added statement comes from the profit and loss account. The statement is simply a re-arrangement of the information contained in the profit and loss account, although the amount of value added cannot be directly linked with any specific balance in the profit and loss account.

A value added statement has several uses. Some of the main ones are summarized below:

1 It provides additional information about the company's performance.
2 It shows the increase in the company's resources.
3 It highlights the proportion of the value added paid to the employees.
4 It shows the contribution paid to the government.
5 It is believed that the information is more useful than the traditional accounting statements in implementing profit schemes, in encouraging employee participation, and in creating a more co-operative working environment.

A value added statement can be seen, therefore, to be something of a political statement. If it is viewed in this light by the employees then it clearly will not achieve some of the benefits claimed for it by its advocates.

Statistical summaries

One of the accounting rules that was dealt with in Chapter 2 was the *periodicity* rule. It was suggested that in order to provide a report for the owners of the business, it was necessary to establish an accounting period of some consistent length. In most circumstances, entities have tended to adopt an accounting period equivalent to twelve calendar months. Such a period is quite an artificial period of time, especially in the case of those entities that have an unlimited life.

In recent years, companies have begun to realize that it may be misleading to present their results purely in terms of this year's results compared with last year's results. Consequently, although there are no legal or professional accountancy requirements, it has become common for companies to include statistical summaries in their annual reports covering a period well in excess of a calendar year.

There is no general agreement on how long such a period should be. Some companies adopt a five year period, whilst others prepare summaries over a ten year period. The contents of such statements, irrespective of the period, is again subject to much variety. The data may include for example, summaries of sales, profit and dividends, assets employed and cash flow. The basic financial data may be accompanied by key statistics and a number of selected accounting ratios. An example of a five year financial summary is illustrated in Exhibit 20.2.

Exhibit 20.2: Example of a five year financial summary

ENERGY PUBLIC LIMITED COMPANY

	19X1	19X2	19X3	19X4	19X5
	£m	£m	£m	£m	£m
Profit summary					
Turnover	£ X	£ X	£ X	£ X	£ X
Profit before tax	X	X	X	X	X
Taxation	(X)	(X)	(X)	(X)	(X)
Profit after taxation	X	X	X	X	X
Minority interest	(X)	(X)	(X)	(X)	(X)
	X	X	X	X	X
Extraordinary items	X	X	X	X	X
Profit for the period	X	X	X	X	X
Dividends	(X)	(X)	(X)	(X)	(X)
Net profit	£ X	£ X	£ X	£ X	£ X
Employment of capital					
Tangible fixed assets	X	X	X	X	X
Fixed asset investments	X	X	X	X	X
Net current assets	X	X	X	X	X
	X	X	X	X	X
Creditors: Amounts falling due after more than one year					
Provisions for liabilities and charges	(X)	(X)	(X)	(X)	(X)
Total net assets	£ X	£ X	£ X	£ X	£ X
Capital employed					
Called up share capital	X	X	X	X	X
Reserves	X	X	X	X	X
	X	X	X	X	X
Minority interests	X	X	X	X	X
	£ X	£ X	£ X	£ X	£ X
Per £1 ordinary share	p	p	p	p	p
Earnings	X	X	X	X	X
Dividend	X	X	X	X	X
Dividend cover - times	X	X	X	X	X

Statistical summaries that cover a long period of time are helpful in establishing trends, but it is important that each year's results have been put on to a consistent basis. Legal and professional accountancy requirements do change over a five to a ten year period, and the company itself may also have altered its accounting policies because of changed circumstances.

If a fair comparison is to be made between the respective periods, it is also essential that some allowance be made for inflation. At a rate of inflation of 5% per annum, for example, prices double over a fifteen year period, and even over a five year period they increase by about 30%.

Employee reports

The 1985 Companies Act pays very little attention to the interests of employees. It has been left largely to employment protection legislation to encourage employee reporting. As a result, many companies now prepare reports specifically for their employees. Such information may be included as a special section in the shareholders' annual report, or a quite separate report may be prepared.

As yet there is little clear guidance about the form and content of employee reports. Thus there is a tendency for them to be just simplified and shortened versions of the shareholders' report. They sometimes use elaborate charts and diagrams, often in many different types, styles and colour of print. In many cases, they make no attempt to translate accounting terminology into the sort of language that everyone can understand, and sometimes their linguistic style is highly condescending. There is still much work to do before the accountancy profession is in a position to produce an acceptable employee report.

As the content and style of employee reports varies so enormously, the student is recommended to collect examples of them. It would be a useful exercise for you to assess their impact on you as a non-accountant, and to find out whether you find their contents useful.

Conclusion

This chapter has examined a number of supplementary statements and reports that might well be found in a company's annual report. All such reports should contain the main financial statements, namely a profit and loss account, a balance sheet, and a statement of source and application of funds, but beyond that the number, type, style and variety will vary from company to company.

Some annual reports may contain the absolute minimum amount of statutory and professional accountancy information, whilst other reports will contain so much information that it is difficult to read it all. However, regardless of the exact format of an annual report, the student who has worked his way through this book should now be in an excellent position to make the most of any such report.

Assignment

For this assignment, you are required to obtain a copy of the annual report of a public limited liability company. It does not really matter what type of company you choose, although you are recommended to obtain the accounts of a manufacturing company as they are more likely to follow the format that has been followed in this book. You are advised to avoid banks, building societies, insurance companies, investment trusts, and unit trusts since the accounts for such entities will probably be somewhat different from the ones that have been described in the last four chapters.

The purpose of the assignment is to help you become more familiar with the contents of an annual report. By having to find out the answers to some fairly detailed questions, you will have to search through the report most carefully. It is hoped that by doing so, you will soon know where to look for certain types of important information.

Required:
Examine the annual report of a public limited liability company, and then answer the following questions (if the report covers a group of companies, answer for the group):

1 What amount was paid to charity during the year?
2 Were there any exceptional items listed in the profit and loss account? If so, what were they, and for how much?
3 What depreciation method(s) did the company adopt?
4 How much was the chairman paid?
5 What was the total amount of dividends paid and proposed?
6 Were there any extraordinary items, and if so, what for and how much?
7 What was the total net book value of the tangible fixed assets?
8 How much ordinary dividend was paid and payable per share?
9 If the company held assets overseas, what rates of exchange did it adopt for converting overseas currencies into sterling?
10 What amount of political donations were paid during the year, and to whom?
11 What was the profit on ordinary activities for the year before taxation?
12 What was the balance on the deferred taxation account?
13 What was the total amount of the minority interest?
14 What was the turnover for the year?
15 What was the total of the shareholders' funds?
16 What were the auditors' fees?
17 How many directors had the company?
18 What was the dividend cover?

19 What amount was paid for the hire of plant and machinery?
20 What was the total of the directors' emoluments?
21 How many employees had the company?
22 What were the principal activities of the company during the year?
23 Were there any qualifications in the auditors' report, and if so, what were they?
24 What method did the company use for valuing its stock?
25 What were the earnings per share?
26 Were the accounts prepared under the historical cost convention?
27 Has the company disclosed details of any conditions or events that were uncertain at the balance sheet date? If so, what were these conditions and events, and has the company been able to estimate their financial effects?
28 Did the company produce any supplementary accounting statements, and if so, what?
29 Did the total of current assets exceed the total of short-term creditors, and if so, by how much?
30 What date were the accounts signed, and by whom?

Appendix 1 Discount table

Present value of £1 received after *n* years discounted at i%

i / *n*	1	2	3	4	5	6	7	8	9	10
1	.9901	.9804	.9709	.9615	.9524	.9434	.9346	.9259	.9174	.9091
2	.9803	.9612	.9426	.9246	.9070	.8900	.8734	.8573	.8417	.8264
3	.9706	.9423	.9151	.8890	.8638	.8396	.8163	.7938	.7722	.7513
4	.9610	.9238	.8885	.8548	.8227	.7921	.7629	.7350	.7084	.6830
5	.9515	.9057	.8626	.8219	.7835	.7473	.7130	.6806	.6499	.6209
6	.9420	.8880	.8375	.7903	.7462	.7050	.6663	.6302	.5963	.5645

i / *n*	11	12	13	14	15	16	17	18	19	20
1	.9009	.8929	.8850	.8772	.8696	.8621	.8547	.8475	.8403	.8333
2	.8116	.7929	.7831	.7695	.7561	.7432	.7305	.7182	.7062	.6944
3	.7312	.7118	.6931	.6750	.6575	.6407	.6244	.6086	.5934	.5787
4	.6587	.6355	.6133	.5921	.5718	.5523	.5337	.5158	.4987	.4823
5	.5935	.5674	.5428	.5194	.4972	.4761	.4561	.4371	.4190	.4019
6	.5346	.5066	.4803	.4556	.4323	.4104	.3910	.3704	.3521	.3349

Appendix 2 Answers to questions

Chapter 1

1.1 (a) To keep a record of the company's day-to-day progress.
(b) To prepare the company's annual financial accounts.
(c) To supply information to the management for decision-making and control.
(d) To operate a system of internal auditing.
(e) To minimize the company's tax liabilities.

1.2 It is required by law. External auditors report to the shareholders on whether the accounts represent a true and fair view (the discovery of fraud is only incidental to this purpose).

1.3 An accountant collects a great deal of information about a company's activities and then translates it into monetary terms - a language that everyone understands. The information that is collected can help a non-accountant do his job more effectively because it provides him with better guidance upon which to take decisions, but the decision is still his. Furthermore, all managers must be aware of the statutory accounting obligations to which their company has to adhere if they are to avoid taking part in unlawful acts.

1.4 No. The preparation of management accounts is for the company to decide if it believes that they serve a useful purpose.

1.5 Yes. These are contained in the Companies Act 1985. In addition, listed companies have to abide by certain Stock Exchange requirements, and qualified accountants are also bound by a great many mandatory professional requirements.

1.6 To collect and store detailed information about an entity's activities, and then to abstract it and summarize it in the most effective way for whatever purpose it is intended to be used.

Chapter 2

2.1 *1* Matching.
2 Historic cost.
3 Quantitative.
4 Periodicity.

5 Prudence.
6 Going-concern.

2.2 *1* Relevance.
2 Entity.
3 Consistency.
4 Materiality.
5 Historic cost.
6 Realization.

2.3 *1* Entity.
2 Objectivity.
3 Periodicity.
4 Prudence.
5 Dual aspect.
6 Realization.

2.4 *1* (a) Prudence.
(b) The long-term services obtained from a professional footballer are highly unpredictable.

2 (a) Realization.
(b) Although it may appear somewhat imprudent to do so, in most cases the risk is usually small in taking profit prior to the receipt of cash.

3 (a) Entity.
(b) The company does not have a legal title to the house.

4 (a) Prudence.
(b) The final profit cannot be known for sometime (although in some cases a proportion of the profit may be claimed if the final outcome is reasonably certain).

5 (a) Materiality.
(b) It would be unduly pedantic to insist on matching the cost of small stocks of stationery purchased in an earlier period with the revenue of a future period.

6 (a) Prudence.
(b) The improvement work may never result in a more successful revenue earning drug. (NB: In certain specific instances, however, earlier period costs on development work may be matched with revenues earned after the work has been completed.)

Chapter 3

3.1 Adam's books of account:

	Account	
	Debit	*Credit*
1	Cash	Capital
2	Purchases	Cash
3	Van	Cash
4	Rent	Cash

	Account	
	Debit	*Credit*
5	Cash	Sales
6	Office machinery	Cash

3.2 Brown's books of account:

	Account	
	Debit	*Credit*
1	Bank	Cash
2	Cash	Sales
3	Purchases	Bank
4	Office expenses	Cash
5	Bank	Sales
6	Motor car	Bank

3.3 Corby's books of account:

	Account	
	Debit	*Credit*
1	Purchases	Smith
2	Cash	Capital
3	Cash	Sales
4	Purchases	Cash
5	Bank	Cash
6	Machinery	Cash

3.4 Davies' books of account:

	Account	
	Debit	*Credit*
1	Bank	Capital
2	Purchases	Swallow
3	Cash	Sales
4	Purchases	Cash
5	Dale	Sales
6	Motoring expenses	Bank

3.5 Edgar's books of account:

	Account	
	Debit	*Credit*
1	Purchases	Gill
2	Ash	Sales
3	Cash	Sales
4	Purchases	Cash
5	Gill	Bank
6	Cash	Ash

3.6 Ford's books of account:

	Account	
	Debit	*Credit*
1	Cash	Sales
2	Purchases	Carter
3	Holly	Sales
4	Purchases	Cash
5	Sales returns	Holly
6	Carter	Purchases returns

3.7 Gordon's books of account:

	Account	
	Debit	*Credit*
1	Purchases	Watson
2	Cash	Sales
3	Moon	Sales
4	Watson	Bank
5	Watson	Discounts received
6	Cash	Moon
7	Discounts allowed	Moon
8	Purchases	Cash

3.8 Harry's books of account:

	Account	
	Debit	*Credit*
1	Cash	Capital
2	Bank	Cash
3	Rent	Bank
4	Purchases	Paul
5	Van	Bank
6	Cash	Sales
7	Purchases	Nancy
8	Motoring expenses	Cash
9	Nancy	Purchases return
10	Mavis	Sales
11	Drawings	Cash
12	Purchases	Cash
13	Sales return	Mavis
14	Nancy	Bank
15	Cash	Mavis
16	Nancy	Discounts received
17	Discounts allowed	Mavis
18	Petty cash	Bank

3.9 Ivan's ledger accounts:

Cash Account

		£			£
1.9.X9	Capital	10,000	2.9.X9	Bank	8,000
12.9.X9	Cash	3,000	3.9.X9	Purchases	1,000

Capital Account

		£			£
			1.9.X9	Cash	10,000

Bank Account

		£			£
2.9.X9	Cash	8,000	20.9.X9	Roy	6,000
30.9.X9	Norman	2,000			

Purchases Account

		£			£
3.9.X9	Cash	1,000			
10.9.X9	Roy	6,000			

Roy's Account

		£			£
20.9.X9	Bank	6,000	10.9.X9	Purchases	6,000

Sales Account

		£			£
			12.9.X9	Cash	3,000
			15.9.X9	Norman	4,000

Norman

		£			£
15.9.X9	Sales	4,000	30.9.X9	Bank	2,000

3.10 Jones' ledger accounts.

Bank Account

		£			£
1.10.X1	Capital	20,000	10.10.X1	Petty cash	1,000
			25.10.X1	Lang	5,000
			29.10.X1	Green	10,000

Capital Account

		£			£
			1.10.X1	Bank	20,000

Van Account

		£			£
2.10.X1	Lang	5,000			

Lang's Account

		£			£
25.10.X1	Bank	5,000	2.10.X1	Van	5,000

Purchases Account

		£			£
6.10.X1	Green	15,000			
20.10.X1	Cash	3,000			

Green's Account

		£			£
28.10.X1	Discounts received	500	6.10.X1	Purchases	15,000
29.10.X1	Bank	10,000			

Petty Cash Account

		£			£
10.10.X1	Bank	1,000	22.10.X1	Miscellaneous Expenses	500

Sales

		£			£
			14.10.X1	Haddock	6,000
			18.10.X1	Cash	5,000

Haddock

		£			£
14.10.X1	Sales	6,000	30.10.X1	Discounts allowed	600
			31.10.X1	Cash	5,400

Cash Account

		£			£
18.10.X1	Sales	5,000	20.10.X1	Purchases	3,000
31.10.X1	Haddock	5,400			

Miscellaneous Expenses

		£			£
22.10.X1	Petty cash	500			

Discounts Received Account

		£			£
			28.10.X1	Green	500

Discounts Allowed Account

		£			£
30.10.X1	Haddock	600			

3.11 Ken's ledger accounts:

Cash Account

		£			£
1.11.X2	Capital	15,000	2.11.X2	Bank	14,000
27.11.X2	Sales	5,000	28.11.X2	Purchases	4,000
			30.11.X2	Bank	1,000

Capital Account

		£			£
			10.11.X2	Cash	15,000

Bank Account

		£			£
2.11.X2	Cash	14,000	3.11.X2	Rent	1,000
30.11.X2	Main	1,000	26.11.X2	Office expenses	2,000
30.11.X2	Pain	2,000	29.11.X2	Ace	4,000
30.11.X2	Vain	3,000	29.11.X2	Mace	5,000
30.11.X2	Cash	1,000	29.11.X2	Pace	6,000

Rent Account

		£			£
3.11.X2	Bank	1,000			

Purchases Account

		£			£
4.11.X2	Ace	5,000			
4.11.X2	Mace	6,000			
4.11.X2	Pace	7,000			
25.11.X2	Ace	3,000			
25.11.X2	Mace	4,000			
25.11.X2	Pace	5,000			
28.11.X2	Cash	4,000			

Ace's Account

		£			£
29.11.X2	Bank	4,000	4.11.X2	Purchases	5,000
30.11.X2	Discounts received	200	25.11.X2	Purchases	3,000

Mace's Account

		£			£
29.11.X2	Bank	5,000	4.11.X2	Purchases	6,000
30.11.X2	Discounts received	250	25.11.X2	Purchases	4,000

Pace's Account

		£			£
15.11.X2	Purchases returns	1,000	4.11.X2	Purchases	7,000
29.11.X2	Bank	6,000	25.11.X2	Purchases	5,000
30.11.X2	Discounts received	300			

Sales Account

		£			£
			10.11.X2	Main	2,000
			10.11.X2	Pain	3,000
			10.11.X2	Vain	4,000
			27.11.X2	Cash	5,000

Main's Account

		£			£
10.11.X2	Sales	2,000	30.11.X2	Bank	1,000
			30.11.X2	Discounts allowed	100

Pain's Account

		£			£
10.11.X2	Sales	3,000	22.11.X2	Sales return	2,000
			30.11.X2	Bank	2,000
			30.11.X2	Discounts allowed	200

Vain's Account

		£			£
10.11.X2	Sales	4,000	30.11.X2	Bank	3,000
			30.11.X2	Discounts allowed	400

Purchases Returns Account

		£			£
			15.11.X2	Pace	1,000

Sales Returns Account

		£			£
22.11.X2	Pain	2,000			

Office Expenses Account

		£			£
26.11.X2	Bank	2,000			

Discounts Received Account

		£			£
			30.11.X2	Ace	200
			30.11.X2	Mace	250
			30.11.X2	Pace	300

Discounts Allowed Account

		£			£
30.11.X2	Main	100			
30.11.X2	Pain	200			
30.11.X2	Vain	400			

3.12 (a), (b) and (c) Pat's ledger accounts:

Cash Account

		£			£
1.12.X3	Capital	10,000	24.12.X3	Office expenses	5,000
29.12.X3	Fog	4,000	31.12.X3	Grass	6,000
29.12.X3	Mist	6,000	31.12.X3	Seed	8,000
			31.12.X3	Balance c/d	1,000
		£20,000			£20,000
1.1.X4	Balance b/d	1,000			

Capital Account

		£			£
			1.12.X3	Cash	10,000

Purchases Account

		£			£
2.12.X3	Grass	6,000			
2.12.X3	Seed	7,000			
15.12.X3	Grass	3,000			
15.12.X3	Seed	4,000	31.12.X3	Balance c/d	20,000
		£20,000			£20,000
1. 1.X4	Balance b/d	20,000			

Grass's Account

		£			£
12.12.X3	Purchases returns	1,000	2.12.X3	Purchases	6,000
31.12.X3	Cash	6,000	15.12.X3	Purchases	3,000
31.12.X3	Balance c/d	2,000			
		£9,000			£9,000
			1. 1.X4	Balance b/d	2,000

Seed's Account

		£			£
12.12.X3	Purchases returns	2,000	2.12.X3	Purchases	7,000
31.12.X3	Cash	8,000	15.12.X3	Purchases	4,000
31.12.X3	Balance c/d	1,000			
		£11,000			£11,000
			1. 1.X4	Balance b/d	1,000

Sales Account

		£			£
			10.12.X3	Fog	3,000
			10.12.X3	Mist	4,000
			20.12.X3	Fog	2,000
31.12.X3	Balance c/d	12,000	20.12.X3	Mist	3,000
		£12,000			£12,000
			1. 1.X4	Balance b/d	12,000

Fog's Account

		£			£
10.12.X3	Sales	3,000	29.12.X3	Cash	4,000
20.12.X3	Sales	2,000	31.12.X3	Balance c/d	1,000
		£5,000			£5,000
1. 1.X4	Balance b/d	1,000			

Mist's Account

		£			£
10.12.X3	Sales	4,000	29.12.X3	Cash	6,000
20.12.X3	Sales	3,000	31.12.X3	Balance c/d	1,000
		£7,000			£7,000
1. 1.X4	Balance b/d	1,000			

Purchases Returns Account

		£			£
			12.12.X3	Grass	1,000
31.12.X3	Balance c/d	3,000	12.12.X3	Seed	2,000
		£3,000			£3,000
			1. 1.X4	Balance b/d	3,000

Office Expenses Account

		£			£
24.12.X3	Cash	5,000			

Tutorial note

It is unnecessary to balance off an account and bring down the balance if there is only a single entry in it.

(d)

PAT

Trial Balance at 31 December 19X3

	£ Dr	£ Cr
Cash	1,000	
Capital		10,000
Purchases	20,000	
Grass		2,000
Seed		1,000
Sales		12,000
Fog	1,000	
Mist	1,000	
Purchases returns		3,000
Office expenses	5,000	
	£28,000	£28,000

3.13 (a) Vale's books of account:

Bank Account

		£			£
1. 1.X3	Balance b/d	5,000	31.12.X3	Dodd	29,000
31.12.X3	Fish	45,000	31.12.X3	Delivery van	12,000
31.12.X3	Cash	3,000	31.12.X3	Balance c/d	12,000
		£53,000			£53,000
1. 1.X4	Balance b/d	12,000			

Capital Account

		£			£
			1. 1.X3	Balance b/d	20,000

Cash Account

		£			£
1. 1.X3	Balance b/d	1,000	31.12.X3	Purchases	15,000
31.12.X3	Sales	20,000	31.12.X3	Office expenses	9,000
31.12.X3	Fish	7,000	31.12.X3	Bank	3,000
			31.12.X3	Balance c/d	1,000
		£28,000			£28,000
1. 1.X4	Balance b/d	1,000			

Dodd's Account

		£			£
31.12.X3	Bank	29,000	1. 1.X3	Balance b/d	2,000
31.12.X3	Balance c/d	3,000	31.12.X3	Purchases	30,000
		£32,000			£32,000
			1. 1.X4	Balance b/d	3,000

Fish's Account

		£			£
1. 1.X3	Balance b/d	6,000	31.12.X3	Bank	45,000
31.12.X3	Sales	50,000	31.12.X3	Cash	7,000
			31.12.X3	Balance c/d	4,000
		£56,000			£56,000
1. 1.X4	Balance b/d	4,000			

Furniture Account

		£			£
1. 1.X3	Balance b/d	10,000			

Purchases Account

		£			£
31.12.X3	Cash	15,000			
31.12.X3	Dodd	30,000	31.12.X3	Balance c/d	45,000
		£45,000			£45,000
1. 1.X4	Balance b/d	45,000			

Sales Account

		£			£
			31.12.X3	Cash	20,000
31.12.X3	Balance c/d	70,000	31.12.X3	Fish	50,000
		£70,000			£70,000
			1. 1.X4	Balance b/d	70,000

Office Expenses Account

		£			£
31.12.X3	Cash	9,000			

Delivery Van Account

		£			£
31.12.X3	Bank	12,000			

(b)

VALE
Trial balance at 31 December 19X3

	Dr	Cr
	£	£
Bank	12,000	
Capital		20,000
Cash	1,000	
Dodd		3,000
Fish	4,000	
Furniture	10,000	
Purchases	45,000	
Sales		70,000
Office expenses	9,000	
Delivery van	12,000	
	£93,000	£93,000

3.14 (a) Brian's ledger accounts:

Bank Account

		£			£
1.1.X4	Capital	25,000	2.1.X4	Rent	2,000
23.1.X4	Cash	6,000	25.1.X4	Petty cash	500
26.1.X4	Ann	5,500	29.1.X4	Savoy Motors	4,000
31.1.X4	Capital	5,000	30.1.X4	Linda	8,000
			30.1.X4	Sydney	2,000
			31.1.X4	Rent	2,000
			31.1.X4	Balance c/d	23,000
		£41,500			£41,500
1.2.X4	Balance b/d	23,000			

Capital Account

		£			£
			1.1.X4	Bank	25,000
31.1.X4	Balance c/d	30,000	31.1.X4	Bank	5,000
		£30,000			£30,000
			1.2.X4	Balance b/d	30,000

Rent Account

		£			£
2.1.X4	Bank	2,000			
31.1.X4	Bank	2,000	31.1.X4	Balance c/d	4,000
		£4,000			£4,000
1.2.X4	Balance b/d	4,000			

Purchases Account

		£			£
3.1.X4	Linda	5,000			
5.1.X4	Sydney	3,000			
15.1.X4	Linda	10,000	31.1.X4	Balance c/d	18,000
		£18,000			£18,000
1.2.X4	Balance b/d	18,000			

Linda's Account

		£			£
22.1.X4	Purchases return	2,000	3.1.X4	Purchases	5,000
30.1.X4	Bank	8,000	15.1.X4	Purchases	10,000
30.1.X4	Discounts received	700			
31.1.X4	Balance c/d	4,300			
		£15,000			£15,000
			1.2.X4	Balance b/d	4,300

Motor Car Account

		£			£
4.1.X4	Savoy Motors	4,000			

Savoy Motors Account

		£			£
29.1.X4	Bank	£4,000	4.1.X4	Motor car	£4,000

Sydney's Account

		£			£
30.1.X4	Bank	2,000	5.1.X4	Purchases	3,000
30.1.X4	Discounts received	100			
31.1.X4	Balance c/d	900			
		£3,000			£3,000
			1.2.X4	Balance b/d	900

Cash Account

		£			£
10.1.X4	Sales	£6,000	23.1.X4	Bank	£6,000

Sales Account

		£			£
			10.1.X4	Cash	6,000
31.1.X4	Balance c/d	14,000	20.1.X4	Ann	8,000
		£14,000			£14,000
			1.2.X4	Balance b/d	14,000

Ann's Account

		£			£
20.1.X4	Sales	8,000	24.1.X4	Sales return	1,000
			26.1.X4	Bank	5,500
			26.1.X4	Discounts allowed	500
			31.1.X4	Balance c/d	1,000
		£8,000			£8,000
1.2.X4	Balance b/d	1,000			

Purchases Returns Account

		£			£
			22.1.X4	Linda	2,000

Sales Returns Account

		£			£
24.1.X4	Ann	1,000			

Petty Cash Account

		£			£
25.1.X4	Bank	500	28.1.X4	Office expenses	250
			31.1.X4	Balance c/d	250
		£500			£500
1.1.X4	Balance b/d	250			

Discounts Allowed Account

		£			£
26.1.X4	Ann	500			

Office Expenses Account

		£			£
28.1.X4	Petty cash	250			

Discounts Received Account

		£			£
			30.1.X4	Linda	700
31.1.X4	Balance c/d	800	30.1.X4	Sydney	100
		£800			£800
			1.2.X4	Balance b/d	800

(b)

BRIAN
Trial balance at 31 January 19X4

	Dr £	Cr £
Bank	23,000	
Capital		30,000
Rent	4,000	
Purchases	18,000	
Linda		4,300
Motor car	4,000	
Sydney		900
Sales		14,000
Ann	1,000	
Purchases return		2,000
Sales return	1,000	
Petty cash	250	
Discounts allowed	500	
Office expenses	250	
Discounts received		800
	£52,000	£52,000

3.15 FIELD

Trial balance at 28 February 19X5

	Dr	Cr
	£	£
Bank	13,000	
Cash	2,000	
Capital		15,000
Creditors		4,000
Debtors	10,000	
Drawings	5,000	
Electricity	4,000	
Furniture	7,000	
Office expenses	3,000	
Purchases	50,000	
Sales		100,000
Wages	25,000	
	£119,000	£119,000

3.16 TRENT

Corrected trial balance at 31 March 19X4

	Dr	Cr
	£	£
Bank (overdrawn)		2,000
Capital		50,000
Discounts allowed	5,000	
Discounts received		3,000
Dividends received		2,000
Drawings	23,000	
Investments	14,000	
Land and buildings	60,000	
Office expenses	18,000	
Purchases	75,000	
Sales		250,000
Rates	7,000	
Vans	20,000	
Van expenses	5,000	
Wages and salaries	80,000	
	£307,000	£307,000

3.17 **SEVERN**

Trial balance at 30 April 19X7

	Dr	Cr
	£000	£000
Advertising	14	
Bank (current)	5	
Bank (deposit)	50	
Bank interest received		1
Capital		100
Cash	8	
Creditors		12
Debtors	30	
Discounts allowed	5	
Discounts received		2
Drawings	45	
Fees received		10
Furniture and fittings	18	
Land and buildings	40	
Motor cars	22	
Motor car expenses	4	
Plant and equipment	37	
Purchases	300	
Purchases returns		15
Rents received		5
Sales		500
Sales returns	20	
Telephone	3	
Wages	44	
	£645	£645

Chapter 4

4.1 **ETHEL**

Trading, profit and loss account for the year to 31 January 19X1

	£
Sales	35,000
Less: Purchases	20,000
Gross profit	15,000
Less: Expenses:	
Office expenses	11,000
Net profit	£4,000

ETHEL
Balance sheet at 31 January 19X1

	£	£
Fixed assets		
Premises		8,000
Current assets		
Debtors	6,000	
Cash	3,000	
	9,000	
Less: Current liabilities		
Creditors	3,000	6,000
		£14,000
Financed by:		
Capital		
Balance at 1 February 19X0		10,000
Net profit for the year		4,000
		£14,000

4.2

MARION
Trading, profit and loss account for the year to 28 February 19X2

	£	£
Sales		400
Less: Purchases		200
Gross profit		200
Less: Expenses:		
Heat and light	10	
Miscellaneous expenses	25	
Wages and salaries	98	133
Net profit		£67

MARION
Balance sheet at 28 February 19X2

	£	£
Fixed assets		
Buildings		50
Current assets		
Debtors	30	
Bank	4	
Cash	2	
	36	
Less: Current liabilities		
Creditors	24	12
		£62

	£	£
Financed by:		
Capital		50
Balance at 1 March 19X2		
Net profit for the year	67	
Less: Drawings	55	12
		£62

4.3 **GARSWOOD**

Trading, profit and loss account for the year to 31 March 19X3

	£	£
Sales (£63,000 − £3,000)		60,000
Less: Purchases (£21,400 − £1,400)		20,000
Gross profit		40,000
Add: Other incomes:		
Discounts received	600	
Investment income received	400	1,000
		41,000
Less: Expenses:		
Advertising	2,300	
Discounts allowed	100	
Electricity	1,300	
Stationery	900	
Wages	38,700	43,300
Net loss		£(2,300)

GARSWOOD

Balance sheet at 31 March 19X3

	£	£	£
Fixed assets			
Machinery			20,000
Office equipment			10,000
			30,000
Investments			4,000
Current assets			
Trade debtors		6,500	
Other debtors		1,500	
Bank		300	
Cash		100	
		8,400	
c/fwd		8,400	34,000

	£	£	£
b/fwd		8,400	34,000
Less: Current liabilities			
Trade creditors	5,200		
Other creditors	800	6,000	2,400
			£36,400
Financed by:			
Capital			
Balance at 1 April 19X2			55,700
Less: Net loss for the year		(2,300)	
Add: Drawings		(17,000)	(19,300)
			£36,400

4.4 (a) LATHOM

Trading account for the year to 30 April 19X4

	£	£
Sales		60,000
Less: Cost of goods sold:		
Opening stock	3,000	
Purchases	45,000	
	48,000	
Less: Closing stock	4,000	44,000
		£16,000

(b) Under current assets as the first item.

4.5 (a) RUFFORD

Trading account for the year to 31 March 19X5

Stock method	1		2		3	
	£	£	£	£	£	£
Sales (£82,000 – £4,000)		78,000		78,000		78,000
Less: Cost of goods sold						
Opening stock	4,000		4,000		4,000	
Purchases (£48,000 – £3,000)	45,000		45,000		45,000	
	49,000		49,000		49,000	
Less: Closing stock	8,000	41,000	16,000	33,000	4,000	45,000
Gross profit		£37,000		£45,000		£33,000

(b) For the year to 31 March 19X6, other things being equal, method 1 would result in a *higher* gross profit than by using method 2 (whereas the reverse would be true in the year to 31 March 19X5).

4.6

STANDISH

Trading, profit and loss account for the year to 31 May 19X6

	£	£
Sales		79,000
Less: Cost of goods sold:		
Opening stock	7,000	
Purchases	52,000	
	59,000	
Less: Closing stock	12,000	47,000
Gross profit		32,000
Less: Expenses:		
Heating/lighting	1,500	
Miscellaneous	6,700	
Wages and salaries	17,800	26,000
Net profit		£6,000

STANDISH

Balance sheet at 31 May 19X6

	£	£
Fixed assets		
Furniture and fittings		8,000
Current assets		
Stock	12,000	
Debtors	6,000	
Cash	1,200	
	19,200	
Less: Current liabilities		
Creditors	4,300	14,900
		£22,900
Financed by:		
Capital		
Balance at 1 June 19X5		22,400
Net profit for the year	6,000	
Less: Drawings	5,500	500
		£22,900

4.7 **WITTON**

Trading, profit and loss account for the year to 30 June 19X7

	£	£
Sales		30,000
Less: Cost of goods sold:		
Purchases	14,000	
Less: Closing stock	2,000	12,000
Gross profit		18,000
Less: Expenses:		
Office expenses	8,000	
Motor car: depreciation (20% × £5,000)	1,000	9,000
Net profit		£9,000

WITTON

Balance sheet at 30 June 19X7

	£	£
Fixed assets		
Motor car		5,000
Less: Depreciation		1,000
		4,000
Current assets		
Stocks	2,000	
Debtors	3,000	
Cash	500	
	5,500	
Less: Current liabilities		
Creditors	1,500	4,000
		£8,000
Financed by:		
Capital		
At 1 July 19X6		3,000
Net profit for the year	9,000	
Less: Drawings	4,000	5,000
		£8,000

4.8 CROXTETH

Trading, profit and loss account for the year to 31 July 19X8

	£	£	£
Sales			85,000
Less: Cost of goods sold:			
Opening stock		4,000	
Purchases		70,000	
		74,000	
Less: Closing stock		14,000	60,000
Gross profit			25,000
Less: Expenses:			
Depreciation: delivery vans (30% × £40,000)	12,000		
shop equipment (10% × £8,000)	800	12,800	
Shop expenses		7,200	20,000
Net Profit			£5,000

CROXTETH

Balance sheet at 31 July 19X8

Fixed assets	£ *Cost*	£ *Accumulated depreciation*	£ *Net book value*
Delivery vans	40,000	24,000	16,000
Shop equipment	8,000	3,200	4,800
	£48,000	£27,200	£20,800
Current assets			
Stock		14,000	
Bank		2,000	
		16,000	
Less: Current liabilities			
Creditors		4,800	11,200
			£32,000
Financed by:			
Capital			
Balance at 1 August 19X7			35,000
Net profit for the year		5,000	
Less: Drawings		8,000	(3,000)
			£32,000

Tutorial note

Accumulated depreciation:

Delivery vans: £12,000 (b/f) + £12,000 = £24,000.

Shop equipment: £2,400 (b/f) + £800 = £3,200.

4.9 (a) Calculation of the depreciation charge for the year to 31 August 19X9:

		£	£	£	£
1	Land				—
2	Buildings: 2% × £150,000			=	3,000
3	Plant at cost	55,000			
	Less: scrap value	5,000			
		50,000 × 5%		=	2,500
4	Vehicles at cost		45,000		
	Less: Accumulated depreciation at 31 August 19X8		28,800		
			16,200 × 40%	=	6,480
5	Furniture at cost		20,000		
	Less: Scrap value		2,000		
			18,000 × 10% =	1,800	
	Additions at cost		3,000		
	Less: Scrap value		300		
			2,700 × 10% =	270	2,070
Total amount of depreciation (charged to the profit and loss account for the year to 31 August 19X9)					£14,050

(b)

BARROW

Balance sheet (extract) at 31 August 19X9

Fixed assets	*Cost*	*Accumulated depreciation*	*Net book value*
	£	£	£
Land	200,000	—	200,000
Buildings	150,000	63,000	87,000
Plant	55,000	40,000	15,000
Vehicles	45,000	35,280	9,720
Furniture	23,000	14,670	8,330
	£473,000	£152,950	320,050

4.10

PINE

Trading, profit and loss account for the year to 30 September 19X2

	£	£
Sales		40,000
Less: Cost of goods sold:		
Purchases	21,000	
Less: Closing stock	3,000	18,000
Gross profit		22,000
Less: Expenses:		
Depreciation: furniture (15% × £8,000)	1,200	
General expenses	14,000	
Insurance (£2,000 − £200)	1,800	
Telephone (£1,500 + £500)	2,000	19,000
		£3,000

PINE

Balance sheet at 30 September 19X2

	£	£	£
Fixed asset			
Furniture			8,000
Less: Depreciation			1,200
			6,800
Current assets			
Stock		3,000	
Debtors		5,000	
Prepayments		200	
Cash		400	
		8,600	
Less: Current liabilities			
Creditors	5,900		
Accrual	500	6,400	2,200
			£9,000
Financed by:			
Capital			
At 1 October 19X1			6,000
Net profit for the year			3,000
			£9,000

4.11

DALE

Trading, profit and loss account for the year to 31 October 19X3

	£	£	£
Sales			350,000
Less: Cost of goods sold:			
Opening stock		20,000	
Purchases		240,000	
		260,000	
Less: Closing stock		26,000	234,000
Gross profit			116,000
Less: Expenses:			
Depreciation: office equipment	7,000		
vehicles	4,000	11,000	
Heating and lighting (£3,000 + £1,500)		4,500	
Office expenses		27,000	
Rates (£12,000 − £2,000)		10,000	
Wages and salaries		47,000	99,500
Net profit			£16,500

DALE

Balance sheet at 31 October 19X3

	£ *Cost*	£ *Accumulated depreciation*	£ *Net book value*
Fixed assets			
Office equipment	35,000	21,000	14,000
Vehicles	16,000	8,000	8,000
	£51,000	£29,000	22,000
Current assets			
Stocks		26,000	
Trade debtors		61,000	
Prepayments		2,000	
Bank		700	
		89,700	
Less: Current liabilities			
Trade creditors	21,000		
Accruals	1,500	22,500	67,200
			£89,200

	£	£
Financed by:		
Capital		
At 1 November 19X2		85,000
Net profit for the year	16,500	
Less: Drawings	12,300	4,200
		£89,200

4.12 (a) ASTLEY

Adjustments for accruals and prepayments for the year to 30 November 19X4

	Electricity	*Gas*	*Insurance*	*Rates*	*Telephone*	*Wages*
	£	£	£	£	£	£
Cash paid during the year	26,400	40,100	25,000	16,000	3,000	66,800
Add: Prepayments at 1 December 19X3	—	—	12,000	4,000	—	—
	26,400	40,100	37,000	20,000	3,000	66,800
Less: Accruals at 1 December 19X3	5,200	—	—	—	1,500	1,800
	21,200	40,100	37,000	20,000	1,500	65,000
Add: Accruals at 30 November 19X4	8,300	—	—	6,000	—	—
	29,500	40,100	37,000	26,000	1,500	65,000
Less: Prepayments at 30 November 19X4	—	4,900	14,000	—	200	—
Charge to the profit and loss account for the year to 30 November 19X4	£29,500	£35,200	£23,000	£26,000	£1,300	£65,000

(b) Balance sheet at 30 November 19X4

	£
Current assets	
Prepayments (£4,900 + £14,000 + £200)	19,100
Current liabilities	
Accruals (£8,300 + £6,000)	14,300

4.13

DUXBURY

Trading, profit and loss account for the year to 31 December 19X3

	£	£
Sales		95,000
Less: Cost of goods sold:		
Purchases	65,000	
Less: Closing stock	10,000	55,000
Gross profit		40,000
Less: Expenses:		
Depreciation: delivery van (20% × £20,000)	4,000	
Office expenses (£12,100 + £400 − £500)	12,000	
Provision for doubtful debts (5% × £32,000)	1,600	17,600
Net profit		£22,400

DUXBURY

Balance sheet at 31 December 19X3

	£	£	£
Fixed assets			
Delivery van at cost			20,000
Less: Depreciation			4,000
			16,000
Current assets			
Stocks		10,000	
Trade debtors	32,000		
Less: Provision for doubtful debts	1,600	30,400	
Prepayment		500	
Cash		300	
		41,200	
Current liabilities			
Trade creditors	5,000		
Accrual	400	5,400	35,800
			£51,800
Financed by:			
Capital			
Balance at 1 January 19X3			40,000
Net profit		22,400	
Less: Drawings		10,600	11,800
			£51,800

4.14 (a) BEECH

Balance sheet (extracts) at	19X4	19X5	19X6	19X7
	£	£	£	£
Current assets				
Trade debtors	60,000	55,000	65,000	70,000
Less: provision for doubtful debts (10%)	6,000	5,500	6,500	7,000
	54,000	49,500	58,500	63,000

(b) Profit and loss accounts: increase/decrease in provision for doubtful debts:

	£	£
Year to:		
31 January 19X4		6,000 (New)
31 January 19X5	5,500	
Less: Provision at 31 January 19X4	6,000	500 (Decrease)
31 January 19X6	6,500	
Less: Provision at 31 January 19X5	5,500	1,000 (Increase)
31 January 19X7	7,000	
Less: Provision at 31 January 19X6	6,500	500 (Increase)

4.15 ASH

Trading, profit and loss account for the year to 31 March 19X5

	£	£
Sales		150,000
Less: Cost of goods sold:		
Opening stock	10,000	
Purchases	80,000	
	90,000	
Less: Closing stock	15,000	75,000
Gross Profit		75,000
Less: Expenses:		
Bad debt	6,000	
Depreciation: furniture (10% × £9,000)	900	
Electricity (£2,000 + £600)	2,600	
Increase in provision for doubtful debts (£21,000 − £6,000 = £15,000 × 10%) − £1,200	300	
Insurance (£1,500 − £100)	1,400	
Miscellaneous expenses	65,800	77,000
Net loss		£(2,000)

ASH
Balance sheet at 31 March 19X5

	£	£	£
Fixed assets			
Furniture at cost			9,000
Less: Accumulated depreciation (£3,600 + £900)			4,500
			4,500
Current assets			
Stocks		15,000	
Trade debtors (£21,000 − £6,000)	15,000		
Less: Provision for doubtful debts	1,500	13,500	
Prepayment		100	
		28,600	
Less: Current liabilities			
Trade creditors	20,000		
Accrual	600		
Bank overdraft	4,000	24,600	4,000
			£8,500
Financed by:			
Capital			
Balance at 1 April 19X4			20,500
Less: Net loss for the year		(2,000)	
Add: Drawings		(10,000)	(12,000)
			£8,500

4.16 ELM

Trading, profit and loss account for the year to 30 June 19X6

	£	£	£
Sales (£820,000 – £4,000)			816,000
Less: Cost of goods sold:			
Opening stock		47,000	
Purchases (£645,000 – £2,000)		643,000	
		690,000	
Less: Closing stock		50,000	640,000
Gross profit			176,000
Add: Other incomes:			
Discounts received		500	
Interest on investments		800	
Decrease in provision for doubtful debts (£42,000 × 5% – £2,300)		200	1,500
			177,500
Less: Expenses:			
Advertising		3,000	
Depreciation: furniture (15% × £12,000)	1,800		
vehicles (£35,000 – £7,000 × 20%)	5,600	7,400	
Discounts allowed		400	
Electricity (£3,200 + £300)		3,500	
General expenses		28,900	
Rates (£6,000 – £1,000)		5,000	
Telephone		1,300	
Wages and salaries		77,600	
			127,100
Net profit			£50,400

ELM
Balance sheet at 30 June 19X6

	£	£	£
Fixed assets	*Cost*	*Accumulated depreciation*	*Net book value*
Furniture	12,000	3,600	8,400
Vehicles	35,000	12,600	22,400
	£47,000	£16,200	30,800
Investments at cost			5,000
Current assets			
Stocks		50,000	
Trade debtors	42,000		
Less: Provision for doubtful debts	2,100	39,900	
Prepayment		1,000	
Bank		400	
Cash		100	
		91,400	
Less: Current liabilities			
Trade creditors	13,000		
Accrual	300	13,300	78,100
			£113,900
Financed by:			
Capital			
Balance at 1 July 19X6			73,500
Net profit for the year		50,400	
Less: Drawings		10,000	40,400
			£113,900

4.17 LIME

Trading, profit and loss account for the year to 30 September 19X7

	£	£
Sales		372,000
Less: Cost of goods sold:		
Opening stock	36,000	
Purchases	320,000	
	356,000	
Less: Closing stock	68,000	288,000
Gross profit		84,000
Less: Expenses:		
Bad debts	13,000	
Depreciation: office equipment (£44,000 − £4,000 × 25%)	10,000	
Insurance (£1,800 − £200)	1,600	
Loan interest	7,500	
Loss on disposal of office equipment (£4,000 − £3,000 − £500)	500	
Miscellaneous expenses	57,700	
Provision for doubtful debts (10% × £93,000 − £13,000 − £2,000) (increase)	6,000	
Rates (£10,000 + £2,000)	12,000	108,300
Net loss		£(24,300)

LIME

Balance sheet at 30 September 19X7

Fixed assets	£	£	£
Office equipment at cost (£44,000 − £4,000)			40,000
Less: Accumulated depreciation (£22,000 − £3,000 + £10,000)			29,000
			11,000
Current assets			
Stocks		68,000	
Trade debtors (£93,000 − £13,000)	80,000		
Less: Provision for doubtful debts	8,000	72,000	
Prepayment		200	
		140,200	
Less: Current liabilities			
Trade creditors	105,000		
Accrual	2,000		
Bank overdraft	15,200	122,200	18,000
			£29,000

	£	£
Financed by:		
Capital		
Balance at 10 October 19X6		19,300
Less: Net loss for the year	(24,300)	
Add: Drawings	(16,000)	(40,300)
		(21,000)
Loan (from Cedar)		50,000
		£29,000

4.18 TEAK

Trading, profit and loss account for the year to 31 December 19X8

	£	£
Sales		164,000
Less: Cost of goods sold:		
Opening stock	2,800	
Purchases (£83,000 − £6,000)	77,000	
	79,800	
Less: Closing stock	15,800	64,000
Gross profit		100,000
Add: Incomes:		
Building society interest (£700 + £800)	1,500	
Dividends (£100 + £600)	700	
Interest from Gray	500	2,700
		102,700
Less: Expenses:		
Depreciation: plant & equipment (30% × £50,000)	15,000	
vehicles (£64,000 − £16,000) × 25%	12,000	
Office expenses (£39,000 + £1,200 − £9,000)	31,200	
Vehicle expenses	12,600	70,800
Net profit		£31,900

TEAK
Balance sheet at 31 December 19X8

	£	£	£
Fixed assets	*Cost*	*Accumulated depreciation*	*Net book value*
Plant and equipment	50,000	45,000	5,000
Vehicles	64,000	28,000	36,000
	£114,000	£73,000	41,000
Investments at cost			5,000
Current assets			
Stocks		15,800	
Short-term loan		10,000	
Trade debtors		13,200	
Debtors (£800 + £600)		1,400	
Building society deposit		20,000	
Cash at bank and in hand		400	
		60,800	
Less: Current liabilities			
Trade creditors	22,200		
Accrual	1,200	23,400	37,400
			£83,400
Financed by:			
Capital			
Balance at 1 January 19X8			66,500
Net profit for the year		31,900	
Less: Drawings (£6,000 + £9,000)		15,000	16,900
			£83,400

Chapter 5

5.1 MEGG

Manufacturing account for the year to 31 January 19X1

	£000	£000
Direct material:		
Stock at 1 February 19X0	10	
Purchases	34	
	44	
Less: Stock at 31 January 19X1	12	
Materials consumed		32
Direct wages		65
Prime cost		97
Factory overhead expenses:		
Administration	27	
Heat and light	9	
Indirect wages	13	49
		146
Add: Work-in-progress at 1 February 19X0		17
		163
Less: Work-in-progress at 31 January 19X1		14
Manufacturing cost of goods produced		£149

5.2 **MOOR**

Manufacturing, trading, and profit and loss account for the year to 28 February 19X2

	£	£	£
Sales			250,000
Cost of sales:			
Direct materials consumed:			
Stock at 1 March 19X1	13,000		
Purchases	127,500		
	140,500		
Less: Stock at 28 February 19X2	15,500	125,000	
Direct labour		50,000	
Prime cost		175,000	
Factory overheads		27,700	
		202,700	
Add: Work-in-progress at 1 March 19X1		8,400	
		211,100	
Less: Work-in-progress at 28 February 19X2		6,300	
Manufacturing cost		204,800	
Add: Stock of finished goods at 1 March 19X1		24,000	
		228,800	
Less: Stock of finished goods at 28 February 19X2		30,000	198,800
Gross profit			51,200
Administration expenses		33,000	
Selling and distribution expenses		10,200	43,200
Net profit			£8,000

5.3 STUART

Manufacturing, trading, and profit and loss account for the year to 31 March 19X3

	£000	£000	£000
Sales			1,932
Cost of sales:			
Direct materials consumed:			
Stock at 1 April 19X2	38		
Purchases	1,123		
	1,161		
Less: Stock at 31 March 19X3	44	1,117	
Direct labour		330	
Prime cost		1,447	
Factory overheads		230	
		1,677	
Work-in-progress: at 1 April 19X2	29		
at 31 March 19X3	42	(13)	
Manufacturing cost		1,664	
Finished stock: at 1 April 19X2	67		
at 31 March 19X3	65	2	1,666
Gross profit			266
Administration expenses		112	
Miscellaneous expenses		16	128
Net profit for the year			£138

STUART

Balance sheet at 31 March 19X3

	£000	£000	£000
Fixed assets			
Plant and machinery at cost			594
Less: Accumulated depreciation			199
			395
Current assets			
Stocks: raw materials	44		
work-in-progress	42		
finished goods	65	151	
Debtors		184	
Bank		7	
		342	
Less: Current liabilities			
Creditors		335	7
			£402

	£000	£000
Financed by:		
Capital		
At 1 April 19X2		264
Add: Net profit for the year		138
		£402

5.4 THE DAVID AND PETER MANUFACTURING COMPANY

Manufacturing, trading, and profit and loss account for the year to 30 April 19X4

	£000	£000	£000
Sales			420
Cost of sales:			
Direct materials consumed:			
Stock at 1 May 19X3	12		
Purchases	100		
	112		
Less: Stock at 30 April 19X4	14	98	
Direct labour		70	
Prime cost		168	
Factory overhead expenses:			
General factory expenses	13		
Heat and light ($\frac{3}{4}$ × £52,000)	39		
Rent and rates ($\frac{2}{3}$ × £42,000)	28		
Depreciation of equipment (15% × £360,000)	54	134	
		302	
Work-in-progress: At 1 May 19X3	18		
At 30 April 19X4	16	2	
Manufacturing cost		304	
Finished goods: At 1 May 19X3	8		
At 30 April 19X4	22	(14)	290
Gross profit			130
Administration salaries		76	
General office expenses		9	
Heat and light ($\frac{1}{4}$ × £52,000)		13	
Rent and rates ($\frac{1}{3}$ × £42,000)		14	112
Net profit for the year			£18

THE DAVID AND PETER MANUFACTURING COMPANY
Balance sheet at 30 April 19X4

	£000	£000	£000
Fixed assets			
Equipment at cost			360
Less: Accumulated depreciation (£180 + £54)			234
			126
Current assets			
Stocks:			
Raw materials	14		
Work-in-progress	16		
Finished goods	22	52	
Debtors		116	
Cash		18	
		186	
Current liabilities			
Creditors		102	84
			£210
Financed by:			
Capital			
At 1 May 19X3			218
Net profit for the year		18	
Less: Drawings		26	(8)
			£210

5.5 **JEFFREY**

Manufacturing, trading, and profit and loss account for the year to 31 May 19X5

	£000	£000	£000
Sales			693
Cost of sales:			
Direct materials:			
Stock at 1 June 19X4		17	
Purchases		180	
		197	
Less: Stock at 31 May 19X5		20	
		177	
Direct labour		200	
Prime cost		377	
Factory overhead expenses:			
General expenses	60		
Plant depreciation (20% × £160,000)	32	92	
		469	
Work-in-progress: At 1 June 19X4	21		
At 31 May 19X5	30	(9)	
Manufacturing cost		460	
Manufacturing profit (20%)		92	
Market value of goods produced		552	
Purchases of finished goods		55	
		607	
Finished goods stock: At 1 June 19X4	26		
At 31 May 19X5	29	(3)	604
Gross profit on trading			89
Gross profit on manufacture			92
			181
Office expenses		127	
Office equipment depreciation (10% × £30,000)		3	130
Net profit for the year			£51

JEFFREY
Balance sheet at 31 May 19X5

	£000	£000	£000
Fixed assets	*Cost*	*Depreciation*	*Net book value*
Plant	160	102	58
Office equipment	30	12	18
	£190	£114	76
Current assets			
Stocks:			
Raw materials	20		
Work-in-progress	30		
Finished goods	29	79	
Debtors		89	
Bank		6	
		174	
Less: Current liabilities			
Creditors		156	18
			£94
Financed by:			
Capital			
At 1 June 19X4			58
Add: Net Profit for the year		51	
Less: Drawings		15	36
			£94

5.6 CLARICO

Manufacturing, trading and profit and loss account for the year to 30 June 19X6

	£000	£000	£000
Sales			1,570
Cost of sales:			
Direct materials comsumed:			
Stock at 1 July 19X5		120	
Purchases	450		
Carriage inwards	22	472	
		592	
Less: Stock at 30 June 19X6		102	
		490	
Direct labour		142	
Prime cost		632	
Factory overhead expenses:			
Electricity ((£16 + £4) × 80%)	16		
Plant depreciation (20% × £110)	22		
Rent and rates ((£70 + £15 − £25) × 60%)	36		
Indirect wages	48	122	
		754	
Work-in-progress: At 1 July 19X5	40		
At 30 June 19X6	74	(34)	
Manufacturing cost		720	
Manufacturing profit (10%)		72	
Market value of goods produced		792	
Purchases of finished goods		30	
		822	
Finished goods stock: At 1 July 19X5	48		
At 30 June 19X6	76	(28)	794
Gross profit on trading			776
Gross profit on manufacture			72
			848
Administration expenses:			
General	39		
Electricity ((£16 + £4) × 20%)	4		
Rent and rates ((£70 + £15 − £25) × 40%)	24		
Wages	26	93	
c/fwd		93	848

	£000	£000	£000
b/fwd		93	848
Selling and distribution expenses:			
Sales expenses	56		
Wages	18		
Delivery van expenses (£12 + £3 − £2)	13		
Delivery van depreciation (25% × £36)	9	96	
Other expenses			
Increase in provision for doubtful debts ((10% × £800) − £55)		25	214
Net profit for the year			£634

CLARICO
Balance sheet at 30 June 19X6

	£000	£000	£000
	Cost	*Depreciation*	*Net book value*
Fixed assets			
Plant	110	62	48
Delivery vans	36	27	9
	£146	£89	57
Current assets			
Stocks:			
Raw materials	102		
Work-in-progress	74		
Finished goods	76	252	
Trade debtors	800		
Less: Provision for doubtful debts (10%)	80	720	
Prepayments (£25 + £2)		27	
Cash		7	
		1,006	
Less: Current liabilities			
Trade creditors	265		
Accruals (£4 + £15 + £3)	22	287	719
			£776
Financed by:			
Capital			
At 1 July 19X5			252
Add: Net profit for the year		634	
Less: Drawings		110	524
			£776

Chapter 6

6.1 **MARGO LIMITED**

Profit and loss account for the year to 31 January 19X1

	£000
Profit for the financial year	10
Tax on profit	3
	7
Proposed dividend (10p × £50)	5
Retained profit for the year	£2

MARGO LIMITED

Balance sheet at 31 January 19X1

	£000	£000	£000
Fixed assets			
Plant and equipment at cost			70
Less: Accumulated depreciation			25
			45
Current assets			
Stocks		17	
Trade debtors		20	
Cash at bank and in hand		5	
		42	
Less: Current liabilities			
Trade creditors	12		
Taxation	3		
Proposed dividend	5	20	22
			£67
Capital and reserves		*Authorized*	*Issued and fully paid*
Share capital (ordinary shares of £1 each)		£75	50
Profit and loss account (£15 + £2)			17
			£67

6.2 **HARRY LIMITED**

Profit and loss account for the year to 28 February 19X2

	£000	£000
Gross profit for the year		150
Administration expenses (£65 + (10% × £60))	71	
Distribution costs	15	86
Profit for the year		64
Taxation		24
		40
Dividends: Ordinary proposed	20	
Preference paid	6	26
Retained profit for the year		£14

HARRY LIMITED

Balance sheet at 28 February 19X2

	£000	£000	£000
Fixed assets			
Furniture and equipment at cost			60
Less: Accumulated depreciation			42
			18
Current assets			
Stocks		130	
Trade debtors		135	
Cash at bank and in hand		10	
		275	
Less: Current liabilities			
Trade creditors	25		
Taxation	24		
Proposed dividend	20	69	206
			£224

Capital and reserves	*Authorized, issued and fully paid*
Ordinary shares of £1 each	100
Cumulative 15% preference shares of £1 each	40
	140
Share premium account	20
Profit and loss account (£50 + £14)	64
	£224

6.3 **JIM LIMITED**

Trading and profit and loss account for the year to 31 March 19X3

	£000	£000	£000
Sales			270
Less: Cost of goods sold:			
Opening stock		16	
Purchases		124	
		140	
Less: Closing stock		14	126
Gross profit			144
Less: Expenses:			
Advertising		3	
Depreciation: Furniture and fittings (15% × £20)	3		
Vehicles (25% × £40)	10	13	
Director's fees		6	
Rent and rates		10	
Telephone, insurance and stationery		5	
Travelling		2	
Wages and salaries		24	63
Net profit			81
Corporation tax			25
			56
Proposed dividend			28
Retained profit for the year			£28

JIM LIMITED
Balance sheet at 31 March 19X3

	£000 *Cost*	£000 *Accumulated depreciation*	£000 *Net book value*
Fixed assets			
Vehicles	40	20	20
Furniture and fittings	20	12	8
	£60	£32	28
Current assets			
Stocks		14	
Debtors		118	
Bank		11	
		143	
Less: Current liabilities			
Creditors	12		
Taxation	25		
Proposed dividend	28	65	78
			£106
	£000	£000 *Authorized*	£000 *Issued and fully paid*
Capital and reserves			
Ordinary shares of £1 each		£100	70
Profit and loss account (£8 + £28)			36
			£106

6.4 **CYRIL LIMITED**

Trading, profit and loss account for the year to 30 April 19X4

	£000	£000	£000
Sales			900
Less: Cost of goods sold:			
Opening stock		120	
Purchases		480	
		600	
Less: Closing stock		140	460
Gross profit			440
Add: Income:			
Investment income			5
			445
Less: Expenses:			
Advertising		2	
Auditors' remuneration		6	
Bank interest		4	
Directors' remuneration		30	
Depreciation: Buildings	28		
Vehicles	9	37	
General expenses		15	
Repairs and renewals (£4 – £2)		2	
Wages and salaries		221	317
Net profit			128
Corporation tax			60
			68
Dividends: Proposed ordinary (10p per share)		50	
Preference paid		15	65
Retained profit for the year			£3

CYRIL LIMITED

Balance sheet at 30 April 19X4

	£000 Cost	£000 Accumulated depreciation	£000 Net book value
Fixed assets			
Freehold land and buildings	800	130	670
Motor vehicles	36	27	9
	£836	£157	679
Investments at cost (Market value £35,000)			30
Current assets			
Stocks		140	
Debtors		143	
Prepayment		2	
		285	
Less: Current liabilities			
Bank overdraft	20		
Creditors	80		
Taxation	60		
Proposed dividend	50		
Accrual	6	216	69
			£778
			Authorized, issued and fully paid
Capital and reserves			
Ordinary shares of £1 each			500
Cumulative 10% preference shares of £1 each			150
			650
Share premium account			25
Profit and loss account (£100 + £3)			103
			£778

6.5 **NELSON LIMITED**

Trading, profit and loss account for the year to 31 May 19X5

	£000	£000
Sales		800
Less: Cost of goods sold:		
Opening stock	155	
Purchases	400	
	555	
Less: Closing stock	195	360
Gross profit		440
Add: Income:		
Investment income		22
		462
Less: Expenses:		
Administration expenses (£257 + £13)	270	
Auditors' fees	10	
Debenture interest (12% × £100)	12	
Directors' remuneration	60	
Depreciation: Furniture and fittings (12.5% × £200)	25	
Wages and salaries (£44 − £4)	40	417
Net profit		45
Corporation tax		8
		37
Dividends: Ordinary - interim	20	
- proposed	5	
Preference (paid and payable)	10	35
Retained profit for the year		£2

NELSON LIMITED
Balance sheet at 31 May 19X5

	£000	£000	£000
Fixed assets			
Furniture and fittings at cost			200
Less: Accumulated depreciation (£48 + £25)			73
			127
Investments at cost (market value £340,000)			335
Current assets			
Stock		195	
Debtors		225	
Prepayment		4	
Cash at bank and in hand		5	
		429	
Less: Current liabilities			
Creditors	85		
Corporation tax	8		
Proposed dividends: Ordinary	5		
Preference	5		
Accruals (£13 + £6)	19	122	307
			£769
Capital and reserves		*Authorized*	*Issued and fully paid*
Ordinary shares of £1 each		500	400
Cumulative 5% preference shares of £1 each		200	200
		£700	600
Share premium account			50
Profit and loss account (£17 + £2)			19
Shareholders' funds			669
Loans:			
12% Debentures			100
			£769

6.6 KEITH LIMITED

Trading, profit and loss account for the year to 30 June 19X6

	£000	£000
Sales		2,100
Less: Cost of goods sold:		
Opening stock	134	
Purchases	1,240	
	1,374	
Less: Closing stock	155	1,219
		881
Add: Income:		
Investment income		4
		885
Less: Expenses:		
Advertising	30	
Auditors' remuneration	12	
Debenture interest (10% × £70)	7	
Directors' remuneration	55	
Electricity	28	
Insurance (£17 − £3)	14	
Depreciation: Machinery (20% × £420)	84	
Vehicles (25% × £80)	20	
Increase in provision for doubtful debts ((5% × £300) − £8)	7	
Office expenses	49	
Rent and rates	75	
Wages and salaries	358	739
Net profit		146
Corporation tax		60
		86
Dividends: Proposed ordinary (400,000 × 10p)	40	
Preference	4	44
Retained profit for the year		£42

KEITH LIMITED
Balance sheet at 30 June 19X6

	£000	£000	£000
	Cost	*Accumulated*	*Net book*
Fixed assets		*depreciation*	*value*
Machinery	420	236	184
Vehicles	80	60	20
	£500	£296	204
Investments (market value £30,000)			28
Current assets			
Stock		155	
Trade debtors	300		
Less: Provision for doubtful debts (5%)	15	285	
Prepayment		3	
Bank		7	
		450	
Less: Current liabilities			
Creditors	69		
Corporation tax	60		
Proposed dividend	40		
Accruals (£7 + £12)	19	188	262
			£494
		Authorized	*Issued and*
Capital and reserves			*fully paid*
Ordinary shares of £0.50 each		300	200
Cumulative 8% preference shares of £1 each		50	50
		£350	250
Profit and loss account (£132 + £42)			174
Shareholders' funds			424
Loans:			
10% Debentures			70
			£494

Chapter 7

7.1 DENNIS LIMITED

Statement of source and application of funds for the year to 31 January 19X2

	£	£
Source of funds		
Profit before tax (£60 – £26)		34
Issue of shares for cash (£800 – £700)		100
		134
Application of funds		
Purchase of land (£700 – £600)		(100)
		34
Increase/decrease in working capital:		
Increase in stocks (£120 – £100)	20	
Increase in debtors (£250 – £200)	50	
(Increase) in creditors (£220 – £180)	(40)	
Movement in net liquid funds:		
Cash (£10 – £6)	4	£34

7.2 FRANK LIMITED

Statement of source and application of funds for the year to 28 February 19X2

	£	£
Source of funds		
Profit before tax (£40 – £30)		10
Adjustments for items not involving the movement of funds:		
Depreciation (£100 – £80)		20
Total generated from operations		30
Funds from other sources:		
Issue of debentures		60
		90
Application of funds		
Purchase of investments		(100)
		(10)
Increase/decrease in working capital:		
Increase in stocks (£190 – £160)	30	
Decrease in debtors (£220 – £110)	(110)	
Decrease in creditors (£160 – £200)	40	
Movement in net liquid funds:		
Increase in cash balances (£10 + £20)	30	£(10)

7.3 STARTER

Statement of source and application of funds for the year to 31 March 19X3

	£	£
Source of funds		
Profit		4,000
Adjustment for item not involving the movement of funds:		
Depreciation		2,000
Total generated from operations		6,000
Funds from other sources		
Capital introduced		20,000
		26,000
Application of funds:		
Purchase of van		(10,000)
		16,000
Increase/decrease in working capital:		
Increase in stock	1,000	
Increase in trade debtors	5,000	
(Increase) in trade creditors	(2,500)	
Movement in net liquid funds:		
Increase in bank balance	12,500	£16,000

7.4 GREGORY LIMITED

Statement of source and application of funds for the year to 30 April 19X4

	£000	£000
Source of funds		
Profit before tax		75
Adjustments for items not involving the movement of funds:		
Depreciation (£180 – £100)		80
		155
Funds from other sources		
Issue of loans		50
		205
Application of funds		
Dividends paid	(35)	
Tax paid	(18)	
Purchase of plant (£550 – £400)	(150)	(203)
		2
Increase/decrease in working capital		
Increase in stocks (£90 – £50)	40	
Decrease in debtors (£50 – £70)	(20)	
(Increase) in creditors (£55 – £45)	(10)	
Movement in net liquid funds:		
(Decrease) in cash balances (£2 – £10)	(8)	£2

7.5 PILL LIMITED

Statement of source and application of funds for the year to 31 May 19X5

	£000	£000
Source of funds		
Profit before tax		580
Adjustments for items not involving the movement of funds:		
Depreciation (£60 + £40)		100
Total generated from operations		680
Funds from other sources:		
Issue of shares for cash (£550 − £500)		50
		730
Application of funds		
Dividends paid (£150 + £250 − £100)	(300)	
Tax paid (£170 + £150 − £220)	(100)	
Purchase of fixed assets ((£800 − £600) + (£250 − £200))	(250)	
Repayment of loans (£190 − £40)	(150)	(800)
		(70)
Increase/decrease in working capital		
Increase in stocks (£540 − £400)	140	
Increase in debtors (£200 − £180)	20	
(Increase) in creditors (£300 − £270)	(30)	
Movement of net liquid funds:		
(Decrease) in cash balances (£320 − £120)	(200)	£(70)

7.6 BRIAN LIMITED

Statement of source and application of funds for the year to 30 June 19X6

	£000	£000
Source of funds		
Profit before tax		115
Adjustments for items not involving movement of funds:		
Depreciation	35	
Loss on sale of vehicle	3	
Increase in provision for doubtful debts	1	39
Total generated from operations		154
Funds from other sources:		
Sale of vehicle		12
		166
Application of funds		
Dividends paid	(20)	
Tax paid	(52)	
Purchase of vehicles	(75)	147
		19
Increase/decrease in working capital		
Decrease in stocks (£60 – £50)	(10)	
Increase in debtors (£100 – £80)	20	
Decrease in creditors (£53 – £60)	7	
Movement in net liquid funds:		
Increase in cash balances (£8 – £6)	2	£19

only a book value

Vehicles a/c

30/6/86	Balance b/d	150,000	30/6/87	Disposal a/c	25,000
	Bank	75,000	30/6/87	Balance c/d	200,000
		225,000			225,000
1/7/87	Balance b/d	200,000			

Prov. for Dep.

30/6/87	Disposal a/c	10,000	30/6/86	Balance	75,000
	Balance c/d	100,000		P+L a/c	35,000
		110,000			110,000

Disposal a/c

30/6/87	Vehicles	25,000	Prov. for dep.	10,000
			bank	12,000
			Loss on Sale	3,000

Chapter 8

8.1 BETTY

Accounting ratios year to 31 January 19X1:

1 Gross profit ratio:

$$\frac{\text{Gross profit}}{\text{Total sales revenue}} \times 100 = \frac{£30}{£100} \times 100 = \underline{\underline{30\%}}$$

2 Net profit ratio:

$$\frac{\text{Net profit}}{\text{Sales}} \times 100 = \frac{£14}{£100} \times 100 = \underline{\underline{14\%}}$$

3 Return on capital employed:

$$\frac{\text{Net profit}}{\text{Average capital}} \times 100 = \frac{£14}{\frac{1}{2}(£40 + £48)} \times 100 = \underline{\underline{31.8\%}}$$

4 Current ratio:

$$\frac{\text{Current assets}}{\text{Current liabilities}} = \frac{£25}{£6} = \underline{\underline{4.2 \text{ to } 1}}$$

5 Acid test:

$$\frac{\text{Current assets} - \text{stock}}{\text{Current liabilities}} = \frac{£25 - £10}{£6} = \underline{\underline{2.5 \text{ to } 1}}$$

6 Stock turnover:

$$\frac{\text{Cost of goods sold}}{\text{Average stock}} = \frac{£70}{\frac{1}{2}(£15 + £10)} = \underline{\underline{5.6 \text{ times}}}$$

7 Debtor collection period:

$$\frac{\text{Trade debtors}}{\text{Credit sales}} \times 365 = \frac{12}{100} \times 365 = \underline{\underline{43.8 \text{ days}}}$$

8.2 JAMES LIMITED

Accounting ratios year to 28 February 19X2:

1 Return on capital employed:

$$\frac{\text{Net profit before taxation and dividends}}{\text{Shareholders' funds}} \times 100 = \frac{£90}{\frac{1}{2}\,(£600 + £620)} \times$$

$$= \underline{\underline{14.8\%}}$$

2 Gross profit:

$$\frac{\text{Gross profit}}{\text{Sales}} \times 100 = \frac{£600}{£1{,}200} \times 100 = \underline{\underline{50\%}}$$

3 Mark-up:

$$\frac{\text{Gross profit}}{\text{Cost of goods sold}} \times 100 = \frac{£600}{£600} \times 100 = \underline{\underline{100\%}}$$

4 Net profit:

$$\frac{\text{Net profit before taxation and dividends}}{\text{Sales}} \times 100 = \frac{£90}{£1{,}200} \times 100$$

$$= \underline{\underline{7.5\%}}$$

5 Acid test:

$$\frac{\text{Current assets} - \text{stocks}}{\text{Current liabilities}} = \frac{£275 - £75}{£240} = \underline{\underline{0.83 \text{ to } 1}}$$

6 Fixed assets turnover:

$$\frac{\text{Sales}}{\text{Fixed assets (NBV)}} = \frac{£1{,}200}{£685} = \underline{\underline{1.75 \text{ times}}}$$

7 Debtor collection period:

$$\frac{\text{Trade debtors}}{\text{Credit sales}} \times 365 = \frac{£200}{£1{,}200} \times 365 = \underline{\underline{60.8 \text{ days}}}$$

you give your debtors 60.8 days to pay their debts

8 Capital gearing:

$$\frac{\text{Long-term loans}}{\text{Shareholders' funds and long-term loans}} \times 100 = \frac{£100}{£720} \times 100$$

$$= \underline{\underline{13.9\%}}$$

owners invested in business – Shareholders' funds

Extent to which company is financed by debt

8.3 Accounting ratios year to 31 March 19X3:

		Mark Limited	*Luke Limited*	*John Limited*
1	Return on capital employed: Net profit before taxation and dividends / Shareholders' funds × 100	£64 × 100 / £250 = 25.6%	£22 × 100 / £327 = 6.7%	£55 × 100 / £290 = 19.0%
2	Capital gearing: Preference shares + Long-term loans × 100 / Shareholders' funds + Long-term loans	No preference, shares or long-term loans	£20 × 100 / £327 = 6.1%	£10 + 100 × 100 / £390 = 28.2%

8.4 HELENA LIMITED

Accounting ratios 19X2 to 19X6:

		19X2	19X3	19X4	19X5	19X6
1	Gross profit: $\frac{\text{Gross Profit} \times 100}{\text{Sales}}$	$\frac{£30 \times 100}{£130}$	$\frac{£40 \times 100}{£150}$	$\frac{£60 \times 100}{£190}$	$\frac{£70 \times 100}{£210}$	$\frac{£75 \times 100}{£320}$
		= 23.1%	= 27.7%	= 31.6%	= 33.3%	= 23.4%
2	Mark-up: $\frac{\text{Gross profit} \times 100}{\text{Cost of goods sold}}$	$\frac{£30 \times 100}{£100}$	$\frac{£40 \times 100}{£110}$	$\frac{£60 \times 100}{£130}$	$\frac{£70 \times 100}{£140}$	$\frac{£75 \times 100}{£245}$
		= 30%	= 36.4%	= 46.2%	= 50%	= 30.6%
3	Stock turnover: $\frac{\text{Cost of goods sold}}{\text{Average stock}}$	$\frac{£100}{\frac{1}{2}(£20+£30)}$	$\frac{£110}{\frac{1}{2}(£30+£30)}$	$\frac{£130}{\frac{1}{2}(£30+£35)}$	$\frac{£140}{\frac{1}{2}(£35+£40)}$	$\frac{£245}{\frac{1}{2}(£40+£100)}$
		= 4 times	= 3.7 times	= 4 times	= 3.7 times	= 3.5 times
4	Trade debtor collection period: $\frac{\text{Average trade debtors} \times 365}{\text{Credit sales}}$	$\frac{\frac{1}{2}(£45+£40) \times 365}{£130}$	$\frac{\frac{1}{2}(£40+£45) \times 365}{£150}$	$\frac{\frac{1}{2}(£70+£40) \times 365}{£190}$	$\frac{\frac{1}{2}(£100+£70) \times 365}{£210}$	$\frac{\frac{1}{2}(£150+£100) \times 365}{£320}$
		= 119.3 days	= 103.4 days	= 105.7 days	= 147.7 days	= 142.6 days
5	Trade creditor payment period: $\frac{\text{Average trade creditors} \times 365}{\text{Credit purchases}}$	$\frac{\frac{1}{2}(£20+£20) \times 365}{£110}$	$\frac{\frac{1}{2}(£25+£20) \times 365}{£110}$	$\frac{\frac{1}{2}(£25+£25) \times 365}{£135}$	$\frac{\frac{1}{2}(£30+£25) \times 365}{£145}$	$\frac{\frac{1}{2}(£60+£30) \times 365}{£305}$
		= 66.4 days	= 74.7 days	= 67.6 days	= 69.2 days	= 53.9 days

8.5 HEDGE PLC

Accounting ratios:

1 Dividend yield:

$$\frac{\text{Nominal value per share} \times \text{Declared dividend rate}}{\text{Market price per share}} = \frac{£1 \times 7\%}{£3.5} = 2\%$$

2 Dividend cover:

$$\frac{\text{Net profit after taxation}}{\text{Ordinary dividends}} = \frac{£70,000}{£35,000} = 2 \text{ times}$$

3 Earnings per share:

$$\frac{\text{Net profit after taxation}}{\text{Number of ordinary shares in issue}} = \frac{£70,000}{£500,000} = 14\text{p}$$

4 Price/earnings ratio:

$$\frac{\text{Market price per share}}{\text{Earnings per share}} = \frac{£3.50}{£0.14} = 25$$

8.6 (a)

STYLE LIMITED

Accounting ratios:

		19X5	19X6
1	Gross profit: $\frac{\text{Gross profit} \times 100}{\text{Sales}}$	$\frac{£525 \times 100}{£1,500} = 35\%$	$\frac{£600 \times 100}{£1,900} = 31.6\%$
2	Mark-up: $\frac{\text{Gross Profit}}{\text{Cost of goods sold}} \times 100$	$\frac{£525 \times 100}{£975} = 53.8\%$	$\frac{£600 \times 100}{£1,300} = 46.2\%$
3	Net profit: $\frac{\text{Net profit} \times 100}{\text{Sales}}$	$\frac{£275 \times 100}{£1,500} = 18.3\%$	$\frac{£250 \times 100}{£1,900} = 13.2\%$
4	Return on capital employed: $\frac{\text{Net profit}}{\text{Shareholders' funds}} \times 100$	$\frac{£275 \times 100}{\frac{1}{2}(£900 + £1,000)} = 28.9\%$	$\frac{£250 \times 100}{\frac{1}{2}(£900 + £1,250)} = 23.3\%$
5	Stock turnover: $\frac{\text{Cost of goods sold}}{\text{Average stock}}$	$\frac{£975}{\frac{1}{2}(£80 + £100)} = 10.8 \text{ times}$	$\frac{£1,300}{\frac{1}{2}(£100 + £200)} = 8.7 \text{ times}$
6	Current ratio: $\frac{\text{Current assets}}{\text{Current liabilities}}$	$\frac{£500}{£80} = 6.3 \text{ to } 1$	$\frac{£1,000}{£210} = 4.8 \text{ to } 1$
7	Acid test: $\frac{\text{Current assets} - \text{stock}}{\text{Current liabilities}}$	$\frac{£500 - £100}{£80} = 5 \text{ to } 1$	$\frac{£1,000 - £200}{£210} = 3.8 \text{ to } 1$

		19X5	19X6
8	Trade debtor collection period:		
	$\frac{\text{Trade debtors} \times 365}{\text{Credit Sales}}$	$\frac{£375 \times 365}{£1{,}500}$ = 92 days	$\frac{£800 \times 365}{£1{,}900}$ = 154 days
9	Trade creditor payment period:		
	$\frac{\text{Trade creditors} \times 365}{\text{Purchases}}$	$\frac{£80 \times 365}{£995}$ = 30 days	$\frac{£200 \times 365}{£1{,}400}$ = 53 days

(b) *Brief comments*

The company increased its sales in 19X6 by £400,000 (26.7%). It appeared to achieve this by reducing its profit on goods sold, but the increased activity probably resulted in additional expenses. As a result, even in absolute terms, its net profit was down from £275,000 to £250,000. It should also be noted there is no explanation why an amount was not set aside for taxation or provision made for a dividend either in 19X5 or in 19X6.

Its liquidity position is still healthy, even if its debtor collection period (based on year-end figures) has increased substantially (as has the time it is taking to pay the creditors). This may be a deliberate policy to stimulate sales or it may be that it has been too busy to encourage its customers to settle their debts.

Not surprisingly, the cash position has deteriorated and at the end of 19X6 the company was in overdraft.

Increased trading activity does not always guarantee survival if the company cannot settle its debts as they fall due, and unless it becomes more efficient in this respect, in the long term, the company's future could be uncertain.

Chapter 9

9.1 *Financial accounting* is mainly concerned with supplying information to the external users of an entity.

Management accounting is concerned with producing information for use within an entity.

9.2
1 Elements
2 Units
3 Direct and indirect
4 Fixed and variable
5 Controllable and non-controllable
6 Relevant and irrelevant
7 Responsibility
8 Normal and abnormal

9.3
1 General board of directors
2 Divisions
3 Factories or works
4 Functions
5 Cost centres

9.4 A clearly defined area of responsibility which is charged with its own identifiable operating costs. A cost centre may take the form of a department, an area, a machine or an individual (such as a salesman).

Chapter 10

10.1 1 FIFO:

			£
1,000 units	@ £20	=	20,000
250 units	@ £25	=	6,250
Charge to production			£26,250

2 LIFO:

			£
500 units	@ £25	=	12,500
750 units	@ £20	=	15,000
Charge to production			£27,500

3 Periodic weighted average:

Units	*Value*
	£
1,000 @ £20	20,000
500 @ £25	12,500
1,500	£32,500

Average = $\frac{£32,500}{1,500}$ = £21.67

Charge to production = 1,250 × £21.67 = £27,088

10.2 MATERIAL ST 2

	Stock	*Units*	*Total stock value*	*Average unit price*
			£	£
1.2.X2	Opening	500	500	1.00
10.2.X2	Receipts	200	220	
		700	720	1.03
12.2.X2	Receipts	100	112	
		800	832	1.04
17.2.X2	Issues	(400)	(416)	
		400	416	
25.2.X2	Receipts	300	345	
		700	761	1.09
27.2.X2	Issues	(250)	(273)	
28.2.X2	*Closing stock*	£450	£488	

10.3 Closing stock calculations:

1 FIFO:

800 units	@ £12	=	£9,600

2 LIFO:

			£
600 units	@ £12	=	7,200
200 units	@ £10	=	2,000
800			£9,200

3 Continuous weighted average:

	Stock	*Total stock* *Units*	*Value*	*Average unit price*
			£	£
1.1.X3	Purchases	2,000	20,000	10
31.3.X3	Issues	(1,600)	(16,000)	
		400	4,000	
1.2.X3	Purchases	2,400	26,400	
		2,800	30,400	10.86
28.2.X3	Issues	(2,600)	(28,236)	
		200	2,164	
1.3.X3	Purchases	1,600	19,200	
		1,800	21,364	11.87
31.3.X3	Issues	(1,000)	(11,870)	
		800	£9,494	

10.4 Calculation of closing stock:

	Units	*Value*
		£
Total receipts:	240	1,692

Periodic weighted average price: $\frac{£1,692}{£240}$ = £7.05

Total issues: 195 units – all issued at £7.05 = £1,375

	£	*Units*
In stock at 30.4.X4 *Less* issues:		
£1,692 – £1,375 =	317	45 (240 – 195)
Add: Stock at 1.4.X4	120	20
Closing stock at 30.4.X4	£437	65

10.5 STEED LIMITED

Trading Account for the year to 31 May 19X5

	FIFO	*LIFO*	*Periodic weighted average*	*Continuous weighted average*
	£	£	£	£
Sales	500,000	500,000	500,000	500,000
Less: Cost of goods sold:				
Opening stock	40,000	40,000	40,000	40,000
Purchases	440,000	440,000	440,000	440,000
	480,000	480,000	480,000	480,000
Less: Closing stock	90,000	65,000	67,500	79,950
	390,000	415,000	412,500	400,050
Gross profit	£110,000	£85,000	£87,500	£99,950

10.6 IRON LIMITED

(a) Pricing the issue of materials to production

1 First in, first out (FIFO):

Total receipts = 2,400 litres
Total issues = 2,200 litres

Therefore closing stock = 200 litres @ £5 per litre = £1,000

2 Last in, first out (LIFO):

Closing stock position at 31 December 19X4:

		£
October receipts:	All issued in December	
June receipts:	400 litres issued in July	
	400 litres issued in December	
April receipts:	300 litres issued in May leaving	
	100 litres in stock @ £3.00 per litre =	300
January receipts:	100 litres issued in February leaving	
	100 litres in stock @ £2.00 per litre =	200
Closing stock value:		£500

3 Periodic weighted average:

Total value of receipts = £9,600
Total receipts = 2,400 litres

Therefore periodic weighted average price per litre = £4.00.
Value of stock = £4 × 200 litres = £800

4 *Continuous weighted average:*

Month	*Quantity*	*Stock balance* *Value*	*Average price per litre in stock*	*Issued at per litre*
	(litres)	£	£	£
January	200	400	2.00	
February	(100)	(200)		2.00
	100	200		
April	500	1,500		
	600	1,700	2.83	
May	(300)	(849)		2.83
	300	851		
June	800	3,200		
	1,100	4,051	3.68	
July	(400)	(1,472)		3.68
	700	2,579		
October	900	4,500		
	1,600	7,079	4.42	
December	(1,400)	(6,188)		4.42
	200	£891		

(b) Calculation of gross profit

Method	(1) *FIFO*	(2) *LIFO*	(3) *Periodic weighted average*	(4) *Continuous weighted average*
	£	£	£	£
Sales	20,000	20,000	20,000	20,000
Less: Cost of goods sold:				
Purchases	9,600	9,600	9,600	9,600
Less: Closing stock	1,000	500	800	891
	8,600	9,100	8,800	8,709
Conversion costs	7,000	7,000	7,000	7,000
Manufacturing cost	15,600	16,100	15,800	15,709
Gross profit	£4,400	£3,900	£4,200	£4,291

Chapter 11

11.1 SCAR LIMITED

Overhead apportionment January 19X1:

	Production Department *A*	*B*	*Service Department*
	£000	£000	£000
Allocated expenses	65	35	50
Apportionment of services department's expenses in the ratio 60: 40	30	20	(50)
Overhead to be charged	£95	£55	—

11.2 BANK LIMITED

Assembly department - overhead absorption methods:

1 Specific units:

$$\frac{\text{Total cost centre overhead}}{\text{Number of units}} = \frac{£250,000}{50,000} = £5 \text{ per unit}$$

2 Direct materials:

$$\frac{\text{Total cost centre overhead}}{\text{Direct materials}} \times 100 = \frac{£250,000}{500,000} \times 100 = 50\%$$

Therefore 50% of £8 = £4 per unit

3 Direct labour:

$$\frac{\text{Total cost centre overhead}}{\text{Direct labour}} \times 100 = \frac{£250,000}{1,000,000} \times 100 = 25\%$$

Therefore 25% of £30 = £7.50 per unit

4 Prime cost:

$$\frac{\text{Total cost centre overhead}}{\text{Prime cost}} \times 100 = \frac{£250,000}{1,530,000} \times 100 = 16.3\%$$

Therefore 16.3% of £40 = £6.52 per unit

5 Direct labour hours:

$$\frac{\text{Total cost centre overhead}}{\text{Direct labour hours}} = \frac{£250,000}{100,000} = £2.50 \text{ per direct labour hour}$$

Therefore £2.50 of 3.5 DLH = £8.75 per unit

6 Machine hours:

$$\frac{\text{Total cost centre overhead}}{\text{Machine hours}} = \frac{£250,000}{25,000} = £10 \text{ per machine hour}$$

Therefore £10 of 0.75 = £7.50 per unit

11.3 CLOUGH LIMITED

Pg. 216

(a) Overhead absorption for March 19X3 - Production department:

1 Direct labour hours:

$$\frac{\text{Total cost centre overhead}}{\text{Direct labour hours}} = \frac{£150{,}000}{30{,}000} = £5 \text{ per DLH}$$

Therefore for order number 123 : £5 × 5 = £25

2 Machine hours:

$$\frac{\text{Total cost centre overheads}}{\text{Machine hours}} = \frac{£150{,}000}{10{,}000} = £15 \text{ per MH}$$

Therefore for order number 123 : £15 × 2 = £30

Selling price of order number 123	*Direct labour hours*	*Machine hours*
	£	£
Direct materials	20	20
Direct wages	25	25
Prime costs	45	45
Overhead	25	30
Total cost	70	75
Administration + profit (50%)	35	37.50
Selling price	£105	£112.50

(b) As the department appears more labour intensive than machine intensive, use the direct labour hour method.

11.4 BURNS LIMITED

Overhead absorption schedule – April 19X4:

Departments	*Processing*	*Assembling*	*Finishing*	*Administration*	*Work study*
	£	£	£	£	£
Direct labour	—	—	—	65,000	33,000
Allocated costs	15,000	20,000	10,000	35,000	12,000
				100,000	
Apportion:					
Administration (50:30:15:5)	50,000	30,000	15,000	(100,000)	5,000
					50,000
Work study (70:20:10)	35,000	10,000	5,000	—	(50,000)
Overhead to be absorbed	£100,000	£60,000	£30,000	—	—

Calculation of absorption rates:

Processing department: $\frac{\text{TCCO}}{\text{Machine hours:}} = \frac{£100{,}000}{25{,}000} = £4 \text{ per MH}$

Assembling department: $\frac{\text{TCCO}}{\text{Direct labour hours}} = \frac{£60{,}000}{30{,}000} = £2 \text{ per DLH}$

Finishing department: $\frac{\text{TCCO}}{\text{Direct labour cost}} \times 100 = \frac{£30{,}000}{120{,}000} = 25\%$

Total cost of producing unit XP6:

	£	£
Prime cost		47
Overhead:		
Processing (£4 × 6 MH)	24	
Assembling (£2 × 1)	2	
Finishing (25% × £12)	3	29
Total cost		£76

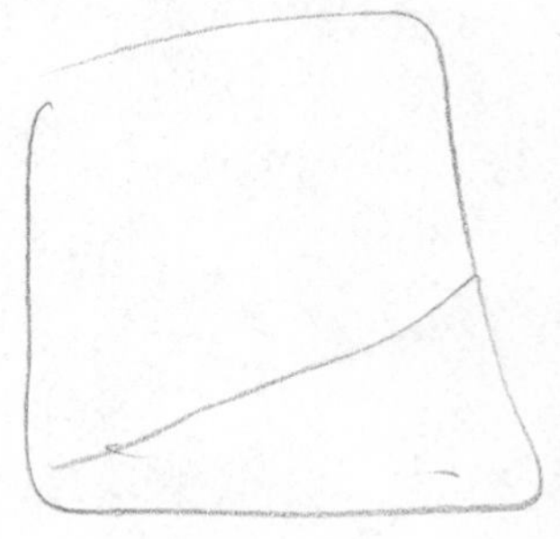

11.5 OUTLANE LIMITED

(a) *Overhead charge – direct labour cost method:*

Pg. 218

	Contract 1	Contract 2
Direct labour cost:		
DLH × rate per hour = 100 × £3.00	£300	£300
Therefore overhead to be absorbed (100%) =	£300	£300

(b) *Overhead charge – machine hour rate method:*

Overhead absorption schedule

	Apportionment Method	*L* £000	*M* £000	*N* £000	*O* £000
Administration	Total number of employees	40	30	20	10
Depreciation of machinery	Depreciation rate	22	8	10	40
Employer's National Insurance	Total number of employees	4	3	2	1
Heating and Lighting	Cubic capacity	6	3	1	5
Holiday pay	Total number of employees	8	6	4	2
Indirect labour cost	Number of indirect employees	4	3	2	1
Insurance: machinery	Capital cost	11	4	5	20
property	Floor space	4	3	2	2
Machine maintenance	Maintenance hours	15	12	9	6
Power	Kilowatt hours	30	50	90	60
Rent and rates	Floor space	20	15	10	10
Supervision	Total number of employees	20	15	10	5
Overhead to be absorbed		184	152	165	162
÷ Total Machine hours		92	38	165	27
= Overhead absorption rate		£2	£4	£1	£6

Machine Hours Overhead Absorption rate = TCCO / Machine Hours = 184,000 / 92,000 = £2

Department	*Contract 1* Machine hours	Absorption rate	Total	*Contract 2* Machine hours	Absorption rate	Total
		£	£		£	£
L	60	2	120	20	2	40
M	30	4	120	10	4	40
N	10	1	10	10	1	10
O		—	—	60	6	360
Total overhead to be absorbed			£250			£450

11.6 SARAH LIMITED

Overhead absorption schedule for June 19X6:

Cost centre	*Production* *D*	*P*	*Service* *1*	*2*	*3*
	£000	£000	£000	£000	£000
Method 1: specified order of closure					
Allocated costs	45	35	160	71	34
Apportion the service cost centre costs in the following order (different orders are possible):					
1 (55:20:15:10)	88	32	(160)	24	16
				95	
2 (45:40: - :10)	45	40	—	(95)	10
3 (50:10)	50	10			(60)
Overhead to be absorbed	£228	£117	—	—	—
Method 2: Ignore inter-department servicing					
Allocated costs	45	35	160	71	34
Apportion the service cost centre costs as follows:					
1 (55:20)	117	43	(160)	—	—
2 (45:40)	38	33	—	(71)	—
3 (50:10)	28	6	—	—	(34)
Overhead to be absorbed	£228	£117	—	—	—

Chapter 12

12.1 One which contains both financial and cost accounts.

12.2 One in which the cost accounts are kept quite separate from the financial accounts, and there is little double-entry connection between them.

12.3 A method of costing designed to suit the particular circumstances in which goods are manufactured or services provided.

12.4 An application of costing methods devised to suit the circumstances in which information is presented to management.

Chapter 13

13.1 POLE LIMITED

Marginal cost statement for the year to 31 January 19X2

	£000	£000
Sales		450
Less: Variable costs:		
Direct materials	60	
Direct wages	26	
Administration expenses: variable (£7 + £4)	11	
Research and development expenditure: variable (£15 + £5)	20	
Selling and distribution expenditure: variable (£4 + £9)	13	
		130
Contribution		320
Less: Fixed costs:		
Administration expenses (£30 + £16)	46	
Materials: indirect	5	
Production overhead	40	
Research and development expenditure (£60 + £5)	65	
Selling and distribution expenditure (£80 + £21)	101	
Wages: indirect	13	270
Profit		£50

13.2 GILES LIMITED

(a) (i) *Break-even point*

In value terms:

$$\frac{\text{Fixed costs} \times \text{sales}}{\text{Contribution}} = \frac{£150}{(£500 - £300)} \times £500 = \underline{\underline{£375{,}000}}$$

In units:

	£
Selling price per unit (£500 ÷ 50)	10
Less: Variable cost per unit (£300 ÷ 50)	6
Contribution per unit	£4

$$\frac{\text{Fixed costs}}{\text{Contribution per unit}} = \frac{£150{,}000}{£4} = \underline{\underline{37{,}500 \text{ units}}}$$

(ii) *Margin of safety*

In value terms:

$$\frac{\text{Profit} \times \text{sales}}{\text{Contribution}} = \frac{£50 \times 500}{£200} = \underline{\underline{£125{,}000}}$$

In units:

$$\frac{\text{Profit}}{\text{Contribution per unit}} = \frac{£50{,}000}{£4} = \underline{\underline{12{,}500 \text{ units}}}$$

(b) Break-even chart

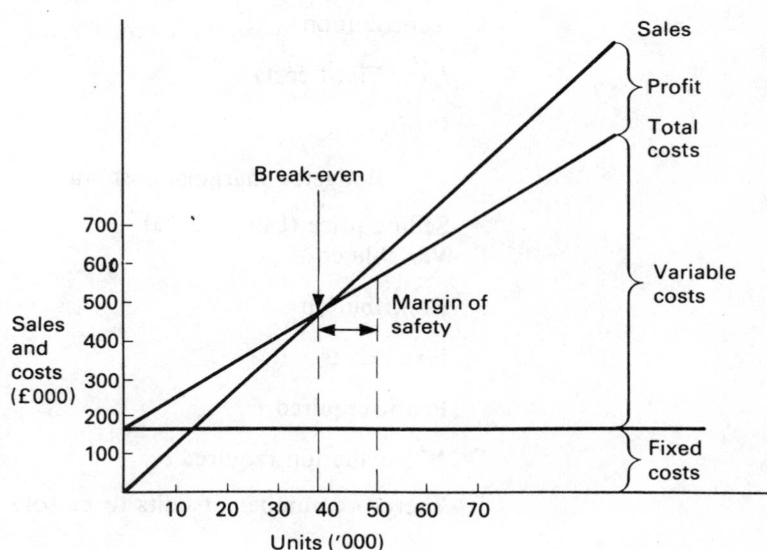

13.3 AYRE LIMITED

Since the company makes a profit of £100,000 on sales of £750,000, all the fixed costs must have been covered. A rise in sales, therefore, of £250,000 (£1,000,000 − £750,000) giving an increase in profit of £150,000 (£250,000 − £100,000) means that the increased variable cost was £100,000. Therefore the profit/volume ratio is 60% (150/250 × 100) and the variable cost of sales must be 40%.

Year to 31 March 19X3	*Budget* £000	*Actual* £000
Budget sales	1,200	1,000
Less: Variable costs (40%)	480	400
Contribution	720	600
Less: Fixed costs (60% × £1,000 − profit of £250)	350	350
Budget profit	£370	£450

13.4 CARTER LIMITED

Marginal cost statement year to 30 April 19X3

	Per unit £	*Total (50,000 units)* £000
Selling price	40	2,000
Variable cost	24	1,200
Contribution	£16	800
Less: Fixed costs		350
Profit		£450

Budgeted marginal cost statement year to 30 April 19X4

Selling price (£40 − 20%)	32	
Variable costs	24	
Contribution	£8	830*
Fixed costs		380
Profit required		£450

*Contribution required

Therefore number of units to be sold $= \frac{830,000}{8} = $ 103,750 units.

103,750 units will have to be sold in 19X4 to make the same amount of profit as in 19X3 if the company reduces its selling price per unit by 20% and increases its fixed costs by £30,000 per annum.

13.5 PUZZLED LIMITED

Option 1 Reduce the selling price by 15%:

	£
New selling price per unit	8.50
Variable cost per unit	7.50
Contribution per unit	£1.00

Therefore break-even = $\frac{\text{Fixed costs}}{\text{Contribution per unit}}$ = $\frac{£40{,}000}{£1.00}$ = 40,000 units

Option 2 Improve the product:

	£
Selling price per unit	10.00
New variable cost per unit	8.80
Contribution per unit	£1.20

Therefore break-even = $\frac{\text{Fixed costs}}{\text{Contribution per unit}}$ = $\frac{£40{,}000}{£1.20}$ = 33,333 units

Option 3 Advertising campaign:

Selling price per unit	10.00
Variable cost per unit	7.50
Contribution per unit	£2.50

Therefore break-even = $\frac{\text{Fixed costs}}{\text{Contribution per unit}}$ = $\frac{£40{,}000 + £15{,}000}{£2.50}$

= 22,000 units

Option 4 Improve factory efficiency:

Break-even = $\frac{\text{Fixed costs}}{\text{Contribution per unit}}$ = $\frac{£40{,}000 + £22{,}500}{£2.50}$

= 25,000 units

Conclusion

The advertising campaign would require fewer extra units to be sold in 19X5 compared with 19X4 in order to break-even; 22,000 units compared with 16,000 (£40,000 ÷ £2.50).

This is still a very large increase (37.5%) in one year, although fewer than the other options. Would the campaign also have to be repeated in future years? Has the company got the immediate cash resources in order to carry out the campaign?

13.6 MICRO LIMITED

Budgeted contribution per unit of limiting factor for the year:

$$\frac{£250{,}000}{50{,}000} = \underline{\underline{£5 \text{ per direct labour hour}}}$$

Contribution per unit of limiting factor for the special contract:

	£	£
Contract price		50,000
Less: Variable costs:		
Direct materials	10,000	
Direct labour	30,000	40,000
Contribution		£10,000

Therefore contribution per unit of limiting factor:

$$\frac{£10{,}000}{4{,}000} = \underline{\underline{£2.50 \text{ per direct labour hour}}}$$

Conclusion
The special contract earns less contribution per unit of limiting factor than does the *average* of ordinary budgeted work. It may be profitable to accept it, therefore, if either it displaces less profitable work or surplus direct labour hours are available. A careful assessment should be undertaken to ascertain whether much more profitable work would be found than is the case with the contract already being considered. It would be unwise to accept the proposal contract if it will displace other more profitable contracts which could arise in the near future.

Chapter 14

14.1 MORAY LIMITED

	Units
Total budgeted sales: January–June 19X1	2,270
Add: Desired stock at 30 June 19X1	450
	2,720
Less: Opening stock at 1 January 19X1	320
∴ Required production units	2,400

$$\text{Monthly average production} = \frac{2{,}400}{6} = \underline{\underline{400 \text{ units}}}$$

14.2 JORDAN LIMITED

Budgeted production for the six months to 31 December 19X1:

19X2		*Sales (units)*	*Production (units)*	*Balance (units)*
1.7	Balance b/f	—	—	100
31.7	Sales	70	—	30
	Production		200	230
31.8	Sales	140	—	90
	Production		280	370
30.9	Sales	350	—	20
	Production	—	180	200
31.10	Sales	190	—	10
	Production	—	180	190
30.11	Sales	150	—	40
	Production	—	140	180
31.11	Sales	120	—	60
	Production	—	40	100

14.3 DALTON LIMITED

	Units
Total budgeted sales: January to June 19X3	1,090
Less: Expected opening stock at 1 January 19X3	100
	990

Average monthly production required ∴ = 165 (990/6)

Note that: Opening stock − sales = stock remaining + monthly production = closing stock.

19X3	O/stock	− sales	=	stock remaining	+	monthly production	=	c/stock
January	100	− 90	=	10	+	165	=	175
February	175	− 150	=	25	+	165	=	190
March	190	− 450	=	(260)				

165 units produced in both January and February will not enable the company to meet its monthly budgeted sales figure for March 19X3. In order to do so, it could produce 295 units (165 + 260/2) in both January and February, and produce 150 units per month in March, April, May and June. This would enable the company to meet its budgeted April sales figures, and to achieve a reasonably smooth production flow. However, it would mean that by the end of June 19X3, the budgeted closing stock will be 200 units compared with 100 units at 1 January 19X3.

The calculations are as follows:

19X3	O/stock	– sales	=	stock remaining	+	monthly production	=	c/stock
January	100	– 90	=	10	+	295	=	305
February	305	– 150	=	155	+	295	=	450
March	450	– 450	=	0	+	150	=	150
April	150	– 150	=	0	+	150	=	150
May	150	– 130	=	20	+	150	=	170
June	170	– 120	=	50	+	150	=	200

Whether the company would wish to adopt this policy is debatable. It might wish, for example, to keep a minimum number of units in stock (perhaps 100 units) at any one time. This would mean increasing the number of units produced in 19X2, because according to the above figures, the company would be left with only 10 units ready for sale at the end of January 19X3. Another 295 units would, however, be immediately ready for sale in February 19X3.

14.4 TOM LIMITED

1 Direct materials usage budget:

	Number of units						
Month	30.4.X4	31.5.X4	30.6.X4	31.7.X4	31.8.X4	30.9.X4	*Six months to* 30.9.X4
Component:							
A6 (2 units for X)	280	560	1,400	760	600	480	4,080
B9 (3 units for X)	420	840	2,100	1,140	900	720	6,120

2 *Direct materials purchase budget:*

	30.4.X4	31.5.X4	30.6.X4	31.7.X4	31.8.X4	30.9.X4	Six months to 30.9.X4
Component A6							
Material usage (as above)	280	560	1,400	760	600	480	4,080
Add: Desired closing stock	110	220	560	300	240	200	200
	390	780	1,960	1,060	840	680	4,280
Less: Opening Stock	100	110	220	560	300	240	100
Purchases (units)	290	670	1,740	500	540	440	4,180
Price per unit	£5	£5	£5	£5	£5	£5	£5
Total Purchases	£1,450	£3,350	£8,700	£2,500	£2,700	£2,200	£20,900
Component B9							
Material usage (as above)	420	840	2,100	1,140	900	720	6,120
Add: Desired closing stock	250	630	340	300	200	180	180
	670	1,470	2,440	1,440	1,100	900	6,300
Less: Opening stock	200	250	630	340	300	200	200
Purchases (units)	470	1,220	1,810	1,100	800	700	6,100
Price per unit	£10	£10	£10	£10	£10	£10	£10
Total purchases	£4,700	£12,200	£18,100	£11,000	£8,000	£7,000	£61,000

14.5 DON LIMITED

Direct labour cost budget:

	Quarter 30.6.X5	31.7.X5	31.8.X5	*Three months* to 31.8.X5
Grade:				
Production (units)	600	700	650	1,950
Direct labour hours per unit	3	3	3	3
Total direct labour hours	1,800	2,100	1,950	5,850
Budgeted rate per hour (£)	4	4	4	4
Production cost (£)	7,200	8,400	7,800	23,400
Finishing (units)	600	700	650	1,950
Direct labour hours per unit	2	2	2	2
	1,200	1,400	1,300	3,900
Budgeted rate per hour (£)	8	8	8	8
Finishing cost (£)	9,600	11,200	10,400	31,200
Total budgeted direct labour cost	£16,800	£19,600	£18,200	£54,600

14.6 GORSE LIMITED

1 Sales budget:

Quantity	Selling price £	Sales volume £
10,000	100	1,000,000

2 Production quantity budget:

Sales budget (units)	Closing stock (units)	Opening stock (units)	Production required (units)
10,000	2,000	(4,000)	8,000

3 Materials usage budget:

Component	Component usage	Production (units)	Total component usage (units)
XY	5	8,000	40,000
WZ	3	8,000	24,000

4 Materials purchase budget:

	Component XY	Component WZ	Total £
Budget usage	40,000	24,000	
Stock increase (25%)	4,000	2,400	
Purchase quantities	44,000	26,400	
Cost price per unit	£1	£0.50	
Purchase values	£44,000	£13,200	£57,200

5 Direct labour budget:

Grade	Production budget	Budgeted hours per unit	Total budgeted hours	Budget labour rate per hour £	Total direct labour cost £
Production	8,000	4	32,000	5	160,000
Finishing	8,000	2	16,000	7	112,000
			48,000		£272,000

6 Budgeted profit and loss account:

	Per unit	Total
Sales units		10,000
	£	£
Sales revenue	100.00	1,000,000
Less: costs:		
Production (see workings)	52.50	525,000
Total factory cost	£47.50	475,000
Administration, selling and distribution		275,000
Budgeted profit for period 6		£200,000

Workings:	£	£
Unit cost:		
Direct materials:		
Component XY: 5 × £1	5.00	
WZ: 3 × £0.50	1.50	6.50
Direct labour:		
Production: 4 × £5	20.00	
Finishing: 2 × £7	14.00	34.00
		40.50
Production overhead:		
$\frac{£96,000}{48,000}$ = £2 per DLH × 6		12.00
		£52.50

14.7 FLOSSY LIMITED

Cash budget for the three months to 31 March 19X7

	January	*February*	*March*
	£000	£000	£000
Receipts:			
Debtors (Workings 1)	1,900	2,950	2,450
Sales of plant and equipment	—	—	30
Sale of short-term investments	60	—	10
	£1,960	£2,950	£2,490
Payments:			
Trade creditors (Workings 2)	1,150	1,850	1,510
Other creditors	450	500	600
Capital expenditure	—	470	—
Short-term investments	—	40	—
Tax	150	—	—
Dividends	200	—	—
	£1,950	£2,860	£2,110

	January £000	*February* £000	*March* £000
Monthly net cash flow	10	90	380
Opening balance	15	25	115
Closing balance	£25	£115	£495

Workings:

1 Trade debtors

Sales	2,000	3,000	2,500
Add: Opening debtors	200	300	350
	2,200	3,300	2,850
Less: Closing debtors	300	350	400
Cash from trade debtors	£1,900	£2,950	£2,450

2 Purchases

Cost of goods sold	1,200	1,800	1,500
Add: Closing stock	120	150	150
	1,320	1,950	1,650
Less: Opening stock	100	120	150
Purchases for each quarter	1,220	1,830	1,500
Add: Opening trade creditors	110	180	160
	1,330	2,010	1,660
Less: Closing trade creditors	180	160	150
Cash to trade creditors	£1,150	£1,850	£1,510

14.8 CHIMES LIMITED

Option 1 Keep the factory open

Production capacity		45%
	£000	£000
Sales revenue		135.5
Less: Variable cost of sales:		
Direct materials	63	
Direct labour	27	
Variable overhead:		
Factory	18	
Administration	13.5	
Selling and distribution	9	130.5
Contribution		5
Less: Fixed costs:		
Factory	10	
Administration	8	
Selling and distribution	6	24
Budgeted loss		£(19)

Option 2 Close the factory

	£000
Costs:	
Redundancy and other closure costs	(30)
Property and plant maintenance	(10)
Re-opening costs	(20)
	(60)
Less: Saving in fixed overheads	30
Net cost of closure	£ (30)

Decision

As the factory will still make a contribution during the year to 30 June 19X8, the factory should be kept open. However, there may be other non-cost factors also to take into account.

Chapter 15

15.1 X LIMITED

		£
1	Direct materials cost variance:	
	Actual price per unit × Actual quantity = £12 × 6:	72
	Less: Standard price per unit × Standard quantity for actual production = £10 × 5:	50
		£22 (A)
2	Direct materials price variance:	
	(Actual price − Standard price) × Actual quantity = (£12 − £10) × 6:	£12 (A)
3	Direct materials usage variance:	
	(Actual quantity − Standard quantity) × Standard price = (6 − 5) × £10:	£10 (A)

15.2 MALCOLM LIMITED

		£
1	Direct materials cost variance:	
	Total actual cost	32,400
	Less: Standard quantity for actual production × Standard price = (50 × 120) × £5:	30,000
		£2,400 (A)
2	Direct materials price variance:	
	(Actual price − Standard price) × Actual quantity = (£6* − £5) × 5,400:	£5,400 (A)
	*£32,400 / 5,400	
3	Direct materials usage variance:	
	(Actual quantity − Standard quantity) × Standard price = (5,400 − 6,000*) × £5:	£3,000 (F)
	*(120 units × 50 kilograms)	

15.3 BRUCE LIMITED

		£
1	Direct labour cost variance:	
	Actual hours × Actual hourly rate = 1,000 × £6.50:	6,500
	Less: Standard hours for actual production × Standard hourly rate = 900 × £6.00:	5,400
		£1,100 (A)
2	Direct labour rate variance:	
	(Actual hourly rate − Standard hourly rate) × Actual hours = (£6.50 − 6.00) × 1,000:	£500 (A)
3	Direct labour efficiency variance:	
	(Actual hours − Standard hours for actual production) × Standard hourly rate = (1,000 − 900) × £6.00:	£600 (A)

15.4 DUNCAN LIMITED

		£
1	Direct labour cost variance:	
	Actual direct labour cost	97,200
	Less: Standard hours for actual production × Standard hourly rate = (10 × 1,200) × £8:	96,000
		£1,200 (A)
2	Direct labour rate variance:	
	(Actual hourly rate − Standard hourly rate) × Actual hours = (£9* − 8) × 10,800:	£10,800 (A)
	$*\frac{£97,200}{10,800}$	
3	Direct labour efficiency variance:	
	(Actual hours − Standard hours for actual production) × Standard hourly rate = (10,800 − 12,000*) × £8:	£9,600 (F)
	*1,200 × 10 DLH = 12,000	

15.5 ANTHEA LIMITED

		£
1	Fixed production overhead variance:	
	Actual fixed overhead	150,000
	Less: Standard hours of production × F.OAR = 8,000 × £15:	120,000
		£30,000 (A)
2	Fixed overhead expenditure variance:	
	Actual fixed overhead − budgeted fixed overhead = £150,000 − £135,000:	£15,000 (A)
3	Fixed overhead volume variance:	
	Budgeted fixed overhead − Standard hours of production × F.OAR = £135,000 − (8,000 × £15):	£15,000 (A)
4	Fixed overhead capacity variance:	
	Budgeted fixed overhead − (Actual hours worked × F.OAR) = £135,000 − (10,000 × £15):	£15,000 (F)
5	Fixed overhead productivity variance:	
	Actual hours worked − Standard hours of production × F.OAR = (10,000 − 8,000) × £15,000:	£30,000 (A)

15.6 ANTHEA LIMITED

Control ratios:

1 Efficiency:

$$\frac{\text{SHP}}{\text{Actual hours}} \times 100 = \frac{8{,}000}{10{,}000} \times 100 = \underline{\underline{80\%}}$$

2 Capacity:

$$\frac{\text{Actual hours}}{\text{Budgeted hours*}} \times 100 = \frac{10{,}000}{9{,}000} \times 100 = \underline{\underline{111.1\%}}$$

$$\text{*}\frac{£135{,}000}{15}$$

3 Activity:

$$\frac{\text{SHP}}{\text{Budgeted hours}} \times 100 = \frac{8{,}000}{9{,}000} \times 100 = \underline{\underline{88.9\%}}$$

15.7 OSPREY LIMITED

		£
1	Fixed production overhead variance:	
	Actual fixed overhead	120,000
	Less: Standard hours of production × F.OAR = $(600 \times 10) \times \left(\frac{£125{,}000}{500 \times 10}\right)$:	150,000
		£30,000 (F)
2	Fixed overhead expenditure variance: Actual fixed overhead − Budgeted fixed overhead = £120,000 − £125,000:	£5,000 (F)
3	Fixed overhead volume variance: Budgeted fixed overhead − Standard hours of production × F.OAR = £125,000 − (6,000* × £25):	£25,000 (F)
4	Fixed overhead capacity variance: Budgeted fixed overhead − (Actual hours worked × F.OAR) = £125,000 − (4,900 × £25):	£2,500 (A)
5	Fixed overhead productivity variance: (Actual hours worked − Standard hours of production) × F.OAR = (4,900 − 6,000*) × £25:	£27,500 (F)

*600 units × 10 standard hours

15.8 OSPREY LIMITED

Control ratios:

1 Efficiency:

$$\frac{\text{SHP}}{\text{Actual hours}} \times 100 = \frac{6{,}000}{4{,}900} \times 100 = 122.4\%$$

2 Capacity:

$$\frac{\text{Actual hours}}{\text{Budgeted hours}} \times 100 = \frac{4{,}900}{5{,}000} \times 100 = 98\%$$

3 Activity:

$$\frac{\text{SHP}}{\text{Budgeted hours}} \times 100 = \frac{6{,}000}{5{,}000} \times 100 = 120\%$$

15.9 MILTON LIMITED

		£
1	Operating profit due to sales variance:	
	Total actual sales	99,000
	Less: Actual quantity × Standard variable cost = 9,000 × £7:	63,000
		36,000
	Less: Budgeted units × Standard margin = 10,000 × £3*:	30,000
	*(£10 − 7)	£6,000 (F)
2	Selling price variance:	
	Actual selling price × budgeted selling price) × Actual units sold = (£11* − 10) × 9,000:	£9,000 (F)
	$\frac{*99,000}{9,000}$	
3	Sales volume variance:	
	(Actual quantity − Budgeted units) × Standard margin = (9,000 − 10,000) × £3:	£3,000 (A)

15.10 DOE LIMITED

		£
(a) *1*	Operating profit due to sales variance:	
	Total actual sales (120 × £28)	3,360
	Less: Actual quantity × Standard variable cost = 120 × £20:	2,400
		960
	Less: Budgeted units × Standard margin = 100 × £10:	1,000
		£40 (A)
2	Selling price variance:	
	(Actual selling price − Budgeted selling price) × Actual units (£28 − 30) × 120	£240 (A)
3	Sales volume variance:	
	(Actual quantity − Budgeted units) × Standard margin (120 − 100) × £10:	£200 (F)

15.10 DOE LIMITED (Contd)

(b) *1* Total sales value variance:

(Actual sales value × Budgeted quantity) − Budgeted selling price = (120 × £28) − (100 × £30) = £3,360 − 3,000: **£360 (F)**

2 Selling price variance:

See (a) *1* above: **£240 (A)**

3 Sales volume variance:

(Actual quantity − Budgeted quantity) × Budgeted selling price = (120 − 100) × £30: **£600 (F)**

15.11 JUDITH LIMITED

(a) *1* Efficiency ratio:

$$\frac{\text{SHP}}{\text{Actual hours}} \times 100 = \frac{(5 \times 2{,}200)}{(4 \times 2{,}200)} \times 100 = \underline{\underline{125\%}}$$

2 Capacity ratio:

$$\frac{\text{Actual hours}}{\text{Budgeted hours}} \times 100 = \frac{8{,}800}{(5 \times 2{,}000)} \times 100 = \underline{\underline{88\%}}$$

3 Activity ratio:

$$\frac{\text{SHP}}{\text{Budgeted hours}} \times 100 = \frac{11{,}000}{10{,}000} \times 100 = \underline{\underline{110\%}}$$

(b) *1* Sales margin operating profit variance due to sales:

	£
Actual sales = 2,200 × £145:	319,000
Less: Actual quantity × Standard cost = 2,200 × £125:	275,000
	44,000
Less: Budgeted units × Standard margin = 2,000 × £25:	50,000
	£6,000 (A)

2 Sales margin selling price variance:

(Actual selling price − Budgeted selling price) × Actual units = (£145 − 150) × 2,200: **£11,000 (A)**

3 Sales margin sales volume variance:

(Actual quantity − Budgeted units) × Standard margin = (2,200 − 2,000) × £25: **£5,000 (F)**

(contd)

15.11 JUDITH LIMITED (Contd)

4	Direct materials cost variance:	
	Actual quantity × Actual price = 2,200 × £72:	158,400
	Less: Standard quantity for actual production × Standard price = (7 kilos × 2,200) × £10:	154,000
		£4,400 (A)
5	Direct materials price variance:	
	(Actual price − Standard price) × Actual quantity = (£9 − 10) × (2,200 × 8):	£17,600 (F)
6	Direct materials usage variance:	
	(Actual quantity − Standard quantity) × Standard price = ((8 × 2,200) − (7 × 2,200)) × £10:	£22,000 (A)
7	Direct labour cost variance:	
	Actual hours × Actual hourly rate = (4 × 2,200) × £6:	52,800
	Less: Standard hours for actual production × Standard hourly rate = (2,200 × 5) × £5:	55,000
		£2,200 (F)
8	Direct labour rate variance:	
	(Actual hourly rate − Standard hourly rate) × Actual hours = (£6 − £5) × (4 × 2,200):	£8,800 (A)
9	Direct labour efficiency variance:	
	(Actual hours − Standard hours for actual production) × Standard hourly rate = (8,800 − 11,000) × £5:	£11,000 (F)
10	Fixed production overhead variance:	
	Actual fixed overhead:	65,000
	Less: Standard hours of production × F.OAR = (2,200 × 5) × £6:	66,000
		£1,000 (F)
11	Fixed production overhead expenditure variance:	
	Actual fixed overhead − Budgeted fixed overhead = £65,000 − (£30 × 2,000):	£5,000 (A)

15.11 JUDITH LIMITED (Contd)

12	Fixed production overhead volume variance: Budgeted fixed overhead – (Standard hours of production × F.OAR) = £60,000 – (11,000 × £6):	£6,000 (F)
13	Fixed production overhead capacity variance: Budgeted fixed overhead – (Actual hours worked × F.OAR) = £60,000 – (8,800 × £6):	£7,200 (A)
14	Fixed production overhead productivity variance: (Actual hours worked – Standard hours of production) × F.OAR = (8,800 – 11,000) × £6:	£13,200 (F)

(c) Standard cost operating statement for the period

	Adverse	Favourable	£
Budgeted profit (£25 × 2,000)			50,000
Sales volume variance (£25 × 200)			5,000
Standard margin of actual sales			55,000
Sale price variance (£5 × 2,200)			(11,000)
Actual margin of actual sales			44,000
Cost variances:	*Adverse* £	*Favourable* £	
Direct materials:			
Price		17,600	
Usage	22,000		
Direct labour:			
Rate	8,800		
Efficiency		11,000	
Fixed production overhead:			
Expenditure	5,000		
Capacity	7,200		
Productivity		13,200	
	£43,000	£41,800	(1,200)
Actual profit			£42,800

Chapter 16

16.1 PROSPECT LIMITED

Calculation of net cash flows:

Year to 31 March	19X1	19X2	19X3	19X4	19X5	19X6
	£000	£000	£000	£000	£000	£000
Cash receipts						
Trade debtors (Working 1)	1,800	2,360	2,740	2,880	1,920	400
Sale of project	—	—	—	—	—	50
	1,800	2,360	2,740	2,880	1,920	450
Cash payments						
Purchase of project	1,000	—	—	—	—	—
Trade creditors (Working 2)	1,350	1,770	2,160	1,990	1,260	150
Expenses	210	220	240	250	300	—
Taxation	—	40	70	100	100	10
	2,560	2,030	2,470	2,340	1,660	160
Net cash flows	£(760)	£330	£270	£540	£260	£290

Workings:

Year to 31 March						
1 Trade debtors						
Sales	2,000	2,400	2,800	2,900	2,000	—
Less: Closing trade debtors	200	240	300	320	400	—
	1,800	2,160	2,500	2,580	1,600	—
Add: Opening trade debtors	—	200	240	300	320	400
Cash received	£1,800	£2,360	£2,740	£2,880	£1,920	£400
2 Trade creditors						
Purchases	1,600	1,790	2,220	1,960	1,110	—
Less: Closing trade creditors	250	270	330	300	150	—
	1,350	1,520	1,890	1,660	960	—
Add: Opening trade creditors	—	250	270	330	300	150
Cash purchases	£1,350	£1,770	£2,160	£1,990	£1,260	£150

16.2 BUCHAN LIMITED

Payback period:

Year	*Investment outlay*	*Cash inflow*	*Net cash flow*	*Cumulative cash flow*
	£	£	£	£
1	(50,000)	8,000	(42,000)	(42,000)
2	—	16,000	16,000	(26,000)
3	—	40,000	40,000	14,000
4	—	45,000	45,000	59,000
5	—	37,000	37,000	96,000

Payback period therefore = 2 years 7.8 months*

*Net cash flow becomes positive in Year 3. Assuming the net cash flow accrues evenly it becomes positive during July: (26/40 × 12) = 7.8 months (i.e. 2 years and 7.8 months).

16.3 LENDER LIMITED

$$\text{Accounting rate of return} = \frac{\text{Average annual net profit after tax} \times 100}{\text{Cost of the investment}}$$

$$= \frac{\frac{1}{5}\,(£18{,}000 + £47{,}000 + £65{,}000 + £65{,}000 + £30{,}000 \times 100}{£100{,}000}$$

$$= \frac{45{,}000 \times 100}{100{,}000}$$

$$= \underline{\underline{45\%}}$$

Note: Based on the *average* investment the ARR

$$= \frac{£45{,}000}{\frac{1}{2}(£0 + £100{,}000)} \times 100$$

$$= \underline{\underline{90\%}}$$

16.4 LOCKHART LIMITED

Net present value:

Year	*Net cash flow*	*Discount factor*	*Present value*
	£000	@ 15%	£000
1	800	0.870	696
2	850	0.756	643
3	830	0.658	546
4	1,200	0.572	686
5	700	0.497	348
Total present value			2,919
Initial cost			2,500
Net present value			£419

16.5 MOFFAT LIMITED

Internal rate of return:

Year	*Net cash flow*	*Discount factors*		*Present value*	
	£000	5%	7%	£000 @ 5%	£000 @ 7%
1	230	0.952	0.935	219	215
2	370	0.907	0.873	336	323
3	600	0.864	0.816	518	490
4	420	0.823	0.763	346	320
5	110	0.784	0.713	86	78
Total present value				1,505	1,426
Initial cost				1,450	1,450
Net present value				£55	£(24)

Internal rate of return

$$= \text{Positive rate} + \frac{\text{Positive NPV}}{\text{Positive NPV} + \text{Negative NPV}} \times \text{Range}$$

$$= 5\% + \frac{55}{55 + 24} \times 2\%$$

$$= 5\% + 1.4\%$$

$$= \underline{\underline{6.4\%}}$$

16.6 MARSH LIMITED

1 Payback

Year	*Investment outlay*	*Cash inflow*	*Net cash flow*	*Cumulative cash flow*
	£000	£000	£000	£000
1	(500)	50	(450)	(450)
2	—	200	200	(250)
3	—	225	225	(25)
4	—	225	225	200
5	—	100	100	300

Therefore payback $= 3 \text{ years} + \frac{(25 \times 12)}{225} = \underline{\underline{3 \text{ years } 1.3 \text{ months}}}$

16.6 MARSH LIMITED (Contd)

2 Accounting rate of return:

$$\frac{\text{Average annual net profit after tax} \times 100}{\text{Cost of the investment}}$$

$$= \frac{\text{£000 } (100 + 250 + 250 + 200)}{4}$$

$$= \frac{200}{500} \times 100$$

$$= \underline{\underline{40\%}}$$

Note: If the average cost of the investment is used:

$$= \frac{200}{\frac{1}{2}\,(\text{£}0 + 500)} = \frac{200}{250} \times 100 = \underline{\underline{80\%}}$$

3 Net present value:

Year	*Net cash flow*	*Discount factor*	*Present value*
	£000	@ 15%	£000
1	50	0.870	44
2	200	0.756	151
3	225	0.658	148
4	225	0.572	129
5	100	0.497	50
Total present value			522
Initial cost			500
Net present value			£22

4 Internal rate of return:

Year	*Net cash flow*	*Discount factor*		*Present value*	
	£000	@ 15%	@ 17%	@ 15%	@ 17%
				£000	£000
1	50	0.870	0.855	44	43
2	200	0.756	0.731	151	146
3	225	0.658	0.624	148	140
4	225	0.572	0.534	129	120
5	100	0.497	0.456	50	46
Total present value				522	495
Initial cost				500	500
Net present value				£22	£(5)

$$\text{IRR} = \text{Positive rate} + \frac{\text{Positive NPV}}{\text{Positive NPV} + \text{Negative NPV}} \times \text{Range}$$

$$= 15\% + \frac{22}{22 + 5} \times 2\%$$

$$= 15\% + 1.6\%$$

$$= \underline{\underline{16.6\%}}$$

Index

Index

Abbreviated accounts, 109
Abnormal gain, 224
Abnormal loss, 224
Absorption, 204-8, 211, 213, 214
  comprehensive example, 208-11
  costing, 173, 184, 213, 214, 220, 224-5, 226, 227, 228, 265, 276
  direct labour cost method, 205-6, 207
  direct labour hours method, 206, 208
  direct material cost method, 205, 207
  machine hours method, 206-8
  methods, 205-8
  over-recovery of overhead, 214, 215
  pre-determined absorption rates, 213-5
  prime cost method, 206, 207
  rate methods, 205-7
  rate methods (exhibit), 207-8
  specific units method, 206, 207
  under-recovery of overhead, 214, 215
Account, 1, 5, 7, 13, 16, 17, 20, 21, 22, 31, 32, 33, 34, 35, 36, 37, 39, 41, 42, 44, 45, 54, 55, 56, 60, 61, 67, 68, 69, 87, 103, 114, 125, 144, 145, 149, 151, 155, 162, 163, 191, 214, 221, 299, 302, 303, 304, 305, 306, 307, 308, 309, 310, 311, 312, 317, 318, 321, 322
  notes to, 308
Accountancy, 5, 13
  associations, 9
  bodies, 8, 9, 10, 22, 299
  institutes, 9
  profession, 1, 5, 8, 9-10, 13, 22, 315, 317, 319-21, 326
  requirements, 300
Accountant, 4, 5, 6, 7, 8, 9, 10, 13, 14, 15, 18, 19, 20, 21, 22, 23, 31, 54, 55, 74, 75, 103, 104, 125, 132, 144, 149, 165, 173, 174, 178, 180, 185, 186, 204, 232, 243, 244, 284, 293, 300, 308
Accounting, 1, 2, 3, 4, 5, 6, 7, 8, 10, 11, 13, 15, 16, 17, 18, 19, 20, 22, 23, 24, 31, 34, 35, 54, 55, 96, 106, 165, 173, 174, 179, 184, 186, 192, 204, 292, 301, 317, 318, 320, 321
  data, 16, 144
  function, 3, 6, 7, 177, 246, 263, 301
  information, 4, 9, 10, 11, 12, 15, 22, 29, 75, 118, 165, 179
  language, 4
  loss, 56
  period(s), 15, 16, 18, 23, 34, 35, 39, 41, 55, 62, 63, 64, 66, 67, 68, 69, 74-5, 126, 127, 137, 319, 324
  policy, 22, 311, 326
  principles, 20, 54
  procedure(s), 5, 11, 18
  profit, 54-5, 56, 74-5, 111, 125-6, 130, 132
  rate of return, 286-7
  rate of return disadvantages, 287
  rate of return (exhibit), 286
  ratios, 144-65, 324
  rules, 12, 13-24, 29, 54, 125, 220, 324
  rules (questions), 24-25
  standards, 21
Accounting Standards Committee, 317, 322
Accounting Standards Steering Committee, 322
  statements, 13, 15, 20, 23, 126, 144, 149, 324
  system, 1, 4, 8, 13, 16, 19, 23, 24
  technician, 9
  techniques, 4
  terminology, 29, 34, 63, 253, 326
  world, 1-12
  world (questions), 12
  year, 67
Accounts (see account)
Accrual(s), 18, 20, 66-7, 74, 113, 133, 314
  adjustments, 61, 66-7
  adjustments (exhibit), 67
  basis, 18
Accrue, 66
Accrued income, 314
Accumulated depreciation, 65-6, 96
Acid test ratio, 148-9, 154
Activity(ies), 183, 213, 227, 229, 232-3, 239, 304
Activity apportionate method, 201-2
Actual costs, 266, 268

Actual hours(s), 265, 266
Actual profit, 279
Acquisitions, 304
Additional depreciation adjustment (ADA), 320, 321
Additional statements, 317-26
Adjustments
 for accruals (exhibit), 67
 for bad debts, 68-69
 for doubtful debts (exhibit), 69-70
 pre-payments, (exhibit), 68
Administration, 96, 182, 211
 budget, 244, 246, 247
 cost centre, 222
 expenses, 264
 function, 176, 177
 manager, 177
 overhead, 182, 211-2, 222-3
 overhead absorption method, 211-2
Administrative expenses, 309, 310, 311
Advance corporation tax (ACT), 111
Adverse variance, 214, 215, 268
After tax profit, 311
Agrarian world, 15
Allocation, 183, 200-1, 214
Allowed hours, 266
Analysing accounts, 162-3
Analysts, 162, 173
Angle of incidence, 232-3
Annual accounts, 14, 15, 39, 45, 110-11, 162, 163, 174, 299, 300, 303
Annual financial accounts, 3
Annual general meeting, 111, 306
Annual reporting, 3
Annual reports, 109, 299-326
 assignment, 327-8
 contents, 301-2
 promotional material, 301
 specialist reports, 301-2
 supplementary statements, 302
Answers to questions, 330-427
Application of funds, 127, 128, 315, 316
Appropriation, 58
Appropriation account, 105
Apportionment, 201-4, 211, 214
Articles, 304
Asset(s), 6, 16, 64, 109, 146, 312, 318, 321, 323, 325
Assets employed, 324
Assignment, 327-8
Associated company, 307-8, 311, 315, 316
Association of Accounting Technicians, 9
Assumptions, 13, 74
Audit, 9
Auditing, 5, 8, 9
 standards, 305
Auditor(s), 5, 303, 304, 305, 306
Auditors' report, 302, 303, 305-6
Auditors' remuneration, 311
Authorized share capital, 107-8, 114
Average trade creditor payment period ratio, 151, 154
Average trade debtor collection period ratio, 150-1, 154
Axioms, 13

Bad debt(s), 18, 61, 68-9
 adjustments, 61, 68-9, 70
Balance sheet(s), 6, 56, 57, 60, 64, 66, 67, 68, 69, 92, 111, 112-4, 125, 137, 148, 161, 163, 222, 299, 301, 302, 307, 311, 313, 314, 315, 321, 326
 disclosure of fixed assets (exhibit), 66
 format, 312
Balancing account, 321
Balancing accounts, 39-41
 exhibits, 39-41
Bank account, 15, 30, 33, 34, 39, 128
Bank balances, 125, 126, 127, 132
Bank borrowings, 311
Bank deposit account, 318
Bankruptcy, 5-6
Banks, 11
Basic accounting practices, 11
Basic accounting rules, 22, 23, 24
Basic costing methods, 223-4, 225
Basic costing principles, 173-84
Basic costing principles (questions), 184
Basic costing techniques, 225
Basic financial statements, 54-75, 96
 comprehensive example, 71-4
 exhibit, 57-9
 questions, 75-86
Basic rules of accounting, 12, 13-24
Batch costing, 223
Batches, 223
Bias, 21
Board of directors, 176, 177, 180, 303, 304, 305, 313
Book entries, 132
Book-keeper, 32, 35, 39
Book-keeping, 1, 2, 6-7, 19, 29, 62, 90, 173, 220, 228
 system, 32
Books of account, 6, 7, 17, 23, 31, 35, 220
Boots and shoes, 223
Borrowing, 292, 318
Bought-in materials and services, 323
Boundary rules, 14-6, 22, 23
Branches of accounting, 4-8
Break-even, 231-4
 chart, 232-3
 chart (exhibit), 232-3
 graph, 232-3

Budget, 225, 243-56, 262, 284, 292
  administration, 246
  committee, 246, 263
  definition, 243-4
  essential features, 244
  period, 245-6, 263
  procedure, 245-8
Budgetary control, 225, 239, 243-56, 262, 263
  features, 244-5
  questions, 257-61
Budgeted balance sheet, 247
Budgeted hours, 266, 267
Budgeted profit and loss account, 247, 279
Budgeting, 173, 243-56, 263, 280, 292
  nature, 243-5
  process, 246-8
  process (exhibit), 247
Building costs, 264
Building maintenance, 201
Building societies, 11
Bus fares, 34
Business, 15, 126, 144, 145, 146, 150, 174
  entity(ies), 8, 96, 106
  managers, 2, 20
  organisations, 3
  profitability, 4
  proprietors, 106, 107

Called-up share capital, 313, 314
Canteen cost centre, 181, 201
Canteen expenses, 88
Canteen staff, 201
Capacity ratio, 266, 267
Capital, 33, 55, 74, 104, 106, 107, 113, 114, 145, 146, 313, 314, 315, 322, 323, 325
  account(s), 33, 104, 105
  and reserves, 113, 114, 313, 314
  employed, 175, 325
  expenditure, 55, 63, 248
  expenditure budget, 247
  expenditure programme, 292
  gearing ratio, 153, 155
  income, 55
  investment, 164, 280, 284-93
  investment appraisal, 173, 284-93
  investment finance, 284
  investment profitability, 284
  investment (questions), 293-6
  reserve, 113, 114
  reserve account, 114
  section, 59
  source of funds, 291-2
Car parks, 291
Cardiff, 109, 300
Carriage inwards, 91
Cash, 17, 18, 19, 33, 34, 54, 55, 66, 67, 68, 74, 126, 127, 128, 129, 130, 131, 132, 150, 222, 223, 284-5, 316
  accounts, 33, 34, 36, 37, 39
  at bank, 33, 312, 314
  balances, 125, 126, 127, 132, 316
  budget, 244, 246, 247, 248
  department, 177
  discounts, 33, 34
  flow, 133, 186, 324
  flow accounting, 17
  in hand, 33, 36, 312, 314
  paid, 18, 23
  payments, 55
  position, 125, 126, 128
  receipts, 55
  received, 18, 23, 33, 288, 292
  sales, 34, 36, 150
  terms, 37, 248
Central government, 2, 8, 9, 162, 173
Certified accountants, 9
Chairman, 19, 303, 305
Chairman's report, 302, 303-4, 306
  signature, 305
Charges, 325
Charitable donations, 305
Charity, 10, 11, 14
Chartered accountants, 9, 306
Chartered Association of Certified Accountants, 9
Chartered Institute of Management Accountants (see Institute of Cost and Management Accountants)
Chartered Institute of Public Finance and Accountancy, 9
Cheques, 32
Chief accountant, 19
Choice of accounts, 32-5
Cleaning, 201
Closing stock(s), 34, 87, 147, 149
  adjustment, 61, 321
  of raw materials, 89
  work-in-progress, 88, 89
Coding system, 184
Commerce, 9, 22
Commission (error of), 45
Company, 3, 5, 6, 8, 11, 17, 19, 21, 24, 89, 103, 107, 108, 109, 111, 114, 118, 145, 147, 148, 151, 153, 155, 161, 162, 163, 164, 165, 174, 175, 176, 177, 178, 182, 183, 184, 211, 212, 213, 228, 233, 238, 253, 254, 256, 262, 265, 283, 289, 291, 292, 299, 300, 301, 302, 303, 304, 305, 307, 308, 309, 310, 311, 312, 313, 314, 315, 316, 320, 321, 322, 324, 325
  account legislation, 118
  account(s), 11, 21, 103, 106-18, 299, 308
  accounts (comprehensive example), 114-8

accounts (questions), 119-24
articles, 304
balance sheet, 112
balance sheet (exhibit), 112-4
chairman, 19
efficiency, 303
head office, 177, 178, 211
productivity, 303
profit and loss account (exhibit), 112
prospects, 304
secretary, 301, 305
types, 108
Companies (see Company)
Companies Act
-1948, 299
-1967, 299
-1976, 299
-1980, 299
-1981, 299
-1985, 11, 21, 106, 109, 299, 300, 306, 307, 308, 309, 311, 312, 313, 316, 326
Companies House, 109, 300, 301
Comparative figures, 21, 308, 312
Compensating error, 45
Complete reversal of entry (error of), 45
Component parts, 89, 185
Computer-based systems, 29, 31
Computerized accounting, 179
Computerized recording systems, 19
Computerized system, 32
Concepts, 13
Conservatism, 20
Consistency rule, 20-1, 23, 24
Consolidation, 308
Construction industry, 15, 182-3
Consumables, 309, 314
Continuous weighted average method of pricing stock, 190, 191-2, 193-4
exhibit, 191-2
Contract costing, 223
Contribution, 229-39
changes (exhibit), 230-1
Control, 3, 7, 8, 10, 33, 39, 175, 184, 185, 200, 211, 214, 215, 243, 244, 246, 253, 262, 264, 280
of resources, 5
ratios, 265-8
ratios (exhibit), 267-8
Conventional accounting, 17
Conventions, 13
Corporate Report, 322
Corporation tax, 11, 113-4, 148, 292, 311, 323
Cost, 17, 18, 87, 185, 194, 221, 225, 227, 228
accounts, 221
Cost accounting, 7, 8, 173
Cost and management accounting, 96, 97, 165, 171-296
Cost and Management Accountants, 9
Cost book-keeping, 7, 8, 173, 220-3, 224
integral system, 220-3
integrated system, 220-3
interlocking system, 220
system(s), 97,224
system (exhibit), 222-3
Cost centre(s), 178, 179, 180, 181, 183, 184, 196, 200-15, 222-3, 246, 248
budget(s), 254, 262
general, 180
manager, 200
miscellaneous, 180
Cost data, 220-6
Costing, 7, 173, 175, 184, 185, 220, 223, 243
advantages, 175
basic methods, 223-4
books, 224
coding system, 179-80, 184
documentation, 179-80, 184
historical review, 173-5
implementation, 175-80
integral system, 174
interlocking system, 174
methods, 223-4, 225
principles, 173-84, 224, 225
principles (questions), 184
procedure, 179, 180-4
records, 228
system, 7, 174, 179, 180, 184, 211, 220, 239
techniques, 224-6
Cost of goods sold, 56, 62, 63, 147, 149
Cost of sales, 23, 54, 310, 311, 312, 323
adjustment (COSA), 320, 321
Cost-plus, 183, 212, 213
Costs (see Cost)
Cost structure, 182-3
Cost variances, 265, 269, 279
Credit, 31, 32, 45
control, 151
purchases, 151
sales, 34, 37, 150
terms, 35, 37, 126, 129, 130, 148, 150
Creditor, 2, 6, 8, 33, 34, 45, 107, 127, 131, 132, 133, 145, 151, 162, 173, 222, 223, 316
accounts, 33, 35
Creditors
amounts falling due after more than one year, 313, 314, 325
amounts falling due within one year, 313, 314
Cumulative preference shares, 108

Current (definition), 148
Current account(s), 104, 105
Current asset(s), 58, 59, 113, 132, 148, 149, 312, 313, 314, 325
 investments, 312, 314
 ratio, 148, 154
 section, 59, 68
Current cost accounting (CCA), 320-1
Current cost accounts, 321
Current cost reserve account, 321
Current liability(ies), 59, 111, 113, 114, 132, 148, 149
 section, 67
Current purchasing power (CCP), 319, 321
 accounting, 319, 320
Current standards, 263-4
Current value accounting, 319-21
Current value school, 319-21
Customer, 20

Data processing manager, 293
Debenture(s), 109, 114, 126, 132, 292, 304, 315, 318, 320
 interest, 109, 292
Debit(s), 31, 32, 45
Debt(s), 5, 70, 107, 125, 126, 162
Debtor(s), 33, 34, 45, 127, 131, 132, 133, 145, 148, 223, 312, 314, 316
 accounts, 33, 45
 collection period, 151
Decision-making, 5, 7, 8, 74, 173, 175, 227, 234, 239
Decorating, 223
Deferred income, 314
Department, 176, 178, 184, 248
Department of Trade and Industry, 9
Depreciation, 22, 63, 131, 132, 287, 309, 311, 315, 318, 320, 323
 adjustments, 61, 63-6
 charges, 311
Development costs, 182, 313
Developments, 304
Direct cost(s), 88, 89, 181, 183, 185-96, 200, 214
 definition, 88
 questions, 196-9
Direct expenses, 88, 89, 182, 195-6, 229
 question, 196-9
Direct labour, 88, 89, 182, 194-5, 196, 229, 238, 254, 264-5
 cost absorption rate method, 205-6, 207-8
 cost budget, 247
 cost variance, 268, 269
 efficiency variance, 268, 269, 270
 hours, 213, 238
 hours absorption rate method, 206, 208
 rate variance, 268, 269
Direct material(s), 88, 89, 182, 185-94, 195, 196, 229, 238, 254, 262, 264-5
 cost, 89
 cost absorption rate method, 205, 207-8
 cost budget, 247
 cost variance, 268, 269
 price variance, 268, 269
 purchasing budget, 247
 usage budget, 247
 usage variance, 268, 269
Direct production cost, 181
Director(s), 5, 110, 304, 306, 313, 314
 emoluments, 311
 remuneration, 110
 report, 302, 303, 304-5, 306
 report (contents), 304-5
 report (signature), 305
 valuation, 113
Disabled persons, 305
Disclosure of information, 109, 299-302
Discount table, 288, 292, 329
Discounted cash flow (DCF), 287-91
Discounting, 287-8
Discounts allowed, 33
Discounts received, 33-4
Disposals, 304
Distribution budget, 248
Distribution costs, 309, 310, 311
Distribution function, 176
Dividend(s), 108, 110-1, 112, 114, 127, 131, 132, 146, 152, 221, 303, 304, 311, 314, 315, 316, 323, 324, 325
 cover ratio, 152, 154
 paid, 110, 131, 132, 303, 310, 311, 315
 proposed, 110, 303, 310, 311
 rate, 151
 received, 223, 311
 yield ratio, 151-2, 154
Division, 176, 177, 178, 179
Divisional board of directors, 177-8, 180
Divisional head office, 17, 178
Divisional performance, 303
Divisions, (see Division)
Doctor, 103
Documentation, 179-80
Donations, 305
Double entry, 41, 67, 90
 book-keeping, 2, 19, 24, 29, 30, 37, 41, 45, 46, 54, 56, 60, 67, 68, 69, 88, 127, 220-1
 effect, 36, 89
 format, 23, 220
 procedure(s), 39, 44-68, 69
 process, 41
 system, 56, 87, 96
Doubtful debt(s), 20, 61, 68-70, 75
 adjustments, 61, 68-9, 70

adjustments (exhibit), 69-70
Drawings, 34
account, 34
office, 201
Dual aspect concept, 38
Dual aspect rule, 18-9, 23, 24, 29, 30-2, 220

Earnings per share (EPS), 152, 155, 310, 311
Edinburgh, 109, 300
Efficiency, 149, 150, 303
Efficiency ratios, 145, 149-51, 154, 266, 267
Elements of cost, 88, 182, 221, 225, 263
Employee(s), 1, 2, 3, 5, 8, 16, 107, 110, 151, 162, 164, 173, 175, 176, 194, 195, 201, 243, 245, 264, 300, 301, 302, 304, 322, 323, 324, 326
accounts, 301
remuneration, 194
reports, 317, 326
employer, 5
holiday pay, 195
national insurance contributions, 194, 195
pension fund contributions, 194, 195
Employment costs, 89, 323
policy, 305
protection legislation, 326
Engineering, 223
Entering transactions in accounts, 35-7
Entity(ies), 10, 14-5, 16, 19, 20, 22, 24, 30, 31, 32, 33, 34, 37, 55, 87, 97, 103, 106, 107, 110, 111, 112, 125, 126, 144, 145, 146, 147, 148, 149, 150, 151, 165, 175, 176, 178, 184, 200, 214, 244, 245, 246, 247, 248, 253, 256, 262, 263, 264, 266, 280, 284, 308, 315, 318, 320, 322, 324
concept, 106
rule, 14-5, 22, 111
Equipment, 313
hire, 196
Errors
commission, 45
compensating, 45
complete reversal of entry, 45
omission, 45
original entry, 45
principle, 45
Estimating accounting profit, 74-5
Ethical rules, 13, 14, 19-22, 23
Exceptional variances, 279
Executive option scheme, 315
Executorship, 7
Expected standard, 263
Expenditure, 23, 55, 63, 147, 220, 248, 309
Expenses, 18, 55, 89, 96, 126, 178, 179, 254
Explanation, 1
External auditors, 5
External customers, 323
External purposes, 114
External reporting, 173, 293
External user purposes, 114
Extraordinary item(s), 146, 152, 310, 311, 315, 316, 325
Extremism, 21

Factory, 89, 176, 177, 179
administration expenditure, 247
canteen costs, 181
cost, 211, 222
management, 88
manager, 177, 180
other costs, 182
overhead(s), 182, 200-11, 222-3
overhead absorption method, 200-8
overhead absorption method (comprehensive example), 208-11
overhead budget, 247
overheads (see Overhead)
production cost centres, 222
service cost centre costs, 201-4
service cost centre costs (apportionment methods), 201-2
service cost centres, 222
space, 238
Fashion industry, 245
Favourable variance, 214, 215, 268
Fibres' division, 180
Final accounts, 61
Final dividend, 111
Finance expenses, 96
Financial accounting, 2, 3, 7-8, 29-170, 173, 175, 184, 220, 221, 243, 293, 302
accounts, 3, 17, 46, 118, 155, 245
analysts, 2, 8
book-keeping system, 7
data, 7, 303
period, 87
ratios, 265 (see also Chapter 8)
recording system, 174
records, 174
reporting, 174
reports, 322
results, 303
statements, 54, 55-9, 60, 137, 302, 305, 306, 307-16
Finished goods, 87, 92, 222, 223, 309, 314
stock account, 89, 222
Finished product, 224
Finished stock, 89, 92
First-in, first-out (FIFO), 186-8, 189, 190, 192-3, 194
pricing method (exhibit), 187-8
Fittings, 313
Fixed assets, 55, 59, 63, 64, 66, 74, 96, 112,

Fixed assets (contd)
114, 126, 127, 131, 132, 150, 292, 305, 309, 312, 313, 315, 318, 321, 325
adjustment, 321
disclosure (exhibit), 66
investment, 310, 311, 312, 313, 314, 315
turnover ratio, 150, 154
Fixed budget, 253-6
Fixed costs, 183-4, 225, 227-39
Fixed expenditure, 247
Fixed overhead, 264-5
Fixed production capacity variance, 268, 269, 270
expenditure variance, 268, 269, 270
overhead variance, 268, 269, 270
productivity variance, 268, 269, 270
volume variance, 268, 269, 270
Fixtures, 313
Flexed, 253, 266
Flexed budget, 253-6
exhibit, 255-6
Flexing, 254
Floor area, 201
Folio, 31, 32
Football association, 13
Forecast, 245
Formal notes, 310, 311, 312, 313, 314
Format of accounts, 60–1
exhibit, 60-1
Fringe benefits, 323
Fully paid share capital, 108, 114
Function(s), 177, 178
Functional budget(s), 248-53, 256
illustrative example, 248-53
Funds, 107, 127-8, 132, 137
from other sources, 131, 132, 315, 316
statements (see source and application of funds)
Future developments, 304

Gearing adjustment, 320
General administration expenditure, 247
General board of directors, 177, 178, 180
General cost centre, 180
General meeting, 303, 306
General overhead expenditure, 247
General public, 2, 8, 162, 173
General reserve account, 114
Geographical areas, 176
Glass industry, 224
Going concern rule, 16, 22, 24
Goods, 33, 34
Government, 301, 322, 323, 324
Goodwill, 313, 315, 316
Gross assets, 300
Gross loss, 56
Gross profit, 56, 62, 96, 147, 309, 310, 311, 318
ratio, 146-7, 154
Gross replacement cost, 321
Group accounts, 307-8
comparative figures, 308
funds statement (see group source and application of funds)
notes to the accounts, 308
Group balance sheet, 308, 312-4
Group profit and loss account, 308, 309-12
Group published balance sheet (exhibit), 312-4
Group published profit and loss account (exhibit), 310-1
Group source and application of funds, 308, 314-6
exhibit, 315-6
Group statement of source and application of funds (see Group source and application of funds)
Group value added statement, 323

Head office, 211
Health, 291
Health authorities, 9
High geared, 153
Hire purchase, 292, 300
Historic cost, 23, 59, 64, 65, 75, 317
accounting (HCA), 17, 75
accounts, 318, 319
balance sheet, 320, 321
convention, 305, 317
profit, 320
profit and loss account, 320-1
rule, 17, 23
Holding company, 308, 310, 311
accounts, 308
balance sheet, 313
Horizontal analysis, 163
Horizontal format, 60, 87, 309, 312
Hotel, 163

Ideal standard(s), 263
Immaterial items, 19
Income, 7, 18, 23, 55, 96, 126, 220, 226, 309
Income from other fixed asset investments, 310, 311
Incomplete work, 89
Indebtedness, 4, 19, 144, 148
Indirect cost(s), 88, 89, 181, 183, 185, 194, 195, 200-15
definition, 88
overhead apportionment (exhibit), 203-4
questions, 215-9
Indirect expenses, 88, 89, 196, 200

Indirect factory costs, 214
Indirect labour cost, 8, 89, 195, 200
Indirect material cost, 88, 89, 200
Indirect production cost, 181, 182
Industrial relations, 164
Industrial revolution, 2, 106
Industry, 8, 9, 22
Inflation, 17, 64, 75, 163, 288, 317-22, 326
  adjusted reports, 317-22
  current position, 321-2
  definition, 317-8
  effects, 317-8
  index, 319
Information for decision-making, 7
Information for management system, 3
Insolvent, 125
Institute of Chartered Accountants in England and Wales, 9
Institute of Chartered Accountants in Ireland, 9
Institute of Chartered Accountants of Scotland, 9
Institute of Cost and Management Accountants (now Chartered Institute of Management Accountants), 9
Intangible assets, 309, 312, 313
Integral cost book-keeping system (exhibit), 221-2
Integral system, 174, 220
Integrated system, 200
Interdepartmental service costs, 202
Interest, 105, 109, 223, 323
  payable, 310
  payments, 153
  receivable, 310, 311
Interim dividend, 110
Internal accounts, 311
Internal auditors, 5
Internal balance sheet, 301
Internal management, 114, 293, 307
Internal profit and loss account, 301
Internal purposes, 118
Internal rate of return (IRR), 287, 289-91
  exhibit, 290-1
  problems, 291
Interlocking system, 174, 220
Interpretation of accounts, 137, 144-65
  illustrative example, 156-61
  questions, 165-70
  questions to be asked, 164
Interest payable and similar charges, 310, 311
Investment, 1, 7, 113, 312, 313, 316, 325
  income, 323
  ratios, 145, 151-3, 154
Investor(s), 2, 8, 106, 152, 162
Iron and steel industry, 106
Iron and steel making, 224
Issued share capital, 108, 114

Joinery, 223
Job costing, 223
Joint Stock Companies Act 1856, 106
Journalist(s), 2, 8, 162, 173

Key factors, 237-9
  exhibit, 238-9
Key statistics, 303

Labour, 88, 89, 194-5, 221, 238
Land and buildings, 305, 313, 314
Language, 4
Last-in, first-out (LIFO), 188-90, 193, 194
  pricing method (exhibit), 189
Leasing, 292, 300
Ledger(s), 31, 32, 220
  account(s), 31-2, 37, 38, 39, 41, 45, 46, 60, 61, 65-6, 67, 70
  account entries (examples), 35-6
  account (example), 37-8
  account format (exhibit), 32
Legal department cost centre, 181
Legal function, 6
Legal requirements, 303, 317, 324, 325-6
Legal restrictions, 103, 107
Legal title, 17, 23, 74
Level of activity, 246-7, 248, 254, 256, 263, 266
  changes (exhibit), 231
Level of efficiency, 266
Liability(ies), 6, 312, 325
Limited liability, 106-7
Limited Liability Act 1855, 106
Limited liability company (ltd), 3, 5, 9, 11, 14, 15, 24, 103, 106-18, 178, 299, 300
  accounts, 109-10
  balance sheet, 112-4
  comprehensive example, 114-8, directors 110
  disclosure of information, 109
  dividends, 110-1
  loans, 109
  operation, 107-11
  profit and loss account, 111-2
  structure, 107-11
  taxation, 111
  types, 108
Limiting factors, 237-9
  exhibit, 238-9
Listed companies, 113, 300
Liquidation, 5-6, 126
Liquidity, 125, 131, 145, 149, 150, 174
Liquidity ratios, 145, 148-9, 154
Loan capital, 304

Loan(s), 106, 109, 113, 114, 153, 311, 318, 323
Local authority(ies), 11, 14, 180, 181
  taxation, 180
Local government, 2, 8, 9, 162, 173, 224
Long-term bank loans, 114
Long-term borrowing, 292, 321
Long-term creditors, 314
Long-term debt, 292
Long-term investments, 113
Long-term loans, 114, 153, 318
Loss(es), 20, 23, 229, 234
Low geared, 153

Machine cost centre, 178
Machine hours, 213
  absorption rate method, 206, 208
Machine shop department, 176
Main financial statements, 302, 306, 307-16, 326
Mainstream corporation tax, 111
Maintenance, 223
  department, 180
Management, 2, 3, 5, 7, 8, 90, 110, 125, 149, 162, 164, 173, 174, 175, 176, 185, 195, 230, 233, 243, 244, 245, 248, 256, 262, 263, 266, 267, 279, 280, 293, 299, 307, 322
Management accounting, 2, 3, 8, 173, 174
  function, 3
  procedure, 5, 8
  system, 3
Management accounts, 3, 15
Manager, 1, 2, 3, 151, 175, 178, 179, 180, 181, 184, 185, 201, 215, 244, 246, 254, 286, 293, 294
Managerial role, 45
Managership, 2
Manufacturing, 89
Manufacturing account(s), 87-97, 111, 125, 182
  comprehensive example, 92-6
  construction, 87, 90-2
  construction (exhibit), 90-2
  contents, 87-90
  format (exhibit), 88-90
  questions, 97-102
Manufacturing company(ies), 176-8
  organisational structure (exhibit), 177-8
Manufacturing cost(s), 88, 89, 90, 92, 96
  of goods produced, 88, 89
Manufacturing entity, 10, 87, 103
Manufacturing industry, 195
Manufacturing overhead, 88, 89
Manufacturing profit, 88, 89, 90, 92
Manufacturing systems, 224
Marginal cost, 228-39
Marginal costing, 173, 184, 225, 227-39, 265, 276
  activity (effect on profit), 232-3
  activity (effect on profit (exhibit)), 231
  application, 230-3
  application (exhibit), 230-1
  assumptions, 228-9, 230
  criticisms, 233-4
  equation, 230
  formulae, 234-5
  formulae (exhibit), 234-5
  illustrative example, 235-7
  statement (exhibit), 229-30
  system(s), 220
  technique, 228-30
  questions, 239-42
Margin of safety, 232-3, 234, 235
Market, 164
  price, 113
  value, 90
  value of goods produced, 88, 90
Marketing function, 177
Marketing manager, 293
Mark-up ratio, 147, 154
Master budget, 244, 248, 253, 255
Matching rule, 18, 20, 23, 24, 54, 126
Material item, 19
Materials, 88, 89, 183, 221, 322
  consumed, 89
  handling, 201-2
Materiality rule, 19, 23
Mathematical apportionment method, 202-3
Measurement rules, 14, 16-9, 22-3
Mechanized systems, 29, 31, 32
Medium-sized companies, 299, 301
Milk, 223
Minimum disclosure requirements, 301
Minor, 7
Minority interests, 310, 311, 313, 314, 315, 316
Miscellaneous cost centre, 180
Modified accounts, 300
Monetary system, 1
Monetary terms, 16
Monetary unit, 16
Monetary working capital, 320
  working capital adjustment (MWCA), 320, 321
Money, 4, 6, 16
Money measurement rule, 16, 17, 22
Motor car(s), 30, 34
Motorway, 223

Nationalized industries, 9
Net assets, 314, 325
Net book value, 66, 96, 150, 313
Net cash flow, 284-5, 287, 288, 289, 291
Net current assets, 313, 314, 325

Net liquid funds, 132, 316
Net loss, 56
Net present value (NPV), 287-9, 291
  exhibit, 288-9
  problems, 289
Net profit, 56, 104, 112, 146, 149, 152, 223, 286, 303, 310, 311
Net profit ratio, 147, 154
Net replacement cost, 321
Nominal value, 114
Non-accountant(s), 1, 3, 4, 8, 9, 10, 11, 29, 37, 38, 45, 70, 74, 106, 118, 127, 133, 136, 137, 144, 165, 220, 225, 243, 262, 278, 280, 302, 322, 326
Non-company balance sheets, 112
Non-factory overhead, 183, 211-3, 214
  absorption methods, 211-3
Non-group companies, 311
Non-limited liability entity, 107
Non-profit and loss items, 126
Non-qualified accountants, 9
Normal loss, 224
Not-for-profit entity, 10, 14
Nuts and bolts, 223

Objectives, 21, 175, 245, 246
Objectivity rule, 21, 23
Obsolescence, 64
Obtaining information, 162
Office equipment, 19
Office expenses, 34
Omission (error of), 45
Opening stock, 34, 62, 87, 147, 149
  of raw material, 89
  work-in-progress, 88, 89
Operating capability, 320-1
Operating profit, 309, 310
Operating statements (in standard costing), 278-9
  exhibit, 279
Operation costing, 223, 224
Operational format, 309-10, 311
Operational research, 4
Ordinary dividend, 152, 153, 292
Ordinary shareholders, 146
Ordinary shares, 108
Organization, 1, 3, 10-11
Organizational structure, 175-8, 184, 185
  exhibit of a manufacturing company, 177-8
  exhibit of a pyramid format, 176
Original entry (error of), 45
Other creditors, 314
Other debtors, 314
Other direct expenses, 88, 89
Other external charges, 309
Other income(s), 310, 311, 323
Other indirect expenses, 88, 89
Other interest receivable and other income, 310, 311
Other operating charges, 309
Other operating income, 309, 310, 311
Other rerserves, 313, 314
Overdraft facilities, 292
Overhead(s), 88, 89, 181, 182, 195, 200-15, 221, 222-3
  absorption (exhibit), 207-8
  budget(s), 247, 248
  methods of absorption, 205-7
Over-night deposit accounts, 132
Over-pricing, 215
Over-recovery of overhead, 214, 215
Over-trading, 126
Own work capitalized, 309
Owner, 2, 7, 10
Ownership, 2

Pacioli, 2
Paid dividend, 110, 152, 303, 310, 311
Partner(s), 10, 11, 104, 105, 111
Partnership, 10-1, 14, 103-6, 110, 111, 112, 118
  accounts, 104-6, 112
  accounts (exhibit), 104-5
  entity(ies), 107, 108, 109
  management, 103-4
Partnership Act 1890, 11, 104
Patents, 313
Payback, 284-6, 287
  disadvantages, 285-6
  exhibit, 285
Payments on account, 314
Pension costs, 311
Pensions, 323
Period of account, 15
Periodic weighted average method of pricing stock, 190-1, 193
  exhibit, 190-1
Periodicity rule, 15, 16, 17, 20, 22, 324
Personnel, 303
  department cost centre, 201
  function, 177
Petty cash, 34
Planned conditions, 265
Planned costs, 192
Planned price, 192
Planning, 3, 7, 175, 184, 185, 211, 214, 264, 280
Plans, 225
Plant and machinery, 313
Plant hire, 196
Political donations, 305
Postulates, 13
Post-trial balance adjustments, 61-71

Practical rule(s), 13, 18
Practising accountant, 6
Pre-determined absorption rates, 213-5
Pre-determined rate, 213
Preference dividend, 146, 152, 153, 292
Preference share capital, 152
Preference shares, 108, 113, 114, 153, 292
Premium, 114
Pre-payment(s), 18, 20, 66, 67-8, 74, 133, 314
  adjustments, 61, 66, 67-8
  adjustments (exhibit), 68
  basis, 18
Price (factor in standard costing), 264-5
Price/earnings (P/E) ratio, 153, 155
Price variance, 264, 268
Prime cost, 88, 89, 182
  absorption rate method, 206, 207-8
Principal activities, 304
Principal reports, 302, 303-6
Principle (error of), 45
Principles, 13, 20, 54
Private bank account, 15
Private company(ies), 108, 109, 300, 301
Procedures, 13
Process(es), 181, 229, 262
Process costing, 224
Product(s), 88, 89, 176, 181
  division, 177
Product performance, 303
Production budget, 244, 247, 284
Production capacity, 280
Production cost, 181, 183, 195, 211, 212
  budget, 244, 246, 247
  cost centre, 181, 200, 201-4, 214, 222
Production department(s), 176, 181, 185, 246, 247
Production director, 293
Production function, 176, 177
Production manager, 177, 247
Production/volume ratio, 267-8
Productivity, 303
  ratio, 266, 267
Professional accountants, 125, 300
Professional accounting bodies, 22, 299
Professional accounting information, 306
Professional accounting requirements, 300, 303, 306, 307, 317, 322, 324, 325-6
Profit, 2, 11, 18, 19, 20, 21, 23, 34, 54, 63, 68, 90, 110, 111, 125-6, 127, 131, 132, 144, 145, 146, 147, 152, 164, 182, 189, 229, 231, 232, 234, 245, 287, 305, 315, 318, 321, 323, 324, 325
  centre(s), 178, 184
  measurement, 54-5
  schemes, 324
  variance, 269
Profitability, 19, 125, 146, 215, 283, 291
  ratios, 145-7, 153-4
Profit and loss account, 6, 56, 57, 60, 63, 68, 69, 87, 90, 92, 104, 106, 111-2, 125, 132, 137, 161, 163, 214, 215, 222, 223, 224, 299, 301, 302, 307, 309, 312, 313, 314, 315, 320, 321, 323, 326
Profit and loss appropriation account, 104-5, 112
Profit before extraordinary items attributable to members of the holding company, 310, 311
Profit for the financial year, 310, 311
Profit making entity, 14
Profit on ordinary activities after taxation, 310, 311
Profit on ordinary activities before taxation, 310, 311
Profit/volume ratio, 231-3
Project profitability, 284-91
Project ranking, 291, 292
Promoting a company, 107
Promotional material, 301
Proposed dividend(s), 110-1, 113, 114, 131, 132, 152, 303, 310, 311
Proprietor(s), 2, 14, 15, 20, 21, 32, 33, 34, 39, 41, 54, 63, 68, 106, 111, 125, 126, 144, 145, 147, 318
Provision for doubtful debts, 61, 68-70
  account, 69-70
Provisional trial balance, 61
  rule, 61
Provisions for liabilities and charges, 325
Prudence, 20, 21, 23, 24
Public, 2, 8, 14, 162, 173, 175
Public company(ies), 108, 109, 113, 300, 301, 304, 307
Public limited liability company (plc), 108, 113
Public sector accountants, 9
Public relations department, 162
Published accounts, 299, 300, 307, 308, 316
  additional features, 307-8
  background, 307
Published balance sheet, 312, 316
  exhibit, 312-4
Published financial statements, 307
  additional features, 307-8
Published funds' statements, 315-6
Published profit and loss account, 310-2, 316
  (exhibit), 310-1
Purchased services, 322
Purchases, 33, 34, 62, 74, 87, 126, 147
  account, 34, 39, 89
  of raw materials, 89
Purchasing power school, 319

Qualified accountant(s), 9, 13, 22
Qualified audit report, 306
Quantitative rule, 16, 22
Quantity (factor in standard costing), 264-5
Quantity variance, 268
Quasi-government entities, 9
Quick ratio, 148-9

Railway development, 106
Rate of interest, 287, 289, 292
Rate of return, 287, 289-90
Rates, 180-1, 183, 201
Ratio analysis, 144-65
Ratios, 144-65
  illustrative example, 155-61
  need, 144-5
  summary, 153-5
  trends (techniques), 163
  questions, 165-70
Raw material(s), 87, 89, 180, 185, 224, 238, 309, 314
  costs, 89
  stocks, 223
Realisation rule, 17-8, 23, 54, 68, 126
Realised 17, 90
Receipts, 248
Receiver, 6
Receiverships, 5-6
Reciprocal service costs, 202-4
  apportionment methods, 202-4
Recommended dividend, 304
Recording accounting information, 29-46
  questions, 46-53
Recording cost data, 220-6
  simplified cost book-keeping system (exhibit), 222-3
  simplified financial accounting system (exhibit), 221
  (questions), 226
Recording information, 1, 2, 32-7
Recording system, 1
Reducing balance method of depreciation, 64-5
  formula, 65
Registrar of companies, 109, 300
Related company, 307-8, 310, 311
Relevance (rule of), 21-2, 23
Rent, 183, 221, 223
Rentals, 311
Replacement cost, 64, 321
Report(s), 1, 15
  auditors, 302
  chairman, 302
  directors, 302
  principal, 302
Research and development, 211
  activities, 304
Research and development (contd)
  budget, 247
  cost centres, 222
  expenditure, 182, 247
  overhead, 182, 211, 212, 222-3
  overhead absorption rate method, 212
Reserve(s), 114, 304, 313, 314, 325
  account(s), 114
Responsibility accounting, 178, 180, 246
Responsibility cost centre(s), 178, 179, 180, 184
Retail price index (RPI), 319, 322
Retained earnings, 292
Retained profit for the year, 310, 311
Retained profits, 291-2, 315, 316, 323
Return on capital employed (ROCE) ratios, 145-6, 153-4
Revaluation reserve account, 114, 313, 314
Revenue, 55, 57, 74, 178
  expenditure, 55, 56
  income, 55, 56
  reserve accounts, 114
  reserves, 113, 114, 311
Review of developments, 304
Royalties, 311

Safety, 291
Salaries, 32, 104, 163, 311, 323
  department, 177
Sales, 18, 34, 74, 126, 147, 150, 164, 222, 233, 234, 311, 323, 324
  account, 34, 36, 37, 39
  budget, 244, 246, 247, 248, 284
  forecast, 280, 284
  margin variance, 275-6
  margin variance (exhibit), 277-8
  margin operating profit due to sales variance, 276
  margin due to sales volume variance, 276
  margin due to selling price variance, 276
  price variance, 269
  revenue, 23, 54, 55, 62, 147, 149, 150, 163, 212, 221, 222, 229, 231, 233, 244, 322
  taxes, 323
  value variance, 275-6
  value variance (exhibit), 277-8
  value selling price variance, 276
  value total variance, 276
  value volume variance, 276
  value variance, 275-8
  variances, 265, 275-8, 279
  variances (formulae), 276
  volume variances, 269
Salesman cost centre, 178
School, 233
Sectional performance, 303

Secured assets, 109
Selling and distribution, 211
  budget, 247
  cost centres, 222
  overhead, 96, 182, 211, 212, 222-3
  overhead absorption method, 212
Selling price, 182, 183, 184, 211, 212, 213, 263, 265, 275, 276
Semi-variable costs, 229
Service costs, 181
  centres, 181, 200, 201-4, 214, 222-3
Service costing, 224
Service entity, 10
Servicing, 223
Services, 33, 323
Share, 107, 108, 114, 126, 127, 131, 132, 151, 153, 178, 211, 292, 302, 303, 304, 311, 314, 315, 316
  acquisitions, 304
  capital, 107-8, 110, 112, 114, 305, 307, 314, 324
  disposals, 304
  market price, 151
  nominal price, 151
  of profits less losses of related companies, 310, 311
  premium account, 114, 313, 314
  price, 303
Shareholder(s), 5, 108, 109, 110, 111, 114, 151, 152, 162, 173, 174, 299, 300, 301, 303, 304, 306, 307, 311, 314, 321, 323, 326
  accounts, 300-1
  funds, 113, 114, 146, 153, 314
  employees, 110
  reports, 326
Short-term borrowing(s), 292, 311
Short-term creditors, 314
Short-term investments, 113, 132, 316
Short-term loans, 318
Simplified cost book-keeping system (exhibit), 222-3
Small business(es), 2, 14, 103
Small company(ies), 109, 110, 300, 301
Social security costs, 311
Sole trader(s), 10, 11, 14, 27, 37, 54, 103, 104, 106, 107, 112
  accounts, 54
  entities, 37, 103, 107, 109, 111, 112
  organisation(s), 10, 11
Solicitor(s), 7, 9, 103, 104
Source and application of funds, 125-37, 292, 302, 305, 307, 308, 314-6, 326
  comprehensive example, 133-6
  construction, 128-31
  contents, 127-8, 302
  contents (exhibit), 127
Source and application of funds (contd)
  exhibits, 128-31
  format, 127-8, 326
  recommended format, 131-2
  recommended format (exhibit), 131-2
  questions, 137-43
Source of funds, 127, 128, 131, 291-2, 315, 316
Specialist reports, 301-2
Specific identification method of pricing stock, 186
Specific order costing, 223-4
Specific order of closure method, 202
Specific units absorption rate method, 207-8
Sports grounds, 291
Staff costs, 309
Standard absorption costing, 265
Standard cost, 192, 194, 225, 262-80, 284
  exhibit, 279
  method of pricing stock 192, 194
  operating statement, 278
  types, 263-4
  unit, 264-5
  variances, 278
Standard costing, 173, 192, 194, 225, 239, 256, 262-80
  administration, 263-5
  analysis of variances (exhibit), 269
  operating statements, 278-9
  operating statements (exhibit), 279
  period, 263
  preparation, 264-5
  questions 280-3
  system, 192, 194
  types, 263-4
  unit, 264-5
  variance analysis (illustrative example), 270-5
Standard hour(s), 265, 266, 267
Standard marginal costing, 265
Statements of source and application of funds (see Source and application of funds)
Standards (SSAP's) (see Statements of standard accounting practice)
Statements of standard accounting practice (SSAP's), 13, 21-2, 300, 301
  SSAP 10 (statement of source and application of funds), 128, 131, 132, 315, 316
  SSAP 16 (current cost accounting), 320-1, 322
  SSAP 21 (leases and hire purchase contracts), 300
Statement of value added, 322-4
Stationery, 19
Statistical summaries, 317, 324-6

Statistical summaries (contd)
exhibit, 325
Statistics, 303
Statute, 306
Statutory accounting requirements, 303, 306, 322, 326
Stock, 19, 34, 62, 126, 127, 128, 131, 132, 133, 148, 149, 150, 186-94, 253, 306, 312, 314, 316, 318, 320, 321
account, 62
adjustment, 61, 62-3
adjustment (exhibit), 63
budget, 247
pricing method, 186-94
turnover ratio, 149, 154
valuation methods, 186-94
valuations, 22
Stock Exchange, 108, 109, 299, 300, 301, 303, 307
requirements, 303
Stores control department, 176
Stores ledger account, 191
Straight line depreciation, 64, 65
Sub-period budget(s), 245-6, 263
Subsidiary company, 307, 308, 311, 314, 315, 316
Sundry cost centres, 180
Superimposed costing techniques, 225, 243
Supermarkets, 148
Supervisory management, 195
Supervisory wages, 195
Supplementary reports, 302, 317-26
Supplementary statements, 302, 317-26

Take-over bid, 162
Tangible assets, 312, 313
Tangible fixed assets, 325
Tax, 8, 9, 22, 111, 112, 127, 131, 132, 146, 152, 310, 311, 315, 316, 325
avoidance, 8
computations, 15
department, 177
due, 132
evasion, 8
on profit on ordinary activities, 310, 311
Taxation (see Tax)
Tender prices, 183
Time value of money, 287
Timesheets, 195
Tools, 313
Tool absorption costing, 183, 184, 213
Total assets, 59
Total assets less current liabilities, 313, 314
Total cost, 183, 184
Total cost of sales, 181
Total cost variance, 269
Total factory cost, 182
Total factory overhead, 182
Total manufacturing cost, 90
Total manufacturing costs incurred, 88, 89
Total manufacturing overhead incurred, 88, 89
Total net assets, 325
Total sales variance, 269
Trade creditor, 34-5, 113, 148, 151, 222, 292, 314, 320
accounts, 34
payment period ratio, 151, 154
Trade creditors (see Trade creditor)
Trade debtor, 35, 68, 69, 148, 150, 222, 314, 320
collection period ratio, 150-1, 154
Trade debtors (see Trade debtor)
Trade discounts, 35, 311, 323
Trade unions, 162, 164
Trader, 103
Trading account, 56, 57, 60, 62, 63, 87, 88, 89, 90, 92, 96, 111, 125, 222
Trading activity, 126
Trading entity, 10, 29-46, 54-75, 87
Trading organisation(s), 10, 56, 89
Transport department, 202
Transport industry, 224
Trend analysis, 163
Trends, 147, 150, 151, 162-3, 164, 256, 325
Trial balance, 41-5, 46, 54, 56, 57, 61
adjustments, 61-71
compilation (exhibit), 42-4
errors, 44-5
True and fair view, 21, 22, 23, 305, 306
Trustee, 7
law, 7
work, 7
Trusts, 7
Turnover, 125, 300, 309, 310, 311, 323, 325
Type of expenditure format, 309-10, 311
Types of account, 37
Types of organisation, 1, 10-1
Types of standard, 263-4
Types of transactions, 16

Under-pricing, 215
Under recovery of overhead, 214, 215
Unit, 181, 185, 186, 195, 196, 200, 201, 213, 220, 223, 224, 225, 227, 229, 231, 262, 264-5
cost, 181, 182, 200, 214, 220
cost structure (exhibit), 182
Unit costing, 220, 225
Unit trusts, 11
Unlisted companies, 113
Unqualified audit report, 306
Unquoted companies, 113

Usefulness, 29
User(s), 125, 145, 151, 179, 183
  groups, 21
  of accounts, 20

Value added, 322, 323, 324
  definition, 322, 323
  statements, 317, 322-4
  statements (exhibit), 323
  uses, 324
Value added tax, 311, 323
Vans, 16
Variable cost, 183-4, 225, 227-39
  and changes (exhibit), 230-1
Variable overhead, 229, 264-5
Variable production overhead variance, 268, 269, 270
Variable production price variance, 268
Variable production volume variance, 268
Variance, 214, 215, 245, 253, 254, 256, 262-80
Variance accounting, 225
  analysis (exhibit), 270-5
  analysis (formulae), 269-70
  diagrammatic format (exhibit), 269
Venetian merchants, 2
Vertical analysis, 163, 262-80
Vertical format, 60, 87, 88, 96, 309, 312
Voluntary organisations, 11

Wages, 32, 311, 323
  department, 176
  manager, 177
Water boards, 9
Weighted average method of pricing stock, 190-2
Westernised agrarian system, 15
Will, 7
Working capital, 127-8, 131, 132-3, 316
  movements (exhibit), 133
Work-in-progress, 88, 89, 222, 223, 309, 314
Work study, 4
Work(s), 89, 176
World of accounting, 11, 12
World War 1914-1918, 174
World War 1939-45, 174